K 14 1 B

Personnel administration
by objectives

THE IRWIN SERIES IN MANAGEMENT

CONSULTING EDITOR   JOHN F. MEE   *Indiana University*

Personnel administration by objectives

GEORGE S. ODIORNE
Dean, and Professor of Management
College of Business
University of Utah

1971
RICHARD D. IRWIN, INC. Homewood, Illinois 60430
IRWIN-DORSEY LIMITED, Georgetown, Ontario

© RICHARD D. IRWIN, INC., 1971

First Printing, February, 1971

Library of Congress Catalog Card No. 74–138415
Printed in the United States of America

PREFACE

THE TRADITIONAL COURSE in personnel management is obsolete.

It was pertinent to the 1920s when the field of personnel management originated. At that time laborers were the most important group in the work force. They made up over 40 percent of those gainfully employed. Their working conditions were often unpleasant, unsafe, and undesirable. They formed unions; they constituted a serious source of discontent and comprised a serious social problem to society.

Today personnel management deals with a different work force. The significant groups are the technical, managerial, professional, white-collar, and service employee. Laborers have declined in total numbers, and as a percentage of those gainfully employed. They have achieved higher wages, many benefits, and the strong support of government.

The manager of the future will supervise other professionals, managers, technicians, staff persons, and white-collar workers. He will hire them from the colleges in many instances. Their work will be international in scope. There will be more women workers, more blacks, and new occupations never before imagined as new technology, such as the computer, emerges. Larger and more complex organizations require different approaches to measuring employee performance. Decentralized organizations will demand more skill in working through complex political structures. Joint decisions through committees will be more important to prevent the big errors which come from incomplete information.

At the same time the skilled and unskilled worker will still be with us, and union influence will be pressed with vigor and intelligence, with government intervention playing a stronger role than ever in controlling this relationship.

Many of the assumptions about personnel management as it emerged in the twenties took for granted that its function was to alleviate the physical and psychological discontent of workers, and to a remarkable degree this goal was achieved. In the process, the economics of human resources were subjected to psychology and behaviorial science. It is a presumption in this book that the time is ripe for a return to an economic approach to personnel management and the management of human resources.

v

Thus, this becomes a book of the strategies and tactics of human resources management, with excursions in the appropriate behavioral and social sciences that are required to achieve economic ends, or that provide limiting conditions to the economic demands.

For whom is this book intended?

Two distinct groups should find this approach of value. (*a*) Personnel students in graduate schools of business or in advanced personnel courses in the undergraduate school of business will find this a preparation for the world of the future in managing human resources. (*b*) Operating executives at the policy level of companies or institutions, concerned with managing human resources, will recognize the realism of the approach.

A quick rifflle through the index may show an absence of the cookbook techniques of personnel management which have sometimes characterized personnel courses in the past. Why this omission?

For one thing, the techniques are changing rapidly and, it is predicted, will change even more in the future. In fact, it is the theme of this book that this change is long overdue, in texts and in practice. The new direction is clearly before us in the behavior of the best run firm, and an orderly statement of the new personnel management is in order.

Cases accompany this text, liberally strewn with actual details of method and technique. Included not merely to present techniques for their own sake, they are an ancillary "internal book" accompanying this text as a teaching tool. The purpose of the cases is to provide opportunity to develop decision-making and problem-solving skill in managing human resources. Whatever techniques are included are incidental in purpose.

A word about the case method.

The cases at the end of each chapter are original; the few exceptions have been selected from prior files or writers and have been adapted by permission. The subject matter of the cases relates to the topical matter of the chapter which it follows. These case studies may be used in several ways to supplement the reading and lectures in the course.

1. The instructor may use them for illustrative purposes, to make a point and show practical application of the text and lecture in a simulated real life situation.

2. The instructor might shape the cases to suit his own educational purposes by preparing and assigning specific questions for use as outside writing and research assignments.

3. The recommended use of these cases is as a course-within-a course, to teach decision making and problem solving in personnel administration. In order to achieve this educational objective the following guides are suggested. They have been tested with student groups at the University

of Michigan and at the University of Utah with highly satisfactory results.

I. *Use Standard Questions for Each Case.*

    A. Summarize the facts in this case. Don't mix facts with hunches, or your biases.

    B. What are the major problems in this case? Which one should be solved before all others?

    C. What are some of the major causes of the problem you have chosen to work on? How could the problem have been averted?

    D. What are some optional solutions to the problem? List several options before proceeding to solution.

    E. What is your decision as to the solution; that is, what option did you select as being the best? Which solution will make the maximum contribution to objectives?

    F. Outline a very specific action plan. What should be done, by whom, and how?

II. *Use Small Group Discussions to Enlarge the Learning.*

Rather than asking the class simply to read the case and come in with the facts, the process of analysis and decision making can be sharpened by asking the class to break into several small groups of 6 to 10 members. One of the members is the group leader, and he is to lead a discussion of the case using the standard questions as an agenda. One of the members can serve as a recorder to prepare a verbal summary of his group's analysis for the class. This report isn't intended to provide minutes of the entire discussion, but is rather to report on the conclusions of the group on the standard questions and the answers the group has chosen for them.

III. *Let the Whole Class Discuss the Comparative Analyses.*

After the small group discussion, each group briefly reports on the case and their group's analysis of it. The teacher's role here is threefold: (1) to summarize each group's report and point up differences and likenesses; (2) to engage in discussion leadership, bringing out the quiet student and suppressing the overly talkative, to assure that all issues are presented and discussed as fully as time allows; and (3) to conduct a summary discussion on "what we have learned about the topic of the week and about the decision-making process from this case." These major learning points should be highlighted and summarized.

Often the decision and action points can be tested by role playing the respective positions and action proposed by the study groups. The objective of the cases isn't, of course, to learn the right or wrong answers but to learn through practice a system of decision making and problem solving under uncertainty. In personnel administration, where the answers are often situational, such a skill of situational thinking and systematic approach is more important than pat answers of textbook solutions.

The author's combined academic experience and executive experience in industry convince him that professional management training is not satisfactorily served by the teaching of mere *procedures* of personnel management.

January, 1971   George S. Odiorne

CONTENTS

PART IV. **Advice as an output of the personnel administration department**   **359**

16. RESOLVING ORGANIZATIONAL CONFLICT   361

What is the objective in conflict resolution? The poisons of corporate infighting: *Executive brawling can wreck a company's morale. The "jurisdiction fighter." The culprit: organization. The rebel. What price the intellectual?* Conflict as a vital corporate ingredient: *Constructive "inside" ferment toughens a firm for the struggle outside. "Swamped with advice."* The management of corporate conflict: *Astute managers ride herd on both good and harmful infighting. Fights do not end a war. The answer: tight planning.*

17. PARTICIPATIVE MANAGEMENT AS A GAME   384

What advice should personnel departments produce? The game of participative management: *Step one. Step two. Step three. Step four.* Welcome to participation land. The research evidence on key questions about participative management: *1. Is participation desired by workers? 2. What opposing influences can block participative management? 3. What premises are necessary to affect participative management? 4. What part does perception play in participative management?* Reality in management: *Marvin Bower's views. Douglas McGregor's perceptions. Rensis Likert's perceptions. Success stories and management systems. Source of data. Which group has a grip on reality? What difference would it make? 5. What practical effects will participation have?*

18. DISCIPLINE BY OBJECTIVES   415

The objective—behavior change. Designing the disciplinary system: *The clear listing of a catalog of rules and regulations. Dis-*

PART I

Managing the personnel administration department

SOME OF the objectives of the personnel department affect other units of the organization, and some affect only the internal management of the department. The personnel manager then, is both line to his subordinates, and staff to the rest of the firm. Yet, the two classes of objectives are hardly distinct. The internal management of the personnel department, including setting objectives for the various sections and groups, is aimed at improving the quantity and quality of staff services to nonpersonnel departments, advice to management, control of policies, and research outputs.

This internal management to achieve personnel department objectives to others begins with major goals and tends to divide into logical families of outputs. These areas of managerial concern for a personnel manager comprise this part of the book.

---

chapter 1

THE NEW BREED

At a large midwestern school an interviewer, seeking personnel department recruits, opened his interview with the question: "Can you type?" In six out of eight interviews the student cut the interview short, and, as reports of this shockingly naive—to the students—inquiry were passed along in the placement office grapevine, the last two scheduled never showed up.

"It was obvious that we couldn't possibly be talking about the same job," suavely explained one student.

Such a question would not have been shocking for an applicant 20 years ago, for it was expected that personnel men would be prepared for a long stint at employment interviewing, and typing up interview reports and resume forms was simply part of the job. The point isn't that today's college graduates are snobbish. More of them can type, and even own their own electric portables than ever in the past. For term papers it is a definite advantage. Even their professor who taught them some of the more elegant ideas about the new kind of personnel administration department probably typed his own rough manuscript when he was writing a book.

The point is that the sights of the personnel profession have been raised considerably from its early days in the twenties when personnel administration was in its infancy.

HIGH ROAD VERSUS LOW ROAD

One of the more experienced professionals in the field of Personnel Administration, Professor Dale Yoder, recently suggested that in personnel administration there are two roads—a high road and a low road. Such an idea can be expanded to propose that the New Breed is concerned with matters of high importance rather than of low importance.

The high road is those activities which are concerned with the more

3

contemporary issues of personnel; such as manpower planning for the firm, relating in-company systems to labor markets, applying behavioral sciences to specific problems of recruiting, selection, placement, and training. The high road is paved with matters that concern the president, divisional general managers, plant managers, and key staff department heads. The high road is concerned with company objectives and policies to get the organization to produce results. It illustrates, as Dr. Frederick Harbison has pointed out, that the line between personnel management and general management is becoming thinner and the two are becoming less and less distinguishable.

The low road still exists and will be done by somebody, very possibly much of it by line managers, the lesser staffs of personnel specialists. Such work has well been described in the early texts in personnel administration and is still found as the major kind of activity in many personnel departments who treat their responsibilities as a narrow, technical specialty akin to traffic, purchasing, or plant maintenance. Studies of the activities of personnel departments done in the thirties and forties showed a strong attention to such procedural matters. Where such procedures did not exist, it was a matter of concern to the personnel manager that system and precedures for detailed processing of personnel as they entered the firm, worked there, and separated should be expanded and improved.

Among such areas of concern for personnel departments as adapted in abridged form from one of the more extensive surveys are those shown in Figure 1–1.[1]

FIGURE 1–1

Hiring
Does your company use an application blank?
Who fills it out, the interviewer or the applicant?
Do you obtain written references?
Use outside sources of supply?
Have a written qualification card?
Does the personnel department have full authority to hire?
Do you require physical exams?
Do you utilize tests for hiring new employees?
What are your procedures for recruiting new employees?
Employee services
Rest rooms for employees?
Do you have an aid station?
A lunch room?
Do you follow up new employees for success on the job?

[1] The items in this list are adapted from one prepared for a survey by Stanley Matthewson in 1930 and repeated in 1940, based on 231 companies employing 1,795,000 employees. The researcher stated them to be fairly indicative if not conclusive about the state of the art in personnel. It is presented here in modified form as an interesting and instructive picture of what personnel administration was concerned with through 1940. Taken from Scott, Clothier, Matthewson, and Spriegel, *Personnel Management* (3d ed; New York: McGraw-Hill, 1941), p. 519 ff.

FIGURE 1–1 (continued)

A magazine for employees?
A company hospital?
An employee's library?
Do you have a formal safety program?
Legal aid for employees?
A recreation room for employees?
Company provided loan fund for employees?
Company housing?
Maintain a store or commissary for employees?

Methods of wage payment
Straight time to direct labor?
Straight piece rate?
Gang piece rate?
Piece rate with a guaranteed minimum?
Task and bonus rate (Gantt)?
Other incentive plans for hourly workers?
Measured day rate?
Severance pay for involuntarily separated employees?

Employee security programs
A mutual benefit association?
Group life insurance?
Accident insurance?
Pension system?
Health insurance?
Credit Union?
Savings and Loan association?
Stock purchase plan?
Guaranteed annual wage?
Profit sharing plan?
Bonus plan?
Seniority system for laying off workers?
Employee representation?

Employee training and development
Formally train new employees on the job?
Foremanship training classes?
Special courses for employees such as Americanization?
Company schools?
Employ cooperative students?
Tuition refund plan for night school attendance?
Are classes held on company time or employees'?
An active suggestion system?
Social and recreational organizations?
Athletic organization?

Personnel research and control
Do you keep records of labor turnover?
Do you keep an employment expense budget?
Job analysis?
Rating scales for evaluating performance?
Community surveys of wages and salaries periodically?
Do you maintain promotional replacement charts?
Do you repeat employment tests for progression?
Do you survey attitudes and opinion of employees?

Even for the experienced eye this list seems to describe the major gamut of the personnel administration functions, except labor relations. The fact that many firms today could not answer affirmatively to many of the items might be cited as evidence that the technical aspects of personnel administration have not been fully adopted.

Many of the items on the list are still pertinent today. Many others, including a somewhat shortened list of various kinds of wage payment plans have disappeared from the scene. Other issues which would not receive a major affirmative response would include many items of employee services—simply because they are so commonplace they are taken for granted. It is most unlikely that a firm does not have rest rooms, even where the law didn't require it. In other cases the social climate simply rejects other kinds of personnel practices which were considered evidence of progressive management when this list was first circulated. Company housing, the company store, and similar provision for the total life style of the employee off the job as well as on it, is no longer generally accepted as necessary. The old company town and company store was written off as paternalistic, and, if not ridiculed, was generally pressured out of existence. Other maintenance factors such as the company chaplain, and similar benefits have been quietly set aside. New ones may have been added such as blood banks, reading racks, and coke machines.

Today a policy of nice-things-for-employees is most often found in isolated work environments where they provide a functional purpose. The paper mill located miles from the nearest city, or the mining operation in an isolated stretch of wilderness must provide stores, barbershops, housing, and perhaps recreation facilities for the employees and their families. Such matters, however, are generally associated with individual plants or mills of a company, and not with total corporate personnel administration.

We might safely conclude that most of the functions which are listed, plus some new ones, are most apt to be found in the lowest echelons of plant personnel management in the firm. The plant personnel manager in an isolated plant is more likely to find the list familiar than the corporate personnel director, members of his staff, or personnel managers in units such as research laboratories, sale offices, corporate or divisional headquarters.

WHAT MAKES THE NEW BREED?

The new brand of personnel man is not so designated because he has simply thrown out the old activities and substituted a lot of new-fangled ones like programmed instruction and sensitivity training. The difference is one of higher level orientation in his approach to his job. A commonly used diagram to show the structure of management functions is presented in Figure 1–2.

The study of Matthewson, and several others less comprehensive, bear

FIGURE 1-2

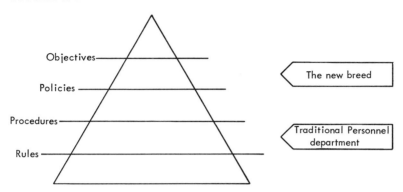

out the assumption that for most of its early years, the field of personnel administration was concerned mainly with procedures and rules, without directly assuming responsibility for policy, or for objectives except as they could be teased out of a mass of procedures.[2] Indeed, old texts taught in major colleges and universities in personnel administration courses in the thirties and forties have often been prescriptive books, training students in procedures. More current texts and current revisions of older authors reflect the change in emphasis toward an objectives orientation.

Although a few more successful leaders in personnel administration had proposed from the beginning that the personnel function should be headed by a vice president, reporting to the president of the firm, it was not a common condition until the decade of the sixties and is certainly not universal today. The reasons are clear. In many instances the orientation of the personnel manager himself was too procedural, too rules-oriented to be comfortable in the company of executives whose interests were at the objectives and policy level. In other cases the top management of firms was insufficiently interested in human resources to see the advantages of clear objectives for the management of managers, of professionals, and the need for innovative and far thinking objectives for managing human resources.

The decade of the sixties saw a revision of the thinking of top management toward the importance of human resources. At a theoretical level, the realization of the importance of human resources had been highlighted by Theodore Schulz in his presidential address at the American Economic Association where he pointed out that investment in human capital was perhaps a better explanation of our economic growth than growth in conventional capital.[3] He pointed out that indeed our great expenditures in

---

[2] W. Scott, R. Clothier, W. Matthewson, and J. Spriegel, Personnel Management (3d ed.; New York: McGraw-Hill, 1941).

[3] T. Schultz, "Investment in Human Capital," *American Economic Review*, March, 1960, pp. 1–17, and also "Capital Formation by Education," *Journal of Political Economy*, December, 1960, 571–83.

education were a form of capital formation, which was not treated as such because accounting conventions had not seemed compatible with such treatment. Economically, however, this investment in education, health services, mobility, and other expenditures paid handsomer returns than conventional investment.

The general climate of the times emphasized manpower and its significance. Placing manpower upon a par with unemployment as a major area of concern, under the Manpower Act the Manpower Report of the President was initiated, thus providing high-level national interest in the issues of personnel policy at the level of the whole economy, and forcing it into the consciousness of managers. Unemployment became less tolerable, and a small rise in unemployment brought tremors to the nation's capital that reflected itself in a variety of national manpower programs aimed at alleviating it. The office of the secretary of labor moved from one of major emphasis upon labor peace and encouragement of collective bargaining to that of manpower. The militancy of blacks and other minority groups erupting into violence in our cities pointed up the high level of unemployment among this group, signaling a materialistic revolution based upon their inability to share in the fruits of capitalism, and the need for remedial programs to avert future disorder.

Even greater than the problems at the lower end of the economic spectrum, if less noisy, was an increasing attention to the problems of managing high-talent manpower. After the Russians launched Sputnik, a great resurgence of interest arose in our technical achievements, culminating in an eight-year *tour de force* of engineering and technology which produced the first step of man on the moon in 1969. During this period the investment in research and development expanded enormously, until by the end of the decade it was said that 95 percent of all of the money ever spent on research had been spent in the past seven years. Inside corporations, the emphasis in personnel was forced to make some radical turns.

THE MANAGEMENT OF MANAGERS

Where the traditional personnel man of the past had been kept busily occupied with factory workers and their affairs, the new breed of the sixties and beyond was moving into the management of managers, and the management of professionals. At the same time he was required to cope with employing unemployables, dealing with unions which were mature, powerful, and clearly materialistic rather than idealistic in purpose.

It was in the management of managers that the new breed found his greatest level of acceptance as a member of the top management team of the firm. The movement from specialist to generalist, called by Thomas Roberts "The Vital Shift," called for new and imaginative programs to assist technically trained experts to adjust to the broader responsibilities of managing managers.[4]

It was here that the personnel manager and the general manager or president found a common set of concerns. It was apparent that the matters which concerned presidents, executive vice presidents, general managers, and major department heads were personnel and human resource matters, not in labor relations nor in employee services and morale, but in managerial levels.

For one thing the literature in which executives were interviewed, or in which they stated their views in public revealed this concern. A sample of the quotations and statements of business leaders during the middle and late sixties on the subject can be presented as representative of the trend.

The big mistakes I've made—the ones that cost me the most personal and private pain—have been mistakes I've made in selection.—*Company President*

The man who finds a sure way of identifying a good general manager early will make a fortune.—*Executive Vice President*

I read everything the behavioral scientists are writing but a lot of it doesn't check with my personal experience and I need some guides as to what is reliable and what's pure speculation by some long-hair.—*Personnel Vice President*

When we make a mistake in compensation, such as in bonus calculation, the effects last a long time. We get into quits, law suits, and good men who slow up.—*President*

A more systematic academic study was done by the author using a population of 175 company presidents attending executive development seminars, soliciting their viewpoint with respect to their most important areas of concern. This was supplemented by another study conducted in conjunction with the American Life Convention of Chicago in preparation for a series of problem-centered roundtables for 90 presidents of life insurance companies. The results of both showed two major characteristics.

1. The technical, financial, commercial, and other "specialist" problems observed by presidents about their own situation was widely divergent. Insurance company executives had their own special problems, as did manufacturing, banking, utility, electronic, aerospace, and retailing chief executives.

2. The common areas of concern among chief executives were predominantly that of managing the human organization, and most especially the key people who reported directly to them. These common, chronic areas of concern in the management of managers are presented in Figure 1–3.

It was apparent that these were areas in which the personnel depart-

---

[4] Thos. S. Roberts, *The Management of Managers* (Bureau of Industrial Relations, brochure) (Ann Arbor: University of Michigan, 1968).

ment should be able to display some competence. The selection, promotion, training and development, coaching, performance records and inventories, compensation problems of managing managers were reported by these presidents to be their most chronic and troublesome.

It was equally apparent that the procedures for hiring, testing, examining, rating, and managing workers which had been the staple fare of personnel departments needed some major upgrading to be applied to the higher levels.

FIGURE 1–3

Some Common Areas of Management and Personnel Department Concern in Managing Managers

In managing managers there are some areas of concern which are chronic, recurring, and although often postponable, are not cancellable. They include those things which can seldom be delegated to subordinates since they are about those very subordinates and matters of interest to them.

1. *Pay raises.* Should the pay of a subordinate be increased, decreased, or left the same? How should salary increase funds be allocated among the respective subordinates?

2. *Bonuses.* Upon what basis should available funds for managerial bonuses be distributed? How can this distribution be made so as to reflect actual contribution to the surplus which created the bonus? How can windfalls be prevented? How can hard luck be taken into consideration?

3. *Promotability.* What are the elements in present performance which can be used to predict success or failure of the man who is promoted to a higher level job? How does his present performance stack up against these indicators? To the extent that bad performance would be a bar to promotion, how good is his most recent performance record?

4. *Performance reporting.* For purposes of filing accurate records of the performance of the man in his job for the past period, what entries should be made about his achievements and his failure to achieve?

5. *Coaching and improvement counseling.* What matters in his recent performance should be discussed with the man? What results areas need betterment? In which ones is he doing an exceptionally fine job?

6. *Management development.* Is there any kind of formal educational effort to which he might be sent which could promise to improve his performance? Should he go to seminars? Should he attend a course? Should he join an association? Should he be given assignments which would enlarge his experience?

7. *Assignment for the future.* With respect to future jobs or tasks within his present job, are there any changes which should be made? Should new responsibility be delegated?

The one common element in all of these areas of concern is that they require discriminatory judgment about the man's job performance and his professional capacity as a manager.

As Professor Wilmar Bernthal of Colorado stated it, the traditional maintenance function of personnel usually accepts the existing organization structure, management climate, and top management policies as given and attempts to perform a multitude of housekeeping chores within this given system.[5] The new role of internal consultant on organizational health calls for him to assess the effect of changes outside the firm, such as the human resources revolution and technological change. Based upon this he applies systems and becomes an educator of management.

The present emerging role of the personnel manager has been pointed up in a study of personnel staff conducted by Cornell University through polling members of the American Society for Personnel Administration. As a professional, the study concludes, the personnel man meets only one of five criteria for that appellation—he works full time for pay at the job. His dominant personal characteristics were a greater loyalty to the profession than the firm, a high level of education, and an intent to remain in the profession.[6] From this study we might conclude also that the new breed, more oriented to his firm and its objectives than traditional professional goals, is to be found at the top of the personnel organization rather than in a lower level staff position.

The effect of such adherence to traditional patterns among the larger numbers of persons in the field leaves the key positions open to the new breed, the man who is oriented more toward his organization's goals than those of his profession. This isn't to suggest that the traditional things won't still be done, perhaps better and with more sophistication than before. It does alter their character, however, converting them from ends into means. Figure 1–4 shows diagramatically how the modern personnel manager, and his staff, relate to the organization of which they are a part.

FIGURE 1–4
The relationship of personnel to corporate goals

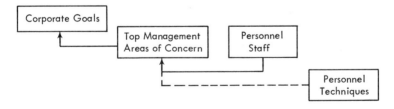

1. For the top manager the objectives of the firm, such as profit, growth, return on investment, high revenue, and low expense lead naturally to devising the major means for getting them. These means include managers who are competent, are available for high responsibilities, respond to motivational efforts, and can manage major areas of the business with competence.

[5] Wilmar Bernthal, "New Challenges Demand That We Change Roles," *The Personnel Administrator*, Vol. 13, No. 6 (December, 1968), pp. 33–38.

[6] G. Ritzer, H. Trice, and S. Gottesman, "Profile of a Professional—A Research Study," *The Personnel Administrator*, Vol. 13, No. 6 (December, 1968), pp. 1–8.

2. For the personnel executive the *means* seen by the chief executive become *ends* for his organization. He sees the goals of selection of good managers, operating a sound inventory system for high talent manpower, operating ingenious and functional compensation systems as ends for successful personnel effort and a contribution to the firms objectives.

His staff in turn becomes the doers and appliers of the existing personnel techniques to the solution of these major and recurring problems. They also will conduct other recurring and stable functions for all levels of the organization, providing advice, service, control, and research for the entire organization as service is demanded or opportunity to serve is seen.

SUMMARY: THE NEW BREED

The new breed is more likely to be top management goals-oriented than techniques-oriented; he is more concerned with results sought than activities conducted.

1. He is conversant with the changes occurring outside the firm which will have an effect upon his results, including changes in population, labor markets, the new generation, and values of middle-class people.

2. He is systematic in his goals definition, using the objectives as criteria for defining achievement in his own organization, and designs systems which will bring about similar behavior in others.

3. He is flexible in changing techniques to meet objectives and resists the strong natural impulse to alter goals to fit the procedures available to solve them.

4. He prizes innovative behavior above routine or problems solving behavior, in the operation of his own department and in the systems which he develops for the larger organization.

5. He is an agent of change in the organization where new objectives or new conditions call for change.

For the professional personnel man, or the student entering personnel administration to work, or for top management viewing its own department, such general statements won't suffice, however. It is necessary that yardsticks for judging personnel department be applied against the existing practices. These, of course, are more than internal checks of the personnel department, for the personnel function should show its greatest effects in the larger organization of which it is a part, rather than inside the offices of the personnel staff.

QUESTIONS AND PROBLEMS

1. How would you relate Yoder's High Road and Low Road to the promotability of a personnel manager?

2. How would training increase the investment in human capital for an employer?

3. If the concerns of top management and the personnel manager are alike, how would this affect the work of the personnel department?

4. "The new personnel manager is closer to being a general manager than a narrow technical specialist." Discuss critically.

5. List six ways in which the new breed is really new. List six ways in which he is the same old technician.

THE GRAND OLD MANUFACTURING COMPANY CASE—PART A [7]

During the fall of 1966 a new assistant director of Personnel Administration was brought in from the outside to strengthen the personnel staff at corporate headquarters at Grand Old Manufacturing, headquartered in New York City. The 50-year-old firm was known as a Blue Chip corporation, with steady growth and regular earnings. It had been served by its corporate personnel administration department under a vice president for 30 years, was considered professional and modern.

Among the moves suggested by the new assistant director was the institution of an annual personnel managers conference to assist in the upgrading of the personnel department, to clarify objectives, and to make the department more modern and professional.

The meeting was held in a midtown hotel for three days and was attended by corporate, division, and plant personnel managers, as well as personnel managers from the research laboratories, engineering, and accounting departments. The following is a summary of the proceedings of the first day of that meeting.

THE JOB OF THE PERSONNEL MAN

It was pointed out by Vice President Hull that the function of the Personnel Manager can vary greatly. He can be a man who does little more than keep track of things, handle routine matters, and solve problems which arise. On the other hand, he can be a man whose influence is felt by the operators as one who substantially helps them with ideas and assistance in bringing about change and improvements, which result in lower costs, more efficient operations, and hence in greater profit. It is this kind of

---

[7] Note: This case is designed for team group study. Divide the class into subteams to study separate areas of the personnel program at G.O.M., identify problems, and prepare solutions.

personnel man we want each of our personnel managers in Grand Old Manufacturing (GOM) to be. This can come about or not come about, depending upon each person. Each of us can create the kind of personnel job and the kind of acceptance and influence we want to have for ourselves and GOM.

The kind of person who is really effective, and creates this position of influence and contribution for himself, is the person who fills the following criteria well:

1. He is a student of personnel, well versed in good personnel practices and programming so that he has the tools to work with in his field.
2. He needs to be a practical person, one who can discard impractical theories, and one who can adapt sound theories to practical working programs which will appeal to practical operations.
3. He must be a man who, because of his personal qualities, can gain the acceptance and confidence of managers and a man to whom they will look for recommendations and a man whose judgment they will accept because they feel he is right.
4. He needs to be a man with the drive, determination, and tenacity to get things done. Frequently it takes more of these qualities when one must influence others than when one can merely take the action himself.
5. He should have a feeling of urgency—that tomorrow isn't good enough if it can be done today. This is highly important when working in a field of intangibles, such as personnel, where there are no rigid schedules to be met and where time can easily slip by unnoticed. While many of the jobs in personnel can be very time consuming, it is very easy to be distracted by lengthy discussions or telephone conversations and the desire to keep up with pertinent reading material. Often a careful marshaling of time and a sense of urgency are needed in order to maximize accomplishment.

ATTITUDE SURVEY

These highlights of the Michigan survey were presented by the vice president as a foundation for many of the subjects that were touched on during the week's conference sessions.

It was pointed out that the survey was undertaken only after full agreement that we would be prepared to take action where the survey disclosed that action was needed. As a basis for the topics to be surveyed, about 50 of our top-management people met in three seminar groups once each week for five weeks. As a result of these seminars, a group of policies were formulated which constituted the basis of the survey. These were policies agreed upon as matters which we expected to have carried out in practice and which we would take steps to correct if we found they were not being carried through into practice.

In general, the survey indicated that GOM is considered a better than average company to work for. In other words, our survey results are better than the average of large companies, as judged from the experience of the University of Michigan and Chicago U. Interestingly, also, our survey results are considerably better than the forecasts made by our executives who forecast how they thought the questions would be answered. This again indicates the favorableness and the optimism of our people.

It is known that some of the most favorable responses came from the Consumer Products activities in which much of the personnel effort has been concentrated over the past few years. Some of the least favorable responses came from the staff groups. Before definite conclusions can be drawn, further analysis is needed.

The survey also reveals the same tendency that surveys in other companies have shown, namely, a tendency for supervisors to rate their performance higher than their subordinates rate them. This is particularly noticeable on such human factors as knowing and understanding their men, listening and explaining, getting participation, commending and rewarding good performance, letting men know where they stand, and promoting the most capable people. In each of these, the subordinates do not think their supervisors do as good a job as the supervisors would rate themselves. On the other hand, in connection with production matters, such as getting the work done promptly and efficiently, the subordinates say that the supervisors do even a better job than the supervisors rate themselves.

The survey indicates our employees feel that we are too tolerant of incompetence in GOM. In fact, only 1 percent feel that the company is too harsh in its treatment of people who are incompetent.

Salary Administration comes in for criticism both with regard to level of pay and in wanting to know salary ranges and salary opportunities, where such information has not yet been disseminated. Our employees also feel that what should count most in getting salary increases, such as good performance, sometimes does not count as much as it should. Supervisors tend to be more critical of the administration of salaries than nonsupervisors.

Some criticism is directed at the Salary Administration Program as such, and some criticism is directed simply at the administration of it by managers and supervisors.

There appears to be a lack of knowledge and appreciation of our benefit programs both as to what the benefits are and as to the amount that is being spent on benefits by the company. Also, there is a feeling that the Blue Cross should be improved.

In the area of promotion, 65 percent report that it is very important for them to be promoted, and 88 percent feel that they are qualified for promotion now. These are extraordinarily high figures, indicating a great consciousness in this area. There is a sizable number of the employees who do not feel that the best qualified person is promoted, or that we do as good a job as we should in recognizing the proper factors in promotion. Also, there is some criticism in the number of outsiders who are hired rather than promoting from within. Part of this shows a need for better communication and explanation and quite possibly a need for a better job in selecting those to be promoted in some cases.

A third of those surveyed indicate that they have never had a performance review, and a fourth of the supervisors report that they have never held one with their subordinates. This is an area for improvement along with an indicated need for better coaching in many places in the supervisory ranks.

The survey shows a heavy reliance on the house organ, annual report, and other printed materials, which is a compliment to them. It shows less reliance, however, than in many companies on information coming from supervisors to their men. This may well indicate that the supervisors need to be kept better informed so that they themselves can pass information on to their people.

It was to be expected that the survey would develop many items where improvement could be made. This will be true of any survey in any company. It is quite encouraging to note that our survey overall produced good results, and that among the areas in which our results were very favorable compared with other companies were the following:

1. Clarity of duties.
2. Absence of conflicting instructions.
3. Training.
4. Handling of grievances or complaints.
5. Promptness in getting decisions.
6. Good opinion of immediate supervisor.
7. Supervisors feeling that they are part of management.
8. Employees feeling that their work is important and useful.
9. Individuals and families having a good opinion of GOM.
10. Employee confidence in their future with GOM.

Discussion questions

What are the major problems you see? What solutions?

chapter 2

THE HUMAN RESOURCES
REVOLUTION

"As societies achieved maturity in
the twentieth century two things happened;
real income rose . . . and the structure
of the work force changed . . ."

WALTER WHITMAN ROSTOW

THE STAGES OF ECONOMIC GROWTH

WHEN PERSONNEL MANAGEMENT first emerged as a business profession about 1920, industrial wage earners comprised the largest single percentage of occupations. It is not surprising, then, that the major emphasis in personnel management was focused upon this group. The fact that the wage-earner group had risen steadily and reached its peak at that time further makes plausible, if not imperative, the substance of personnel management in its earliest form. The fact that the labor force has changed drastically since that time, and that personnel administration techniques and social science research have not changed accordingly, is less logical.

The presumption of this text is that personnel management and social science rooted in the past has been made irrelevant by change. Changing patterns of economic activity have reflected themselves in the changed occupational pursuits of people in our society. Personnel management, which was soundly based in 1920 on the nature of work in that day, emphasized the management of workers, of coping with their organizations, and alleviating their discontents.

Today's worker is a different breed than the worker visibly before the earlier architects of personnel management. The educated employee—the manager, the engineer, and white collar worker—is the significant employee today. Social science, too, has often failed to keep abreast of

17

this change, with the result that an inordinate amount of research deals with problems which are no longer vital.

If we select 1920 as the beginning of modern personnel administration, we can picture the kinds of problems it was designed to alleviate. It was a high water mark in the division between "capital and labor," and the possibilities of class conflict were very much before the owners and the public. The labor movement, although firmly committed by that time to job-oriented unionism, was still viewed as having class struggle potential.

The length of the working day was reduced to eight hours in steel in 1923 after many years of insistence that the mills could not run with less than 12-hour shifts. Yet, many workers were alive who remembered 70-hour work weeks as ordinary. Small wonder that the personnel administration of the time was oriented as one historian puts it:

The study of the worker's fitness for the job, his psychology, and the conditions which by making him ambitious, contented and willing worker, tend to increase his efficiency. . . .[1]

The social orientation of early personnel management

Large-scale personnel management found its origins in 1917 shortly after America entered World War I. The committee on Classification of Personnel in the army was created by the War Department to uncover special qualifications of the hundreds of thousands of men flowing from industry into the army. Seven thousand officers and men interviewed and classified over 3 million men and placed over 1,200,000 of them according to their findings.[2] This provided an unprecedented stimulus to American employers to adapt these principles to the personnel problems of industry.

After the war a group of the key figures formed a consulting firm to do research and consult for employers in applying these techniques to industry. The earliest textbook in personnel was drawn from the experience of that firm—The Scott Company—with some 40 clients.

The economic and social climate were ripe for such a movement. The scientific management movement of the Taylor, Gilbreth, Gantt school had made wide gains, and the possibilities of applying scientific methods to personnel was appealing. Socially, there was much discontent among the millions of hourly workers, who comprised the largest single occupation of the day. The War had accelerated unionism, and the postwar Bolshevik campaigns had created uneasiness among employers about the pooled brute power of this group. The possibility of misunderstanding through poor communication seemed inevitable where workers in a

---

[1] C. W. Wright, *Economic History of the United States* (New York: McGraw-Hill, 1949), p. 606.

[2] Scott, Clothier, Matthewson, and Spriegel, *Personnel Management* (3d ed.; New York: McGraw-Hill, 1941), p. 519 ff.

single work force might number in thousands, and bosses were impersonal and faceless individuals.

To overcome this now large-scale barrier against individual treatment of workers similar to that which had existed between the farmer and his helper, or the small shopowner and his hands, the personnel movement was confronted with four commonly held attitudes of management toward their mass groups of workers. The changing of these four widely held attitudes comprised the personnel platform of the 1920's. Thus, personnel objectives were rooted in correcting managerial fallacies:

1. *The commodity treatment of labor is wrong.* Since the early stages of capitalism it had been accepted that wages were responsive to supply and demand. Where labor was plentiful wages would be low; where labor was scarce labor wages would be high. Carried out to its ultimate conclusions, Ricardo and Malthus could be considered architects of personnel policy—gloomy but precise. The Clayton Act of 1914 had written into public policy certain limits on injunctions on the justification that labor was not subject to antitrust laws since it was not a commodity.

2. *The worker is not a machine.* The depersonalization of the man–boss relations could often be attributed to simple impossibility to think of workers in any other sense than as a productive mechanism. Labor could be considered as Hands, not whole men, and viewed as contributors to cost under the economics of cost accounting without regard for the ultimate consequences.

3. *Paternalization is too superficial.* In the face of rising union memberships, suits over safety conditions, strikes, and the rising political influence of labor, many employers began to see a direct relationship between restrooms, good lighting, visiting nurses, recreation programs, bulletin boards, and other "nice things for nice people" and the productivity of people at work. The ultimate failure of such obvious paternalism, in which the employer became the father-substitute through his counseling and benefit programs was already apparent and the personnel men were calling for broader statesmanship in management of workers.

4. *The national asset approach involves government.* The memory of the regimentation of the war economy still fresh, it was apparent that treatment of worker's problems as management of a national asset was rising. Child labor laws, minimum wage and hour, safety, and workmen's compensation laws were enacted during this period. Many employers following World War I and for the three decades afterward saw the practicality of doing voluntarily that which would be done for the employees by government if denied by private firms. There was much evidence that employee demands for security were not to be denied. The only choice open to private industry was whether to give it voluntarily—and get credit for doing so—or to go down fighting and still pay when it became enacted into law. Shorter work hours, child labor, premium pay for overtime, safety laws, workmen's compensation, and a host of other benefit plans for employees helped create a climate for personnel management to emerge.

As a result of personnel administration the traditional concepts of labor were in a state of upheaval. Simplistic images of the worker produced policies which proposed that "the other fellow works for pay and should ask no more." Such policies were attacked vigorously on all fronts by personnel management specialists. This new doctrine suggested that:

1. The minds, attitudes, aptitudes, and morale of workers was important to the firm.

2. The worker had rights which went beyond the receipt of pay for services rendered, and that such rights ranked equally with those of stockholders or customers.

3. Individual rights of workers were important and should be considered by their supervisors in industry.

4. Democracy at work was considered to be just as much a right of the citizen at work as in the community, and participation in the decisions which affected him was a right which should be extended to the job as a normal extension of our democratic system.

Much of this philosophy was expounded through hortatory and evangelistic lectures, and by inspirational speeches. More fundamentally, there had begun to emerge in the field a more systematic study of men at work, mainly through the application of psychology to industry. Hugo Munsterberg at Harvard was a source of some dismay to his peers in the psychological sciences when he turned his attention to the factory and office. By 1925, however, it was common for testing, interviewing, counseling, and other measurement methods to be used in hiring and promotion of employees.

The Hawthorne experiments and their aftermath

A breakthrough in the application of scientific study to the employment relationship took place in some experiments at the Hawthorne works of the Western Electric Company in Chicago.[3] Extending over several years, these experiments began as a test to measure the effects of lighting intensity upon operator output in making telephone equipment. Despite the best scientific controls which varied the intensity of light and measured correlative output, it soon became apparent that there was something else at work which was controlling output. All the evidence indicated that something in the social organization of the workers was causal, and the engineer immediately retreated from the scene.

---

[3] F. Roethlisberger, and N. Dickson, *Management and the Worker* (Harvard, 1940).

They were replaced by a team of psychologists, sociologists, and anthropologists, mainly from Harvard. They studied for some five years the effects of pay, rest pauses, free lunches, and other tangible stimuli upon worker output and were left finally with clear-cut evidence that the social organization of the workers and their attitudes were more controlling over productivity than physical conditions or pay—far more controlling than had previously been imagined. Formal organizations designed to achieve technical objectives are also accompanied by informal organizations which are designed to meet the emotional needs of workers. These informal organizations control the behavior of members, and can be a force favorable to productivity, or can effectively sabotage management objectives, inspection systems, work standards, cost measures, and all of the other measures of scientific management.

The impact of Hawthorne's findings was immense for several reasons:

1. The measurements taken had been directly among workers in factories. The reader could see the faces of the workers, and read their actual comments. They were neither abstractions nor sentimental platitudes, but actual statements in vernacular from the workers.

2. It was an application of science to human affairs in a way which had seldom been done on such an extensive basis before. The anthropologist, whose findings previously had been obscure and perhaps whimsical matters concerning the Kawkuit Indians or the Trobriand Islanders had great impact when they dealt with Irish, Polish, and Italian working girls in a Chicago factory.

3. The composition of the work force was still seen as being comprised, in majority, of laborers on an hourly basis. The censuses of 1930 and 1940 were to reveal the beginning of a shift away from that proportion that has been commonplace knowledge today. In its time, however, anything which promised solutions to the "labor problem" was of utmost importance.

4. It opened the door for countless other studies in factories by social scientists. (Of late called "behavioral sciences," with some reservations on the part of geneticists and others whether or not certain of their work and methodology really justified the term science as it studies behavior).

The conclusion which quickly imposed itself upon personnel management was that the worker was at once an economic, psychological, and social entity, and must be managed accordingly.

At the same time it was a clearly minor part of the personnel management apparatus to deal with the employee who occupied a technical, managerial, or professional position in industry. Managers, it was quickly made clear to the people pressing for modern personnel management, were exempt from these kinds of techniques. For a personnel manager to be concerned with anybody making over $10,000 a year would be an impertinence, and as for engineers, sales managers, and other staff persons, they were too small in numbers to bother with. The key issues, the dynamite laden ones, were those dealing with workers.

Despite the rising evidence that the unskilled work focre was shrinking as a portion of the whole work force, unions gave added impetus to the *worker emphasis* in personnel.

The rise of unions and their impact upon personnel management

Labor union membership, which had risen to over 5 million members by 1920, had fallen to some 3.7 millions of members by 1922, and remained at about this level until the beginning of the depression in 1929. Between 1926 and 1930 the level of strikes fell to the lowest levels since the early 1880's. The advent of the New Deal under Franklin D. Roosevelt in 1933 began a "green light" period for organized labor. Within a year the gain in membership offset the losses since 1923, and by the end of 1937 was at 7.3 million. It leaped to 8.5 million members by 1940, and at the end of World War II in 1945 was at 15 million members. It reached a peak in excess of 18.9 million in 1958 and thereafter began a decline in absolute numbers which continued until unionization of government employees rose rapidly in the sixties.

This rise of union strength had many effects, one of the significant ones being that it kept the attention of personnel managers strongly oriented toward the management of workers.

That American personnel managers paid special attention to labor unions during a period of greatest growth is not surprising, nor should it be implied that any other course was open to them. The function of unions was as a vehicle and administrative agency for worker protest, and they came to "exercise a proprietary interest over labor protest," as Richard Lester has put it.[4] It established this power through economic power in part, but also the possibilities of unions becoming servants of revolution was not overlooked. Mainly through political appeal to the workers and political backing of government unions gained increasing power.

By 1955 the composition of the work force in which unionism was rooted was changing; so, too, was the nature of union activity. The militancy of unions so prevalent in their youthful stages was tempered with the aging of their leaders, the institutionalization of its functions, and its integration into the community.

Typical of its changing role in the fifties was the relationship it had with the independent or uncommitted intellectual in pulpit, college lecturn, and editorial office. In its earlier and more militant days the union

---

[4] For an insightful look at the changing role of labor, see Richard Lester, *As Unions Mature* (Princeton, 1959).

was a focal point of liberal reform, and a vehicle for betterment of society in the eyes of the intellectual. Many actually joined its ranks and turned out mimeographed broadsides, made and wrote speeches, and did statistical and legal studies to arm its advocates of "more." As unions achieved many of the objectives for which they had militantly fought, but still continued to press for job control and economic advantage for their members, the intellectuals began a retreat from their defense.

For the professor in the small liberal arts college in 1959 it was less of an idealistic crusade to uphold the cause of the exploited laborer, who made more money working in a steel mill or driving a truck than the English teacher did for teaching. In his courses of instruction in the arts of composition and in the structure of the modern novel, he was more apt to assign *The Organization Man* or *The Man in The Gray Flannel Suit* as supplementary reading than readings depicting the plight of the horny handed son of toil. During the sixties his moral fervor turned more to civil rights and the war in Vietnam than unionism.

As the pure economic nature of the labor management struggle became clearer, many of the intellectuals who had served on the staffs of the unions retreated to the campus. There they moved into neutral postures as arbitrators, urging the creation of "third forces" to exert the public interest in the grubby two-sided struggles for job control, wages, and slices of the growing economic pie. More and more, as the labor-management-relationship true character emerged as a struggle for economic advantage, the disenchantment of the intellectual liberal rose at the two-sided "buck grabbing contest," as one of them ruefully put it.

For the true professional in trade unionism there had been no change. Unions obtained emoluments for the membership or they lost their jobs. Intellectuals in unions had never enjoyed the full confidence of the operating leadership.[5] Such key roles were reserved for the line steward, the business agent, the international rep, the pork chopper, who, when older and slower, might become a labor statesman. The intellectual was no longer at the response end of the buzzer in the union leader's office. Who needs 'em? If the intellectual became disillusioned with the unions, it was only himself to whom he could point as his deceiver.

Gompers had made clear what union goals were: "More." The ultimate disenchantment for the intellectual came with the presidential elections of 1968, when substantial numbers of union members avoided Humphrey and Nixon, and cast their ballots for George Wallace. Among them was a local of the United Automobile Workers in Flint, Michigan who a mere 30 years before had been one of the locals involved in the famous "sit-down strikes" in the General Motors plants there. At that earlier time,

---

[5] Harold Levinson, *The Intellectual and the Labor Movement* (Harper & Row, 1957).

when Governor Murphy of Michigan had called out the National Guard to protect private property from possible usurpation by the union mob, many a worried capitalist had equated the sit down and occupation of private property by the unions as a first step to Bolshevism. Yet, a mere 30 years later the successes of unionism in gaining benefits, guaranteed annual wage, pensions, and high pay had moved them into the most conservative position on the spectrum.

Other observers had noted that the teamsters union in New York City had not supported the Democrat Beame, nor the Liberal Republican candidate John Lindsay, but rather had leaped to the support at the polls of ultra conservative candidate Buckley. Having something substantial to lose, they began to act like conservators, resisting invasions of their property rights. The crusade and idealistic purposes of the thirties, when unions fought for organization and bargaining rights, had been sold to the intellectual as a moral crusade. In final essence, however, it had turned out that union members were crass materialists after all. Having won the right to earn a buck, they now aimed to hang onto it. The intellectual who chose to ignore such a clear aim, or worse, tried to change it, had little to decry but his own naïveté if he had made little progress in attempting to climb aboard the labor movement and steer it.

The emergence of the new Human Resources Approach

Supervisory training during the 1930's was a desultory and ill-aimed affair for the most part. The Hawthorne experiments had led to the conclusion that workers' discontent must also be allayed by training foremen in human relations, since it was the first line supervisor who controlled the working climate and psychological atmosphere in which the great mass of troublesome workers functioned. Under such circumstances, foreman training was merely another procedure, like restrooms, guards on machines, coffee breaks, and rest pauses to make more workers contented. Few training courses, if any, were designed to improve the productivity of the department through enlarging the managerial leadership, administrative, organizational, or decision-making skills of foremen.

Management, under such a rationale, was human relations. "Management," one popular viewpoint went, "is getting results through people." The assumptions were that if the foreman used his authority sparingly and permitted wide latitude to workers they would be more contented, because, it was presumed, they all had a highly developed sense of independence and desire for freedom from orders and directions. Granted this freedom and independence of action on the job, they would devote their energies toward producing, with new zest, high quality goods at the lowest possible cost.

If there was any consideration that the foreman himself was a resource to be developed and improved (beyond serving his workers' needs for contentment), it was seldom divulged. During World War II a great shortage of foremen heightened the foreman's economic importance, and quick training courses to teach managerial skills in six two-hour sessions were presented to thousands of defense workers before they were placed in charge of production.

At the end of World War II a whole host of problems, growing out of the need for more managers, more technicians, more engineers, and more staff people who could innovate, began to plague companies.

1. Continued high-level prosperity feeding upon wartime savings required plant and sales expansion.

2. The new policy of decentralization, breaking large organizations up into smaller more manageable units, called for more persons with general management skills.

3. The technical breakthroughs of the war were converted into commercial invention. Electronics, chemistry, and atomic energy and space technology were but a few of the areas which bred demand for more technical manpower.

4. Inflation and rising costs created a demand for better accounting systems, more industrial engineers, systems specialists, and the management of paper work.

5. The failure of firms to train managers during the depression, coupled with a manpower shortage in the civilian economy during the war years was accelerated by retirements of older managers, many of whom had continued in their position during the war. The management manpower gap was considerable, and focused attention upon management development.

6. Rising labor costs and inflationary wage increases in negotiated contracts following the war caused many firms to press aggressively for mechanization and labor-saving equipment and devices. The term "automation" became a synonym for replacing workers. This drive for mechanization and automation accelerated the demand for technical, managerial, and professional persons who would engineer and install the new systems. It had the reverse effect upon workers themselves and eliminated worker positions at an even faster rate.

While this steady, urgent restructuring of the work force was occurring, many personnel departments plodded along applying the techniques and procedures of the 1920's. Social scientists continued to pursue research which called for equalized power between boss and worker, almost universally proving that permissive management was superior to dictatorial styles, if the upheaval of the exploited masses was to be averted. The slow dissolution of this class and its vastly improved condition was unnoted.[6]

[6] Harold Levitt, Review of Rensis Likert "New Patterns of Management" in *Personnel Psychology*, 4, 1964.

THE KEY ECONOMIC RESOURCE TODAY

During the late fifties it became apparent that organization planning, manpower planning, manpower selection, management development, technical personnel management, and a whole host of new problems relating to managing managers and high-talent manpower were the vital ones to the firm from an economic viewpoint. Often the personnel department, engaged in plant gate employment and grievance handling, proved too busy to be concerned, and such matters became the province of special staff assistants to general management.

In part, this changed emphasis has gone unnoticed because other matters affecting the management of personnel intervened. Certainly one of the least noticed has been the economic reconstructing of the wage and salary distribution. In the typical company which makes and sells goods on a national basis, the division of income of the employees is unequal, as might be illustrated by Figure 2–1.

FIGURE 2–1

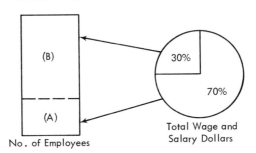

In the bar graph on the left we note that the division of employees shows about 25 to 30 percent in the category (A) "Technical, Managerial, or Professional." This presumes that the firm has a research program, a marketing staff, legal, personnel, purchasing, traffic, accounting, and supervisory persons on its payroll. Category (B) are the wage earners or clerical employees. The pie chart on the right shows a typical distribution of wage and salaries paid to the same groups.

• The technical, managerial, and professional groups, although smaller in number, will receive more in salaries and other payments than the entire wage group.

• In some businesses this may run in the ratio of 25 to 75 of persons to salary dollars received, in other words, the managerial, professional, and technical staffs comprise only 25 to 30 percent of the total number of employees but are paid 70 to 75 percent of the total wage and salary payments made to all of them.

As Mr. Albert Watters, then Vice President Personnel of General Foods put it, "The distribution of labor costs between the two groups makes it apparent that the significant group from the viewpoint of the economics of the firm are the professional and managerial groups."[7] The implications of this for personnel management, he suggests, are that personnel management in the future will be geared to the "classes and not the masses."

This ratio, which examination of 100 company records shows is typical of the modern corporation, varies according to the special characteristics of each firm, but holds for the majority of firms, considered as an average.

1. The company with extremely high labor content in its product price will probably find that the costs of wage labor will be a higher percentage of total labor cost than for companies with lower labor costs.

2. Firms with low labor costs as a percent of total expense are more apt to have a concentration of that labor cost clustered up in technical, managerial, and professional salaries.

From this it logically follows that as automation, mechanization, and the increased use of purchased materials and parts are put into practice to eliminate direct labor costs, the more this tendency is accelerated. This can be illustrated by Figure 2–2, which illustrates the nature of the business firm. The firm is the great buyer and seller in our society. The things it buys are labeled as *inputs*. The things it sells are labeled *outputs*. The process in between, of converting the inputs into outputs, is often termed the process of *production*. The outputs may be goods, or they may be services which are sold to users.

FIGURE 2–2
The nature of the firm

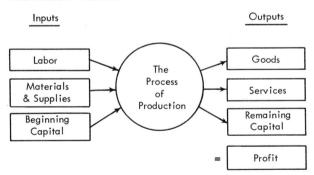

THE NATURE OF THE FIRM

The inputs are labor, material or supplies, and capital. The outputs are these same things converted into goods or services which are sold. The

---

[7] Address, Bureau Industrial Relations, University of Michigan, Ann Arbor, June, 1960.

firm also has capital at the end of the process. The purpose of this entire process is *profit*. The objective of the management of the firm is maximizing that profit. ✓

In a later chapter more will be said about the nature of this firm, and how the substitutability of capital for other factors may improve profitability, especially the substitutability for labor.

In terms of our problem at hand, however, we can consider labor inputs in terms of the *mix* of that labor, since the change in this mix is the most drastic change that has occurred to affect personnel management. The strategic use of this labor input is the proper subject matter of this book—the management of human resources. Returning to the changes in current labor markets and labor mix, we can conclude in the above terms.

• *Labor input* can be classified into a number of major categories:

Managerial   Skilled
Administrative staff   Unskilled
Technical and professional   Semiskilled
Clerical and white-collar workers

The alteration in this mix which has crept up on the field of personnel management has been decline in the number of semiskilled and unskilled, and the rise of those occupations at the top half of the list. We'll examine this trend in some detail later.

TABLE 2–1
Professional and managerial employment † (in thousands)

| Year | Professional, kindred and technical occupational group | | Managerial occupational group | |
	Number employed	Percent of total employment	Number employed	Percent of total employment
1947	3,795	6.6	5,795	10.0
1950	4,490	7.5	6,429	10.8
1955	5,782	9.2	6,442	10.2
1960	7,475	11.2	7,067	10.6
1965	8,883	12.3	7,340	10.2
1970	11,000	13.5	8,400	10.3
1975	12,900	14.5	9,200	10.4

† Eric Vetter, *Manpower Planning for High Talent Personnel,* Bureau of Industrial Relations, University of Michigan, 1968.
SOURCE: *Manpower Report of the President,* 1967, pp. 211 and 274.

Returning to Figure 2–2 showing the *nature of the firm*, we note that *Labor* as one of the input factors has many facets, and that in fact the labor mix shifts. This changing mix can be caused (and has in recent years) by some of these forces:

1. Rising wages among the lower level skills has made it economical to

increase the capital input, replacing labor with machines, equipment, and devices.

2. New instruments and control mechanisms have made it possible to replace many occupations previously considered feasible only for human discretion and judgment.

3. The rising wage cost has made it economical to purchase materials and supplies abroad or from smaller firms rather than putting in labor.

4. This increase in the input of capital, as well as the changing systems of production, requires more technical, managerial, and professional kinds of labor.

The economics of the firm and the alterations in the labor market have changed the mix in such a way that high-talent personnel became the key human resource, and personnel management was attuned to this existing economic structure, without ignoring or neglecting its now lessened traditional tasks.

HUMAN RESOURCES AND PROFIT

From the economic viewpoint it is apparent that the input mix which is high on capital and high on managerial and technical talent produces profit. Considering the profit contribution which can be imputed to human resources is vastly more complex than simply buying and selling manual labor.

In the simpler and more rudimentary market economy we could describe the economics of buying and selling labor through the mechanism of the firm in this way:

> The firm purchases the labor power from the market and uses it in production to create goods and services which it sells at a price in excess of the cost of labor and materials. This surplus comprises profit, which is measured as a rate of return to capital. The value added, which can be imputed to labor, is its contribution to profit.

The unit of input here is always labor, which is a cost. Yet, a more sophisticated look at the results of labor input for staff services, research, engineering, marketing, tax, legal, traffic, personnel administration, public relations, and operations researchers requires different measurement. A more apt description of the present estimation of the economic value of labor should include these considerations:

The rate of profit (profitability) is shaped by two major variables:
1. The earnings (revenues minus cost of goods sold minus selling costs minus overhead)
2. The investment (fixed capital such as plant; plus working capital such as inventories, cash, accounts receivable)
This means that the performance of technical and managerial resources can

improve profitability through either *increasing earnings* or *decreasing invest-ment.*[8]

1. The sales manager may increase volume, or cut selling costs or both to contribute to profit.

2. The manufacturing manager may cut unit costs by improving efficiency, reducing waste, utilizing materials, and is mainly measured by his cost performance.

3. The engineering manager may be measured by his cost reductions in processes or products, or in unit costs of services used in production (power house, utilities, etc.).

4. The staff man may improve profitability by decreasing investment. He may reduce inventories through operations research, may improve cash flow and reduce cash requirements through data processing. The accountant may cut billing procedures and the credit manager tighten collections to reduce the capital invested in receivables.

All of these examples are profitability-enhancing activities. The activities of the personnel man are designed to enhance the effectiveness of all of these activities by ensuring that qualified, trained, and experienced persons fill each of these kinds of positions.

The personnel manager of the sixties and seventies became increasingly concerned with enhancing profit through the people who contribute to the profitability of the firm.

The major contribution of the human resource in a business was no longer its energy and labor power. Decision making, analysis, innovation, organization, and application of knowledge; mental, verbal, and written skills comprise the vital profit-producing activities of labor.

Personnel management became the management of brainpower more than muscle power. The new median worker was an educated professional.

THE NEW MANAGEMENT OF HUMAN RESOURCES

If we consider the economically significant "new median" employee as a professional, a technician, or a manager, it becomes patently absurd to engage in arguments which pervaded the early personnel management movement. The consideration of the median employee today must be along the lines of a *human resource*. This complex resource provides value added in the economics of the firm by directing, changing, controlling, organizing, and innovating inside the processes of production and conversion. Is this median worker a machine? If so, he's a complicated device,

---

[8] James Bullock, "Responsibility Accounting," *Management of Personnel Quarterly*, No. 4, 1965.

more complex than the computer in function and more versatile than the cybernetic machine in being able to set his own goals. In the sense of automatically repeating his own actions again and again like a punch press, he's most unlike a machine, for his work is seldom a replica of itself.

Paternalism simply died for today's median worker. Not, at least, paternalism of the older model in which the superior leader or owner could adopt the father image. If a company invades the privacy of the manager or manipulates him through testing and appraisals, it is rare for such manipulation to continue without resistance. The ability of the educated human who is today's worker includes great ingenuity in deciding his own goals and methods. If paternalism works for awhile in some organizations, it can hardly be expected to last, since the leaders and paternalists are becoming surrounded by persons of greater knowledge and sophistication, which can be applied to making themselves free of such restrictions.

The paradox of the second revolution

In the face of this new emphasis upon the better educated, the technically and professionally trained, the high-talent man, came a concurrent revolution of the low-credential population, mainly blacks. While personnel departments vigorously pressed programs of college recruiting, management development, technical colloquia, and early identification of high-talent personnel, the streets of the major cities were wracked by riots. Those whose inability to pass the screens of education, placement, testing, and credentials were without jobs in larger numbers. This inability to participate in the fruits of the corporate system produced intolerable living conditions, disintegration of the family and the social structure of the ghetto, and produced violent reactions.

The top management of the major corporations reacted vigorously. The presidents of General Motors, Ford, and Chrysler joined to personally change the employment directions of their firms to open the doors to more unemployable blacks. Hiring centers were set up in the ghettos to recruit the illiterate, the ex-convict, the drop out, and the otherwise unemployable. Special foreman training sessions on hiring and handling the hard core unemployed were tooled by training departments.

This anomaly, of emphasis upon seeking out high talent and low talent simultaneously, placed severe stress upon personnel departments. As the black revolution continued and grew, the dichotomy became more apparent. A credentials revolution of major proportion emerged. The common ingredient was the increased emphasis upon human resources and stress upon personnel administration techniques. The traditional tools were strained at both ends of a spectrum. They neither solved the problems of the high talent nor of the hard core. The search for a common thread led back again and again to basic objectives. The phrase "Management by Objectives," [9] first coined by Peter Drucker in 1954 in his *Practice of Management,* became more pertinent, and specific techniques of defining objectives and managing in such a way that they would be achieved, shifted the attention of personnel managers from methods to end results sought.

Around this concept of management by objectives the possibilities of finding a common approach to the range of practical and difficult problems of personnel administration began to emerge.

1. It had no preconceptions about method, only a systematic way of defining goals, with a far wider range of permissible behaviors which could be applied to their achievement.

2. As attention to objectives increased, faith in prior definitions of policy and of former criteria used in recruiting, selection, placement, training, and supervising employees declined.

3. Findings of the behavioral and social sciences began to fall into perspective, with some findings proving themselves of great relevance, and others being shown as without great significance.

4. The techniques themselves were expanded, widened, and amenable to much more generous interpretation than in the past. Less cook book and doctrinaire approaches to activities proved successful as more and more leading firms made Management by Objectives their modus operandi.

Under an MBO approach, human resources emerged as the vital ingredient to corporate success. Yet, it remained an "ingredient," a means, and a constraint in the ultimate drive to achieve objectives which were economic at their core.

Is labor a commodity? Perhaps more than we would like to admit. The implications of referring to unskilled laborers as a commodity in 1914 might have been an unconscionable exploitation, degradation, and indignity in human relations. Such dangers are substantially less for today's worker where objectives are predominant. Stripped of the possibility of exploitation and the loss of dignity for the worker implicit in a commodity theory, there may be ample justification for a *new commodity theory,* perhaps best designated as a *human resource approach* to the management of employees. Obstinate avoidance of looking at the economic effects of human resources, and the guidance of complex human activity toward useful goals for the firm, may result in drastic economic losses.

Does this new commodity theory of labor imply that the social, psychological, and cultural factors in management of human resources are trivial or nonexistent? Most certainly not. They are vital *means* of utilizing

---

[9] George S. Odiorne, *Management by Objectives—A System of Managerial Leadership* (New York: Pitman, 1965).

talent and human resources to achieve corporate goals. The regressive mind which would return us to the twenties by declaring that all such cocial science nonsense is irrelevant is missing the significance of its contribution.

Social science is a powerful means to economic goals in managing the firm and its human resources toward objectives. As a vital tool, it behooves the manager and student of management to enquire and utilize such knowledge to its utmost, keeping the economic objectives of his organization close at hand as guides.

Personnel as a user of social science

Modern social and behavioral science has developed many new tools of research, and has applied them vigorously. In doing so, they have often assumed to carry their research results forward into the area of prescription and application to management problems in what one management scholar has described as a "Take Over." [10] Often his nominative findings conflict with business objectives.

The ultimate test of whether the behavioral scientists make a contribution to management practice is a function of the problems he works on. Where he finds better ways to attain corporate objectives he is accepted. In this regard there is much to be desired. The nature of corporate objectives is economic, legal, contractual, and cultural, and corporate objectives change. The anecdote of the economics professor who responded to the amazed observation that his exams hadn't changed in 20 years by stating, "That's all right, we change the answers every year," has a certain amount of poignant truth in management practices. The situation changes and the answers to the same questions differ. The new behavioral techniques are only as good as the questions they ask and their contribution to goal attainment.

Solving the problems of the twenties and thirties through behavioral research in the seventies is of little economic import to the firm which needs answers for the seventies and eighties. The management of human resources to achieve company goals in the next decade will send the personnel manager of our time again and again to the basic research in the behavioral sciences for clues to shape personnel policy and practice for today's labor force, working in today's market economy. Studies which provide clear guides for the postwar world of 1945–50 are historically interesting, but from a policy viewpoint may be distracting and irrelevant.

In the ensuing pages we will deal with a systematic appraisal of human resources and the management methods and policies required for their effective use.

---

[10] Lyndall Urwich, speech before the Academy of Management, 1963.

QUESTIONS AND PROBLEMS

1. In what ways does the history of the personnel profession color the work and status of the personnel manager today?
2. If you were starting a new personnel department for a small to medium firm, what two functions would you begin with? Why?
3. "The best approach to employee benefits and personnel management is to wait until they ask for it, then give it to them when it is inevitable." Would you agree or disagree with this statement. Why?
4. Can personnel administration contribute to profit? How?
5. What has made the Hawthorne experiments be noted as a hallmark in personnel administration?
6. Why were unions first considered to be conspiracies?
7. "Labor unions are monopolies and should be brought under the control of the antitrust laws of the United States." Do you agree or not? Why?
8. What caused the disenchantment of the intellectual with the labor movement, and what were its effects?
9. During the early seventies the "Hardhats" were much sought out by the conservative political groups and were welcomed in the White House. How would you explain this conservatism of the labor movement?
10. What affect did the rise of technology have upon the composition of the labor force during the sixties?
11. What are the various classes of labor inputs in a firm, and how is their value determined?
12. How has the manpower revolution created a demand for more knowledge of the behavioral and social sciences?

THE GRAND OLD MANUFACTURING COMPANY CASE—PART B

The first personnel conference for the personnel managers from Grand Old Manufacturing had begun with presentations on "The Job of the Personnel Man," and a factual summary of the results of a recent survey made by the University of Michigan. The discussion had been light, and many of the personnel managers from outlying plants and divisions expressed a desire to see a tally of the actual results of the survey. It was agreed that a summary tally would be prepared and distributed. Further discussion brought out the suggestion that every employee receive the raw data in tally form. It was agreed that this would be done locally.

The next presentation dealt with the placement and selection program. Vice President Hull stressed that selection was close to the heart of the personnel function and was of vital significance to the future of the firm. This presentation included a step by step plan being presented, for the first time, for college recruiting. Following this, a review of the performance appraisal program was given.

The following memorandum was filed by the man giving each of these presentations:

SUMMARY OF THE PLACEMENT AND SELECTION PROGRAM

The accumulation of information on individuals within the GOM organization is designed to satisfy a basic management objective which says, "Building an adequate and effective management force which will carry GOM to the dollar and volume goals that have been set is one of the most critically important problems."

The information you can put together and record about people, their performance, skills, and so forth is essential in the realization of this objective. The personal records will assist in this identity if properly supported with accurate information.

The function of centralized personal records may be stated as follows:

A. They provide the most complete and uniform source of personnel information on management and premanagement employees.
B. Serve as major source of identification of individuals with potential.
C. Provide information that can be effectively utilized in the advice and counsel relating to placement of people.
D. Provide information to assist in the development of individual programs for further accumulation of experience and growth of individuals.
E. Provide primary source of factual and evaluative information in acquainting General Office management with individual qualifications.

Indirectly, we accumulate information in the personnel files on approximately 3,500 exempt employees plus an undisclosed additional number of young men not classified as exempt, yet revealing potential or growth possibilities that demands evaluative information.

The information that should be fed into these records is as follows:

1. Personal Qualifications Inventory.   This is a statement by the individual on personal information, education, work experience, and interests

and is, perhaps, the most important single piece on information that can be acquired.

2. Personal Qualification Inventory Supplement.   This is an extension of the first record that brings to light changes in education and work experience as well as interests and is submitted by the individual.
3. The pictures and negatives.   The importance of these is self-explanatory.
4. The patterned interview.   It is accepted that this is a vital bit of information acquired at the prehiring point for all new employees. On those individuals in the organization that are promotable regardless of the degree, this information is essential so that the management group will have adequate information on which to assist in evaluation of the person.
5. The test scores.   This is principally a prehiring instrument, yet again very important especially on highly promotable people.
6. Appraisal data.   This includes: (1) management appraisals, (2) analysis of potential, (3) progress reports. These are designed to measure job performance, skills, certain strengths or weaknesses, each helping to form a pattern giving information for the proper development and placement of individuals.

It has been revealed that promotion is a primary concern to the majority of the people in this company. The proper replacement of management is also a basic goal of the company. Promotion from within is a cardinal principle within GOM. It is, however, impossible to satisfy these basic objectives of the company and its people without the centralized accumulation of factual information that will assist in the evaluation and placement of these people, and the accumulation of this information is a responsibility the individual personnel people must accept and then take the added step of submitting it to the centralized personnel files.

The reasonable conclusion, then, as to what you can do to assist would be as follows:

1. Follow through to make sure all exempt people have completed and submitted a Personal Qualifications Inventory or supplement.
2. Provide the centralized files with copies of all pattern interviews and other evaluative data that you now have or will obtain in the future.
3. Bring to our special attention employees who have been identified as promotable.
4. Advise of all vacancies at locations either actual or projected for which qualified candidates may be located within the company. As previously stated, the identity of promotable men is a function that demands attention of all concerned. It is a constantly changing condition and these changes must be reflected through proper evaluative information based upon facts and the facts then made available for the personnel files of

each of the individuals. With complete and correct information on the personnel of GOM a more perfect and satisfying growth and development can follow and this is a responsibility you must assume.

A STEP-BY-STEP RECRUITING PLAN FOR GOM

I. Determining the needs for college recruits in GOM

    A. Number of personnel needed to fill
       1) Current openings
       2) Long-range needs
    B. Quality (education, experience, personal characteristics)
       1) Technical
       2) Liberal arts
       3) Business
       4) Advanced degrees
       5) Special needs
    C. How the Personnel Administration Department surveys the needs of the divisions and staffs
       1) September inquiry to division and staff
       2) January inquiry to division and staff
       3) Special requests
       4) Selling good candidates without requisitions
    D. Define the need for "long-range" recruiting
       1) Advancement into management
       2) Advancement into technical or special areas
       3) For replacements

II. Picking schools to recruit

    A. Geographical location
       1) Cost of inviting people in
       2) Travel to and from
       3) Ease of communication
       4) Company reputation (local)
       5) Frequency of contacts—socal, professional, etc.
       6) Easier to know local schools
    B. Course offerings
       1) Number of colleges or schools within a university
       2) Match your needs
       3) Range of offerings
    C. Academic standards
    D. School admission standards
    E. Previous experience in recruiting

III. Scheduling campus visits

    A. Making initial contacts
        1) *Aways* the placement director
        2) One year ahead—the *goal*
    B. The prerecruiting visit
        1) Make arrangements in advance to call on placement officer
        2) Don't waste placement officer's time
    C. Let the placement office know about your needs one to two months in advance and confirm the visit—10 days ahead (call or write)
    D. Handling changes in plans
        1) Cancel in advance
        2) Advise of changes
    E. Advise PAD of schedules for
        1) Spring graduates by October 30
        2) Winter graduates by June 30
    F. Check special recruiting trips with PAD as they occur
    G. Company literature should be sent two months prior to visit

IV. Conduct of recruiters on campus

    A. The art of turning down boys
    B. Relations with placement people
        1) Protect their position
        2) Don't go around them
    C. Be prompt
    D. Keep on schedule
    E. Luncheon arrangements
    F. Overnight arrangements
    G. "Who's the customer here?"
    H. Use money carefully
    I. "How much pressure on boy?"

V. Screening interviews on the campus

    A. Obtain from him
        1) A resumé you can keep
        2) Get vital statistics—age, marital status, academic record, extracurricular record, work record
        3) Get his *aims* clear
            a) Geographical limits
            b) Job limits—types
            c) Health

    d) Availability
    e) Ultimate career goals
    f) Salary expectations
B. Allow for questions from students—five minutes (sell the company)
C. Tell student what the next step will be within specific date limits
D. Records
    1) Resumé of student with notes on margin
    2) Use back of resumé for *immediate* notation

VI. Using faculty and placement people on the campus

A. Faculty
    1) Cautious—more interested in student than the company
    2) Use sparingly—and in areas of their authority
    3) Don't try to "use" him to sell the company
B. Placement people
    1) This is primary contact—they are more "your" representative than anybody on campus
    2) Respect their position
    3) Don't always insist on top man in placement department
    4) NEVER offer "favors"—maybe Christmas gifts if tactful
    5) Don't "talk down" to them
    6) Never make an offer to faculty or staff on recruiting trip
    7) Keep placement department informed of all negotiations

VII. Inviting to headquarters or office

A. Make "invite" decision at time of campus interview—subject to review
B. Make a master schedule of visits planned
C. From master schedule make out detailed student itinerary
D. Allow flexibility for student on date
E. Write warm but not clubby letter of invitation—*sell* always
F. Ask for return call, wire, or letter. Suggest they call collect. Letters are preferable.

VIII. Corresponding with recruits

A. EVERY person talked to gets a letter explaining his exact status
B. *NO* letters (See Exhibits A & B)
    1) Be tactful
    2) Don't reflect on the *man's* qualities
    3) Sell the company
    4) Be especially prompt—one month maximum

　　　　5) Don't become personally involved—handle them all alike
　　　　6) Be brief
　　C. Conditional offer letters
　　　　1) Candidate has visited office and been agreed upon to hire
　　　　2) Offer states the job clearly
　　　　3) Salary stated
　　　　4) Location stated if known
　　　　5) Offer conditional upon passing physical
　　　　6) Request written reply
　　　　7) Follow up if no reply comes—may wait three months
　　　　8) SELL the job
　　　　9) Be warm, friendly, not flowery
　　D. Other letters
　　　　1) Military follow-up
　　　　2) Refusal follow-up (military)
　　　　3) After visit "No" letter

IX.　The recruit's visit to company

　　A. Importance—the key part in recruiting
　　B. Have right schedule set up for man—send resumé and check-list one day ahead to people who will interview prospect
　　C. Handling man on arrival
　　　　1) Handle his expenses
　　　　2) Brief him on the day's activity
　　　　3) Start him on interviews
　　　　4) Have luncheon with small group of staff where he can relax
　　　　5) Have him take tests, if any
　　　　6) Pattern interview if still actively interested in hiring
　　　　7) Allow time for man to talk about views—ask questions
　　　　8) Sell the WHOLE company
　　　　9) Sell your activity
　　　10) Wind up day
　　D. Keep rigidly to schedule—don't lag
　　E. Do all introductions carefully
　　F. Give brief explanation of who interviewer is that he's meeting
　　G. Thank GOM staff man for his time, check his impressions same day

X.　Clinching the deal

　　A. Sell the whole company
　　B. Sell division or activity second
　　C. Remember—good men have many offers
　　D. Answer questions candidly

E. Don't exaggerate or OVERSELL
F. Don't make promises that can't be delivered
G. Emphasize company interest in *individual* progress
H. Don't haggle over pay
I. Don't be whipsawed on job or pay
J. Know your bargaining power and flexibility
K. Be well briefed on common questions about GOM

XI. Placement and follow-up

A. Placement
  1) Advise man's boss of any arrangements made at hiring in writing
  2) Provide full background on man to his new boss (except Vocational Audit)
  3) Don't oversell a candidate to manager
B. Follow-up
  1) Get progress report, send copy to New York after first six months, thereafter once a year
  2) Visit with man if in that location
    a) Suitability of work
    b) How well he likes job
  3) Checks with manager—formal and informal
  4) Salary progress
  5) Any change of interest
  6) Is reassignment indicated?
  7) If terminated or quits—reasons why
  8) Let him know others are interested in him
  9) Regular "How Am I Doing" talks
  10) Management appraisal

XII. Salaries

A. Personnel Policy Committee approved salary schedules
B. Bargaining for exceptional men
C. What other industry is paying this year (NICB report)
D. Avoid upgrading your own offer to a man
E. Don't try to cut corners—pay the approved rate
F. Report salary problems in recruiting in writing to New York—be *specific* and *factual*
G. SELL the benefit package
H. Sell stability of company
I. Know and explain incentive plans where they apply—give realistic picture.

XIII. Training of recruiters

    A. Company recruiting policies
    B. Responsibility to schools and students
    C. What to expect from schools and students
    D. Recruitment ethics
    E. Company-wide manpower needs
    F. How to evaluate a student
        1) Screen
        2) Pattern interview on visit to office
        3) Management interviews
        4) Application blank
        5) Comments of faculty and placement people
        6) Subjective observation
        7) Questions and answers
    G. How to sell the company
    H. Year-round contact with schools
     I. Contacts with placement office
     J. Contact with student group
    K. Referrals
    L. Use of literature and aids
    M. Interviewing skills
    N. Skill in pattern interviewing
    O. Knowledge of tests and their uses

EXHIBIT A
"No" letter after campus visit

Dear Mr. _____:

Recently I had the pleasure of talking with you in connection with the Grand Old Manufacturing Company recruiting activity. We appreciate very much your interest in investigating our company and the time you gave me.

We have now had an opportunity to explore the areas in which you are interested. Nothing encouraging having developed, we regret to advise you that we do not have a position to offer you at the present time. We wanted to be prompt in giving you this information so as not to interfere with any employment decisions you might be in the process of making.

Again, our sincere thanks for your interest. If an opening should develop in the near future which we feel might be of interest to you, we should like to feel free to contact you.

                              Sincerely,

EXHIBIT B
"No" letter after New York visit

Dear Mr. _____:

It was certainly a pleasure having you with us recently. We sincerely hope that the full day's activities proved interesting to you and that you had a pleasant trip back to _____.

EXHIBIT B (continued)

A great deal of time has been spent in going over all of the material which we assembled in hopes that we could fit you into one of the positions in GOM. I am sure that we explained at the time of your visit that we are interested in offering only those positions we feel would offer a real challenge and opportunity for you. At the moment, _____, we do not have a position to offer you.

We wanted to be prompt in sending this information on to you as we know that you are giving some consideration to employment with other companies. We all wish to thank you for your sincere interest in our company. If anything should develop in the future which would suitably utilize your excellent qualifications, you can be sure you will be given further consideration.

Sincerely,

THE APPRAISAL SYSTEM IN GOM

The session on appraisal was devoted primarily to the three-step procedure to locate and identify promotable people within GOM. By way of review, this procedure is outlined as follows:

Step 1. Working from a list of all exempt people within a section, a responsible manager of that section should, in a short oral report to a representative from Personnel, indicate the people on the list who are unlikely to advance to a level much beyond their present. This manager should give good reasons for making such a value judgment, such as "nearing retirement," "has a limiting health condition," "has failed to perform well in responsible positions in the past," etc. Step 1, therefore, is a screening process whereby roughly one third of the people on the list of exempt people within this section are eliminated from further consideration. Caution should be exercised to prevent the manager from summarily eliminating a person without a sound reason.

Step 2. A management appraisal interview should be conducted in which the qualifications of each person who "passes" Step 1 is discussed in detail by the man's immediate superior. During this interview emphasis should be placed on facts, not opinions.

Step 3. Those people who appear to possess potential for advancement on the basis of a management appraisal should be given a patterned interview and tested (ordinarily the Wonderlic Personnel test, the SRA Nonverbal form, and the McMurry-Johnson Number Relations test are enough to give a fair measure of a man's basic intelligence—our reasons for giving these tests in the first place). The test scores and a write up of the patterned interview should become a permanent part of the file of the person considered as well as a copy of the management appraisal interview.

In this three-step process the management appraisal should play the largest part in determining potential of an incumbent. The patterned interview and the tests are supplementary and provide facts about the man's background, interests, and aspirations that would be helpful to those who are considering the man for a transfer or promotion.

If a conscientious job is performed in all three steps of this procedure, it is our expectation that a better job will be done in locating those people within the organization who have the potential to make significant contributions to company objectives over the long run.

Since the first step in the three step appraisal procedure is self-explanatory and since more personnel people within GOM have had training in the use of the patterned interview, there seems to be only one step of the procedure that requires explanation, that is Step 2 or the management appraisal. It is our intention here to spell out rather concisely the purpose of the interview and the methods to be employed in conducting the interview, rather than the procedure whereby some of the information gathered in the interview may be used in making a final evaluation of the man's present performance and potential.

Purpose

The purpose of management appraisal is to evaluate people, i.e., give management information as to how individuals fit into their jobs for the purpose of taking constructive remedial action or to highlight potential. Although many of the textbooks say that merit rating can also be used to get material with which to counsel an individual, many industrial psychologists feel that this concept is wrong for many reasons that we will not attempt to explain here. Our chief interest in the management appraisal is to find and identify promotable people within the organization. Thus, it is used as a management tool and not necessarily as a basis for counseling with an employee.

How to conduct the appraisal interview

The management appraisal is a field type of merit rating. Three people are involved—the interviewer, rater (the employee's supervisor), and the employee or the subject. However, the subject need not know that he is being rated, and, for obvious reasons, it is probably best that he be unaware that he is one of the subjects of an appraisal program. The interviewer and the rater are the only persons involved in the actual appraisal interview. It is very desirable and, in most cases, imperative, that the interviewer be at as high a level or higher than that of the rater (In terms of position within the company.) Thus, for example, if a division comptroller is to be interviewed and asked to rate his chief accountant, the interviewer would logically be the division personnel manager rather than the newly hired personnel trainee. Since it is the interviewer's responsibility to bring the rater down to earth, to check for inconsistencies, and to follow through and probe on many of the questions, it is desirable that he have a fair measure of aggressiveness. He also should be someone who inspires confidence; the rater must be certain that the information he divulges will be treated in the most confidential manner.

The interviewer must find a private place where he and the rater can talk without being overheard and where they are free from distraction. A private office with a secretary taking incoming calls is the most desirable. The first thing that the interviewer should do, once he gets together with the rater, is to explain the program and to sell the rater on it. Unless the rater is convinced the program is worthwhile, the value of the appraisal will be reduced substantially. The following are some things to keep in mind when you "sell" the rater:

1. Whether the rater is consciously aware of it, or not, he is constantly making ratings and evaluations of those people reporting to him as they perform various duties from day to day throughout the year. Thus, appraisal is nothing new or mysterious to the rater. If an employee is late in turning in a report, for example, his boss (the rater) is inclined to "rate" the man down somewhat. If, on the other hand, he should turn in a good report on time, the employee would get a "good" rating in that particular instance. It would be safe to say that almost anything a subordinate does is rated by the superior, either good or bad, and this is as it should be.

2. However, the difficulty comes when the superior called into *his* boss's office and is asked to give an appraisal of the man's qualifications for a promotion. If he is pushed for an on-the-spot appraisal, he is bound to be influenced by the overweighing of recent occurences. There would be a tendency, for example, to ignore or lose sight of all the good things the employee had done in the past year if the subject had torn the fender off the boss's car in the company parking lot just the night before.

3. Even if he is given a few hours to think it over, his rating or appraisal might not be as objective as it might be if the rater were aware of all the areas to be examined and if he had the help of an impartial third person whose sole responsibility was to see that he did a good job in this rating.

4. The management appraisal method of inventorying the qualifications of personnel is as fair and as objective as any we know. If properly conducted, a management appraisal interview will turn up enough facts about the man's work performance to enable the rater, with the help of the interviewer, to make a good evaluation of the subject's potential.

5. Since during the interview the rater only talks about facts and avoids his own personal opinions, he is not actually sitting in judgment of his subordinate, but is merely acting as a reporter. Thus, he should not feel that he is playing a game with a subordinate's future nor should he feel that his rating will be as susceptible to error as are the great majority of other appraisal systems. Instead of allowing an overweighing of a recent occurrence, for example, the interviewer will, through his questioning, force the rater to remember the good as well as the bad and draw

out a good number of incidents of performance by the subject. If presented properly, these should be strong selling points for the management appraisal system.

The appraisal interview, then, is simply a process whereby the interviewer forces the rater to recall how the man being rated performed in various instances, so that when the entire appraisal is reviewed a fairly clear picture emerges of what the man has been doing. This provides a basis for making a logical, objective prediction of what the man will do in the future.

After the rater has been sold on the purpose of doing the rating and the method to be employed, there remains the task of going through the appraisal form and getting answers to as many questions as possible. The controlling factor here is the amount of information that the rater has about the subject. For example, if the subject has never conducted a meeting, item 12, (Exhibit C) which deals with the ability to conduct meetings might be skipped, or if the person being rated does not have any customer or outside contacts, item 30 (Exhibit C), which deals with this subject would not be covered. Furthermore, there will be questions asked that the rater cannot answer because he doesn't have sufficient knowledge in the area questioned. For example, item 25 (Exhibit C), the ability to accept criticism, if the subject has never been criticized, the rater would have no basis for a valid answer.

In all, there are about four instances when the interviewer will ask the rater for a subjective opinion:

1. When he asks how well the subject is doing his job.
2. When he asks for the subjects strong and weak points.
3. When he, at the end of the appraisal, asks for an overall rating of the subject.
4. When he asks the rater's opinion on the subject's promotability.

Other than in these cases the interviewer should strive to deal exclusively with facts. It is not enough for the rater to say, for example, that the subject has quite a bit of imagination and creativity. The real question is, what has this man even created that is original. It is not enough for the rater to say that the man works well under pressure. The test is, has the man ever become disorganized or unduly excited and, if so, what were the reasons and situations surrounding the disorganization and excitement. It is the interviewer's job to keep the rater talking about facts rather than opinions.

A well-conducted management appraisal interview will probably prompt the rater to consider his subordinate from angles that he had never considered before; it can be an education to the rater as well as a source of good appraisal information. By the time he has completed the interview the rater may have an entirely different idea about his subordinate's capabilities than he had before he started the interview. In addition, and probably more important, is the fact that a responsible manager, who must later make a decision whether or not to promote or relocate the subject, will be armed with quite a bit of information about the man's on-the-job performance.

EXHIBIT C

Rater _____ _____ 1st ___ 2nd ___ 3rd Rater
          Name   Position

MANAGEMENT APPRAISAL FORM – PART II
(CONFIDENTIAL WHEN COMPLETED)

Name _____ Date _____

Job Title _____ Ranking _____ of _____

Department, Division, Plant or Office _____ How long in this position _____

Came with company _____ Age _____
                    Date   Position   Present Age

How well is he doing the job? _____
                    How does his performance compare with last year or previous periods;

with other doing similar work? _____

Strong points _____
                    What is he doing unusually well?

Weak points _____
          What are his outstanding weaknesses? (Every one has some weaknesses, if this employee is to be

developed, helped to overcome his limitations, and properly placed, it is imperative that all of his weaknesses, shortcomings

and limitations be brought to light.)

1. Appearance, dress and manner _____
                    Are they appropriate for the position?

2. Technical qualification _____
                    Is it excessive?   If not qualified, where is he weak?

3. Industry _____
                    Is he lazy?   Does he work too hard?

4. Energy, initiative and drive _____
                    Is he a "self-starter?"   Does he find obstacles challenging?

                    Is he a "doer?"

5. Expense and cost consciousness _____
                    Does he watch the pennies?   Enough?   Too closely?

6. Ability to plan and organize _____
                    Is his work and that of his subordinates systematically laid out and organized?

                    Does he anticipate contingencies?

7. Creativity and imagination _____
                    What has he ever created that is genuinely unique and original?

EXHIBIT C (continued)

8. Adaptability and resourcefulness _____
If conditions change suddenly radically, how quickly and effectively can he adapt
himself to them? _____ ☐

9. Accuracy _____
Can his reports invariably be accepted with no checking whatever? ☐

10. Personal selling ability _____
Can he overcome resistance and close the hard ones? ☐

11. Promotional ability and showmanship _____
What flair has he for the unusual, colorful and dramatic? ☐

12. Ability to conduct meetings _____
How well organized, well presented and interesting are his meetings? ☐

13. Willingness to support company policies and instruction with which he is not in agreement _____
Is it whole-hearted, or does
he simply give them lip service? With reference to Ind. Relations, Purchasing, Financial, Operating policies, etc.
If he gives only lip service, why? Does it show itself? Is his attitude constructive or destructive? ☐

14. Attitudes toward superiors _____
Is he resentful, cooperative or obsequious? (a "bag carrier" or a "brown noser")? ☐

15. Ability to get along with associates _____
How well is he liked, accepted and trusted? ☐

16. Leadership and ability to handle men _____
What is his philosophy of Leadership: autocratic, participative or helpless
("doesn't know what to do", a "hand wringer" no direct leadership)? ☐

17. How well does he delegate _____
Does he delegate at all?   To what extent does he delegate responsibility without
authority? ☐

18. Concern with detail _____
To what extent does he bury himself in unimportant detail? ☐

19. Development of subordinates _____
Whom, specifically, has he developed? ☐

20. Pets and favorites _____
Does he prefer "yes men" as subordinates? ☐

21. Self-reliance _____
Is he a "leaner?"   How well does he stand on his own feet?   To what extent does he habitually
tell the boss what he wants to hear? ☐

22. Willingness to accept responsibility for his and his subordinate's errors, etc. _____
Does he "pass the buck" and alibi?
Will he admit that he is wrong? ☐

EXHIBIT C (continued)

23. Ability to follow through decisions _____
Can assignments given him be forgotten?
[ ]

24. Ability to work under pressure _____
To what extent does it create panic or disorganization in him?

What is his reaction to pressure?
[ ]

25. Ability to accept criticism _____
Is he prone to resent it or pout and sulk?   What does he do afterward?
[ ]

26. Ambition _____
Is he content to remain at his present level?   What aspirations does he have?   How realistic are they?
[ ]

27. Willingness to accept direction _____
Is he a troublemaker or is he too docile?
[ ]

28. Analytical ability _____
Can he come up with practical and realistic solutions to problems?   Are they usuable?
[ ]

29. Trading or negotiating skill _____
Is he a hard bargainer?   Does he usually get his money's worth?
[ ]

30. Skill in handling customer (or outside contacts) relationships _____
How well is he respected, liked and accepted?

How influential is he with them?   Can he keep them in line?
[ ]

31. Ability to present and sell ideas to superiors _____
How many and what kinds of ideas has he presented and sold?
[ ]

32. Ability to handle discipline _____
How taut a ship does he run?
[ ]

33. Ability to handle labor relations _____
Is he an appeaser, a compromiser, a hard and clean bargainer, or a reactionary?

Does he know a "good deal" when he sees it?
[ ]

34. How "people minded" rather than "work centered" is he? _____
How sensitive is he to the needs and feelings of others?

Does he think of people in the same terms he does of machines?
[ ]

35. Capacity to stand up against superiors _____
To what extent does he fight for his convictions?
[ ]

EXHIBIT C (concluded)

36. Ability to face issues squarely _____
    Is he prone to avoid coming to grips with unpleasant issues?   Does he procrastinate?

Does he indulge in wishful thinking? _____

37. Tendency to act on short vs. long range basis_____
    How impulsive is he?   Is he prone to jump at conclusions?

To act in terms of momentary expendiency?   To make snap judgments?
Off-the-job factors _____

    Health _____
        What conditions are affecting his work or threaten to?

    Home _____
        What conditions are affecting his work or threaten to?

    Finances_____
        What conditions are affecting his work or threaten to?

    Habits _____
        What about drinking?   Gambling (including the horses)?   Women?

What has been done to help him?_____
        What specific weaknesses and limitations have been recognized?

        What steps have been taken to help the individual to overcome them?

What do you plan to do? _____
        What further steps are contemplated to help the individual to overcome his weaknesses and

limitations and build himself for higher level responsibilities?

Overall Rating: _____ Outstanding (1)_____ Meeting expectations (2)

        _____ Not meeting expectations (3)_____ Unsatisfactory (4)

Is he best fitted for decision making _____or advisory _____ responsiblity?

Why? _____

Is he promotable?   _____ Yes   _____ No

To what? _____
        It must be remembered that a mistake in making a promotion is costly not only to the employer; it is even more

costly to the employee.
When?_____
        Before any promotion is made, it is imperative that the demands of the higher

Why or why not?_____
        level position are studied in detail and fairly definite specifications established.

        These must include standards not only for skills and experience, but also

        for intelligence, ability to initiate, to make decisions, to administer discipline,

        to plan and organize, to exercise leadership, and to show self-reliance and

        administrative ability. Unless the candidate meets the requirements in all these

        respects, he will probably be over his head in the position to which he has been

        promoted.

_____   _____
    Rater   Interviewer

chapter 3

NEW YARDSTICKS FOR MEASURING PERSONNEL DEPARTMENTS

IT IS MUCH easier to describe what personnel department activities are than it is to define the difference between an effective one and an ineffective one. The reason is that often the personnel department is conducting its affairs without yardsticks of excellence and merely rates itself against certain checklists of *activities* which are carried on.

It is here that the systems approach comprises a useful discipline. The systems approach is more *output* oriented than activity oriented, the activity having little virtue of its own, but only as it adds values to the resources being put into the department. As shown in the diagram in Figure 3–1, many personnel departments have been excessively concerned in recent years with activity, and somewhat less about inputs. They have lamentably, all too often, been oblivious to outputs, or even to the fact that there should be definable outputs which are worth the inputs consumed and the activities conducted.

FIGURE 3–1

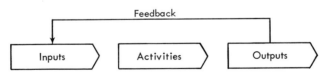

The system called management by objectives proposes that the first step in managing would be a clear definition of the outputs expected. This would be followed by obtaining resources to achieve them, and finally the conduct and control of the activities. As we've noted, dramatic changes in technology have produced a world of technical and professional employees that differs drastically from the early days of personnel in the 1920's and beyond. Because the composition of the work force is changing, the objectives of personnel and industrial relations departments are changing.

In 1920, almost half of our employees were blue collar. Today, blue-collar workers make up somewhere over 20 percent. In 1920, the research bill in the United States was less than $100 million. In 1967, it ran in excess of $23 billion. In 1920, approximately 150 firms had research departments. Today, over 16,000 firms have research programs or departments.

In 1920, the industry of the United States was primarily a national industry which engaged in foreign trade. Today, great international divisions operate foreign enterprises manned by foreign nations operating on American investment and along the lines of American technology and American management principles.

In 1920, staff positions such as market researcher, operations researcher, personnel researcher, organization planner, and the like were nonexistent. Today they are common.

Since 1920 we have seen the creation of entire new business staff professions such as accountants, computer programmers, quality control and reliability experts and industrial engineers. Mechanization has been supplanted by automation in both factory and office. Larger accumulations of capital, more stable money systems, the gains of creative chemistry, space technology, electronics, atomic energy, and the rising influence of government in the employment relationship have all changed the personnel job.

Such changes call for new activities for personnel departments. How can you evaluate whether or not your personnel administration staff is adequate, its activities germane, its effectiveness high?

At present we find five major yardsticks which are being used to audit and evaluate personnel departments. They include the following:

1. You might audit yourself by comparing your personnel programs with those of other companies, especially the successful ones.

2. You might base your audit on some source of authority, such as consultant norms, behavorial science findings, or simply use a personnel textbook as a guide.

3. You might rely upon some ratios or averages, such as ratios of personnel staff to total employees.

4. You might use a compliance audit, to measure whether the activities of managers and staff in personnel management comply in policies, procedures, and rules, using what I would call the internal audit approach.

5. Finally, and my own personal recommendation—you might manage the personnel department by objectives and use a systems type of audit.

Let's look at each audit system in turn:

1. *Copying other companies.* It is pretty natural and not without some

merit that we should try to imitate the successful. If we learn that GE, IBM, RCA, Dupont, or General Foods is practicing a certain kind of personnel technique, it is not surprising that we tend to imitate them. They are successful in the overall results which their companies achieve. We presume that copying individual programs is to increase the likelihood of achieving similar overall results from their experience for our own.[1]

Yet, the model which calls for imitating the best isn't without dangers. We may imitate the wrong things. We might copy some irrelevancies rather than the fundamental germ of the idea. We may copy something which was designed to meet a specific local problem within the model firm, but which doesn't suit the needs of our own firm and its problems. Even worse, we may imitate those things which a few isolated individuals, whose low work pressure permits them to appear most frequently at conventions as speakers, declare to be their company practice, but which the great bulk of their managers have never practiced, nor do they intend to ever try.

Many personnel and training men fall into the self-deluding habit of describing their own desires and plans to outsiders in terms that would create the impression that their firms are smoothly operating monolithic machines which have none of the real-life problems and obstreperous people which you and I always seem to encounter in our own shops.

Learning from another's experience is valuable if you can learn all of the details of that experience. Short of that, constructing new programs based on copy-cat thinking might mean borrowing the other fellows' troubles along with his gains.

2. *Basing your audit on some outside authority.* A second method of devising yardsticks for evaluating your personnel department is to find an expert authority and adopt his criteria.

a. The search for experts who will do our thinking and decision making for us often starts with a checklist. A list of all the personnel functions and a rating scale of how well each is done usually comprises the basic audit instrument. This list can come from a textbook, from a manual, or from some commonly applied audit. The University of Minnesota's Triple Audit would be one such example, or the Industrial Relations Counselors Procedure another.[2] There are many such lists, many of which are constructed by copying from the others.

b. Consultant's observations comprise another type of expert or authoritative rating. The consultant has visited and worked for numerous firms. He has a well stocked memory drum of personnel practices he has seen

---

[1] Such an approach accounts for the great success of the American Management Association in attracting managers to its seminars, conferences, and courses. Their credo "education of management by management" has proven one of the most attractive aspects.

[2] Dale Yoder, *Manpower Management* (New York: McGraw Hill, 1961).

elsewhere. He will tell you how your personnel program stacks up against the others he has seen. He may also tell you how to correct any short-comings.

c. Behavior science research findings is one of the most amazing sources of expert knowledge in recent years, against which present practices are rated. Such norms as Theory X or Theory Y, Managerial Grid, and Auto-cratic-Democratic scales would be examples of norms and values which are proposed by academic research types as tests of personnel administra-tion effectiveness. The X guys are bad, the Y types are the good guys, and so on.[3]

The common ingredient to all such standards for personnel depart-ments is that they are general in scope and are applied to specific depart-ments, located in specific companies, at a specific time. Not without some uses in obtaining ballpark estimates of how you compare with others, such authoritative guides are a poor beginning point for measuring per-sonnel effectiveness. As ultimate criteria they have many shortcomings.

3. *Measuring your department against an average* is closely related to the others in that it is the practice of counting things and rating the find-ings against some averages. The ratio of personnel people to other em-ployees, the ratio of professional staff to clerical staff, the ratio of mana-gers to workers, or the ratio of offers to acceptances in college recruiting are common terms in personnel department evaluation efforts. This can be calculated in dollars to results ratios, percentages of total workforce ratios. Negroes, females, impending retirements, turnover, absenteeism, are examples of averages we use. In the use of personnel statistics, the use of averages of one kind or another is commonplace. Frequently, it is enlightening and useful.[4]

Some limitations do exist here. Such statistics only have meaning as internal control devices, not as evidences of success or failure. When the statistics for your firm are matched against the averages for all firms, or even for leading firms, you may be committing a blooper in logic. To some, the use of averages or statistics is mistaken for managing by objectives.[5]

4. *Measuring compliance against policy, procedure, and rules out in the work force and sales office* is the fourth approach to evaluating the per-formance of personnel departments. Increasing in frequency, the trend seems to be toward turning the dirty job of conducting such inspections over to the internal auditing department. The steps in preparing such audits goes about as follows:

a. The personnel department in cooperation with the internal auditor

---

[3] These uses and limitations of this source are discussed in Chapter 17.

[4] Figures for turnover, for example, are estimated and published annually by the U.S. Department of Labor, usually in their official publication "The Monthly Labor Review."

[5] *Ibid.*

takes out the policy and procedure manuals on employment, selection, testing, grievance handling, time off with pay, leaves of absence, and all of the areas of concern, and converts it into a checklist.

b. From some commonly available checklists they add others and compile it into an internal auditor's guide to policing the line organization on behalf of the personnel department.

c. The internal auditor, along with the regular duties of checking revenue and expense procedures, probes into personnel practices and issues a compliance or noncompliance report. The personnel department is thus removed from the unpleasant task of being policemen. When the report is unfavorable, they are then properly sympathetic and helpful in correcting the deficiencies.

As a kind of manipulative system, it helps protect the good guy image of the personnel department. As one personnel manager put it, "It's really a wonderful plan. The auditors are all viewed as snoopers and SOB's anyhow."

The main advantage of the system is that it takes the personnel department out of the role of controller and turns it into a service and advice department, which is a softer and more pleasant image. The disadvantage is that it turns over to the controller some personnel functions and may not be as cleverly concealed as we suppose. The general manager who gets a favorable financial audit, but is clobbered because he has varied from a personnel policy for good reason, will hardly welcome innovative suggestions from the personnel people. It also implies that exact slavish conformity to every personnel regulation and rule is to be placed in the same category as a violation of the rules for handling cash receivables, inventories, billings, and purchase orders. There is a difference between personnel practices respecting people, and accounting practices regarding control of cash. Each in its way has some useful purpose. Auditing people for their management of cash is nothing more than removing temptation—a Biblical kind of work. Intervening between manager and subordinate by strict definition of every detail of that relationship is hardly Biblical, or even human.

5. The objectives approach to auditing personnel departments is the fifth approach. Did it set sound objectives? How well did it achieve the objectives which it set for itself? Measuring results against objectives for personnel departments offers the best chance for integrating the personnel department into the parent organization which created and sustains it.

Yet, an anomalous situation exists in many firms. The personnel management development and the training departments have been leaders in espousing management by objectives for other managers, but have been amazingly reluctant at installing the same system in their own shop. The reasons given often include such evasions as "our work is to intangible and can't be measured." This invites two immediate questions:

1. How can you be so insistent that everyone else do something which you yourself evade?
2. If your output is so vague that it can't be described or measured, what would the company be missing if it were eliminated?

The plain facts are: Many personnel departments are being managed by objectives. They do it and find it exciting and helpful. They are more successful than those which do not manage by objectives.

What is success for a personnel department?

Personnel departments don't produce tangible products. They produce intangible softwares. These intangible softwares are made and sold for a captive market consisting of line departments and other staff departments, plus top management. By applying management by objectives to your personnel department, you are able to use a marketing approach to personnel department administration.

A marketing approach to personnel administration? The beginning point for managing the personnel function by objectives is to determine that we are in the business of making and selling certain kinds of products for a captive market. What is this captive market? It consists of those departments which produce and sell the hardware or are themselves staff departments to these same producers and sellers.

The purposes of the firm are to make and sell such things as automobiles, chemicals, soap, or cereals. Or, to produce and sell some kind of consumer services which will be sold such as insurance protection, investment advice, or education.

The purposes of its own captive departments such as personnel, public relations, traffic, legal, and the like, are to help the hardware departments succeed or to help the top management of the firm manage the organization.

It is the loss of insight into its own purposes which gets personnel departments into low repute inside its own firm, or leads to its being crippled in size, budget, and effectiveness.

It is precisely in this regard that the four criteria for auditing personnel departments can contribute to its lower effectiveness rather than raising its effectiveness. Outside authorities, behavorial sciences, practices of other firms, ratios, compliance with policy and consultants have value only to the extent that they impel the personnel department in your organization toward the objectives of your customers. The demand for personnel services is a derived demand. Personnel functions are like an organ which depends upon the entire organism for its sustenance. At the same time, it comprises a part of the organism and strengthens it by performing a vital function.

What are the stages in setting sound objectives for the personnel department? Since the personnel department is primarily a producer of soft-wares, it must research its market and find out what its customers, the primary producing departments, need, want, or will buy. This requires line objectives be reasonably clear. In too many cases the line departments are unclear on where they are going and the personnel department is trying to help him get there.[6]

If operating departments are not clear on objectives, the personnel department has a challenge—to train them in setting objectives, appraising performance against objectives and administering salaries by objectives.

With these primary department objectives, the personnel department has the basis for establishing its own targets. As an intangible software department, it works at an organization-wide level. And, it should be working on five-year plans, with one-year objectives and commitments to them.

RELATING SHORT-RUN AND LONG-RUN PLANNING

Continuing to do the same things over and over, with occasional changes in activity as targets of opportunity are seen within reach, seems to be a common pattern in personnel departments. As one personnel executive stated an all too typical viewpoint, in an interview:

Frankly, we don't try to work too far into the future. For one thing we are terribly busy getting our work done. For another, our problems are so different from the production departments that we can't really foresee what they will be six months ahead, to say nothing of five years from now. We have a lot of things we'd like to do, but they are sort of on the back burner, and if the climate is right and we get the right chance to sell ourselves we might get to them some-day, but meanwhile we are pretty busy and have a fine crew of hard working people on our staff.

The fallacy in such thinking can be pointed up in three conditions that are admitted by the statement.

1. The department is so busy getting "there," that it doesn't have time to figure out where it is going.

2. It admits of no specific multiyear plans which are presented regularly for installation or approval by management, nor desire to consider them. That which might be foreseen will be first noted as a crisis.

3. "Fine, hard working people" gives no assurance that the outputs of their hard work are going in the proper direction, only that the general level of activity will be high.

The differences noted between production and personnel staff work

---

[6] For a fuller discussion relating to line departments see George S. Odiorne, *Personnel Policy* (Columbus, Ohio: C. E. Merrill, 1963).

are, of course, very real. The production people produce hardware which can be counted or measured, whereas the personnel department produces intangibles, which must be measured in *indicators,* especially constructed to measure the unmeasurable. There is a natural discipline of *things* and *items* in production or sales, and managing by objectives in a rudimentary way is forced by the situation. This natural forcing of objectives does not occur in personnel, and therefore *it is much more necessary that it be worked unremittingly.* If this is not done, the result will be activity feeding upon itself and becoming less and less related to output and consequences for the firm.[7]

The multiyear plan

The relationship between the multiyear plan and the single year's objectives for each staff member, controlled perhaps by quarterly reviews can be illustrated in Figure 3–2.

FIGURE 3–2
Diagram showing relationship of five-year plan to first year's objectives.

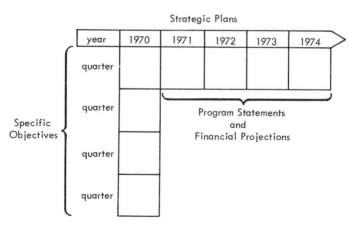

The five-year period is arbitrarily chosen for purposes of illustration, and any natural multiyear period might be chosen in its place. The relationship between the five-year plan and the first year of it can be explained as follows:

1. The top personnel manager and his key staff heads develop a five-year strategic plan, showing major program statements with attending financial projections for major innovations, or problem-solving programs, or problem-prevention projects for each year of the next five years.

---

[7] N. Maier, J. Hooven, and R. Reed, *Superior Subordinate Communications* (AMA Research Report 52) (New York, 1962) demonstrates this point.

2. This is an estimated, projected, and frankly conjectural statement based upon the best estimates of what these problems will be and what innovations will be called for during that period. They file firm statements of financial requirements to execute such programs with the higher levels of management as part of their annual budget statements.

The five-year plan is redone each year, dropping the year just completed and adding the next year beyond the fifth. Thus, the plan becomes a "walking man" plan.

Such a moving plan means that the years beyond the first year are not commitments, since making such commitments might be inadvisable in a changing business. They start with the assumption that "other things being the same (which they never are), here is what we would see as our plans for the next five years." As the future years move closer and become the immediate year ahead, the individual commitments to achieve specific targets should be obtained. This is the ordinary Management by Objectives (MBO) system.

3. The five-year plan is a specific annual document, produced in time to provide a framework for individual departmental budgets and specific personal objectives for the personnel chief and all of his staff.

4. The staff work for such a plan is often done by the personnel research staff, although any major section head may add to it by filing program statements and financial estimates which can become part of the five-year plan.

Is such a plan in operation anywhere? In operations of large corporations it is a customary kind of management system. The Dupont management system is perhaps one of the earlier applications of it. The most visible example is the management of the automobile industry, which in 1928 went to the annual model change in order to bring order to its managerial system, and to enhance its marketing potential.[8] In this industry with respect to product planning, the pattern shown in Figure 3–2 would come out as following:

Typical pattern of five-year planning for product development and change in the automobile industry.

Year

1. *This year.* The objectives of the majority of employees in the company will be to make and sell this year's model, in sufficient numbers, quality, and cost to generate a specific target profit.
2. *Next year's model.* The purchasing and engineering staffs are to complete all tooling for the next year's models. This tooling will be pur-

---

[8] Alfred Sloan, *My Years with General Motors* (New York: MacFadden-Bartell, Inc., 1965).

chased or made internally in order that next year's model will be
launched as specified on time.

3. *The year after next model.* All engineering of the year after next model
will be completed and the engineering plans and drawing turned over
to tooling for execution of the tooling stages as scheduled. This means
that renderings of the model will have been received from styling,
feasibility studies for manufacturing completed, models made and
tested, and turned over to tooling within one year. (This is engineering
by objectives.)

4. *The year after the year·after next model.* The styling studios will prepare renderings of the approved line of cars as chosen by higher management from amongst the alternatives prepared in advance styling.
This styling will include interiors, exteriors, and will incorporate the
results of market research, new government safety regulations, and
changes in tastes. The renderings will be completed and turned over to
engineering in one year.

5. *The year four years from now.* Advanced styling will have produced a
range of possible styles from which the upper management can select
the styles actually to be completed through to production and sales.
This range should include cars not yet ready for the public taste, as well
as contingency plans for unforeseen changes in competitive markets or
consumer tastes. Such a wide range permits free latitude to the most
imaginative minds and bold thinking. In some cases working models of
such advance styles may be made on a prototype basis and market
tested, or released confidentially in private showings, or even in public shows.

Of course this model doesn't take a rigid format and the people working
under it are subjected to the customary surprises which come when they,
being seers and making prophecies, are confronted with reality.[9] Yet, it
lends order and managerial system to what could well be a disastrous
confusion.

The uses of the five-year plan

A number of specific managerial uses of the five-year plan become
apparent when we see it in operation.

1. It permits the establishment of objectives for jobs, programs, or
departments which are working in software and creative areas. The stylist,
the staff man, the engineer are not producing cars, they produce ideas,
software, drawings. The judgments made that such designs will sell five

---

[9] R. House, and A. Filley, *Managerial Process and Organization Behavior* (Glenview, Illinois: Scott-Foresman), p. 208 suggests that research shows flexible plans
are more effective than fixed or stable plans.

years from now are never perfect, and will be made by higher levels of management who assume this responsibility for risk.

2. Advance areas will always be less likely to have certainty and immediate feedback than those areas close to production and selling. *Milestones*, dates, budgets, program completions become their objectives.

3. It requires that people be committed to achieving their stated programs and plans for the immediate year, and provides a basis for managing the great majority of managers and staff during the immediate year.

The major difference between the five-year plan and the system of managing by objectives is that objectives call for commitments. These are promises by responsible people to somebody whose opinion is important that a person will try to produce something specific within specific limits of time, cost, quality, etc.

Its application to the personnel function

While the organization of automobile production is interesting, that, of course, isn't the point here. The model can be used effectively for the management of the personnel department.

1. The five-year plan calls for attention to the conditions of the future, including external matters such as population projections, labor market changes presently visible, and major social and political trends which would have a bearing upon personnel department objectives in the future.

2. It calls for close attention to the internal direction of the firm, in terms of products, processes, expansion, changes, in markets, and the present and future structure of the employee and management roster.

3. It requires a systematic attention to new techniques being used by others in the profession, and the study and perhaps development of new tools which may be required to solve tomorrow's problems.

4. It calls for periodic, perhaps annual, review of the present functions of the personnel department to see if any of them have become redundant. What is your present product line? Who is buying it? Is the market growing or declining? What present activities should be cut or diverted into more fruitful areas of concern? With such a multiyear plan in hand, individual objectives can be established for the personnel department.

At the beginning of each year, every staff member in the personnel department should be required to make a commitment to his immediate superior, with respect to three kinds of responsibilities. They should reflect what this staff member intends to contribute on his job during that period, with perhaps some quarterly indicators and measuring points noted in advance.[10]

---

[10] *Ibid.*

These three kinds of objectives should include, in ascending order of importance, the following kinds of goals:

A. Regular routine chores.   In this category he states those regular, ordinary recurring responsibilities for which he accepts responsibility. The outcome here should be stated in terms of average expected outcome but should always include a range of high and low expectations as well. The importance of stating objectives of this kind in a range cannot be over-estimated.

No personnel man worth his salt would reasonably expect that he can predict exactly how many college graduates or computer programmers he will hire during the coming year. He could state the range of expected successes and failures. This is more than a ballpark guess because it is based on present levels in stating the average expected. The lower level of expectation is the figure below which he must inform the boss in time to take action, if he fails. The highest expected outcome states the most optimistic possibility and would indicate superior performance.

It is always a mistake to set targets for a single outcome in regular duties. Even more foolish are those managers who simply take last year's outcome and add 2 percent.

The first major mistake in setting personnel objectives is to set a single target rather than a range of possible outcomes. The second is to give a man a single responsibility area upon which his entire performance will be measured. Such areas of routine responsibility should be stated to permit trade-offs of one outcome for another.

You could get all the college recruits you need if you could have an unlimited budget for recruiting. Budget compliance must be a trade-off responsibility with head count of campus hires. You could operate with no grievances for a whole year but labor costs would go through the roof. You must trade off certain numbers of grievances in order to keep labor costs down. Grievance levels often are trade-offs for labor cost levels. The number of regular responsibilities must include the trade-offs of cost, quantity, quality, service, and time pressures.

B. Problem-solving objectives.   The second major category of objectives for personnel departments begins where the regular routine responsibilities leave off.[11] They consist of immediate and on-the-spot problems which exist in the organization that the personnel department must solve. Usually they are found in the indicators for the routine responsibility. An indicator running below minimum acceptable levels is a problem. A problem very specifically stated is the best kind of objective possible. Every staffer in your personnel department should be identified as responsible

---

[11] George S. Odiorne, *Management Decisions by Objectives* (Englewood Cliffs, N.J.: Prentice-Hall, 1969) expands upon this class of objective.

for some problem or problems on which he will work. This doesn't mean he will solve two problems per year. He may solve only part of one or he may solve a dozen. The key point here is that he has two or more in front of him at all times. They are before him with a known order of priority and an agreement with his boss that they are important. Also, what priorities exist for their solution.

C. Innovative goals. The hardest of all to measure but probably the area of greatest contribution for personnel departments is that of innovating, introducing changes or raising the quality of employee relations to higher levels than before. This may mean introducing new ideas from the outside which will enhance the performance of the customer departments. It means keeping abreast of new developments which might contribute to such growth. It means making orderly feasibility studies of their application to your business. It means making intelligent and aggressive action in installing new programs and making them work.

This trio of categories—routine, problem solving, and innovative—comprises an ascending scale of excellence in personnel work. It also comprises an ascending scale of need fulfillment for the people involved, whether you prefer Maslow's hierarchy of needs, or Herzberg's motivation and maintenance factors.

More important, it attunes the personnel program, budget, and staff toward the needs of the parent organization, not to some theoretical, unrelated checklist of audit items. The personnel departments make available only those items of advice, service, or control which its market research among its customers shows that they need, have asked for, or can be sold.

Should personnel departments sell their wares to other departments?

The personnel man can take the position that selling isn't part of his job description, otherwise he'd have joined the sales department or marketing staff. Such beliefs lead to these standard errors of the frustrated personnel staff man:

He sees the line manager as an enemy who seeks to frustrate him—an obstacle on the path to professional success—rather than as a customer whose needs must be met and around which his wages must be shaped.

He relies too heavily on faith in top-management backing to knock down the barriers to his programs.

When line managers won't buy his wares, he cites this as proof of their autocratic nature, incompetence, or uncooperative nature. He creates a special island empire and either abandons the project or goes it without line help. Often the personnel department has ogre images which they have attached to some of the most influential managers.

To survive, he measures his success more and more in intradepartmental terms: the number of programs installed—trainees covered—forms approved or processed—man-hours devoted to each project—and similar symptomatic measures.

Ultimately, he is a likely candidate to start searching for more felicitous grounds, a more enlightened management climate, or a more progressive company where all obstacles to his plans will be removed.

Strategies for success:

> Know your client and design your product catalog to suit his needs. Be ready for opportunities.

> Produce tangible results early in the game. Build major projects on prior success.

QUESTIONS AND PROBLEMS

1. Where do you begin applying a system of management by objectives to personnel management?

2. How have changes in personnel objectives since 1920 changed the activities required of the personnel department?

3. What are the advantages and disadvantages of copying the leading firms in their personnel programs?

4. If behavioral research has contributed so much to personnel managers, then why can't we rely upon it fully for guides to operating our personnel department?

5. "I'd like to have you come to my company and evaluate the success of my personnel program." If you received such a request, what would you look for first?

6. How could long-run planning and short-run work be split into distinct activities in personnel departments? How would you start to alleviate this shortcoming?

7. Give some examples of how a "walking-man plan" would look in college recruiting for a company.

8. "Our business is so uncertain, even for a few months ahead, so I can't see any advantage in a five-year plan." How would you refute such an argument by a personnel manager?

9. Why are routine goals less indicative of organizational excellence than innovative goals?

10. "The personnel department should wait for people to ask for help and not push its services where they are not wanted." Discuss this statement.

11. How would you start a "product catalog of outputs for the personnel department"? Where would you start?

GRAND OLD MANUFACTURING COMPANY CASE—PART C

The first companywide personnel management conference started after lunch with a discussion of the reporting procedures of the various division and plant personnel management departments to the central personnel administration staff. Several of the individual managers stated rather warmly that since the policy of the company was for decentralization they could see little real need for such reports. Vice President Hull stated that the only real reason for it would be to improve communications among personnel men in various locations so that the achievements and experiences in one location could be promulgated to others. Pat Murphy, a long-time personnel manager in a large division in the West stated that he felt that it was really a concealed way of trying to control them, and that he wouldn't like to report.

A new central office personnel research department was explained, and a discussion of its role held by the group. The liveliest discussion of the day took place between Jason Rombard, the corporate training director, and the field personnel managers. There was a great deal of conviviality back and forth during this presentation and Jason received a loud hand when it was complete. The minutes are attached.

PERSONNEL MANAGER'S NARRATIVE REPORT

The subject of a personnel manager's periodic report was presented at the Personnel Management Conference. It was suggested that this report might be used in conjunction with an interchange bulletin that would be circulated amongst all personnel managers of the company. The possibility of following a uniform format following this pattern was discussed by the personnel managers:

1. Accomplishments and projects completed
2. Projected plans (this portion would include projects launched even though not completed)
3. Ideas wanted or offered

The items of general interest would then be extracted and placed in the interchange bulletin which would be circulated to the personnel managers of the company.

Some expressed the thought that this would entail preparation of another report, requiring time and effort. Others were of the opinion that this would not mean additional work due to the fact that their present procedure required preparations of such a report for their divisional managers. It was pointed out by some that the routine nature of their activities would not be newsworthy except on rare occasions.

There was expressed the desire on the part of many to receive information regarding activities of other locations.

The format of the personnel interchange bulletin was outlined as follows:

1. Accomplishments
2. Projected plans
3. Ideas wanted or offered
4. Other news and announcements

Interest was expressed with regard to news and announcements that might come from the GOM Personnel Administration Department, as well as information with regard to location activities.

With regard to the channels of communication, the divisional personnel managers expressed the desire to preserve their established channnels. Therefore, it was their desire to have reports from the field funneled through their office and the outgoing communication in the form of a personnel interchange bulletin to also come through their respective offices.

The details relative to the mechanics of this project were left for further research.

Final Result: This item has been tabled temporarily.

PERSONNEL RESEARCH AND PROGRAMMING ACTIVITIES

A comparison was made between research in the physical sciences and the human sciences. Results generally are much more definitive and conclusive in physical research. This arises largely from the fact that such research can be more carefully controlled, such as in temperature, pressure, contamination, etc. Nonetheless, there is vast literature today that reflects the great amount of research being done in the human sciences, of which personnel administration is an applied area.

Most of the published research results are the product of universities, colleges, etc. A great deal of research is done in industry; however, it is primarily for different purposes than academic research. For these reasons, industrial personnel research isn't as prevalent in published form. Personnel research in industry, for example, is almost always done with a particular application in mind, and is seldom done merely for the general interest of gathering information in some area.

Personnel research can encompass a wide variety of subjects. One common area of investigation is the validation of tests for the selection and placement of employees. Research can also be done in evaluating interviewing techniques used by individuals, in reference checking; however, it can and should go far beyond these areas. It includes attitude surveys, studies in salary administration, group interactions, manpower needs, training programs and their effectiveness, etc.

At present time the Research Department as such is only a couple of weeks old. There has therefore been no program outlined as yet for any definite long-term research. Assistance with the pulling together of the survey results has been the principal concern assigned at the present. Assistance with salary studies is about to be undertaken in the area of clerical salaries.

Other projects have been assigned to the members of the department, and these are already being worked on. These consist of the handling of this conference, arrangements for the four Company Management Courses, Communications Conferences, Education Assistance Program, editing of communications, manuals, assisting with the intra and interdepartmental reports, etc.

In general, the role of this department can be described as one of assistance to the personnel staff people of the organization. Actual research will not be done for specific locations, but opportunities to assist with setting up such research projects would be welcome because of the resulting overall coordination of personnel research throughout the corporation.

PLANT TRAINING SERVICES

The training services function for plants is a service to plant operating management in the identification of training needs, the formulation of training content, and the design of appropriate training procedures or methods.

The principal problems confronting training as viewed from the General Office are:

1. Continuity—keeping established and adopted training procedures alive and in continual use.
2. Getting operating management to recognize and accept standard training procedures as regular operating procedures and not something "extracurricular."
3. Keeping operating management aware that control over operating costs and our competitive position requires that everything that we do must be done continually better. Training in its various forms and application is the principal controllable variable that helps people accomplish our principal goal of "working smarter, not necessarily harder."

The principal problems confronting training as viewed from the field were stated thus:

1. The recognition of the difficulty of keeping alive and in use the regular

training procedures by getting operating management to accept these procedures as curricular rather than extracurricular.

2. The tendency of the General Office to be "top heavy" in the design of some training procedures. There is a continual need for keeping training programs and procedures simply designed and easily adapted to to daily work routines.

3. Some programs (Work Simplification, for example) have been too much a "one-shot approach"—crash programs—rather than set up as a repetitive procedure. It was felt that we need to set our sights on more repetitive and refresher type training on particularly the more important training procedures instead of trusting that one thoroughgoing installation training will suffice.

4. There is a feeling that perhaps we have relied too long and too exclusively on the conference method. It is felt that there is a need for injection into our training program subjects where men are "taught" rather than always trying to accomplish the same results through the conference method.

5. The field personnel managers see a definite need for some sort of central audit or follow-up procedure to assist them in keeping alive the procedures and practices that have been established through some formal training effort.

6. In the field, it is felt that there is too little evidence of awareness and interest on the part of top divisional managers in the training efforts and procedures that are being carried out in the field.

7. The need for keeping training materials up-to-date through the simple expedient of reissuing in different colored folders, stamping materials "revised, 1959," etc.

The personnel managers and operating management men present were assured that all of these constructive observations will be given very careful attention and put into practice where applicable in all future training designs. The remainder of the session was a refresher discussion of the more basic and continuous training procedures which must be kept in continual use. These were:

The Supervisor Selection Procedure
The New Supervisor Introductory Training Procedure
The Maintenance Training Procedure
Work Simplification
The New Employee Orientation Procedure
The Management by Objective Procedure

Discussion questions

What problems do you see here? What solutions?

chapter 4

PERSONNEL POLICY
BY OBJECTIVES

IN THE AGE of cybernetics and the decline of respect for centralized authority, the definition and purposes of policy have changed radically.[1] Under earlier and more traditional definitions of policy, it was a form of ready-made decision, the answer to questions not yet asked, a guide to action. In one sense it was like a Newtonian physics, there were laws and rules and regulations which relied heavily upon the essential rightness of the laws and policies. "I realize that you may not be able to see the immediate logic of the policy, but believe me the navy has been in operation for 200 years and the policy it enforces has grown out of the experience of hundreds of thousands of men going back to John Paul Jones"—thus hears the recruit when he observes that the policy seems to be downright foolish since it prevents the immediate job at hand from being done. The roots of the ready-made decision type of policy lay in these factors:

(1) *Experience is the basis for policy.* It presumes that the errors of the past have produced means of preventing undesirable outcomes in the future. The reason the company policy prohibits any petty cash funds in local units is bad experience in the past when such funds led to shortages. The reason for the policy on daily scrubbings of the deck is because it was discovered at some time in the distant past that this prevented disease on a crowded sailing vessel at sea for years. The effect is also one of enforcing seniority-rule of the old hands over the young. Such an effect in recent years has bred rebellion against the rules.

(2) *"Superior information" as the basis for policy.* In the conduct of foreign affairs, policy is often explained when challenged by casual observers as being founded on "information which is available to us through

---

[1] Eugene J. Koprowski, "Cybernetics and the Death of God," *Management of Personnel Quarterly,* Vol. 7, No. 4 (Winter, 1968), pp. 17–27.

secret intelligence sources which cannot be made available to all without jeopardizing the source and the mission itself." The plant manager has knowledge of certain planned capital improvements and personnel changes which he is not free to divulge, but which dictate a policy that does not seem consistent with immediate targets. Furthermore, this confidential advance information cannot be divulged since it would adversely affect the possibility of the master plans being achieved. Thus, the lesser ranks must rely upon the judgment of the top men who set policy, because they alone can freely see such information. It also has the effect of making his judgment unquestionable by lesser levels, a kind of circumstance which conflicts with a rising value system of participation of these lesser ranks in decisions which affect them.

(3) *Consistency as a virtue is often a basis for policy.* A typical policy manual begins with a statement much like this: "In order to achieve uniformity, fairness, equity, and consistency of administration among diverse and perhaps widely separated units of the firm, the following policies have been enacted by the board of directors (executive committee and the like) and will serve as the stable reference point in the conduct of the affairs of the organization." The virtue here lies in the elimination of inequities and the natural tendency of humans to judge their own status by that which others enjoy. If the plumber in one plant gets $5.00 per hour and the plumber in another plant ten miles away with similar work and identical seniority, and both are satisfactory performers, gets $5.10, the former considers himself put upon and discriminated against. In fact, he will describe himself as *underpaid.* The fact that no other employee gets that amount of money, or that plumbers in ten other plants get 50 cents per hour less, becomes irrelevant.

(4) *A theoretical model for policy is the basis for much policy.* The theoretical model, which seems best to satisfy the three conditions for sound policy, has been adopted widely and resembles a triangle.[2] Under such a model the peak of the triangle is the objective (see Figure 4–1) which enlarges into policies or guides to action. These in turn become procedures of detailed explanation of how the policy would be implemented in practice, and finally rules and regulations which state specific prohibitions or instructions or behavior which would comprise compliance.

What traditional policy contributes

Experienced managers, who have found that traditional policy has become a necessary part of their management tool kit, can point to the advantages readily.[3]

---

[2] See Chapter 1.

[3] George S. Odiorne, *Personnel Policy* (Columbus, Ohio: C. E. Merrill, 1963), chapter 1.

FIGURE 4–1
Traditional mode of policy construction

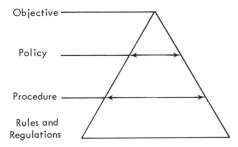

1. It prevents self-canceling and mutually exclusive behavior, but establishes the dimensions of decisions to be achieved even when the specific questions to be answered are not known.

2. It is liberalizing for people since it establishes guides for decision, thus placing them outside the realm of mere personal hunch, bias, and self interest of the decision maker.

3. It produces order, rationality, and a conscious system of achieving results through predictability. This means that control or error prevention has been increased through establishing preset standards for decisions.

4. Good policy produces a uniformity of effort and the losses which could come through individual eccentricities and brilliance is more than offset by the gains in preventing gross errors from failure to adhere to proven ways of doing things.

5. It considers the long-run well-being of the organization and its people which might not be so considered in momentary judgment or hasty decision made without policy guidance.

6. It eliminates the necessity for painful thought and study for problems which might have been foreseen and solved through uniform guides to action, prepared by expert staff after research.

The attack upon traditional policy thinking

While such benefits of policy have been proven by practice, there is a substantial sentiment which suggests that policy is really a tool of authoritarian management, and rather than freeing or assisting the individual is merely another instrument for enforcing raw authority. Generally such criticism emanates from rebels in the organization, many of them young, or perhaps even more frequently from individuals of high intelligence, high levels of education, and whose work is technical in nature. Where the scientist, engineer, or high-level staff expert finds that policy has been established to meet the requirements of sound administrative practice, he seldom dwells long upon the advantages to the organization as a whole, but upon the abrasive nature of its impact upon his own personal freedom to behave as he likes. Often this restriction upon his behavior extends to limiting him in freely practicing his profession. The purchasing policy which forces him to obtain bids when hs scientific sense tells him clearly that there is only one sensible source, and that all others are idiotic, causes him to turn upon policy as restrictive and petty. The asserted value here is *individualism*.[4]

A second kind of revolutionary movement which tends to upset traditional approaches to policy formulation and administration is that of the antiauthoritarian trend, especially among the young. The school system has taught many young people that the unexplained order or rule is offensive and should be questioned. It may subsequently be obeyed if it can be internalized after explanation, but until such time it is to be continually questioned and perhaps resisted if the explanation is either not forthcoming or is unacceptable.

A third source of rebellion against traditional policy thinking lies in the unwillingness to passively accept the absurd as ordinary. A kind of dissonance arises when one sees inconsistency and stark madness in the implementation of purely traditional policy. Joseph Heller's novel "Catch 22," the story of a bomber pilot in World War II, is laden with such lunacies, all of which emerge from policies and regulations which are self-canceling and mutually exclusive. While war itself seems lunatic (which is Heller's major point), such catches exist wherever large organizations exist and generate sensible, rational policies that are self-canceling at the grass roots level of the organization and produce a wild kind of situation which resembles humor. The humor lies in incongruity, a factor which the protagonists are apparently unaware exists, and which they resist acknowledging.

A large university's top management issued two policies to its lesser unit directors. The first was that no faculty member could be paid more than 5 percent of his monthly pay for one evening of extra teaching. It also issued a policy that nobody except the vice president of academic affairs and the professor were entitled to know the professor's salary. Thus, when the Director attempted to compensate his faculty for extra work through initiating an extra pay voucher, he was required to draw it for 5 percent of an amount which he could not know by policy. Questions and protests of the absurdity were bruskly rejected by the administration.

This is an example of the absurd. Large organizations abound in it, most of it visible at the lower levels where the multiplicity of sometimes conflicting policies finally see their ultimate working out.

The church membership which soberly voted to construct a new building using bricks from the old and then with equal seriousness voted

---

[4] David Riesman, *The Lonely Crowd* (New Haven: Yale University Press, 1950).

not to tear down the old building until the new one was ready for services, was guilty of an absurdity of which it was unaware because it didn't consider the operational problems of the contractor.

Such illustrations from real life in large organizations are painfully easy to uncover, and employee humor abounds in such stories. The result is a general loss of confidence in the logic of policy.

A fourth source of discontent with traditional policy making lies in its effects upon human beings. The policy of psychological testing validated upon present employees has the effects of excluding anyone who doesn't conform to the present employee group. This excluded group then becomes deprived of opportunity to work, and it plunges them ultimately into a state of poverty, disease, and crime. The policy doesn't have as its intention the effect of poverty; the actual effect is unintended, and regreted and deplored as a result. However, the causes are direct, tangible, and immediate, and lead to rebellion against the policy system which produces it. The civil service system which was formulated to prevent the evils of the spoils system is rooted on a policy of "merit." The effect, however, although not the purpose, is racial discrimination against people who lack such merit.[5]

A fifth source of discontent with traditional policy is in its effects upon creativity. The innovative inventive mind often functions at its best when it is free of artificial constraints. The requirements of customary administrative neatness, uniformity, and orderliness are antithetical to the more or less shapeless conditions of creative activity. Regular hours, time clocks, stipulated hours of attendance, and detailed reports of activity divert the creative mind from the flow of ideas, the pursuit of solutions, and comprise to such people a major distraction from the important purposes of creating the new, from unique combinations of the old.[6] Surface efficiency produces inventive inefficiency, such persons charge, and attack not only specific policies, but the entire concept of traditional administrative practices founded upon the pyramidal model of policy formulation and administration.

Objectives—the systems approach to policy

The assumption that the absurd, the suppression of individualism, the breaking of rebelliousness, and the losses of human values are necessary concomitants of policy, is widely accepted. "Yes, I realize that there are drawbacks to having policies, but the advantages of having order and

---

[5] Garth Mangum, and L. M. Glenn, *Employing the Disadvantaged in the Federal Service* (Ann Arbor, Michigan: Institute of Labor and Industrial Relations, 1969).

[6] Oskar Morgenstern, "New Uses for the New Knowledge," *Think*, Vol. 34, No. 5 (September–October, 1968) suggests that ideas have greater difficulty breaking through if they involve behavior change than if they are represented by machinery.

sound policy outweigh the individual disadvantages, and the good of the organization must take precedence over individual preferences. After all, where would this company be if everyone could simply go his own way without coordination and consistency among various units?" So goes the rationale for traditional policy. Taken by itself, there is much to be said for this justification. Losses from self-canceling actions, mutually exclusive behavior, and self-negating practices could be costly. Yet there exists a rising level of discontent, especially among behavioral scientists whose research throws some keen insights into these issues. Ralph Stogdill, a behavioral scientist from Ohio State has found that predictability of the pattern of relationships is essential to satisfactory membership in an organization. When there is no clear basis for such prediction of relationships, the people in the group will be dissatisfied with their place, and the effectiveness of the group will suffer therefrom.[7]

The implications of Stogdill's findings could be interpreted as requiring traditional policy, but it might also find that the same predictability could be achieved where each person had clarified his objectives, and his peers have done likewise, and all are aware of the others. Mr. *A* behaves differently from Mr. *B*; because his goals are quite different and Mr. *B* is aware of that difference, he sees no inconsistency between them simply because their actions differ.

Dr. *X* is working on an experiment which is adversely affected by sunlight, so he unilaterally sets his own hours to work evenings. Dr. *Y* has no such limitation in his work so he keeps ordinary working hours. Because *Y* knows *X*'s goals he feels no conflicting emotions over the fact that he is apparently rising each morning while *X* is permitted to sleep until noon. The objectives underlying the behavior being clear, he feels no unfairness and doesn't make a fuss.

On the other hand, if ten female assemblers all arrive on time because they know that promptness and a full crew on hand is necessary for full production, and Mary decides that she needs more time to dress and have breakfast, they would be understandably puzzled and perhaps dismayed if the foreman didn't enforce prompt attendance behavior upon Mary.

While the two situations may seem radically different, they have some common ingredients. The objectives of the assemblers is to assemble, which in turn requires a full crew on hand for all to be successful and make a satisfactory contribution to the objectives of the department.

Uniform objectives probably calls for uniform behavior, where nonuniform or varied objectives can be permitted varied behavior.

Thus, the best policy is one which would allow everyone to behave in

---

[7] Ralph M. Stogdill, *Individual Behavior and Group Achievement* (New York: Oxford University Press, 1959).

that way which would maximize his contributions to his own objectives, without diverting others from the achievement of theirs in the process.

The requirement here calls for a far more intensive attention to objectives than is ordinarily paid them, in those organizations where attention to traditional policy exists. Traditional policy which is activity controlling rather than objectives oriented would appear to be the basis for much of the dissatisfaction which has emerged around traditional policy setting.

The rule of organizations by policy is similar in many respects to rule of law, as Max Weber has pointed out.[8] The presence of rational policy, while it restrains employees from certain kinds of behavior, also can serve to restrain the arbitrary or capricious kinds of behavior possible by management. The prisoner and the guard are in the same jail. Thus, the employee who sees the possibilities of the absurd, the restriction of human values and the like in authoritarian type policy, may be overlooking the fact that he is able to freely see rules which comprise a joint commitment. The management is practically required to rule by them, if they promulgate such policies and procedures.[9]

This is, of course, persuasive in those instances where the issue at hand is one which works both ways. If the company chooses to list causes for discipline in the plant, and attaches certain penalties for such behavior, it must abide by its own standards. If the regulations call for reprimand for the first offense of insubordination, it cannot then discharge Jim Jones for his initial act of insubordination.

This equality is not always cutting equally both ways however. As the French epigram put it, "The law in its majesty prohibits the rich and the poor alike from sleeping on park benches." The fact that the rich are extremely unlikely to have any necessity for violating the law in fact makes them immune. The nature of policy then becomes a restraint upon the choices available to lesser ranks.

From the foregoing we can see that personnel policy—or any organizational policy whatever—is derived from objectives, and obtains its legitimacy from those objectives. The distinctive contribution which policy can make to the decision process is that of providing a test of means, not an inconsiderable matter. One of the effects of this accentuated attention to management by objectives could well lead to the following:

Odiorne's Proposition: A policy should be matched against a corresponding statement of specific objectives, and comprise a set of restraints upon the means by which the specific objective can be pursued.

---

[8] M. Weber, *Theory of Social and Economic Organization* (Oxford University Press, 1947).

[9] A. Filley, and Robert House, *The Management Process* (Glenview, Illinois: Scott Foresman, 1969).

Tying policy constraints to objectives statements

The initial step in making uses of policy is to define the objectives: the condition that would exist in terms of outputs if the objective were well done. This often comprises an ideal of optimal level of output. This can then be followed by reviewing the existing book of policies, the customary practices, and the mores which govern, and extracting from these the specific constraints which must be borne in mind in selecting courses of action and activity to produce the outputs. For example:

The objective of the firm is to bring into its ranks a selected group of college graduates each year. In 1971 we will seek to hire 30 such graduates.

The constraints:

No graduate will be hired at higher pay than his boss.
The company will reimburse candidates for no more than two visits from the campus or his home to the company premises.
Living expense for new hires will be covered for two weeks duration during his period of early employment.

Such a list of constraints could, of course, be enlarged almost indefinitely to such trivia as whether or not the company would pay cab fare or only limousine rates when the graduates come visit the home office. Yet, it is the defining of such constraints that makes for clarity of understanding and the avoidance of disagreement and displeasure on the part of superior and subordinate at a later time. Under such a system, the discussion of objectives and of reversals or amendments of policy which would be necessary to attain these objectives can be agreed upon prior to entering into the effort to achieve the objective.

In practice, the chances are that rather than listing all of the constraints, it becomes simpler if the parties assume the following: "given the objectives which we have agreed upon, and other things being equal, all ordinary policy, law, custom, and practice will be followed in the achieving of these objectives." Since, of course, things are never the same, some required exceptions may be expected and exceptions to policies or practices may be predicted and approved.

Supportive management as a solution

Operating under a system of management by objectives, the customary procedure is for each manager and his subordinate to sit down at the beginning of a period, such as a quarter or a year, and discuss objectives until an agreement upon desired outputs is achieved. These are then confirmed by memo, which becomes the basis for the subordinate's activity, and serves as a basis for the superior's judgments about performance during the period.

It is at this goal-setting stage that most of the undesirable effects are generated or could be eliminated.

Rensis Likert reports that a supportive style of management is productive of higher morale, less turnover, and a generally higher quality level of superior-subordinate relations.[10] This supportive relations, which is generally expressed during the day to day relationship of the two, is shaped most importantly during the goal-setting stage. After the goals have been defined, discussed, and agreed upon, the supportive manager will ask the subordinate a question of key importance: "Is there anything that I could do, do differently, or stop doing during the coming objectives period which would help you be successful in achieving your objectives?"

It is in response to this question that the subordinate should have in hand the exceptions to policy which he would like to obtain approval for. Under such a system, the testing of policy against objectives becomes operational, and the decision to stick with policy, or vary from it is rooted in the basic reasons for policy even under traditional rationale. The ideal conditions for policy, even in the more hidebound and rigid organization, have been that objectives required it. The needed improvement in practice to avoid the serious criticisms of policy thinking is that objectives and their definition be far more clearly defined than in the past. Rather than "policy management," the emphasis becomes "objectives management," in which policy is responsive to and servant of the specific objectives which have been agreed to. If the policy conflicts and should predominate, say, because it is a law of the land, or the administrative ruling of the NLRB, for example, then clearly the objective must be modified if the means of achieving it are not available.

Personnel policy in decentralized firms

As firms grow large they move from organization form A to organization form B. Form A is a functional organization with a single chief and special functions headed by a director of that activity. Under form B each of those reporting to the chief is a general manager who serves much like a captive company president, and to whom the functional heads report.

In the functional form, the personnel manager serves as staff expert for the office of the president (even when he doesn't report directly to him). His policies are designed to guide the personnel actions of all of the functional areas.

In the divisionalized form each of the subordinates reporting to the

---

[10] Rensis Likert, *New Patterns of Management* (New York: McGraw-Hill, 1961).

FIGURE 4–2

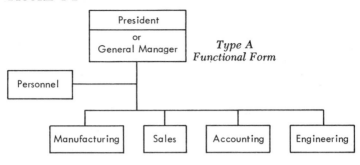

Type A
Functional Form

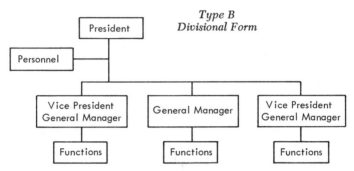

Type B
Divisional Form

president has been delegated responsibility for profitable operation of his division. A common tendency for such persons is to assert a wide degree of independence, and when a specific division is very profitable, it is a commonly observed phenomenon that he widens the degree of independence which exists between him and the corporate executives and staff.

This independence of division from corporation becomes most obvious when the division is an international one. The culture, the values, the nature of the laws in foreign operations, make the adherence to company policy difficult, if not impossible. The result is a rather high level, continuous struggle over the question of adherence to corporation devised policies by divisions whose independence is founded upon achievement of objectives such as profit.

The sources of such problems can be listed as follows:

1. The autonomy of division general managers is threatened by corporate staff who devise policy.
2. Different corporate staff such as personnel and accounting may attempt to devise and enforce conflicting policies.
3. Corporate staff may attempt to police policy conformity based upon fragmentary information.

4. Corporate staff may attempt to implement policy by working directly with their technical counterparts and bypassing the division general manager.
5. Decentralization is often selective upon what policies shall be divisionalized and which will be kept centralized. Labor relations and budgeting are often centralized. Training and personnel research could be either way. Employment of local employees is always wholly decentralized.

Under such circumstances, "company policy" refers to those subjects or matters which will be uniform and consistent among all divisions and sub-units . . . in other words, are centralized. Where the firm is decentralized, no company policy may exist beyond that of a "policy of decentralization" which permits wide discretion, autonomy, and latitude to the divisions. Where such a policy of decentralization exists, the division enjoys freedom from any policy constraints but is free to impose them upon plants and offices which comprise its own subordinate units.

At stake in making such a complex quasi-political system work is that people understand it. For instance, where decentralization is the stated policy and decisions about policy are passed down to the next level, such as the division general manager, it is not uncommon to find that the division manager does not pass that decision-making authority down below himself. In effect, he implements the policy of decentralization by acting out the following: "I am firm and adamant in my belief that decentralization is essential as it comes down from above. I am equally adamant that I must not decentralize decision making to anybody below me in rank."

The result may be the paradoxical requirement that the corporate chief must autocratically direct the division manager to be more democratic in his leadership style, and let others below him make decisions.

The point of this example is not to suggest that paradoxes are necessarily bad, but to point up that, in this case and numerous others, policy statements as constraints on means of attaining objectives calls for policing policy, using sanctions and discipline where necessary.

The similarity of policy to law in personnel matters points up some instructive prescriptions for makers and users of policy.

1. The purpose of law is the attainment of justice and is aimed at controlling *means* and activity. It clearly states that ends do not always justify means.
2. The enforceability of a law is an integral part of it, including often an agency for enforcement, and a procedure for dealing with lapses. This entails the power of a sovereign in one form or another.
3. Much of the law of the society or the policy of a firm consists of a common set of precedents, past decisions, and customary ways of

doing things which are often not written but enmeshed in the ordinary behavior of people.

4. The enforceability of law ultimately rests in the willingness of the governed to be ruled by laws, rather than the vigilance and zeal of the enforcement agents.

Summary

The proposal in this chapter has been that personnel policy, like most managerial policy, has suffered from a lack of clearly defined objectives. A duality exists, much along the lines of the old saw that "authority and responsibility should be commensurate," with respect to the two: A policy should be matched with a corresponding statement of specific objectives and comprise a set of restraints upon means by which the specific objectives can be pursued.

POLICY IS TO CONTROL MEANS, OBJECTIVES DEFINE ENDS

History is filled with examples of inhuman, cynical, and immoral actions perpetrated in the name of a worthy cause. Cortez, in slaughtering the Mexicans for gold, wrote back to his king, "As we fought under the standard of the cross, for the true faith and the service of your Highness, heaven crowned our arms with such success, that, while multitudes of the infidels were slain, little loss was suffered by the castilians." [11]

Machiavelli, an adviser to princes in Italy, was perhaps best identified with the kinds of manipulative policies which leaders should follow in managing a state, the end justifying the means.

While management starts with the definition of objectives, and policies follow, policies comprise a restraint and in some instances, void the objectives.

These constraints are not always mechanical impossibilities, nor are they always based on a logical analysis. They include constraints which grow from moral, ethical, legal, and religious considerations.

Legal restraints. It is not at all uncommon for company policy to be changed because a new law has been passed. Equal employment opportunity laws forced changes of some companies' written policies. The draft laws which require that employees drafted be offered equal or better jobs when they return from their military service, produced affirming policies and some explanatory procedures to implement such policy.

Moral bases for policy. In still other instances policy is rooted in moral codes or practices. While this could begin with such matters as accepting

---

[11] William H. Prescott, *The History of the Conquest of Mexico* (New York: Modern Library, 1941), p. 245.

gifts from vendors at Christmas time, it might also extend to more personal codes of conduct. For many years it was reported that under Thomas Watson, Sr. it was a matter of discharge to have liquor found in your possession in your desk on company premises. Morality, of course, was a relative matter which could be different in a small company in the Bible belt in the Midwest, and in a slum in Philadelphia.

In recent years the attention of scholars and practitioners has turned toward the morality of the human relationship. Is the other fellow an enemy to be destroyed? A slave to be used like an object? A person to be hired for a consideration and ask nothing beyond that? Or perhaps like a child who is to be assisted and aided as long as he is properly obedient? Or another man made in the image of God, who could be better than he now is, and whom all of us have an obligation to help?

It is obvious that in various degrees all of these perceptions of man are held by companies and bosses at one time or another.

If the senior officers of a typical American corporation were to be asked to rate their perception of a typical employee between the three classes shown in Figure 4–3, where do you suppose they might fall?

FIGURE 4–3

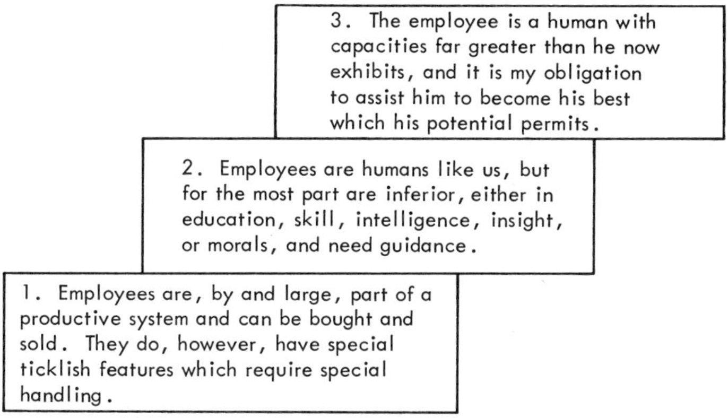

3. The employee is a human with capacities far greater than he now exhibits, and it is my obligation to assist him to become his best which his potential permits.

2. Employees are humans like us, but for the most part are inferior, either in education, skill, intelligence, insight, or morals, and need guidance.

1. Employees are, by and large, part of a productive system and can be bought and sold. They do, however, have special ticklish features which require special handling.

If the top management of the firm adheres to one, they will prescribe certain personnel policies which will differ from policies they write if they adhere to another.

Take, for example, the policy of many years standing in General Mills, Inc. when Charles Bell was president and chief executive officer. Briefly, it provided that no employee with over 15 years service with the firm should be discharged unless such discharge has been reviewed and approved by the office of the president.

The effects were such that new people, who were not going to succeed, were not kicked around from pillar to post, but were released when their inadequacy was discovered. For another, no capricious firings of long service employees could occur. For another, the amount of remedial work which occurred among long-service employees rose rapidly. While the rationale of this policy was always expressed by the officers of the firm as logical, pragmatic, and sensible—a sort of enlightened self-interest—it, in fact, grew out of the attitude of the top man toward other humans.

Religious bases for policy.   In some firms, probably a minority, religious ethical systems comprise a basis for personnel policy. In one large firm located in mid-Pennsylvania, it was a firm policy not to hire divorced persons, and the authority of Biblical injunctions against divorce was specifically stated as the reason for the policy. The LeTourneau earth-moving equipment company for many years sponsored prayer meetings which were attended by all employees, and in numerous other southern firms during the fifties industrial chaplains were extremely influential in instilling a religious code of morality upon personnel policy. The man who drank, cursed, and otherwise misbehaved was either brought to task, discharged, or if known in advance, not hired. Often this came out as a form of ethnology that kept Jews and Blacks from any important positions, or from employment at all beyond a certain percentage.

Ethos as a basis of policy.   Beyond the moral and religious bases, perhaps the most prevalent source of policy as a constraint upon the way objectives can be attained is in the ethos, or prevailing sentiment of the majority of the people in the firm. In many firms, for example, it is simply considered bad form to ask for a raise. If you do an outstanding job, both you, your peers, and your boss will be aware of this, and the boss should have sufficient grasp of the ethos to know that this should be recognized in either pay or promotion. Yet, to barge into the boss's office and specifically ask for a raise is considered out of touch with the way things are done.

This character of an institution, which may even comprise its genius, often consists of unwritten laws and customs, which are rooted in the deeply held beliefs of the majority of those in positions of importance, and accepted by those who work there. It has important influence upon hiring, placement, payment, promotion, demotion, appraisal, and every other facet of personnel policy in the firm.

In a large automobile company it is not uncommon for executives who have failed to achieve objectives consistently to be demoted. If they succeed at the new task, they are considered for elevation once again. In other companies the invitation to accept a demotion is tantamount to being fired, since the loss of face would be too great under the existing customs of the firm.

In one large metal working company it was well known that one of the best ways of succeeding inside the firm was to leave, and rejoin the firm later at a higher rank after succeeding elsewhere. Thus, the young man caught in what he saw as a blind alley would leave and come back later on, on the upward side of the old obstacle. In other firms, the very act of quitting is evidence of disloyalty, which is a cardinal sin, and it would be impossible for that person ever to return in any capacity.

While these examples could be listed almost indefinitely, they illustrate ethos as a source of policy. It should be noted that often these standards and constraints are not written by the top management—in fact may be unwritten—but are policed by the entire organization through a common understanding.

Clearly, objectives for the personnel department must be consistent with the existing value systems, and policies should express those values or they will not be adhered to.

QUESTIONS AND PROBLEMS

1. If you received an assignment to prepare a statement of personnel policies for an organization, what information would you ask for before you began?

2. Despite changes in ideas about management, policy still persists as a basis for guiding action. Is this a logical and useful trend?

3. What is the best avenue to solving the conflict when bright and able people in organizations seem to rebel against policy?

4. Give an example of a policy which seemed to do more harm than good from some organization of your own experience.

5. Is it completely impossible that policy should exist without creating absurd contradictions? How would you achieve this?

6. "We do things informally around here. We, therefore, won't write out our policies, because we like to adapt to the situation." What kinds of problems could you see in this approach?

7. What does the supportive style of management do to the dignity of the manager? Does it make him a servant of his subordinates?

8. A policy statement in a decentralized firm is as follows: "All of the powers of management exist in the management of the corporation except those which are specifically delegated to the divisions." What do you think of this as a statement of decentralization? How would you word it?

9. How does policy differ from objectives? Give an example out of your own experience. From sports? From religion?

10. Does ethics and morality have anything to do with policy? Give some examples.

11. "If you don't have uniform policy, uniformly applied the result is chaos." What would your response to this statement be?

THE MAYFLOWER LIFE
INSURANCE COMPANY CASE *

Background

The Mayflower Life Insurance Company, located in Boston, has assets of $8 billion. In recent years it has experienced rapid growth and to keep pace, the Company installed numerous electric accounting machines—collators, sorters, tabulators, reproducers, etc.—of the IBM variety. The installations have been made in various areas as the need arose. As a result, the Company has a sizable expenditure in machine rental and machine operator costs.

As part of its continuing efforts to improve overall operating efficiency, and more specifically based on a recent campaign to reduce costs, the General Office Manager has requested that studies be made concerning the possibility of combining the separate electric accounting machine operations. At present, separate installations exist in four divisions. The electric accounting machine installations represent only a portion of the total function of each division.

On the surface, this would appear to be a logical area for genuine savings. The same type of electric accounting machines and the same kinds of machine operator skills are to be found in each division. Actual machine usage fluctuates from 20% to 90% depending upon the specific machine and the division in which it is used. The divisions in which the electric accounting machine functions are located are: Group Insurance Service, Dividend Disbursement, Machine Accounting Services, and Claim and Salary Disbursement.

The following briefly summarizes each division's staffing and functions:

GROUP INSURANCE SERVICE DIVISION
Total staff: 142
Number of machine operators: 29 (20% of total staff)
Number of electrical accounting machines: 29
Functions: Maintains and furnishes supplies, general typing, forms control, claim and conversion, statistical control, and key punch operations.
Specific EAM functions: Preparation of reports, billing, accounting, commission work, and annuity maintenance.
This work is highly diversified and is not adaptable to any set repetitive procedure.

---

* Reproduced with permission, L.O.M.A., 1966, and Prudential Insurance Co. of America.

DIVIDEND DISBURSEMENT DIVISION

Total staff: 104

Number of machine operators: 17 (16% of total staff)

Number of electrical accounting machines: 23

Functions: Accounting and disbursement of policy loans, surrenders and dividend checks, maintains dividend records, correspondence and adjustment of records, typing and key punch operations.

Specific EAM functions: Prepares checks for loans, surrenders and dividends, policy loans maintenance, process punched cards for the electronic computer. In general the work may be considered repetitive, permitting specialization of operator skills.

MACHINE ACCOUNTING SERVICES DIVISION

Total staff: 146

Number of machine operators: 69 (47% of total staff)

Number of electrical accounting machines: 92

Functions: Control of transactions involving valuation data, agents' production records, statistical studies, correspondence and adjustments, key punch operations.

Specific EAM functions: Calculation of commissions, premium statements, distribution of premiums by states, preparation of lists for field inspections, process punched card data for the electronic computer.

These EAM functions may also be described as repetitive.

CLAIM AND SALARY DISBURSEMENT DIVISION

Total staff: 101

Number of machine operators: 31 (31% of total staff)

Number of electrical accounting machines: 26

Functions: Makes all salary payments, maintains records of earnings, deductions and tax reports, prepares checks for claim settlements, issues claim summary statements, codes mortality statistics, key punch operations.

Specific EAM functions: Prepares accounting and statistical information for claim payments, and for payroll disbursements, check preparation, available for special jobs from other departments.

In this division, the EAM work is considered to be highly diversified.

Estimated Savings

As a first step, the General Office Manager asked the Planning Division to estimate the potential savings on the assumption that the EAM functions of the four divisions would be consolidated.

The Planning Division obtained actual cost figures for the present set-up of separate installations and estimated comparative costs for a consolidated installation:

Annual Cost of Separate Installations for 170 Machines

Machine rental	$ 523,000
Operator cost	770,000
Total annual costs	$1,293,000

Estimated Annual Cost of Consolidated Unit (160 machines)

Machine rental	$ 513,600
Operator cost	643,000
Total estimated annual costs	$1,156,600

Estimated Annual Savings of Consolidated Unit

Actual cost—separate installations	$1,293,000
Less estimated cost—consolidated unit	1,156,600
Estimated savings	$ 136,400

The Planning Division also suggested that further savings were possible if the Consolidated Unit were to operate on a two-shift basis:

Estimated Annual Cost of Consolidated Unit on Two Shifts (83 machines)

Machine rental	$ 361,200
Operator cost	646,800
Total estimated cost	$1,008,000

Estimated Savings of Consolidated Unit on Two Shifts

Actual cost—separate installations	$1,293,000
Estimated cost—two-shift consolidated unit	1,008,000
Estimated savings	$ 285,000

Savings in machine rentals are estimated largely on the basis of more efficient use of machines. Operator costs have been estimated by multiplying the "operator hours" (the number of hours of operator time needed to do the work represented in machine hours) by the appropriate hourly rate.

In the Planning Division's memorandum to the General Office Manager, containing the estimates of savings, the following comments are included: ". . . the work now being done in four divisions would result in annual savings of $136,400 if the machine operations were consolidated. However, if the consolidated work is put on a two-shift basis, annual savings of $285,000 would be realized.

"Estimated floor space for the consolidated area is about one-half the space presently required. In terms of space value this represents an annual savings of $33,600.

"Other advantages which cannot be analyzed for cost are:

1. With functional use of machines there would be more efficient use of floor space. Also "free time" on a machine should be more available.
2. With systematic scheduling there should be better machine utilization and improved service to dependent divisions.
3. Second shift machine cost is based upon machine hours used. This analysis allows for more hours on a second shift than are needed; thus, a certain amount of flexibility is permitted for unexpected jobs.

The General Office Manager then asked the Personnel Division to review the Planning Report and determine what personnel problems might result from consolidating the EAM operations. A recommendation was also requested as to the feasibility of the consolidation from Personnel's viewpoint.

Memorandum for General Office Manager—(from Personnel Division)

As the Planning Division has thoroughly covered the facets of a consolidated machine operation, we have accepted their conclusions that it is practical from an operational and work-scheduling standpoint. Our studies have been largely confined to personnel problems that would arise from a double-shift operation. In our studies we have drawn on the experience of comparable night operations in other firms in this area.

In evaluating the experience of others we find that their reasons for second-shift operations are based on better service, increased work volume, and the need to tap a new labor market. In no case is the reason parallel to our consideration of savings.

While the importance of cost factors should not be overlooked, neither should we overlook the disadvantages of second-shift operations.

Of initial concern is the disposition of our present IBM operator staff in these four divisions—currently 146 men. Theoretical savings are based on the premise that there will be an even distribution of staff between day and night operations. Thus, the need for daytime operators would decrease to 73 men. Adjustments of supervisory personnel would also be required.

Although the excess operators and supervisors could be assigned to the second shift, we foresee considerable resistance to voluntarily accepting such a transfer. Previously, in one division where a second shift is in operation, we experienced just such difficulties. Very few men were attracted by the bonus pay offer. We believe forced transfers would create serious morale and turnover problems.

If the excess operators were not assigned to the evening operation, they would then be added to the increasing list of displaced and extra persons; and, we would still have to hire the night-shift staff. Such additional hires would largely be made up of persons employed in other daytime jobs. The need for maintenance men to make machine repairs during the second shift also becomes apparent.

In their calculations the Planning Division has reflected savings from the elimination of overtime. This is based on the functionalization of machines to provide sufficient time to accomplish all the work without extra sessions. However, special assignments do occur and any overtime work would then only be completed at the end of the second shift. To add overtime to the second shift—especially if it is staffed by persons holding two jobs—might present personnel and efficiency problems.

We also have considered the work area arrangement in a consolidated machine room. As we visualize the area, there would be row upon row of machines. This would tend to resemble an assembly line or factory-like atmosphere. At present the machine operators do have some contacts with our clerical staff. In a consolidated machine room the operators would be set apart. Perhaps we would encounter personnel problems unique to the company, many of which cannot be anticipated at this time.

We feel that the proposals of consolidating and second shifts must be considered as separate problems.

Conclusion:

With the exception of some possible personnel problems, the consolidation of four areas seems to be a practical and logical move. The advantages of machine functionalization are apparent. It seems desirable to locate such a consolidated machine room in the Office Administration Department rather than in one of the line departments involved. Acceptance of this consolidation by departments involved will depend upon the assurance they are given that it will not have an adverse affect on their service and work schedules.

As for double shifting, we feel that the personnel considerations previously mentioned may outweigh the suggested savings.

It is our recommendation that the machine operations be consolidated; however, we do not recommend that a second shift be established.

The General Office Manager forwarded these reports to the General Managers of the interested divisions. A meeting was arranged to discuss the proposal:

JIM WINTERS: (Dividend Disbursement and Claim and Salary Disbursement Divisions) I have read these reports and I am impressed by the amount of estimated savings. I think I am as appreciative as anyone else of the need to reduce costs. However, as I see it you are asking me to reduce the staff in one of our divisions by 16 percent and in another by 31 percent. Frankly, I have reservations about these savings estimates and I certainly have reservations about our ability to meet schedules and give comparable service.

AL TRENT: (Machine Accounting Services Division) You are asking me to give up 47 percent of one of my divisions. It doesn't leave very much, and it would seem to me that you would be creating another problem. What do we do with the remainder? I doubt that its continued existence could be justified as a division. Yet, I don't see where we can relocate the remaining sections.

JACK PETERSON: (Group Insurance Service Division) This idea of consolidating makes no mention of our situation where we have a great variety of jobs. How can a huge production line operation adapt to diversified nonvolume functions such as ours?

J. WINTERS: Let's get back to these cost and savings figures. For discussion's sake let's concentrate on the savings of $136,400—the consolidation without a second shift.

I notice that Planning says a small planning group is necessary. What's the estimated cost of this group? And doesn't that reduce our savings?

J. PETERSON: If we are going to get service, there's a transportation of work involved. I see no estimate of this item, and just like the planning group this is an annual recurring cost which also subtracts from the estimated savings. What does that leave us with?

A. TRENT: There also are some initial nonrecurring costs which eat into the first year savings. How about moving and installation? I know that our machine operators have comparable skills. But they are still going to need training in the consolidated unit. Who is going to train them? At what cost? And what will happen to our schedules and service?

J. WINTERS: Speaking of service and schedules, all of us have our priorities and deadlines. At present we work these things out in our own areas. What will happen in a consolidated unit when priorities and schedules conflict?

Another thing, when our machine operators have difficulties with certain things, they can readily contact the clerical area in our division and get straightened out. In a consolidated unit they are not going to have that ready access to source material. Nor are they going to have any idea that we have a rush job coming until it hits them. At present we can give them this information in advance.

J. PETERSON: Right now I feel that we have a minimum of personnel problems with our operators. If you consolidate these operations, it seems to me you will create the problems that go along with that sort of mass work environment.

A. TRENT: The Personnel Division had indicated their awareness of that possibility. Still they recommend consolidation; I can't understand Personnel's recommendation. Are these potential problems significant? If they are, and with all the other doubts which we have, I think the estimated savings lose their attractiveness.

Question for Discussion:

As general office manager, what is your conclusion?

chapter 5

ORGANIZATION OF THE PERSONNEL DEPARTMENT BY OUTPUTS

To PRESENT an "ideal" form of organization for a personnel administration department, we might choose a large firm which invests much money in personnel administration and show the reader that firm's organization chart. It shows that the chief personnel officer is a vice president who reports to the president of the corporation. Reporting to him are the major department heads, who each in turn have their own staff supervisors reporting to them. Traditionally this would be considered a pretty good personnel department, with adequate status, and apparently a reasonably generous budget for staff to conduct all of the activities which a well-developed and supported personnel department should have.

Yet, there is a certain amount of uneasiness in many such personnel departments, for they know that when top management changes, the degree of support of the activity may decline. We also might note that in other kinds of organizations, this personnel department simply wouldn't be appropriate at all.

Would, for example, such an organization be suitable for the Detroit Symphony, in which the personnel director is mainly responsible for artists' contracts, dealings with the musicians unions, and handling the personal likes of stars? Or we would hardly suggest that such an organization would be at all relevant for the manager of personnel for the Detroit Lions, where the personnel manager might find himself engaged in such discussion as whether Mel Farr or Nick Eddy should be paid more than the other. Nor would it fit thousands of other organizations, large and small, which could be listed. In part, this is because of the differences in size, although this doesn't seem to be the major difference. The differences in organization of personnel departments lies in the differences in the objectives of the organization for which they provide personnel advice, service, or control. This is why no model or ideal form of personnel department can be prescribed.

Personnel department organization is based upon a derived demand for specific programs by the parent organization, which generates such demands from its own objectives.

When we manage the personnel department by objectives, the organization form is aimed at achieving the objectives of the parent organization, and its senior management. If this seems obvious, it is far from it in actual practice. Most personnel departments in the past have been organized around *activities* to be initiated and conducted within the personnel department rather than around objectives of the firm which it hopes to make a contribution to through applying personnel techniques.

This should not be interpreted as meaning that the "people" problems of the company are to be clustered up in a distinct set of offices. As the late Glenn Gardner, a pioneer in early human relations programs, put it: "By centralizing the personnel function in a personnel department, too many people have assumed that you can centralize human relations." [1]

The debate over the functions of personnel and their relations with line departments has taken more space than deserved, and persists mainly because personnel departments have clutched too much self-assigned responsibility unto themselves. For the line manager to assume responsibilities for business objectives, and then to turn the management of the people who work for him over to a staff department which has no commitments to the line objectives is a foolhardy gesture.[2]

The effect of well-defined personnel administration objectives and policies is that the line organization will deal more effectively with its own "people problems." Beyond this, it should be beneficial to the people themselves, in the sense of permitting them to live up to their best potentialities.

The concept of staff

The role of staff departments has been discussed for many years, since the "general staff" form of organization was first installed in the German army in the last century. Often this idea is covered by generalizations such as "line does, and staff advises" or similar statements. While they are often true, such homilies do not make the specific organization of a staff

---

[1] American Management Association, *Personnel Functions and the Line Organization*, Personnel Series No. 121 (New York, 1948).

[2] Joseph Juran, *Managerial Breakthrough* (New York: McGraw-Hill, 1965) has many original insights on the staff role in management.

department such as personnel operational and leaves too many areas of conflict and ambiguity to be sufficient.

The steps in organization of the personnel department by objectives starts with a definition of several conditions:

What are the major organizational objectives of the parent firm?

What are the major organizational relationships among the various units of the firm?

What are the major problems or opportunities to which the personnel department might contribute solutions—in whole or in part?

What organization form inside the personnel department would maximize the department's contribution?

Let's look at each of these in turn.

MAJOR ORGANIZATION OBJECTIVES

In every organization, objectives can be classified into three major categories, as shown in Figure 5–1. These three classes are designed to meet organizational needs. They also serve as a hierarchy of motives for people working in the organization.

FIGURE 5–1

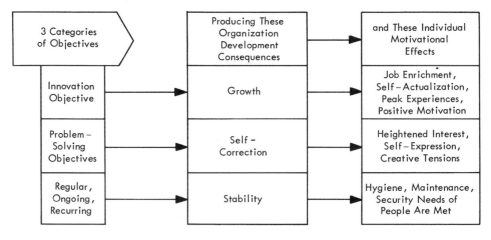

The objectives for the personnel department, which are outlined procedurally in Chapter 9, are derived from a similar set of objectives for each of the major line and staff departments of the firm.

Regular objectives are those ongoing, recurring goals which continue over a number or period of time.

The effects of such regularity upon the firm are good, for it makes the *organization* stable. Stability means that the products will be produced at predictable rates of time and cost, the taxes will be paid promptly, the lawns mowed, employees will come to work at the same time, and paychecks will be ready on Friday. These are relatively predictable, and regularity and predictability are virtues within such a context. The organization will not fall apart because of simple failures.

The effects of regularity and stability upon *motivation of people* is not always beneficial in effects. Boredom, apathy, indifference, and a sense of absurdity often results from such stability. Something more is needed, both for organization development and growth.

Problem-solving objectives to which managers are committed are those objectives which would restore normality and bring back the status quo. Using Simon's definition of a problem as "a deviation from a standard," problems arise when normality and regularity is disrupted, interrupted, or smashed by changes.[3] It requires human ingenuity and vigor to restore the status quo. The act of restoring is problem solving.

In *organization development* effects, problem-solving behavior in the organization means that the self-inflicted wounds which every organization suffers will be recognized and treated by the person closest to the scene of the injury. The organization has recuperative powers to mend itself, renew its dying tissues, and repel attackers from within, such as rising costs, grievances, turnover, and the like. Where an organization is so rigid that it engages in a false worship of stability as an end in itself, it falls into two dangerous tendencies. The first danger is that it will become so rigid that it will break in the face of strong winds from outside. Even more likely, it can become an organizational hemophile, which can bleed to death from small wounds. The hemophile (or bleeder) must be especially careful about injuries since it hasn't the clotting and stemming mechanisms to heal itself. Organizations, like organisms, can become hemophilic. Where all problem-solving authority resides at the top of the organization, and no problem-solving objectives are forced down to the lowest levels, the organization can bleed to death from little cuts because of the delays inherent in centralization of problem solving. Universities in the sixties proved hemophilic, when nobody at lesser levels such as department chairmen, deans, or even vice presidents could solve the problems of student disorder. Government agencies which require Washington approval of every action, the union which calls for clearance at the international level for every proposed solution to problems, and the large corporation which fails to free every supervisor to see and solve problems where they fall, can become hemophiles.

In terms of individual motivation, there is an added zest, creative tensions and added interest in work where the job has problems that tax

---

[3] Herbert Simon, *The New Science of Management Decision* (New York: Harper Bros., 1960).

the incumbent's best abilities to solve them. "Something different every day" is a compliment we pay our work, whereas "the same old rat race" implies that the job is routine and frustrating.

Innovative objectives for managers means that each is committed to try to improve something, even though no problems exist. Such objectives start with a dissatisfaction with the status quo, and presume that there is no one best way of doing a job. Armed with such a vision, the manager seeks change and betterment. Often unmeasurable, but describable, such goals are less likely to succeed, and the risks are higher, but rewards are commensurate for success.

In organizational development, innovative objectives are the substance of growth. It might be growth in sales, profits, or reduction in costs, the improvement of quality, reduction of time required to do something, improvement of service, or in a myriad other ways means that the organization is growing in size or in strength. Where such a climate of growth exists in industry or the economy at large, the company which fails to get commitments from its most important people to innovation will fall behind relatively.

Motivation is highest for people in engaging in this level of behavior. The "peak experience" described by Maslow, the job enrichment of Herzberg, and the self-actualization of the man which behavorial scientists declare to be highest in motivational values is found in this level of objectives.[4, 5]

Economic objectives and personnel organizations

In Figure 5–1 we noted that the objectives of the firm, classified into three major categories, produce objectives which are of immediate concern to the personnel department in its staff role. The first of these is organizational development (OD) and individual motivational effects. This figure and the ensuing discussion implies that the personnel department will provide advice, service, and control in such matters as selection, promotion, compensation, training, research, and other personnel areas which aid and abet the line organization in achieving its objectives.

Economic objectives, or organizational objectives stated in terms of economic consequences, make up the most important basic objectives of the corporation. By its charter it is obliged to consider the economic effects of every action upon investors, and failure to do so in any respect could result in stockholder suits or, even more drastic, attacks upon the stewardship of the management of the firm. The means used to achieve these continuously have been generously interpreted by the courts as

---

[4] A. Maslow, *Motivation and Personality* (New York: Harper & Row, 1954).

[5] F. Herzberg, B. Mausner, and B. Snydeman, *The Motivation to Work* (New York: John Wiley and Sons, 1959).

including a wide range of intervening, secondary, and tertiary activities, including such matters as donating to colleges, assisting local school building programs, and contributing executive time to public service projects. Yet, these do not remove the basic economic purposes which underlie subsidiary objectives.

Noneconomic objectives

Many personnel departments have become excessively focused upon the non-economic objectives, including worker happiness and other means of managing people to the extent that on occasion the entire underlying basis of the corporation is lost in the welter of activity which occurs. Two kinds of risk which are economic in nature need to be noted and kept in mind by the personnel department:

1. The first kind of risk is the *business risk*, which is inherently associated with the field of business endeavor. Such risks rise from the fact that volume of sales activity may fluctuate widely, may be especially susceptible to minor recessions, that the price of the product may not be under the control of the seller, or that unforeseen costs might occur without control of the management. The automobile industry has wider fluctuations than the food industry in sales volume and profits, and tastes of consumers may alter abruptly in response to extraneous factors, including foreign competition. Union actions, labor market shortages or surpluses, governmental regulation, and a myriad of other influences might be included under such risks.

For the personnel department not to be aware of the existence of such risk, and constantly abreast of new problems which arise in this area would be naive and irresponsible.

In one large oil company during the sixties some new regulations upon imports of crude oil radically altered the profit picture of the firm for several years. When the personnel department, along with others, was asked to tighten its belt and suspend programs, bitter recriminations of management stupidity and lack of concern for people were heard.

2. A second category of risk is that of *mismanagement* of the resources and people assembled and put into the enterprise. The economic losses from high turnover, sales compensation which rewards salesmen disproportionately for their effort, or failure to permit creative and problem-solving behavior to function fully and freely in the firm, would be typical examples. Personnel systems which permit the wrong people to move ahead, leaving good people behind, produce inequity or lack of competitiveness in salary and bonus, that fail to keep good records of the quantity and quality of high-talent manpower would be an example of how personnel administration departments might fail to maximize their contribution.

It is primarily in the economic area of risks of mismanagement that the personnel staff can make its greatest contribution.

The listing of the chronic areas of concern in Chapter 1, Figure 1–3, make this point clear. The personnel department is responsive to the business risks of the firm, but uses aggressive strategies of administration in the risk areas surrounding the possible mismanagement of resources.

UNDERSTANDING MAJOR ORGANIZATIONAL RELATIONSHIPS

Another key to the effective functioning of the personnel administration department is that of understanding the major organizational relationships in the firm as a whole. The personnel department does not exist in a vacuum, nor on an island populated only by personnel men. This can often be done effectively by using a modified marketing approach to the personnel function. This approach—adapted from the marketing concept—has these major steps:

a. The identification of the market for personnel staff effort.
b. Specification of the product for each market.
c. A definition of authority and responsibility for making and selling such product to each market within the personnel administration department.

Let's examine each in a little more detail.

a. Identifying the market for personnel's efforts. Large corporations are often divisionalized into major product divisions, geographical divisions, or some combination of the two. Each comprises a different market for personnel, and ordinarily such divisionalized corporations will have personnel departments for each of the major units as well as for the entire firm.

Honeywell, a billion dollar corporation, has a relatively small staff of experts at corporate headquarters, with personnel managers for each of the major divisions, such as the data processing division in Massachusetts. With the data processing division there are many plants, and the larger ones such as Lowell or Wellesley Hills have a plant personnel manager. The market for personnel is diversified. The demands of the personnel staff in the unionized Philadelphia plant are different from those upon the personnel manager at the research laboratory in Hopkins, Minnesota. This isn't merely because of geographical spread, but because each of the divisions and plants has needs which its own personnel department must fulfill. In Honeywell, there is no tight, centralized control to assure uniformity or consistency among divisions in many areas of personnel. Perhaps in labor relations where a common union exists between plants, central coordination exists to prevent being whipsawed by the union, but in training, each division and location decides what and when it will train, or even whether it will train at all. This isn't at all illogical, for each division has special characteristics, goals, and problems which must be managed there. Each too has special business risks which it alone must cope with. The defense or space efforts may differ drastically from the industrial controls or microswitch divisions.

The common ingredient, or uniformity if you will, among the divisions lies in the common task of serving their own market for personnel services.

To the extent that the divisions are markets for personnel, the approach to personnel in each division differs to the extent that the divisions themselves differ in business characteristics and managerial risks. Personnel skills applied are also alike to the extent that the divisions have common characteristics.

A typical breakdown of markets for personnel departments might look somewhat like Table 5–1.

TABLE 5–1

Marketing approaches for various personnel departments in a single firm

Level	Market characteristics for personnel department functions
Corporate Personnel Office	Selects, trains, and develops personnel men for each division and for corporate staff. Provides personnel services for corporate officers, division managers, and key corporate staff. Controls some activity companywide, including labor relations and salary administration. Does personnel research.
Divisional Personnel Departments	Assigns, trains, and develops division and plant personnel administrators. Handles personnel services for divisional executives, plant managers, and sales managers within division. Provides other central services where economically sound.
Plant Personnel Manager	Provides personnel services for plant workers, foremen, superintendents, and plant staff persons. Provides services for employees, maintains records, handles grievances through step 3, and controls wage and salary equity issues.

This listing is not complete, by any means, but is intended to be illustrative of how various levels, as well as special functions, can be used to describe markets. This difference is more clearly pointed up when we move to the next element in analyzing organizational relationship, in order to improve staff functions.

b. Specifying the product of the personnel department. Taking a marketing approach calls for identifying the product of the personnel department. Personnel departments which organize around markets and products are more closely attuned to the corporate objectives than those which follow a check list of personnel activity and follow it regardless of demand. In this approach to personnel we assume that the personnel department is a maker and seller of intangible softwares (nonhardware) to an internal captive market. These products (software) cost something to make and sell and we should constantly scrutinize the content of the product catalog and at least annually revise the list.

Table 5–2 shows a classification system, originally proposed by Juran for staff departments in general, as it might apply to the personnel department. Across the top of the table are listed five major categories for organizing your personnel effort. These are problems in organization which must be answered for each of the three major or four major classes of product which personnel departments can produce.

In studying the chart you may find it instructive to classify your own personnel department. You might be advice oriented, service oriented, control oriented, or research oriented. Having found which seems most descriptive of your goals, you may then move laterally across the table and note the basis of your authority, how your staffing is decided, your organization structure, and what your major product contribution will be. It is unlikely that any personnel department will be purely one of the four types.

TABLE 5–2

How to classify your personnel organization by products produced

Type of product	Basis of authority	Staffing	Organization structure	Output
ADVICE	Technical know-how Experience Acceptance by users	Small group of experts	By functional skills or by projects	Case loads New ideas Problem solutions Evaluation
SERVICE	Technical expertise Special facilities or equipment needed by users	Functional experts and technicians Medium size	By type of service provided	Efficient service
CONTROL	Delegated jurisdiction Defined market Special skill Authority to compel	Matches line organization Large functional group	By departments controlled	Defines procedures Observes practices Checks and corrects others
RESEARCH	Special knowledge Training or education	Small teams of experts	By project	New ideas Innovations Solutions to problems

By checking off on the list in Table 5–3, the kinds of things your personnel department is presently engaged in, you might gain some insights into the basic product position you are presently taking.

TYPES OF PRODUCTS BY PERSONNEL DEPARTMENTS
1. Where the product is advice, the department
    a. Responds to technical requests for solutions.
    b. Keeps abreast of new trends and issues bulletins for solutions.
    c. Initiates problem solving on long-run problems.
    d. Interprets company personnel policies.
    e. Predicts effects of personnel policies and actions for management.
    f. Conducts personnel audits and issues reports.
    g. Trains personnel men, runs annual personnel conferences, etc.
    h. Mediates conflicting opinions on personnel matters.
2. Service-oriented personnel departments
    a. Maintain common use facilities such as lounges, cafeterias, recreational facilities, medical rooms, training rooms.
    b. Provide temporary or short-time personnel for other departments.
    c. Provide testing, interviewing, and employment facilities.
    d. Manage certain facilities such as vending machines, company library.
    e. Maintain files of personnel records.
    f. Do rate setting for factory and office jobs (where no industrial engineering department exists).
    g. Supervise plant security force.
    h. Operate employee services activities including blood bank, employee counseling, car pools, and company store.
    i. Assist employees in associations such as credit union, recreational association, bowling leagues, and amateur performing groups.
3. Control-oriented personnel departments
    a. Operate manning tables and obtain weekly reports on manpower levels.
    b. Assign excess people to new departments, or otherwise furlough them.
    c. Have employee relations representatives in each section to actually handle the grievances in that area.
    d. Have final approval authority for wage and salary increases, and all personnel transactions such as hiring, firing, transferring, suspending, and promoting.
    e. Operate safety program and issue violations notices.
    f. Perform job analysis and set rates for jobs.
    g. Schedule rotational assignments of employees.
    h. Keep personnel records, including performance appraisal, salary progress, any changes in status for employees.
4. Research-oriented personnel departments
    a. Do attitude and opinion surveys of employees.
    b. Survey local and national labor markets for salary competitiveness.
    c. Interview to uncover special problems and their causes.
    d. Maintain continuous surveillance of labor markets, new trends and issue reports, bulletins, and information memos.
    e. Maintain statistical reports on personnel issues such as turnover.

f. Conduct special project type investigation for top management upon request.

Although this checklist could be expanded, and each department will have distinctive goals it must accomplish, the list is typical and illustrative of the kinds of activities which comprise the four major classifications. To get maximum benefit from such an analysis, try the following steps:

1. Place a check beside the listed functions under each of the four categories if they are being done in your own personnel department, or in one which you are analyzing.

2. Next make a simple chart of the percentage of total available staff time and budget which is devoted to each. That chart might look something like Table 5–3.

TABLE 5–3

Product line	% of manpower	% of budget
Advice functions	_____	_____
Service functions	_____	_____
Control function	_____	_____
Research function	_____	_____
Total	100%	100%

If your estimates have been at all accurate, this gives you a picture of how your personnel department is presently organized and setting its goals.

You are then prepared to make a decision as to whether or not this is the product line you wish to be producing, or whether you wish to modify it in any way.

It specifies your product and market position in the firm.

c. *Defining authority and responsibility.* Here are some general guides for fitting your product line and market position more closely to the firm.

1. If your personnel department is located at the corporate headquarters level, it should probably be more oriented toward advice and research as its major product. Never use muscle, only persuasion.

2. If your department is a divisional personnel department, it will include some advice and research, but tend more toward the service kind of product. Sales, often hard sell, may be necessary; so easy on ordering users to buy.

3. If you are in a plant or regional sales personnel department, you will probably have more of the control functions than any of the other two departments. In some cases you'll need delegated power to enforce compliance and correct deviations.

These generalizations won't of course, fit every company. The small firm which has a single plant may be a combination of all three. There are, however, dangers for the personnel department at the corporation level which becomes excessively oriented toward control, unless there are overwhelming reasons why control should be centralized. Multiunit collective bargaining, with a single union, would be one example. There is a loss of reality and a slowing down of decision processes when control is centralized simply for the sake of control. On the other hand, the plant personnel department ordinarily will not have the time, the budget, nor the specialist help to conduct extensive research. In many instances the operation of facilities such as training rooms, computerized personnel records, and similar service functions is more economical at the divisional levels.

The point here isn't to suggest how a specific department should organize its product line and assign authority and responsibility, except to suggest that it should know what its product line consists of, and make a conscious decision as to its suitability to that firm at that time. Where such product decisions have been made consciously the quality of personnel administration in the firm is improved.

PROBLEMS AND OPPORTUNITIES FOR PERSONNEL DEPARTMENTS

The personnel administration department which is geared only to repetitive work may find itself on occasion hard pressed to survive for even such work. The major values of personnel departments are found in those areas of problem solving and innovation which bring new techniques, new findings of behavioral science, and in being abreast of change as it occurs or possibly before. What are some examples which have actually happened within the last decade? How do we organize to handle such problems?

For one thing the rise of the technical specialist and high talent manpower has altered the role which personnel can play in the firm. Finding new climates for work for such people, new systems of incentives, new methods of training and coaching are among the challenges which have arisen, most of which still remain unresolved.

The rise of the international executive is another area of increasing concern which provides an opportunity and a problem for the personnel staff. The stateless corporation without national boundaries is closer to reality than it was ten years ago, and new personnel policies and procedures are called for.[6]

---

[6] See two illustrative studies for the impact for international operations in personnel policy: John L. Lesher and Ralph E. Griffith, "International Compensation," *Business Horizons,* Vol. 11, No. 6 (December, 1968); and Dan S. Moore, "Compensating the Overseas Work Force," *Conference Board Record,* Vol. 5, No. 10, 1968, pp. 44–48.

The rising black revolution and the promise of brown and red Indian revolutions presents a problem and opportunity which caught most personnel departments unawares, with top management making the initial moves and personnel following.

Organization to accommodate change

Much of the recognition of such problems before they have engulfed the organization lies in the strategic work which was outlined in Part 1 of this book. One person who determines to become the company's labor economist (where you don't already have one) can produce some invaluable warning signals for the personnel department staff, even though the professionals in labor economics might fault some of the fine strokes.

The important role of a personnel research section

Very few companies have formally consulted personnel research departments, and while formal organization might attract some undesired attention, getting the function performed is essential.[7] In some large firms the importance is recognized by the size of budget and staff, with one major oil company having 150 personnel assigned to this responsibility. In others a researcher is slipped in here and there in the personnel and industrial relations department as a "job analyst" or "contract researcher" in labor relations. Some of the areas it works in will be in the preparation of the product catalog for the personnel department several years hence.

1. In a rapidly growing firm it might be devising new systems for inventorying quantity and quality of managerial manpower.
2. In a company which is altering its marketing patterns from selling directly to dealers to one of selling mainly to large chains (as in groceries), it might be exploring the alternative ways of costing out early retirement plans for salesmen.

When jet airplanes were first introduced into commercial use, the response of the different airlines to crew-size changes was radically different from line to line. In United Airlines, with the visionary leadership of Charles Mason, their vice president of personnel, United calculated costs and benefits and solved it quickly even though the initial outlay was high. It eliminated the flight engineer position, now redundant, and offered flight training to all displaced flight engineers. If they couldn't

---

[7] Dean F. Berry, *The Politics of Personnel Research* (Bureau of Industrial Relations) (Ann Arbor: University of Michigan, 1967).

qualify for this, or chose not, other alternatives were presented to them until all were placed inside or outside the company.

On another competing airline they waited long after the change had occurred, with the result that if you flew in a Boeing 707 from Detroit to Chicago on United there were three crewmen in the cockpit, but if you flew on a competing line there were four, one of whom was not needed. On still another airline they tried to respond by simply firing the extras, and were subjected to a very long strike in which picket lines surrounded their counters and terminals for many months before they finally settled.

Opportunities for such preventive, innovative, and problem-solving goals in personnel requires that people specifically charged with such output be placed in the personnel organization. Some experts even suggest that in the future personnel staffs will be organized around problems, rather than special, isolated functions.[8]

QUESTIONS AND PROBLEMS

1. What kinds of inefficiencies grow out of the failure of staff departments such as personnel to see their work in terms of its outputs, rather than its activities?

2. What does derived demand mean in personnel work?

3. How does individual manager commitment relate to organization development?

4. Visit a personnel manager and obtain a list from him of three or four major problems facing his company in the personnel department this year. How would you state them in terms of outputs?

5. What is the connection between innovation and motivation?

6. Define the differences between business risks and the risks of mismanagement.

7. What is different about the markets of the corporate personnel staff and that of the divisional or plant personnel staff which might make it hard for a person to move from one position to another?

8. Visit a personnel department and apply the classification system shown in the chapter in Table I. Describe how it would be described in the terminology of this grid and explain.

9. Why should a corporate personnel department refrain from using muscle? After all, aren't they at the top of the heap?

10. What are some of the changes in society, values, or people which could have an effect upon personnel outputs in the coming decade?

11. If you were advising a personnel department on some ideas of research that would help improve personnel functioning, what would you propose?

---

[8] D. A. Lederer, Jr., "Personnel Policies for the 1970's," *Personnel* Vol. 45, No. 5 (September–October, 1968).

GRAND OLD MANUFACTURING COMPANY CASE—PART D

The final presentation at the Personnel Management conference of Grand Old Manufacturing was given by Gary O'Brien, and dealt with the organization of the Personnel Administration Department. The segment of his presentation which brought the greatest attention was that dealing with relations with the divisions. A number of opinions were expressed about the nature of decentralization, the proper role of division, corporate and plant personnel functions, and how much service the corporate staff should provide to the divisions.

The minutes of this session follow:

ORGANIZATION OF PERSONNEL ADMINISTRATION DEPARTMENT

Gary O'Brien, Assistant Director of Personnel Administration Department

The Personnel Administration Department is a corporate staff activity headed by a vice president and director of personnel administration who is responsible to the president. The director of personnel administration is responsible for formulation and revision of personnel policies which attract capable employees to GOM and provide the environment and relationships conducive to high morale, productivity, and creativeness. Such policies become effective when they have been reviewed by the Personnel Policy Committee and approved by the president and are administered and carried out by the operating divisions and departments of the Company.

The vice president's office generally has three responsibilities in executing his duties.

1. The management of the Personnel Administration Department.
2. The competent staffing of the department and provision of technical services to line departments and staff departments in the respective areas of personnel administration.
3. Advice to top management on personnel policy and practice.

The assistant director of personnel administration acts for the vice president of personnel administration in his absence and manages the day-to-day operations of the department, especially in the areas of selection and placement, plant personnel services, research and programming, and of the staff assistant in charge of the guide book and suggestion plan.

Personnel management at the New York headquarters office is handled by the general office personnel manager who has a staff of two people and who reports to the vice president of personnel administration.

The medical director manages the medical records of the Company, initiates medical programs on a companywide basis, directs the activities of consultant doctors throughout the company in all of the various locations, and operates the Medical Department in the New York general office.

The salary and benefits section is headed by a salary administrator. Reporting to him are a staff assistant for salary administration, who maintains salary records and statistics for all company personnel, and the manager of employee benefits. The manager of employee benefits is responsible for Employee Retirement System, Major Medical, Group Insurance, Travel Insurance, and other benefit programs.

The manager of personnel research and programming is responsible for maintenance of contacts with developments outside the Company affecting personnel administration and employee relations as well as internal studies toward the end of improvement of personnel policies and practices.

The manager of selection and placement is responsible for the conduct of college recruiting to fill replacements and to provide a supply of promotable young men from the current graduating classes of colleges, to assist line management of the various operating divisions in the departments in filling job vacancies and in finding positions for persons who require transfers. He is also responsible for the maintenance of personnel records on salaried employees, including personal qualifications inventories, vocational audit information, and records of appraisal. The appraisal activity in the selection and placement department is responsible for conducting appraisals of the performance potential of presently employed managers in the Company as well as improving the appraisal systems presently used in the operating divisions and departments. The staff assistant for maintaining the guide book is responsible for keeping the personnel guide book up to date and for periodically issuing revisions of this guide book. She is also responsible for the functioning of the Suggestion System as a secretary of the General Suggestions Committee of the Company which reports to the president of the Company. She initiates and does staff work on special suggestion promotions and the installation of suggestion systems in new locations.

RELATIONSHIPS WITH OPERATING DIVISIONS AND DEPARTMENTS

It is a Company policy that wherever circumstances permit, staff services such as Personnel should be performed within the division itself as a direct and controllable element of cost, with only such overall Company staff personnel to insure consistency of policies from division to division, proper research in all current developments in the field involved, and the need for officially representing the Company in that field before the public, public authorities, and trade groups. In some instances staff functions such as Personnel can be performed more economically and logically as a central staff unit in order to provide flexibility of assignment and the utilization on behalf of all operations of individual talents which could not be available were the function performed within each division such as a small division.

Personnel administration is, therefore, generally consistent with the decentralization policies of the Company. Each division which can support staff services to do the personnel administration job is by Company policy expected to do this. This means that the division personnel manager and his staff are directly responsible to the division management itself. Its relationship with the central personnel administration department is one of coordination and communication to insure consistency of policies and to look to the central personnel administration department for research and current developments and programs.

The fundamental objective to be kept in mind in guiding the relationship between the corporate personnel administration department and the divisional personnel function is a maximum of cost control and to maintain the profit and loss responsibility of the division chief executive. In order to do this there need be maximum insurance that divisional and department head responsibility is not diluted by assessing him with unnecessary administrative charges over which he has no control.

Discussion questions

1. What major problems do you see here?
2. What are some optional solutions?

EXHIBIT A

Organization of personnel administration department

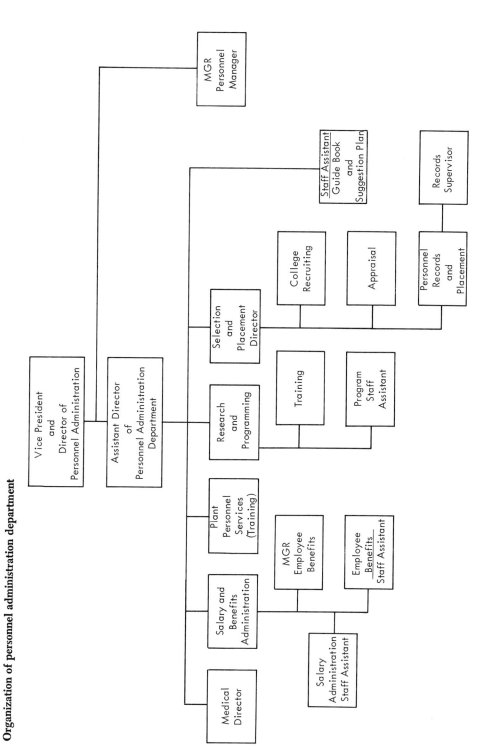

chapter 6

MAKING MBO OPERATIONAL IN THE PERSONNEL DEPARTMENT

STRATEGIES BEING long run, and since in the long run we're all dead, it's unlikely that the typical personnel director and his staff will await the full evolution of multiyear plans before starting to fill in the first year's operational goals. Nor is there any reason they should wait. The staff is on hand, the budget has been allocated, the offices and desks are installed, and there is work waiting in the form of training to be conducted, employees to be hired, salary forms to be processed, and grievances to be adjudicated.

How do you begin in installing MBO in the personnel department? This chapter is a how-to-do-it manual for that purpose.[1]

1. Start at the top of the organization. While it may be possible to initiate an objectives program in a smaller unit such as the training department or employment department, the idea will never really get launched unless the top man is personally active in it. It is even more effective if the highest level line officer in the organization has endorsed and is using objectives as a vehicle for managing his subordinates. In the case of the corporate personnel staff, the general manager should have a hand in defining what he expects from his personnel department. At the plant level the plant manager should be involved in defining what comprises good output from the personnel department.

If the top man doesn't actively take part, a system of sorts can be started if the top man practices a "hands off" policy toward the way things are done at lower levels. If, however, he is resistant to the idea and habit-

---

[1] See also G. S. Odiorne, *Management by Objectives—A System of Managerial Leadership* (New York: Pitman, 1965), chapter 5.

ually second-guesses or interferes with the way that things are done, any attempt to install MBO in a personnel department will probably produce only frustration. This latter condition is not common, however, for the basic logic of managing to achieve objectives has a self-justifying nature.

In one large steel company a number of younger personnel men with an interest in change and improvement attended a seminar on management by objectives. They returned to their job and attempted to install such a system. While it worked very well with their subordinates, who were enthused, the senior personnel officer refused to cooperate or endorse it. Long experienced in labor relations, he seemed to relish baiting the younger men. "Our job is to fight fires. When the bell rings I pack my shirt and run. How can you predict the future when the unions are so hostile and unpredictable?"

His major interest seemed to be in proving that the future was an imponderable, that all questions could be resolved by bringing them to him, and that reliance upon superior experience would take care of all problems. Naturally, the system didn't work and most of the proponents sought employment elsewhere.

The point isn't, of course, that the steel industry resists objectives—for a couple of the best applications in personnel departments have been in the personnel departments of Republic Steel; and other firms such as Pittsburg-Wheeling and J & L Stainless Division and Kaiser's Fontana plant have adopted the system.

The point is that top-management permission or endorsement is a necessary condition, and active participation is a great advantage. Where the top man opposes defining objectives, my suggestion would be to forget it for that firm unless you have a rich wife, a saleable skill, or a monumental ego which accepts failure with equanimity. You are confronted with a person who, perhaps for good and sufficient reasons, firmly intends to make all of the major decisions and as many of the minor ones as possible. To attempt to change him by installing a system is a romantic plan. Once the top man has indicated agreement, the following four steps seem essential:

a. Conduct a *familiarization seminar* or training session for the top man and all of his key subordinates. This might be an in-plant briefing by an inside man with experience, or an outside resource person. It might also be done by sending the group in twos and threes at university seminars which deal with MBO as a system, (not merely as a philosophy). These could include The University of Michigan, University of Utah, American Management Association, and various other organizations.

b. Reach an agreement in installing the system following the familiarization. Define the objective to "install MBO" and define any constraints which exist upon that goal with respect to policies or special conditions.

c. The top man and his key subordinates work out statements of total organizational objectives. This may take place in one or more meetings, often off-premises, which deal with agenda items as the following:

• What is the present condition of the department? What services do we produce? What kinds of advice is asked for? What controls do we have? What research projects do we have under way? Who are the customers for what we produce? Have they changed? Added to? Dropped away?

• If we didn't do anything differently from our present way, where would the department be in three years? In five years? Is this outcome acceptable to us? Where are some goals of what we would like the department to be?

• Given these ideal goals, what could each of the major segments of the department do, or do differently, or stop doing in order to move the whole organization forward in employment? in training? in labor relations? in management development? in wage and salary administration? in personnel research?

At this stage, the time has come for individual section heads to break down into their own areas of responsibility and develop specific targets for contribution to total personnel department goals.

2. *Face to face communication is essential.* Having completed in preliminary form, at least, a general statement of overall personnel department goals, the next stage involves a dialogue between every manager and subordinate manager about the goals for the subordinate for the coming year, with some quarterly indicators of accomplishment built into them. The three stages of installation, of which this dialogue and memo is the second could be pictured as in Figure 6–1.

Following the development of all of the individual statements through face-to-face discussion, confirmed by a memo in each case, an optional but advisable step would be a second general group meeting for the purpose of enhancing teamwork, motivation, and cooperation between units.

1) Each department head presents his departmental objectives to the group. (see Figure 6–2)

2) He answers questions, and any jurisdictional problems, or possible areas of collaboration can be ironed out. The original goals may be polished or amended here.

3) At the end of the first year of operation and thereafter, this meeting takes on heightened significance. Each department section head now has a four-item agenda:

   a) Here are the actual objectives we set for ourselves as we described them to you in our goals meeting one year ago.

   b) Here are the actual achievements after that one year to which we can point.

   c) Here are some of the differences between goals and results and the reasons for those differences.

FIGURE 6–1

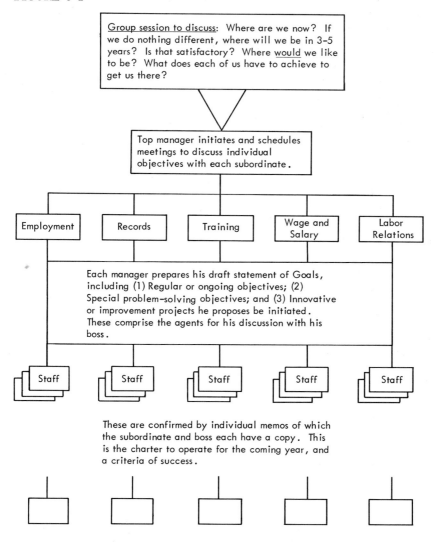

Group session to discuss: Where are we now? If we do nothing different, where will we be in 3–5 years? Is that satisfactory? Where would we like to be? What does each of us have to achieve to get us there?

Top manager initiates and schedules meetings to discuss individual objectives with each subordinate.

| Employment | Records | Training | Wage and Salary | Labor Relations |

Each manager prepares his draft statement of Goals, including (1) Regular or ongoing objectives; (2) Special problem-solving objectives; and (3) Innovative or improvement projects he proposes be initiated. These comprise the agents for his discussion with his boss.

Staff   Staff   Staff   Staff   Staff

These are confirmed by individual memos of which the subordinate and boss each have a copy. This is the charter to operate for the coming year, and a criteria of success.

The subordinate then repeats this same individual conference process with each of his subordinates, initiating and scheduling such meetings to discuss individual objectives with each person.

d) Here are the objectives which we have set for next year, with quarterly review indicators.

The powerful effects of poor group opinion and influence should not be underestimated. The strong influence which a promise or commitment can have upon subordinates is beneficial in stimulating them to change their directions, their behavior, and their attitudes. At the same time, for

FIGURE 6–2

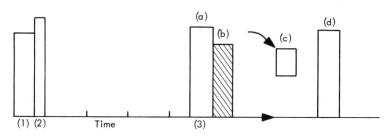

the individual who has bad luck, or through no fault of his own can't meet his commitments, the possibility of facing a group of peers can be strongly unpleasant. In one instance a good manager, caught by hard luck and conditions not under his influence or control, so feared the prospect of facing his colleagues and explaining his failure that he resigned and the company lost a good man. On the other side, the possibility that a fraud can perpetrate a hoax on a group of his peers is rather slim.

3. Set goals with personnel staff heads. The most difficult aspect of setting goals for the personnel department lies in defining *outputs* and not defining *activities*. Because the product is not hardware, it is reasonable to expect that the statements of outputs must be represented by indicators. In many instances we have developed indicators which we presume will reflect changes in some underlying condition.

One tested way of making goals more usable is to write them in such a way that it facilitates their use during the period, and also at the end of the period when it comes time to make judgments about the overall results achieved.

Goals should be stated in a way which will probably affect the man's behavior and results, not simply to set out in writing those activities which he would have performed anyway, even if he hadn't written them on paper.

The two basic tools for goal setting are the *dialogue* and the *memo*. The dialogue between superior and subordinate comes first. Trying to operate a management-by-objectives system by exchanges of memos alone has an extremely poor record of success. The cold and undiscussed memo is more apt to sever or widen relations than consumate an agreement. The cold and undiscussed memorandum has little to commend it where the purpose of communication is to resolve conflict, strike a bargain, or change another's behavior.

Your own departmental organization chart can be the key to the schedule of dialogue-memo sessions. The manager sets objectives with the people who report directly to him. If he wishes to have goals-setting extended down lower in the organization he makes this extension one of the objectives of his subordinates.

The three classes of objectives

At the beginning of the period, the boss asks his subordinates to make appointments with him in the near future to discuss job objectives for the coming period. Ordinarily these will fall into three major job categories, plus any personal development or growth objectives for the man himself.

Before the conference occurs, the boss lists some objectives that he'd like to see achieved in that man's position during the coming year, and has them ready for the meeting with the man. The boss should be especially prepared to discuss new ideas, innovations, and problems to be solved during that year.

In a personal conference, taking as much time as is necessary, review his proposals, tell him your ideas, and discuss the two until an agreement upon objectives for the man for the coming year has been reached. The respective roles of the boss and subordinate for two experienced managers might look something like Figure 6–3.

FIGURE 6–3
The respective roles of boss and subordinate in goal setting

Subordinate proposes	Superior's actions
1. Set standards for his job	Insist upon realistic ones that challenge ability
2. Define measures for results	Ask how arrived at
3. Do detailed analysis	Question methods
4. Suggest alternative actions	Suggest other possible actions where germane
5. Propose one course of action	Force a recommendation from subordinate
6. Predict effect of goals	Get commitments and make them to subordinate

Have two copies of the final draft statement of objectives prepared. One goes in the manager's "operations notebook" and the subordinate gets a copy. The final stage in the goals process is for the boss to ask what he can do to help the man succeed in achieving those objectives. Note his suggestions and keep them with his objectives.

The end product of the system, in tangible terms, is shown in Figure 6–4. The manager's operations notebook consists of a simple three-ring binder, with dividers for each of the managers reporting to him. As a general guide for managing a department by objectives, three pages of objectives should comprise the estimated physical length of the memos. Further documentation of a back-up explanatory nature can be filed separately. This is a summary guide to goals.

How, in a practical sense, can the objectives of a complex job be con-

FIGURE 6–4
Three-page memo of subordinates' job objectives

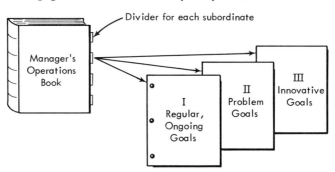

tained on three pages? One successful method for achieving such brevity lies in classifying objectives in the order of importance and complexity.

While a picture of a notebook offers a tangible kind of example, there is another way of viewing the goal-setting process especially when using the three classes.

For most managerial jobs, such a hierarchy of objectives comprises an ascending scale of excellence which can be used to measure performance for purposes of pay, promotion, bonus, selection, coaching, training and development, and delegation.

1. The man who is doing less than his regular responsibility needs

FIGURE 6–5
The hierarchy of objectives

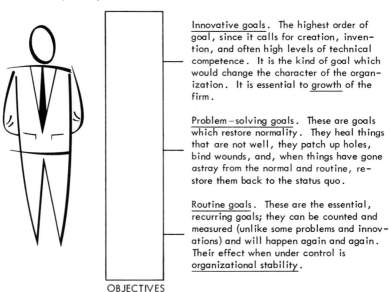

Innovative goals. The highest order of goal, since it calls for creation, invention, and often high levels of technical competence. It is the kind of goal which would change the character of the organization. It is essential to growth of the firm.

Problem–solving goals. These are goals which restore normality. They heal things that are not well, they patch up holes, bind wounds, and, when things have gone astray from the normal and routine, restore them back to the status quo.

Routine goals. These are the essential, recurring goals; they can be counted and measured (unlike some problems and innovations) and will happen again and again. Their effect when under control is organizational stability.

OBJECTIVES

attention to bring him up to this level, and unless he attains that minimum level should not be retained in that position. It may be that he is a learner and should be given time and training. Perhaps he has slipped and needs coaching. Or perhaps the job has changed and he has not, which calls for upgrading by the boss.

2. The manager doing all of his regular duties is filling his job description and is entitled to the same job (at the same pay) for another year. Raises and bonuses should not go to people who achieve all their routine goals, but should be reserved for the smaller group which solves problems or innovates.

3. Problem solving and innovation are levels higher than regular and routine and puts the man into excellence country where the benefits to him should be highest. The man, for example, who is innovating and improving the way things are done in his areas of responsibility, in addition to problem solving and routine, is worth more to the company than the man who is doing less; for example, he is not innovating.

The order in which to set goals

In practice, the order in which goals are set may have an effect upon the overall program of managing by objectives. This is especially true with that special class of employee or professional whose *major function of his work is innovation.* He might be the personnel research manager, the developer of new training courses, or the wage and salary research or labor relations research manager. Often the benefits department will have an individual or two whose main objective is to innovate in the benefit package area.

Such people have similar job objectives to the physical scientist, the developmental engineer, the market researcher, or other staff analyst position. His typical response would be, "But my work is different with each job. How can I predict, measure, or count outputs when every project is all new?"

There is little point in attempting to try to fit such a position into the pattern of goals statements which would work admirably for a plant manager, or a sales manager. His job is indeed different, and requires a different approach. The difference can be illustrated in Figure 6–6.

Thus, the discussion for category II, the innovative job, begins with the question: "What projects are you working on, what new projects are you planning, and what are your plans for the *management* of those projects?" Such a manager's problems are generated in the projects, and the regular things are less significant and come last, generally being limited to reports, meetings, and statistical annual results statements such as budgets, floor space, and similar matters. The *project* is the vital goal-setting medium, and discussion of objective should *start* with the most important.

FIGURE 6–6
Classes of objectives

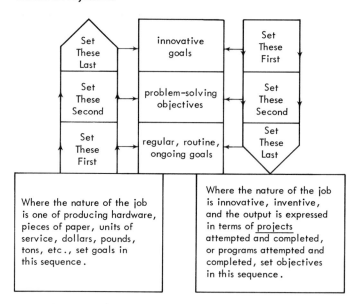

Setting personnel department objectives

Most positions in personnel administration will be of the first category shown in Figure 6–6, a regular service, some advice given to predictable clientele, and some controls in which matters like salary increases or insurance claims come to the department for processing. What then might a set of objectives look like for a typical personnel department job?

Figure 6–7 shows a page which might have been prepared by a manager of college recruiting for a medium sized manufacturing firm. It shows the regular objectives for the position for the coming year, with specific numerical indicators, Note some of the key points in constructing a statement of regular objectives.

1. These regular objectives are only the first page of three, and comprise only regular, ongoing, and repetitive goals. If a goal won't fit onto this form, it is probably because it is innovative or problem solving. Regular goals are always quantifiable, by definition. If it can't be quantified, don't call it regular.

2. Note that listing goals such as "visiting the colleges" or "production" doesn't permit them to be used as guides during the period. Such are *activity* statements. The statement of goal areas should be stated in terms of OUTPUTS for a specific period of TIME. Regular duties are those which occur daily, weekly, monthly, quarterly, or annually, and the time needs to be identical.

FIGURE 6–7

		Levels or indicators of output		
	Objectives statement — manager of college recruiting for the year 1971, and for first quarter 1. Note that these are regular, routine, recurring, and measureable objectives. If they don't fit in this page they are most likely to be innovative or problem–solving goals. Save them. List responsibilities below ONLY in terms of (OUTPUTS / TIME)	P	R	O
		Pessimistic	Realistic	Optimistic
KEY INDICATORS	1. No. of hires/per year 2. Cost per hire/per year			
TRADE–OFF GOALS	. Grade point average/year . % blacks/year			

3. Note that the KEY INDICATORS are listed first. Every job incumbent knows that there are base points around which other objectives resolve. The plant manager knows that production (units per shift) and quality (rejects per shift) count higher than some others, and thus seem to be the KEY objectives.

4. Trade-offs are *"more"* objectives, which also must be accomplished as well as the key objectives. They are called "trade-off" objectives because they *compete* with other objectives. For example, in Figure 6–7 the recruiter might increase the number of hires if he didn't have to stay within certain limits of grade point and cost per hire. He might get more black recruits if he could pay twice the going market rate, but he "trades off" quantity for quality, seeking a balance between numerous objectives rather than seeking a single one. Simon calls this "satisficing" behavior.

If we let a man pursue a single objective, he may achieve that objective but add painfully to the losses somewhere else. Under such a circumstance we list the trade-offs. If we study the skeletal framework of this regular goals statement, we see that down the left column are WORDS, whereas across the top from left to right we require *numbers.*

These numbers comprise indicators of level of output for the areas listed down the left-hand column.

The statement of these numbers is based upon a range of possible outcomes, and has numerous advantages over a single number which comprises the razor's edge between success and failure. These numbers are agreed upon by the boss and subordinate along these lines:

FIGURE 6–8

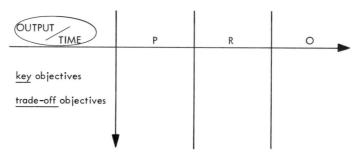

1. Start at *R*, or *realistic* figures. This could be last year's results as tempered by any new facts the two managers are aware of. If nothing else has changed or is to be changed, then reality suggests the same outcome again this year.

2. State the *O* or *optimistic* figure. This could be the best ever done—the record. It is not theoretical because it has been done before, even if only one time.

3. Finally choose the *P* or pessimistic estimate. This is the "exception point" for the subordinate. At any time he realizes that he is apt to fall below this level, he should so inform the boss that his objectives will not be met. This permits the boss some freedom from close control. He knows that unless he hears to the contrary he can assume that the objective will be achieved, or close to it.

This method of setting regular goals provides an instrument panel for the manager to direct his own ship. He knows what normal or realistic is; he knows when he has broken past records, and he knows when a problem exists and he should notify the next highest level.

Any organization which a manager can devise indicators for, he can manage. Any organization which operates without indicators is not being managed, it is drifting.

For the most part, a typical management job should be considered under control if it has 10 to 14 indicators which reflect changes in the underlying conditions. When they get over 15 it may be sensible to review them and see if some can be combined.

What are some indicators for regular personnel department goals?

It is possible from the experience of personnel departments which have been arranged by objectives to suggest some indicators for the various major functions of personnel administration. It is more important, however, that the staff practice devising their own indicators. The quick tendency to judge that personnel goals cannot be described by indicators is not borne out in the successful efforts of the many who have tried.

1. Because the personnel department produces nonhardware items, it

probably has not been working against a natural discipline of "things"; therefore, they have not been forced by the situation to define such measurable goals, and *therefore it is much more necessary* that they get started and try it.

2. There are some specific aids in defining intangibles which have grown out of the new systems approaches to management, which can be applied readily to defining personnel staff goals. These are shown in Figure 6–9, "Setting goals to measure the unmeasurable."

3. If the personnel administration department is to be the agent of change in the organization and adopts management by objectives as its suggested system of managing, appraising, coaching, and promoting line managers, it should be the first to have applied the system to its own internal management. For one thing, the personnel manager will find less credibility in suggesting the MBO system for sales plant and engineering if he is obliged to report that "It's OK for other people but not for us." For another, the experience of operating a staff group by objectives will provide tangible experience which can be used in solving the operating problems of others. Since the least difficulty will be encountered in manufacturing and selling departments, and most difficulty will be encountered in staff departments, this practical experience in managing the personnel department will be invaluable.

FIGURE 6–9
Setting goals to measure the unmeasurable

1. It is often necessary to devise measurements of present levels in order to be able to estimate or calculate change from this level.
2. The most reliable measures are the real time or raw data in which the physical objects involved comprise the measures to be used. (Dollars of sales, tons of output, number of home runs hit.)
3. When raw data can't be used, an index or ratio is the next most accurate measure. This is a batting average, a percent, a fraction or a ratio.
4. If neither of the above two can be used, a *scale* may be constructed. Such scales may be "rate from one to ten," a nominal rating against a check list of adjectives such as "excellent, fair, poor," or one which described "better than" or "worse than" some arbitrary scale. (These are useful but are far less precise than the above.)
5. Verbal scales are the least precise but can be extremely useful in identifying present levels and noting real change. *Verbs* such as "directs," "checks," and "reports" are indicative of actions to be taken.
6. General descriptions are the least useful, but still have value in establishing benchmarks for change. "A clear, cloudless, fall day" is obviously not the same as a "cloudy, foggy, misty day" and the two descriptions could be used to state conditions as they exist and conditions as they should be.
7. The statements of measurement should be directed more toward output than toward *activity*. (Much activity may prove impossible to state in specific terms, whereas results of that activity can be so stated.)
8. In stating results sought or in defining present levels, effort should be made to find indicative, tangible levels and convert verbal or general descriptions into such tangible scales, ratios, or raw measures where possible.
9. If you can't count it, measure it, or describe it, you probably don't know what you want and often can forget it as a goal.

Figure 6–10 presents a representative set of indicators which might appear on the statements of routine objectives of several different personnel department staff heads, in this case, the Training Director.

FIGURE 6–10

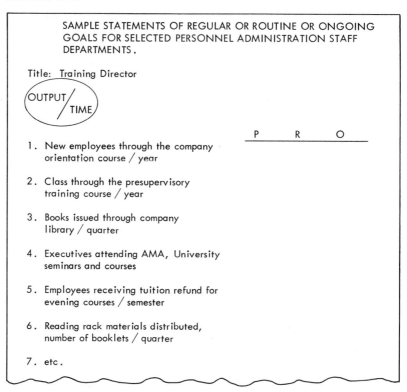

SAMPLE STATEMENTS OF REGULAR OR ROUTINE OR ONGOING GOALS FOR SELECTED PERSONNEL ADMINISTRATION STAFF DEPARTMENTS.

Title: Training Director

OUTPUT / TIME

P   R   O

1. New employees through the company orientation course / year

2. Class through the presupervisory training course / year

3. Books issued through company library / quarter

4. Executives attending AMA, University seminars and courses

5. Employees receiving tuition refund for evening courses / semester

6. Reading rack materials distributed, number of booklets / quarter

7. etc.

It's obvious that these are routine, regular, and recurring. They happened last year, and are now included in the repertory of the department.[2] Any additional programs, new developments installed, shouldn't be included here but stated as either PROBLEM-SOLVING GOALS or INNOVATIVE GOALS. What would a problem-solving goal look like for a training director? Perhaps something like the sample page in Figure 6–11.

The reason this could be treated as a problem-solving objective is that *the result is to return to a status quo,* and heal a self-inflicted trauma which the organization has incurred.

[2] The training director's objectives almost always are "behavior change," and these routine goals suppose a prior effort to identify behavior change desired. See George S. Odiorne, *Training by Objectives* (New York: Macmillan, 1970) for a fuller exposition.

FIGURE 6–11

A SAMPLE STATEMENT OF A PROBLEM-SOLVING OBJECTIVE
FOR A TRAINING DEPARTMENT

I. *Name the problem:* The turnover rate among the newly hired hard core unemployed is 22% per year compared with 11% for the plant at large.

II. *The objectives:* To prepare and conduct a supervisory and plant management training program to reduce this rate from 22 to 11%.
realistic goal: 11% has been realized in some departments and should be attainable here.
optimistic: Some departments in this and other companies have gone as low as 6%.
pessimistic: Anything higher than 15% should be considered a failure for this objective.

III. *Methods and time stages* (plan):

stage	estimated time to complete
a. Interview foremen, plant personnel, study exit interviews	3 weeks
b. Prepare draft of course outline and submit to IR director, plant manager, and training director for approval	2 weeks
c. Test run the program with first group	2 weeks
d. Schedule and conduct sessions for all plant general foremen, and foremen	8 weeks

Once the problem-solving objective is achieved, it might well be absorbed into routine and become an ongoing part of the training department's activities and objectives.

What then might innovative goals look like? Usually there are less of them, they are less susceptible of measurement, and their outcome is far less certain. They are distinguished from problem-solving goals by the fact that they seek *growth* beyond existing levels in volume, quality, cost, time, and other variables. There may indeed be no problem or "level gone wrong" that needs restoring.

It is based upon the purely inventive and innovative talent of the job incumbent to move the organization ahead. Some sample statements of innovative programs which the training director might identify and schedule for the coming period would include:

- Reaching a whole new training population (clerks, executives, women, etc.)
- Introducing a complete new technology not previously used (closed circuit TV, learning lab, programmed instruction)
- Installation of an entire new training department physical plant
- Research project to evaluate the effect of sales training
- Other research projects in which the outcome is not known, the purpose of which is to gather and interpret information.

Cumulating the subordinates into the superior's goals

The regular goals of the superior, in this case the industrial relations or personnel manager, are accumulation of the totals of his several subordinates. In the case of the training director whose regular objectives consist of various populations to be trained, the total of these becomes the regular objective of the superior in reporting to the president.

FIGURE 6–12

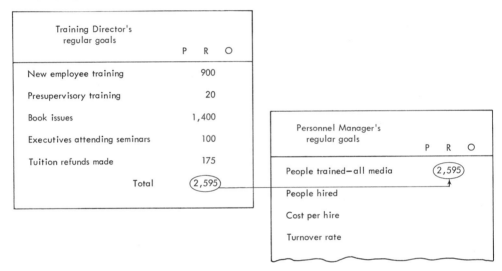

The items which appear on the subordinate's regular goals statement are summarized and the key goals included at the next highest level, in cumulative form.

Thus, the employment manager may have 14 indicators of his performance, but these are summarized for the boss. The labor relations manager, the benefits manager, the salary administrator—each has more detailed indicators for his position than his boss has for that position. If this isn't done, the higher levels of management are staggered under several hundred objectives.

The personnel manager's regular objectives are summary statements of the total objectives of all of the key section or unit heads.

Is it possible to find a ready prepared set of objectives for a personnel department? The chances are slim that they would fit your own department. If the goals statements are couched in output terms, and the boss and subordinate understand them and agree that they are sound guides for the subordinate to act upon during the forthcoming year, then they will be satisfactory, whether or not they meet a textbook requirement.

FIGURE 6–13

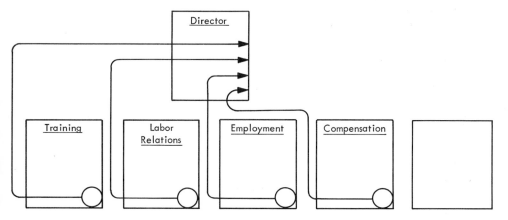

The summarization of goals upward is really nothing new. The whole principle of organization charting has been based upon a similar principle.

The major difference in managing by objectives is that the descriptions which make up the differences between positions are of objectives and outputs, not of activities. If the difference seems trivial, it indeed is not. The difference in effects is enormous.

Delegation, then, becomes the delegation of results sought rather than activity to be conducted. The dialogue-memo has assured agreement rather than ambiguity.

With such a system installed and operating in the personnel department, the difficulties of persuading other departments to use the system, and instruct them in its use, will be eliminated.

If management is getting results through other people, the personnel department should be the best managed department in the organization, and objectives should be clearer there then anywhere else in the firm.

The same summarization method displayed in the previous figure can be used for problem-solving objectives and innovative goals. The personnel manager will have some problems of his own which he is working on without involving subordinates, and he also will be stating to his boss an array of the problems which his department will be solving during the forthcoming year.

Similarly, he will have an array of research projects, developmental programs, and innovative ideas which he will collect from his key subordinates and commit himself upon to the boss.

This emphasis upon outputs rather than activity leads to somewhat less structure of actions by the subordinates, permits a job enrichment by the subordinate to take place through encouraging innovation and problem solving, and avoids the ill effects of overrationalization of activity and work.[3]

While this chapter has been a "cook book" of procedures, we shouldn't lose sight of the giant steps we are taking in philosophy and policy when we manage by objectives in the personnel department.

1. We improve the utilization of the *skills* of the personnel staff man when we concentrate first upon *results* of the application of those skills.

2. The demand for the skills of the personnel staff man, and even the details of those skills are drastically altered if we begin with objectives.

QUESTIONS AND PROBLEMS

1. Why should a program of installing management by objectives start with the board or officers of the firm? Could it be started with a lesser level manager if he had authority to manage his own operation?

2. Management by objectives uses training to move the training out of the class onto the job. Do you agree?

3. Why wouldn't it save time to install a management by objectives program to simply write a memorandum directing it to be used and then distribute it through the mail?

4. Construct a list of ten pitfalls which you could see which should be avoided in installing a management by objectives system.

5. Construct a role play situation for the dialogue between superior and subordinate for setting goals for a personnel manager and the employment manager. Enact it in class with two other persons playing the roles.

6. Why is it commonly stated that "some jobs can't be measured?" Does this mean that it is impossible to set objectives for some jobs?

7. Why should regular objectives have time commitments stated? What is the importance of time as a variable in commitment?

8. Show several kinds of trade offs which students must make in their own objectives. How would these apply to a labor relations manager? An employment manager? A personnel research manager?

9. Why should you start with reality when you are defining goals?

10. Explain how the pessimistic level of indicator can be used as an application of the "exception principle"? Find several examples of the exception principle you use in your own life and list them.

11. How are procedures related to philosophy in management by objectives? Explain for some of the important areas of personnel concern:
    motivation   job enlargement   self actualization

---

[3] For studies on the effects of overly detailed work pattern designs, as opposed to management by objectives, a number of studies by Herzberg, Likert, Kahn, and others are available. R. Guest, "Better Utilization of Skills Through Job Design," *Management of Personnel Quarterly*, Vol. 3, No. 1 (Fall, 1964) is a brief summary of this position.

THE DALLAS OFFICE CASE

PART I

In the early fifties, the rapid growth of Amherst Insurance business out of the Dallas office finally necessitated a large-scale reorganization and decentralization of that branch. The two prime reasons for this were: 1) to cut traveling expenses and 2) to give the salesmen a firmer place in a more concentrated area. Since its inception, the plan has worked well; there are now seven district offices working under the Dallas branch office, and each of these offices is staffed with a district agent, 7 to 12 salesmen, and its own clerical staff.

To facilitate business and give it a more personal touch, each of the district offices is set up as a self-sufficient selling and servicing unit. The salesman usually work from their homes, doing their own underwriting (the home office term for this is "field underwriting"), and reporting regularly to the district office. The district offices, in turn, report all applications, all premiums, and all claims directly to the home office in Amherst, Massachusetts. There they are processed and altered, if necessary, and afterward they are returned to the district office *via the regional office*.

The position of the regional office, after the reorganization, has become supervisory. There are three regional managers there: one for ordinary life, one accident and health, and one group. In addition to attending to their lines of insurance, they also assist in other matters as they arise: training of salesmen, management and personnel advice, occasional legal direction, and so on.

Recently, company president John Nordberg, working in conjunction with the three Dallas regional managers has conceived a plan which he hopes will make the running of the district offices smoother yet. To announce this play, he has written the following letter to each of the seven district agents:

Jeffrey Building
Amherst, Mass.
June 19, 1961

Dear _____,

As you no doubt know, the district office reorganization plan has, to date, proved highly effective. Our sales in the Texas region have increased 21% during the last five years, and we feel that we have been able to service our accounts in a considerably improved manner.

Like most organizational realignments, this plan has not been without its "kinks," however. As a district agent you have had to keep your head turned two ways at once—tending both your salesmen and connections with the home office. While this situation has not been unsatisfactory, I and the three regional managers in Dallas feel it could be improved.

In lieu of this I would like you to start thinking in terms of making one of your salesmen a part-time "Home Office Representative." Hopefully, this position will facilitate many aspects of our business: servicing, sales, and particularly communications between the district, regional, and home offices. I mention the communications problem with emphasis; with our company developing a more complex organizational structure, a more intricate communications pattern becomes necessary.

I have instructed Cecil Pride in the Dallas Office to be at your disposal in an advisory capacity. As a man who has worked extensively in personnel management and sales trainee programs, he should be very helpful.

Feel free to address any questions on your "Home Office Representative" to him, or me. More detailed material on this will be forthcoming shortly.

Yours truly,
JOHN NORDBERG

PART II

Cecil Pride is the Amherst Company's regional agent in Dallas. He has been with the company 14 years, but has been in his current position for only two. His prior experience has been distributed among various aspects of the sales and personnel areas in the business, and he has gained a considerable amount of respect—both from his equals and his superiors. Nordberg has been in steady contact with him on the "Home Office Representative" idea, though, in actuality, Pride has had little to say about it. His own feelings are somewhat negative; he doubts that the district agents will care for this intrusion into the management of their offices, and he doubts also the advisability of the plan on purely organizational grounds. Several times, it has seemed to him that Nordberg is merely complicating the communications apparatus of the company, instead of using the already available channels.

This is not his decision to make, however; for his part he is to assist the seven district agents in selecting a "Home Office Representative" from among their salesmen. Pride has had a hand in training most of these salesmen, and has ready knowledge of their performance through the Dallas files. His background work in sales and personnel management should also serve him well. He knows that some of the district agents will leave the choice to him to a greater extent than others; in several cases he anticipates conflicts.

PART III

The Galveston district office of the Amherst Company is managed by Charles Truslow. He is a quiet, steady worker—very firm in his ways but generally well-liked by the eight salesmen who work under him. His office has run at a somewhat high loss ratio, but Truslow has had more than the usual luck in developing a group of loyal salesmen, all of whom have been with the company for at least three years. The yearly earnings of this force range from $6,000 to $20,000 yearly, a figure Truslow is proud of quoting to outsiders who query him on the success of his office.

Due to his success with salesmen, Truslow was asked, not long ago, to be one of the leaders in a statewide management-personnel relations seminar conducted by three insurance companies with large operations in the Southwest. There, one of his tasks was to outline his criteria for a good salesman, a job which he found to be somewhat puzzling. He had, often in the past, interviewed as many as 25 candidates for one position, but had given little thought to any actual method he might have. When his ideas came out, they were as follows: 1) enthusiasm, 2) willingness to meet people, and 3) desire to earn money. These, however, did not satisfy the participants in the seminar, who asked more specific questions. The transcripts of two of Truslow's answers read as follows:

Q: "Do you place any particular emphasis on college degrees? Or business school degree?"

A: "No, I don't. I don't think it makes much difference one way or another. And actually I've had more success with noncollege students. An eight-year company survey bears this out, and you know some of these college kids come in with awfully big preconceptions. They want to get big quick, come into your office and almost say 'Well, here I am; pay me!' Seem to think their degree entitles them to everything right away. Actually I look on my college experience as a four-year brain stretching period, but it doesn't seem that way any more. I wish it were. As for business administration, well that's pretty general too—and it makes the kids think they're something they're not. We still have to do all the specialized training."

Q: "When you've a choice between a single man and a married man, which do you hire?"

A: "Well, it's hard to generalize here. Really an individual matter you know. I suppose the single man does have a tendency to be footloose; his ambition often gets limited by what he needs to support himself, too. But this isn't always the case."

PART IV

Truslow has now been in receipt of Nordberg's letter for several days; the idea has not irritated him as Pride thought it might. In fact he rather likes the idea, for it will relieve him of a number of the more routine duties which sometimes wear him down, and interfere with some of the more essential duties of his job. Truslow is, however, in somewhat of a quandary about the selection of a "Home Office Representative" from among his sales staff. He is aware that Pride will contact him soon on the problem, and he also senses that there might be differences between them on the choice. At the outset, Truslow has been able to narrow his choice down to two men and he feels Pride will no doubt concur to this point.

Truslow's tentative choice for the position is George Herbert, one of his older and most reliable salesmen. He is the only salesman on Truslow's staff who was with the company before the division into district offices came about, and Truslow considers his length of experience and steadiness a good asset for the new position. Herbert has also been one of the Galveston branch's most productive salesmen and is the top man on Truslow's payroll. In recent years, however, Herbert has had repeated arthritis attacks and has even had to spend some time on crutches. Surprisingly, this has not diminished his productivity, though Truslow feels that a falling off is imminent. Herbert is not a college graduate, coming into the insurance field by way of night school courses in accounting. Later he changed off to sales, and has stayed there ever since; this is his 23d year with Amherst. The only difficulty Truslow has had with Herbert centers around the monthly meeting of the district staff, where Truslow tries to institute "round robin" discussions on Company policies, sales methods, etc. Of late Herbert's attendance has been irregular, a fact that bothers Truslow somewhat, though on reflection he acknowledges the fact that Herbert usually said next to nothing anyway.

The other possibility for the "Home Office Representative" job is Edward Muchard, single, a graduate of Southern Methodist University, and a man possessed with an oft demonstrated ability to work with people. Often in the earlier period of Truslow's employment in Galveston, Muchard helped considerably in the training of new salesmen, and Truslow is openly aware of his abilities as a "man-builder." Muchard has, however, been somewhat of a man of his own will in the office—at least in Truslow's eyes. His sales have been consistent, though he has not quite measured up to Truslow's expectations, vague as they may be. In his moments of deeper consideration, Truslow has admitted that Muchard might make a better "Home Office Representative" than Herbert, but Truslow has always been closer to Herbert, and Herbert in turn has been more subservient. Truslow feels that Muchard's broader interests (sales, personnel, salesman training) might lead him to handle the new position in a rather diffuse manner.

PART V

At the same time the district agents received their letters from Nordberg, Pride also received full word of his role in the new appointments. As yet no further definition of the "Home Office Representative's" position has been forthcoming from Nordberg, and the date designated for appointment is less than a week away. Pride has been able to take care of five of the district offices quite easily; in four of the cases there was little if any choice involved, and in another the situation was resolved by a sales-man declining the new job. Two undecided "spots" remain; one is Gal-veston and the other is San Antonio.

Pride has talked with Truslow by phone in Galveston and is quite fully aware of the possibilities of choice there. He has had to spend more time with that office on account of the several gulf hurricanes which have hit the area in the last four years. Appraisals have been tedious and claims have been extensive—and he has done some special work with the sales-men in view of more hurricane possibilities.

While still doubtful as to the efficacy of Nordberg's position, he has decided to try and make the best of it—and his supervisory advice has been directed accordingly. Pride is familiar with both Herbert and Muchard, and is quite convinced the latter is more apt for the new posi-tion. He is aware of latent personal jealousies between Muchard and Truslow, but desires to have Muchard installed anyway. He feels Much-ard's concern is more for the company as a whole, while Herbert is primarily concerned about the size of his own commission. He admits, with Truslow, that Muchard's ambitions may be limited, but feels that the shift in responsibility would probably bring out his abilities better than the straight-selling work he has been doing. He also fears that Herbert will merely be a "puppet" of Truslow, and contribute little to the unity of the company.

With clash of attitudes between Pride and Truslow impending, unless Pride is very tactful in giving his advice, Pride wishes to know how best to go about his job.

PART II

Personnel administration strategy

Effective use of research outputs

IT IS ONLY in recent times that economists have pretended that economics was a science separate from other social sciences. In the early days of Smith, Ricardo, and Mill the connection was clearly acknowledged. Personnel is not yet a science. The management of human resources, however, is clearly rooted in personnel research, with tentacles in other disciplines as well. For now, however, here are several chapters on the study of the strategies of personnel affected by personnel research. Supply and demand are economic terms but also much involved with public policy, psychology, and sociology. Population as an aggregate source of supply, unemployment as a special problem of supply, and how "quality" is defined in the form of credentials for employment, are clearly made up of intersecting political economic influences. All comprise the warp and woof of personnel and human resources strategy to set goals and achieve them. Thus, our attention to manpower research and its outputs.

chapter 7

FORMULATING A STRATEGY
FOR MANAGING MANPOWER

WHILE THE general climate in management these days tends to favor the annual Management-by-Objectives approach to managing, not everyone is clear on what to do, or how to get started. While it is sensible to get going immediately by agreeing with both superiors and subordinates upon annual objectives, it is also obvious that limiting management to such a limited time span could be costly.

Where any unit manages on a year-by-year basis, it is systematically exploiting the best outputs possible from the existing resources and procedures. This is, of course, a vast improvement over doing things chaotically. For the foreman in the assembly department such may be the limits of his scope, with the longer run strategic decisions being made at the higher levels of the firm, or in staff specialists departments.

For the personnel department however, the first step in managing by objectives is to shape its strategic goals prior to defining yearly or quarterly objectives. What is the difference between strategic and tactical or operational objectives?

Strategic goals are multiyear in time span and are designed to change the character of the organization for the better or avert impending and potential major problems.

Operational or tactical goals are those which are designed to get the most out of the existing resources and execute the next most immediate stages of the strategic goals. For our purposes we consider those operational goals as being one year in length, with quarterly review periods.

These two classes of objectives comprise the major operating system of a personnel department which is operating by objectives. It also helps divide the labor inside the department. The top man, his line advisers (such as a personnel policy committee), and his key staff department heads or subordinates collaborate on the shaping of such strategic goals.

133

The professional staff, the section chiefs and supervisors in employment, recruiting, statistics, records, employee services, wage and salary administration, training, and labor relations will be more preoccupied with operational objectives moving toward strategic objectives. The preface to this part of the book indicates that strategic objectives are far more than rational or logical systems; they are also political, cultural, and social. The corporation is at its root an economic institution, that is, its functions by its charter are to make profits for its shareholders. All strategies are designed to ultimately forward that economic aim. This shouldn't be interpreted narrowly, however, for strategy should be concerned with *long run* (multi-year) economic gain, not merely temporary gain. Thus, in an individual year a firm may spend money in a way that actually does less than maximization of economic gain, in order to maximize long-run economic gain.

We might also note that even in nonprofit, public, and institutional organizations there is an economic dimension of great significance, and economics is of great importance there.

An economic strategy of personnel

In these days of job enlargement, it might be sensible for the professional in personnel administration to show a little initiative in enlarging on his own job. If you are such a man, you might, for instance, cast about for a useful occupation that is being left undone around your shop; then quietly add its duties to your repertory. One suggestion is to become your own company's labor economist. This, of course, assumes that your company doesn't have any existing individual holding this position title; if that isn't true, it might be a sound idea to wait until he has the decency to abdicate.

Such a person on your organization's payroll is extremely unlikely. In fact the functions of the job are largely not being done at all; this fact provides a fine opportunity for you if you presently work at some trade such as personnel manager, salary administrator, personnel researcher, manpower planner, organization planner, employment manager, or labor relations man (between contracts). You might even tentatively set up shop in this role if you are training director and have cool nerves, and nobody else really shows much interest in the job.

This added role doesn't imply that you must quit doing your present job. In fact, you must, in the early stages, insist that this is "just a part of my job" and that you are displaying splendid initiative in assuming this much-needed task. By the time you've gotten well-ensconced in your new function, most people who might wish they had thought of the idea will have been outrun, and your grasp on the job will be firm.

Your quizzical gaze (indicating that you wonder how you can handle both jobs) is partly justified. Clearly you'll have to work harder or longer to get established in the newly-created labor economist spot, but that seems to be the main idea behind job enlargement, doesn't it? Titles aside, what you are undertaking is preparation of the total personnel strategy for your organization. How do you set up shop? There are a number of rather specific tools which you'll need to function as your company's own labor economist; among them are the following:

Get some basic books and reports. You should immediately obtain copies of the current and several past issues of the *Manpower Report to the President.* This comes out annually in March and is a fountainhead of information and ideas. You'll want to be added to the subscription list of the U.S. Department of Labor for their various manpower bulletins and reports, and to be on the mailing list of your state Employment Security Commission, which issues monthly Labor Market Bulletins. These bulletins tell the current standing on employment, unemployment, and other important data about the labor market in the nation and in your area.

You'll also want to have handy the *Statistical Abstract of the United States,* the *Survey of Current Business* (Department of Commerce), and perhaps a good economic news letter such as the National City Bank letter, or similar general economic bulletins so you can keep abreast of current changes in the general economic picture. Add to these a couple of good weekly news magazines, and one of the sounder financial dailies, and you have enough to get started. Later on, when you get your feet on the ground, you can slip in some of the more expensive services such as Prentice-Hall, Bureau of National Affairs (BNA), Commerce Clearing House (CCH), or others which cost more. Not too fast to begin with.

Get as much specific company information as possible. Without too much fanfare, see if you can get yourself on the distribution list for inside company information without arousing too much suspicion that you are either empire building or serving as a spy for the competition. Any manpower statistics which are generated for other purposes should be pretty easy to get. If monthly profit statements are not restricted information, get on the circulation list; get also any other kinds of information which might give you some idea of what the basic economic health of the company is. You might even invest in a share of stock in your company which will entitle you to the same information which all stockholders obtain. The annual report, any SEC statements about the company, copies of officers' speeches and press releases about new products, and similar information about wages, prices, and profits will serve you well. You might even set up a filing system and make memos to file on matters which you learn routinely or which you overhear.

Getting your program under way

There are a number of specific targets you can set out as phase one objectives on your new job. These consist of things you are going to keep under surveillance. Having watched them for a decent period of time, your native ingenuity will tell you what are the important things you might tentatively start emitting brief blurbs about. These might start as little interdepartment memos around the personnel deparment, and gradually expand into personal contacts out in the line departments. Two major areas will become the focal point for your efforts; you can build your program around them: (1) supply of labor and (2) demand for labor.

While these major headings don't seem to be very impressive, once you get started you'll be able to expand them into dozens of subheadings each. By that time you'll be happy you chose only two headings. The mass of things you receive, read, and sort over will be confusing, but most of it will fit into either of these areas. Let's take a quick glimpse at the kinds of things you might find under each heading, and how it might be useful to your company.

Scanning labor supply

What are the general trends in population? Are the various age levels of the population rising or thinning out? Maybe that vice president doesn't realize that while population is rising, the rate of increase isn't. The percent of the total population which is Negro is presently 12 percent, but the percent of the population under age ten which is Negro is substantially higher and in ten years this percentage will have increased drastically.

What is happening in enrollments in the schools? The enrollment in colleges by categories of major is surveyed annually by the dean at the University of Cincinnati. You should keep your chief engineer abreast of what's happening on engineering campuses. How many MBA's will be produced now, and in 1970–75? The figures are there. How many are enrolling in business? Where are the National Merit Scholars going? What does the Placement Council and Frank Endicott of Northwestern predict for the future in campus talent? Are more women going on to college; are many electing business? What is happening in Negro colleges, and in Negro enrollment in all colleges? What are the major curriculum changes in the large universities which supply a majority of the college graduates? These are a few examples of what you might keep an eye on.

Which are the scarce occupations? State and county labor market reports can tell you whether there is now, and will be, shortages ahead in computer programmers, secretaries, machinists, die makers, and the like. This leads to the even more useful kinds of studies you can do about the immediate source of labor for your own company.

While temptation is great to get all wrapped up in these national trends, you'll do better to spend most of your time scrutinizing those things which are of most importance to your own business and your own company. For example, you might keep an eye on the following and be ready to toss in some authoritative information when the occasion demands:

Your old economics text book states that "the labor market is the area within which a person can change his job without changing his residence." This is all fine, except that the labor market is changing in scope. Suppose, for example, that you read in the evening newspaper that a freeway is going to intersect your town. This means that the size of your labor market will be enlarged considerably. You might want to issue a bulletin after you've estimated what this could mean. People in such jobs as manager, engineer, machinist, and many operators can now live and be hired from the new areas which the freeway opens up.

How volatile is the local labor market? In Michigan, for example, labor supply is a function of how prosperous the durable goods industry is at the time (automobiles). A moderate recession usually hits durables sooner than consumer goods, and people delay purchases of durables first. Production falls and there is more help available. In a state like Minnesota, with its emphasis upon agriculture processing, employment reaches fewer red-hot pressures, but also declines less in hard times. Government employment anywhere is usually quite stable, except for some defense and space activities.

What are your local schools producing? Figures from your county superintendent of education can reveal much about the forthcoming supply of labor in your area. What is the percentage of school dropouts in your public schools? Typically, of 100 youngsters reaching the age of 16, about 75 will have graduated and about 25 will not have graduated from high school. Estimating what percent of this year's high school graduating class will be available can be complicated by the effect of the draft and junior college enrollment. But in spite of their delay into the labor market, these young people will, after two or more years, return and provide a more highly trained source of labor.

Women power as a supply source must be handled separately because the employment of women is usually "bimodal," that is, it has two peaks of frequency. The first cluster is the 18–22-year-old group (that is, the group coming from the school system). There is ordinarily a 15-year retirement while the women are raising young children. Then the second cluster occurs as they reenter the labor market. Often they are rusty in secretarial or other skills but are available if retrained. There are numerous benefits—low turnover, high productivity, good work habits—to the employer who can utilize such employees. Simply taking inventory of employees by the classification "female" can be deceiving. You should treat young women and older (let's say more mature) women as two different resources in figuring supply of labor.

In estimating the labor supply situation in your labor market, there are two other inputs which should be noted. The first is returning veterans. The second is the number of potential employees who move into your labor market from other places. This second figure can, of course, be a negative one if more people are moving out than in, such as occurred in the coal mining regions of Pennsylvania, or the textile towns of New England for many years.

In summary, you can estimate supply by taking net gains from education establishments, womanpower (i.e., women returning to the workforce), in-migration, and returning veterans.

Estimating demand for labor

With an estimate of supply of labor in hand, you turn next to making an estimate of demand for some period into the future, say the next two to five years. This is stickier and calls for two kinds of data: (1) an inventory of present employment levels and (2) a forecast of future employment. From these two you can generally come up with your target product: a useful (if not perfectly accurate) forecast of what the critical or short-supply jobs will be in the future. This will help predict what kinds of training needs your company might be faced with, what kinds of jobs may be shorthanded, and what kinds of jobs you might have to go some distance to fill.

Taking inventory.   Getting your hands on the total number of employees and their wage levels in a labor market isn't especially difficult, since it has already been done for you. The Bureau of Employment Security of the U.S. Department of Labor publishes a report, *Employment and Wages of Workers Covered by State Unemployment Insurance Laws.* Your state Employment Security Commission will provide you a list of firms in the county covered by unemployment compensation law. Your state *Directory of Manufacturers* will also help you to establish levels of employment and a list of all firms. (Generally it excludes farm and service employment.) From these sources, plus others which may be locally available (including some letters to other employers), you can construct an accurate inventory of how many employees by major occupational classifications there are in your labor market.

Forecasting demand.   Now things get tougher. As a starter, you can find that a pretty useful skill inventory and forecast in many counties has already been done for you. If you want to conduct such a study yourself or in conjunction with other employers, the methods described in the *Handbook on Labor Market Research,* a publication of the Bureau of Employment Security, U.S. Department of Labor, is one guide. Perhaps an even more accurate method would be merely to survey the 20 to 30 largest employers in your labor market. Normally they will employ more than half of all employees. This shortcut is extremely useful and you can likely come up with an even more useful and accurate predictor of future demand than by surveying every employer. There are three major reasons to explain this anomaly. For one thing, most small employers, such as the local druggist or retailer, really don't have any basis for predicting. Their demand for employees is derived from the general level of business.

Secondly, the general level of business will be based on the growth and prosperity of the few larger employers whose products or service are exported out of your labor market. And last, by breaking down the total number of employees into two major categories (local businesses and export businesses), you will note the existence of a ratio of people employed between them. For example, in Washtenaw County, Michigan (the home county of the University of Michigan) the ratio of people employed in businesses which sell their product outside the county to those producing services for local consumption was .5 of local employment to 1.0 of export employment.

Since this ratio can safely be used to predict that a gain in the export type firms will create an additional one-half job in the local economy, you need to get predictions only from the larger employers (who make up most of the export business employment).

Large company estimates are not perfect by any means, but are vastly more reliable than those of the small firms who have neither information, time, nor resources to make any projections of their future labor needs. Consider the firm which decides to expand its plant toward making consumer durables. It hires 1,000 new employees. It also creates by the multiplier effect 500 other jobs in such things as groceries, cleaning establishments, and the like. The pressure on the labor market then is more than just the 1,000 employees hired. A new plant moving into your area may put even more pressure on the labor market than 1.5, but this is a fairly reasonable estimate.

What should a company labor economist produce?

After scrutinizing existing data, collecting some yourself, and making calculations, you should be able to create something useful for your own management and for the personnel department. Here are the products you might start with and build upon.

A summary report of labor supply. This would inform management and other personnel men what to look for in the labor market in terms of output for the coming year or two. By the time you've added the inputs and subtracted the outputs, you can come up with a net figure of how many people will be around as applicants for jobs. You'll also want to note the retirement patterns, numbers of people moving away, percent of draftees out of the presently employed, and mortality rates. If you keep this up for a couple of years you can make it more meaningful to the reader by telling how it will probably change from the past year or two. If you are forced to forecast, you can always use this hedge, regularly used by the economists: *"If things go in the future as they have gone in the past,* you may expect the shortage of computer programmers, secretaries, and experimental machinists to continue."

A summary report of labor demand.   Here you could call upon some of your general economic indicators to report the general characteristics of the demand for labor. This is a summary analysis of present employment, how your labor market compares with the state and national labor markets, and what big new influences will be working on the local labor market to affect demand in the future. For example, if your labor market has stuck pretty closely in performance to the national pattern, you can draw upon general national forecasts for your own local forecasts. If it has been tied to consumer durables, you can tie onto predictions of those industries, such as automobiles, appliances, and the like. If it is soft goods such as food, you may relate your local predictions to the available national predictions for that industry. One important factor never to overlook is the effect of government employment upon demand and supply of labor. Government is often among the largest employers in your labor market.

If you are in a corporate headquarters, you have a more complex problem because you will probably be dealing with a national labor market and needn't bother with such local labor market data as we've discussed. Ultimately, however, you might want to get people in each location to start maintaining such data for their own location. They could then, incidentally, provide you with copies and you'd have a better grasp of what the situation is in each location.

A list of possible beginning reports or reference volumes is attached as an appendix. This would be a fair start; get and read these regularly for awhile. Keep them at hand and use them as needed.

Your end product is a report. It may simply be an interoffice memo on some facet of the labor market as it would affect your company. This can be distributed to people in personnel such as college recruiting, employment, labor relations, wage and salary, or some selected other individuals who might be interested and receptive. After issuing a few, conduct some casual but meticulous soundings of their effect. If they are being read and understood and some value is being received, you'll start receiving questions asking for interpretation and amplification. Let word-of-mouth advertising be your agent for circulation. One manager who cites it to another creates a demand for it. This isn't simply psychology. It means you are making the product responsive to the needs of your internal captive audience. If it is sparsely distributed and if it is worthwhile (i.e., it tells people things about the labor market they need to know but didn't), you'll find your product in demand. At this stage you can begin expanding it, digging deeper into better resources, and perhaps generating studies upon request.

Why continuous surveillance of labor market is essential

We can identify six areas of economic and technical change which affect jobs and influence skills in our industrial system. These would include scientific management, mergers and consolidations, changes in locations of businesses, shifts in product demand, changes in equipment and process, and automation.

The trend is shifting from the manual and manipulative to the more mental and cognitive types of work. The historical changes in the occupational distribution of the labor force is shown in Table 7–1. In 1900 the

TABLE 7–1
Major occupational groups as a percentage of total labor force, representative years [1]

Occupational group	1900	1947	1960	1975
White-collar workers	17.6	34.9	43.1	47.8
Professional and technical	4.3	6.6	11.2	14.2
Managers and proprietors	5.8	10.0	10.6	10.7
Clerical workers	3.0	12.4	14.7	16.2
Sales personnel	4.5	5.9	6.6	6.7
Blue-collar workers	35.8	40.7	36.3	33.4
Craftsmen and foremen	10.5	13.4	12.8	12.8
Semiskilled operatives	12.8	21.2	18.0	16.3
Laborers (exclusive of farm and mine) ..	12.5	6.1	5.5	4.3
Service workers	9.0	10.4	12.5	14.3
Farm workers.......................	37.6	14.0	8.1	4.5

number of white-collar jobs was less than half the number of blue-collar jobs, whereas by 1975 it is projected to be 44 percent greater. In the blue-collar ranks, only the skilled and highly skilled craftsmen are expected to maintain status quo in the labor market. The greatest employment gains within the white-collar area have been made by the professional and technical employees, who generally have more education and skill.

Previously, the principal demand for white-collar workers was in teaching, banking, government, and insurance occupations. However, today the largest demand by percentage is in industry.

The blue-collar-white-collar shift in the employment force signifies that the primary function of work today is in the distribution of goods—not the production. In the early 1900's 70 percent of the nation's labor force was engaged in production compared with less than 40 percent today.[2]

---

[1] Grant Venn, *Man, Education, and Work*, American Council on Education (Washington: Government Printing Office, 1966), p. 8.

[2] *Manpower Report of the President*, 1970.

The emergence of the "Human Resources Era," (the acquisition, training, placement, and evaluation of personnel), will lead to an expected growth rate in professional employment approximately double the rate for total employment. Employment in clerical occupations is expected to grow about 50 percent faster than total employment. In general, the transition to the Human Resources Era will lead to a relatively rapid growth of white-collar over blue-collar occupations (See Figure 7–1.)

FIGURE 7–1
Projections of growth in one large industrialized state [3]

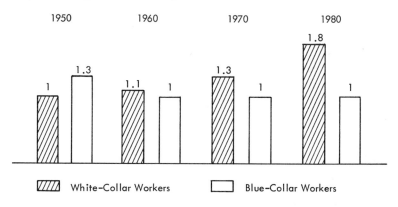

Underlying causes of labor market change

Competitors are constantly researching new ideas and developing new products at an accelerated pace. In many businesses, the rate of inovation is so high that jobs and job skills are created overnight. There is a constant drive, on the part of business firms, to obtain new technical knowledge. Greater emphasis is being placed on research and development, with each new discovery leading to additional research. The ultimate objective is to create new products at a lower cost to consumer. Business must draw from the labor supply to carry out its objectives.

Both internal and external forces create change in business which creates a modified demand for labor; for example, industrial cost accounting, emergence and growth of decentralization, growth of unions resulting in new personnel policies and techniques, and national emergencies. The success in the creation and manufacture of new products is directly related to the competency of existing staff.

As companies enter new product lines, they will demand more en-

---

[3] State of Michigan, *The Michigan Manpower Study* (A report to Michigan Department of Labor, Education, and Commerce). Research conducted by Battelle Memorial Institute, Columbus Laboratories, Ohio (November, 1966), p. S–7.

gineers, scientists, and technicians. In the face of competition, managers will be required to possess a greater working knowledge of accounting, electronic data processing, and applied mathematics and behavioral science. Personnel management, public relations, purchasing, and legal departments will be dealing with new and more complex problems which will require more college trained men. The need for trained people is evident in the high technology industries. Only the highly skilled and well educated can adjust quickly enough to the relatively short life span of products and processes. The life of an invention is shorter than ever before.

With the increased size and complexity of today's business, there is need for an altogether different type of manager. Today's managers must have a high degree of skill in setting objectives and policies, making decisions, organizing and integrating people into the existing organization, planning both long-range and short-range, and directing and controlling large volumes of men and materials.

Model making for manpower planning

One of the more advanced skills of the economist is model making—not the physical kind of model, but conceptual and often diagrammatic. In some cases models can be represented by mathematical models. The major advantages of modeling the situation are these: It clarifies relationships, it describes all of the important variables, and it forces the model maker to seek out data to flesh out his skeletal framework. For the company labor economist, the simpler models are preferable when they are to be presented to nontechnically trained members of the firm's management.

Two sample models are presented below. The first is one used by the Battelle Memorial Institute in studying the characteristics of Michigan's labor force for the next 15 years. The next is a model developed for use in manpower planning for the individual firm by Professor Eric Vetter of Tulane University. You might find these two would work in moving from aggregate labor market analysis to the specific planning for your own firm or organization. Or you might find it better to modify these and develop your own. The end result of these two models should be a perpetual, moving, strategic plan for managing your personnel administration department.

1. *The Battelle Institute's socioeconomic model.* The Battelle Memorial Institute has employed a broad scale socioeconomic model which deals with manpower in Michigan. Battelle Michigan Manpower Study is an analysis of the characteristics of Michigan's labor force in the next 15 years. It's not Michigan, but the model which interests us here.

The methodology utilized in this study was based on a socioeconomic model, which illustrates in capsule form which primary factors affect the

FIGURE 7–2
Main elements of Battelle's socioeconomic model

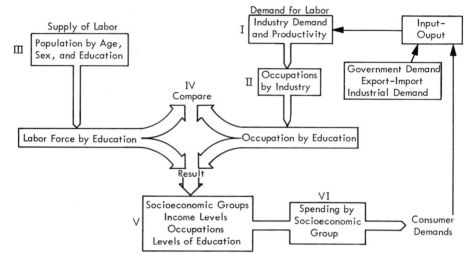

demand as well as the supply for labor in a labor market or geographic area beyond the single firm.

Here are the major elements in the model:

I. Demand for labor: Industry responds to inputs and produces products for consumer consumption. It is necessary that the latest production methods be incorporated in the manufacturing process to insure the quantity and quality of a product in order to satisfy the profit motive.

II. This in turn creates a demand for labor, and stratification of occupation by jobs results. The educational level of these jobs is determined by individual job skills as they relate to our existing technology—thus, the demand for labor is created.

III. Supply of labor: The supply of labor can be broken down into total population, age, sex, and educational level.

IV. A comparison is made of the labor force to see if educational backgrounds are amenable to the requirements established by industry.

V. This results in socioeconomic groups with established income levels, occupations, and educational levels—the educational level determining the quantity of income.

VI. The culmination of supply and demand results in spending by socioeconomic groups. This in turn heightens consumer demand, which ultimately results in an input to industry. The cycle then repeats.

The pressure created by internal and external forces causes business to undergo constant change. When greater harmony exists between the educational level of the labor force and the demand by industry for educated labor, there is a better chance of a thriving economy.

FIGURE 7–3
A procedure for manpower planning

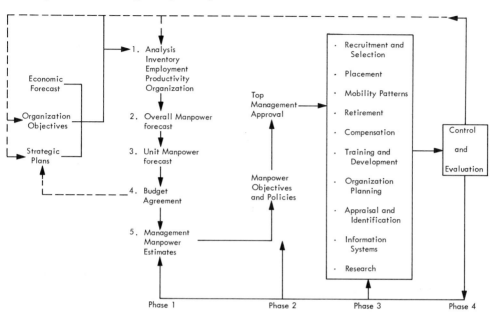

2. The Vetter model for individual manpower planning for the firm.
While the Battelle model is useful for sizing up a larger labor market, a
geographical area, or socioeconomic unit, it is insufficient for the company
labor economist or personnel manager who must forecast and plan manpower needs and resources for his own firm. The model developed by
Professor Vetter comes much closer to that need and is related to the
realities of corporate management. As shown in Figure 7–3, manpower
planning activities can be broken down into four major phases. Into each
of the phases there must be interjected the objectives of the firm, its economic potentials, and strategic plans, including sales forecasts. The four
phases, shown in the diagram, are as follows:

1. An inventory and forecast of manpower demand and supply. This includes an accurate inventory of the present manpower, estimated employment levels for the future, the effects of productivity gains upon
   that employment, and the effects of organization changes such as
   mergers or divisionalization. Each unit forecast of manpower needs is
   integrated into a total manpower forecast and the final manpower estimates of demand and supply are prepared.
2. A statement of manpower objectives and policies for varying periods
   of time into the future are prepared and presented to the top management for approval.

3. Action programs to implement the manpower plan are devised and executed. These programs include recruiting, placement, mobility patterns, retirement planning, adjustments in compensation, training and development planning and programming, organization planning, performance review and other qualitative measurements of manpower, identification of promotable people, the establishment of information flow systems about needs and resources in personnel, and continuing personnel research to identify problem areas and test proposed innovations.

4. The final phase of manpower planning is a continuous review of progress against the plans, and revision periodically for changed conditions or to adjust for progress made.

The significance of the Vetter model has been stated by its designer as follows:

A sound system will enable the planner to avoid omitting some important steps in his work and it will provide some structure and guidance to his efforts. To know what must be accomplished and why it must be accomplished, the manpower planner must develop his planning procedure before he begins his actual planning work.[4]

The human resources approach demands that an integrated plan for every aspect of personnel management be devised. A total manpower plan becomes the guiding system for all other activities in the personnel administration function.

Existing methods of manpower planning

In business today, there are two existing methods used to plan and forecast for manpower resources. The first deals with short-range planning and the second with long-range planning for personnel.

Short-range planning. In the short-range plan major emphasis is placed on filling an immediate need for personnel, a practice which is common among small businesses. It is referred to by some as the "stopgap" method of planning. This approach gives little consideration to company objectives, new markets, new projection methods, competitive influences, and projections of future organizational structure, and the like. It is more concerned with filling positions which have been or soon will be vacated by employees because of quits, deaths, or retirement. New jobs not anticipated need to be filled immediately. The following interview of a small company, Firm X, will illustrate this point.

Firm X has approximately 300 employees. The question was, "How does your firm determine the quality and quantity of manpower it needs?"

---

[4] Eric Vetter, *Manpower Planning for High Talent Personnel*, Bureau of Industrial Relations (University of Michigan, 1968), p. 44.

Answer: At present there is no attempt made to project ahead for organizational planning (growth, changing processes, equipment) with the need for manpower. The firm operates on a short-term basis. Each first line supervisor is required to turn in a report each week indicating (1) present manpower; (2) the need for additional manpower; and (3) when, in time, this additional manpower is needed. Usually "when" is immediately. Often internal transfers solve the problem. In this firm quality is usually determined by one man, the personnel manager. He has been with the firm a considerable length of time and is somewhat familiar with the necessary qualifications for each job in the firm. No job descriptions exist.

Small firms like X can survive with the short-range plan. They rely on stability, and may suffer because market conditions change quickly. Such firms often lack the necessary financial strength or qualified personnel to carry on anything but a short-range planning system.

Long-range planning.   In this type of planning more emphasis is placed on population trends, governmental policies or laws, market projections, future organizational structure, expansion of facilities, equipment, and the like, with particular interest on what relationships exist between these and the following items:

1. The number or quality of personnel presently in the firm (e.g., scientists, engineers, managers)—their backgrounds and technical competence. What implications can be drawn from market research that will help plan this talent reservoir?

2. The sophistication and age of equipment with emphasis on skill requirements.

3. The success of various departments and individual projects completed and the time interval elapsed from organization to the end product.

The single factor which makes a plan of this type so difficult is the inability to accurately forecast the future of the basic business itself. The planner lacks data which will indicate accurately the size, shape, and characteristics of the market, competition, or econcmic trends. There is accordingly no definite information about future supply of skilled people and types of skills needed. Since, as Vetter's model shows, manpower demand is derived from total company plans, long-range manpower planning calls for total company longe-range plans.

The present trend is more in the area of long-range planning, with particular emphasis on eliminating uncertainty. The use of advanced computer techniques and operations research is proving to be helpful in this respect.

Even in large firms the transition from hiring personnel for current estimated needs to long-range forecasting is rather slow. According to one survey of 136 companies in 1961, more hiring is done on current estimated needs (see Table 7–2). Eight years later a resurvey showed a slight trend toward long-range forecasts.

TABLE 7–2

Are you hiring to fill current needs, or needs based on long-range forecasts? [5]

	1961	1969
Hiring based on current estimated needs	70	60
Hiring based on long-range forecasts	19	24
Other (usually a combination)	7	11
N.A.	11	—
Total number of respondents	107	95

Relating short-run to long-run manpower strategies

The difference between short-run and immediate programs, and long-run objectives emerges more in the nature of the result sought than in the time period involved.

Short-run objectives and programs are designed to get the maximum use from the existing resources.

Long-run objectives are those which are designed to change the character of the organization in the future.

Thus, since the future will begin immediately, any action which would change the character of the organization immediately and permanently must be considered a strategic move. Another distinction which might be made is that short-run objectives are probably more in relation to existing problems or crises, whereas long-run objectives are designed to act, innovate, change, prevent problems, or to make things happen in an orderly, rational, and conscious fashion.

The requirements of manpower planning should not call for the powers of prophecy, nor should the manpower planner necessarily be a seer. He should, however, be a systems maker and a skilled maker of long- and short-run objectives.

Most definitions of manpower planning emphasize the static aspects, those of meeting present needs or solving existing problems.

1. The results of the plan hoped for both long- and short-run are stated in terms of outputs or quantifiable end consequences. A useful plan should be stated in terms of "have five available candidates for general management positions" rather than in terms of activity, for example "to conduct development programs for high potential men."

2. The first year of the five-year plan is stated in terms of specific programs and objectives for each of the major units responsible. These one-year goals to which responsible managers of units and staff departments must be committed are not *any* one-year plans, but *first* year plans. These

---

[5] George Odiorne and Arthur S. Hann, *Effective College Recruiting*. Research conducted by the Bureau of Industrial Relations and the University of Michigan, Report 13, 1961, p. 99.

are subject to quarterly review to permit responsiveness to changed conditions and special problems in operations.

3. *The summary strategic plan for managing human resources thus becomes a specific document—the five-year plan, the first year of which is cumulative, objective statements of recruiters, trainers, compensation managers, and the like.*

QUESTIONS AND PROBLEMS

1. How does strategy differ from annual objectives? Give an example from the military, from education, from personnel.
2. List the most important kinds of information which should be kept under surveillance by a personnel researcher in order to make sound strategic decisions.
3. What are the major sources of labor supply?
4. What are some of the influences affecting labor supply?
5. Demonstrate out of some recent events how demand and supply have had an effect upon personnel policy in this country?
6. Does the decline of blue collar workers and the growth of white collar workers mean that unemployment and changes in the labor market will be averted?
7. What things do you see in common between the Batelle Model and the Vetter Model? What differences?
8. What are the bare requirements for short range manpower planning?
9. If you were personnel manager for a small company of 200 employees in manufacturing, what elements would you include in your manpower planning?
10. Prepare arguments on both sides of the question: "Should a company only spend hard money on needs which it can see clearly, and not waste money on vague futuristic problems which may never come to fruition?"
11. Visit several companies and interview them to find out how they plan their manpower needs. Make a brief summary report to the class.
12. What is the use of doing a five year plan when things are sure to change each year anyhow?

GRAND OLD MANUFACTURING COMPANY CASE—PART E

SALARY ADMINISTRATION

The session on salary administration was opened with a review of recent activities of the Salary Administration Department.

Evaluation of positions

It was explained that in accordance with the policies adopted by management, salaried positions throughout the company would be reexamined to determine whether internal relationships had been maintained properly since the salary Administration Program was inaugurated. It was explained that we established approximately 130 benchmark jobs to establish both vertical and horizontal relationships and that these jobs were being used for comparisons with all exempt salaried jobs in the company. It was also explained that these benchmark jobs were evaluated by use of the factor and point system based on job requirements in the areas of knowledge, ingenuity, administrative responsibility, and operating responsibility.

The work being done with the various division and activity salary administration committees was covered. We also explained that we were obtaining survey information on going rates in both the technical and administrative areas and that we are actively surveying office and clerical jobs throughout the country.

Salary administration manual

We covered generally the work that had been done to date in the revision of the current manual and its provisions, and that this work was still in progress.

Communications

The group was informed of the policy adopted in the area of communicating information to employees with regard to grades and salary ranges and that instructions for carrying out this policy would be issued shortly.

Basic elements of salary administration

The eight basic elements in good salary management were discussed and were shown on a chart for the purpose of highlighting and emphasizing the importance of each. These elements were:

<table>
<tr><td>1. Salary policies</td><td>5. Pricing of jobs</td></tr>
<tr><td>2. Defining the job</td><td>6. Administrative guides</td></tr>
<tr><td>3. Evaluating of jobs</td><td>7. Keeping up to date</td></tr>
<tr><td>4. The formal grade structure</td><td>8. Management of salaries</td></tr>
</table>

Following is a summary of the comments made on the preceding eight subjects:

GOM salary policies

1. Maintain salary ranges which recognize differences in the values of positions to the company.
2. Maintain salary ranges which are comparable with those of other employers.
3. Pay salaries which fairly compensate for degree of performance, recognizing varying degrees of proficiency.
4. Increase salaries of promoted employees to recognize increased responsibilities.
5. Give supervisors sufficient authority to administer salaries of those reporting to them.

The job descriptions

In order to carry out these salary policies there must be definite standards of pay. These standards of pay start with salary ranges which are related to the value of the job to the company. In order to determine the salary range for a job we must know what the job is. This is the purpose of a job description. There is certain essential information which we need in a job description for it to fulfill its function. We need:

1. Job title and job number.
2. Basic functions of the job. This is the broad descriptive need for the job.
3. Organizational relationships.
4. Specific objectives and responsibilities of the job.
5. Qualifications of the incumbent as to education, experience, and desirable age.

There is much information in our job descriptions today which is not needed. These are, in the case of supervisory positions, common responsibilities of all jobs, such as:

1. To follow organization lines and require similar procedure from others.
2. To operate within the limits of established Company policies and procedures.
3. To assign duties and delegate responsibilities in accordance with the plan of organization.

4. To see that operations for which he is responsible are efficient and performed within approved cost budgets, etc.

We have two groups of job description:

1. *Nonexempt from wage and hour laws.* Have too many and will be weeded out. Can and should be simple as they apply to large groups doing relatively simple and uncomplicated jobs. For example, a job description of a typist could really be "she types."

2. *Supervisory or management level job descriptions.* Generally, there are variations in duties and responsibilities of this type job requiring, in many cases, individual descriptions. In this area the job description should tell us:

   What the incumbent does
   What decisions he makes
   What recommendations he makes
   What policies he establishes
   What he plans
   What his administrative and function responsibility is
   What controls he exercises, etc.

Evaluation of jobs

We evaluate a job to determine its relationship to other jobs in the company to determine and recognize differences in their value to the operations. This is a simple process in a small group. For example, if you have five people working for you, it is easy to say "John is my most valuable man—Fred is next, etc."

For large groups this becomes more complex and requires some sort of method or system.

GOM uses ranking method done by committees.

PAD, as mentioned, now uses a factor-point method.

We use this method to help us in working with committees on their evaluations.

Grade structure

Grouping of jobs
Scatter
Surveys

Pricing

Establishing of minimums and maximums for salary ranges.

Administrative guides

Helps to supervisors
Hiring—salaries
Administering salaries

Rules for budgetary reasons

Establish centralized control for uniformity throughout the
company

All this for purpose of carrying out company policies

Keeping up to date

Most important

Job descriptions—changes in duties

Nonexempt area

Standardized group descriptions

Exempt

Change job descriptions when duties change

Reevaluate basis revised duties

Get local survey data every six months

After you get it—action—remembering GOM
policies regarding salary levels

Talk to businessmen in community to broaden survey data received

Management of salaries

Management of salaries ranks in importance with management in any
other area.

Good management of salaries is the supervisor conscientiously carrying out GOM Salary Policies in day-to-day management of his area of responsibility.

a. Establishing rates

Hiring new employees is where salary management begins.

Comptrollers' management of salaries in plant offices.

Quality of new personnel kept at high level only by adopting community hiring rates.

Use of surveys of hiring rates, both formal and informal.

Hiring below community hiring rates causes salary progression problems in future—Discussion of hiring zones in manual. (Exhibit A)

Better to hire well-qualified people at suitable rates to get good production and maintain good morale.

First six months of employment considered by many to be most important to company in building and maintaining staff of high caliber.

Analyze performance of employees during this period and reward pro-
ficient employees with the important first salary increase after hire as
permitted by regulations.

Marginal employees during this period should be considered in the
light of the necessity of additional training or the advisability of a
termination.

Questions

b. *Providing increases (Subsequent increases)*

This is a very important area in management of salaries.

Requires recognition of budgetary limitations.

In preparing budgets allow for anticipated increase in level of community going rates.

Conduct surveys of community going rates—use formal and informal surveys.

Prepare detailed analysis of merit increases to be anticipated.

Within budget limitations established as above the dollars allocated for merit increases within a unit should be used during the year to reward the most productive employees. A merit increase is reward for *significantly* improved performance—has no relationship to community going rates, cost of living, etc.

Ranking as we discussed under evaluation of jobs exempt decide who is doing the outstanding job for me? Who is next best?, etc. The last? Deadwood?

An employee performing in a so-so manner, barely meeting job standards is not deserving of a merit increase. We should follow this as a prin-

EXHIBIT A

Office clerical hiring rates (typist—salary grade I)

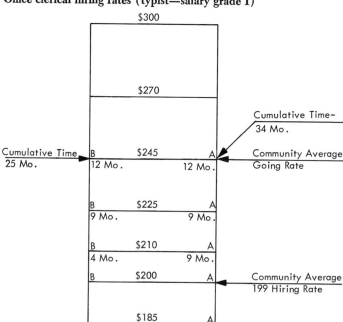

A = Salary progress of typist hired at bottom of Zone 1.
B = Progress of employee hired at community average hiring rates.
        Assumes 7% merit adjustments at minimum time intervals.

ciple of good management and be willing to talk to employees about varying degrees of performance.

FOREMEN'S COMPENSATION

History

Through the years various methods have been used to maintain an equitable relationship between the compensation of foremen and the wage employees they supervise. In some cases this has taken the form of larger and more frequent than normal salary increases which were arbitrarily labeled "merit increases." In addition, bonus arrangements called weekend pools were established to try to compensate further for scheduled extra days.

Results

In general, these plans have not been completely satisfactory. There are several reasons for this:

1. In many instances foremen's salaries have reached a point where they are completely out of proportion to the straight time rates of the wage employees supervised.
2. In many instances the plans have not provided an equitable relationship between the foremen's compensation and the earnings of the wage employees supervised.
3. The plans had to be revised periodically to adjust to changing situations.

Remedy

The company has adopted a uniform plan:

A. It provides for the maintenance of a fair differential between a foreman's base salary and the straight time rate of wage employees supervised.
B. It provides premium compensation for scheduled extended work weeks.
C. It retains the merit increase provision of the Salary Administration Program.

Here is how the plan works:
1. **Base differential salary.** The base differential salary is the initial salary paid a new foreman whether newly hired or transferred from another job and is established on this basis:

A. Foremen: 15% to 25% over the average straight time rate of the top 25% of employees supervised.

B. Assistant Foremen: 10% to 20% over the same wage as noted in "A" above.

When the plan is introduced at a plant, foremen whose base salaries are below the differential rate should have their salaries raised to the differential rate. Foremen's salaries which are above the differential rate are not to be adjusted.

When there are general changes in wage rates or significant changes in the composition of the group supervised, the base differential is to be recalculated. If the new differential is above the salary of the foreman, the salary is to be raised to the differential.

In the case of new foremen who start at the differential rate, care should be taken to avoid dilution or elimination of true merit increases which may have been given over a period of time. In the case of a foreman whose salary was above the differential rate when the plan was introduced, no adjustment for a revised differential rate should be made until the relationship between the foreman's actual salary, the differential rate, and the salaries of other foremen appears to be in proper perspective. (Exhibit B).

EXHIBIT B

Foreman compensation

	Base Differential salary	Actual salary	
		Foreman A	Foreman B
Before introduction of program	None	$525	$615
Program starts (base differential calculated at 125% of average straight time rate of top 25% supervised)	$531		
Adjustment		6	
Adjusted salaries		531	615
New wage contract— differential recalculated	548		
Adjustment		17	
Adjusted salaries		$548	$615
Merit adjustment—Foreman "A"		20	
Adjusted salaries		568	615
New wage contract— differential recalculated	$560		
Adjustment		12	
Adjusted salaries		$580	$615

2. *Premium compensation.* Foremen and assistant formen are to be paid premium compensation for scheduled extended work weeks in excess of 40 hours per week as follows:

A. Reduce the base differential salary to an hourly rate by dividing it by 173 hours. This becomes the hourly rate to use in computing overtime.

B. For scheduled extended work weeks in excess of 40 hours, one and one half times the base hourly rate is to be paid for week days and twice the base hourly rate is to be paid for Sundays and Holidays.

C. Premium compensation is payable only for scheduled extended work weeks in excess of 40 hours. No premium is to be paid for unscheduled, casual, or emergency daily overtime.

EMPLOYEE BENEFITS

1. Communications

Communications about employee benefits was reviewed at some length. It was indicated that techniques in the future will involve new booklets, mailing pieces, employee conferences, visual aids, and other methods which may be developed to be of special assictance to operating divisions.

Disclosure was made of a new insurance type kit which will be given to each salaried nonunion employee. It will consist of a plastic carrying case and a maximum of seven envelopes. Each envelope will include a certificate covering seven of the present employee benefit plans:

Retirement Income Plan
Major Medical
Social Security
Blue Cross
Travel Insurance
Life Insurance—Major Medical Plan
Life Insurance—Retirement Income Plan

The final copy is being approved on this kit. It is planned for distribution during the summer of 1966.

A chart was shown disclosing the costs of fringe benefits in GOM. A summary of that data is attached with this report. (Exhibit C)

2. Blue Cross and Blue Shield

A review was given of the general adequacy of the Blue Cross-Blue Shield and the Major Medical Plans. Charts were shown elaborating on the percent of insurance coverage. A review was also made of the increased costs for both medical charges and benefits paid.

EXHIBIT C

Cost of fringe benefits (as of May 31, 1965) (in 000's)

Total salaries and wages	$75,172,442	100%
GOM cost of benefits		
Retirement plans	$ 2,967,962	3.9%
Death benefit insurance	54,149	.1%
Temporary benefits	90,198	.1%
Blue Cross-Blue Shield	840,903	1.1%
Major medical	46,386	.1%
Social security	1,722,834	2.3%
Workmen's compensation	246,365	.3%
Tuition refund	23,418	.0%
Total		7.9%
Vacations	3,132,185	4.2%
Holidays	2,255,173	3.0%
Total		15.1%

Cost of termination compensation
Cost of sick leave
Cost of funeral leave
Cost of jury pay
    etc.

Total cost fringe benefits
About *20–25%* of salaries and wages paid

3. Retirement plans

A general review was made of the many changes that have come about in the Company retirement plans during the past two or three years. A detailed discussion was held regarding the Variable Feature of the Retirement Income Plan.

A general review of the wage plans was made, with special emphasis on the importance put on the operation of the Retirement Allowance Committees, which consist of both management and union personnel.

It was indicated to the persons present that administrative procedure manuals are now being prepared for each of the retirement plans. It is planned that these will be issued in the summer of 1966.

4. Military leave of absence

A short discussion was held with respect to highlights of the present Company policy about employees entering or coming out of military service. Personnel Administration Department Memorandum No. 9 covers the details to guide local management.

chapter 8

POPULATION—HUMAN RESOURCES IN THE AGGREGATE

VISITORS TO THE U.S. Department of Commerce building in Washington D.C. are often shown a large clock which shows population of the United States. Each hour the net addition to the population of the United States is ticked off, showing an addition each minute to a population now in excess of 200 millions.

The interest of many people in population goes far beyond the mere totaling up of the number of persons included. The study of population—known as *demography*—is a special field of interest, study, and research. It has many other facets than that of the supply and demand for labor, or the wages, hours, and conditions of work, but in understanding personnel management a knowledge of some of the major facts and issues in population are basic to effective personnel and manpower planning. Population study is a basic element in human resource planning.

Growth of population

The dominant fact about world population for the past 300 years has been a rapid growth. World population has grown from 545 million in the year 1650 to a midyear estimated population of 3,419 billion in 1967.

It is not only the absolute number of persons which reduces the amount of available space for each that concern some, but the rate at which the increase is occurring.

The reason for this growth is, of course, the industrial revolution, which has had the effect of lengthening life by eradicating the causes of death (disease, starvation, etc.) and producing a greater well being in humans, thus effecting a general change in population balance.

TABLE 8–1
Growth of world population, 1650–1967

Date	Estimated world population (in millions)	Annual percentage growth during prior period *
1650	545	—
1750	728	0.29
1800	906	0.44
1850	1,171	0.51
1900	1,608	0.63
1940	2,171	0.75
1950	2,380	0.92
1967	3,418	

* Average rates computed by compound interest formula 1970.
SOURCE: Prior to 1940 taken from A. M. Carr-Sanders *World Population* (Oxford: Clarendon Press, 1936), p. 42. The 1940 figure is from the *League of Nations Statistical Yearbook 1941–42*. The following figures are from the Statistical Office of the United Nations. The 1967 total is an estimate applying the previous annual percentage growth to the ensuing years.

In the early days of the industrial revolution and prior to it, an increase in population was considered highly beneficial, in fact, became a measure of national economic health in much the same way national income is viewed today. Yet, there has been increasing concern that population will outstrip the ability of the world to feed everyone. One estimate indicates that if the 1940 rates of population were to continue, the world would hold 21 billion persons by the year 2,240. Such astronomical possibilities were perhaps in the mind of Thomas Malthus when he first proposed his theory of population.[1] In summary form Malthus suggested that population rates tend to increase geometrically, whereas food supply increases only arithmetically. The result, he concluded, was that the human race was doomed to press upon the ability of the earth to support it. The result would be starvation, disease, and other natural consequences of poverty. An alternative which he proposed was that of controls over birth rates through abstinence, or through man made disaster such as wars, which effectively reduce the population.

Although Malthus' gloomy predication was not to come true in the western world, it still stands as a central theory in population studies. The reason the Malthusian theory didn't come true lay in two influences which the gloomy parson could not have foreseen:

1. Great breakthroughs were achieved in the ability of western and industrialized societies to produce. Large formations of capital, stable money systems, and the constant movement forward in production technology, creative chemistry, agricultural science, and, in later years, electronics and atomic energy, have made it possible for some societies to be concerned about overproduction rather than the reverse. The United

[1] Harold G. Moulton, *Controlling Factors in Economic Development* (Washington, D.C.: Brookings Foundation, 1950).

States, for example, comprises only 6 percent of the world population, but produces more than half of the manufactured goods in the world. Indeed, while it is true that population can be limited by subsistence, the growth rate of population has far outstripped the astounding gains in production.

2. A more fundamental change has been the working out of a kind of demographic balance in world population. This is a movement from a population balance based upon high birth rate-high death rate to a balance in which there are low death rates, and also a low birth rate.

The first of these two, the technological revolution, is well known to all of us. The latter, change in balance, is less widely appreciated. It has some importance in managing personnel, especially for firms operating or doing business in world markets.

Birth rates and death rates

In primarily agricultural societies, the balance of population which determines its size, growth, and rate of change was comprised of a high birth rate and a high death rate. The average length of life in primitive, or in agricultural societies, such as the early American society, or in modern China or India was about one third of today's American, Frenchman, or Swede. When transition to an industrialized society occurs, the first things to change in population rates is a decline in the death rate. Later, there follows a decline in the birth rate. This can be pictured in Figure 8–1, which shows the three stages of growth which occur in the movement from agricultural to industrial societies. The important point lies in the transition phase, in which the high birth rate is accompanied by a lowered death rate, with the result that total population grows at an astounding rate.

FIGURE 8–1
The effects of stage of economic growth from agricultural to industrial upon population size and growth rates

	Stages of Economic Growth		
	Agricultural	*Transition*	*Industrialized*
Birth rate	High	High	Low
Death rate	High	Low	Low
Effect on population size	Stable or declining	Extremely high rate of growth	Stable or slow growth

This effect has been observed in European countries, and in Japan as well. In nations like India, China, or most South American nations, the effect of industrialization in a population explosion has yet to be fully realized. The effects of industrialization and the resultant population rise upon Asia as a whole, already holding over one billion inhabitants, is nearly incomprehensible.

The possibilities of long-run stability of population after complete industrialization holds a glimmer of hope, but severe problems will be presented from the transition meanwhile.

The possibilities of migration

In the face of such stresses growing from differential rates of population growth, the possibilities of migration of people from one place to another is theoretically a solution. We see workers from Italy, Spain, and Greece moving to Germany to work in factories today. This drains off surplus agricultural workers during the Transition stage into areas where labor shortages exist. The movement of braceros or "wet backs" from Mexico to work in southwestern and western laborer jobs, or of Puerto Ricans to New Jersey are other examples. Yet, confronted with a present excess of some 200 million or more excess farmers in India, these examples are paled into insignificance.

The greatest barriers to such migration are not economic, but rather social, political, and cultural, which are less likely to bend to economic necessity. It is to be expected, however, that international mobility of labor may increase rapidly in the future, and whether or not it completely solves the problem will be of sufficient magnitude to comprise a management problem for firms operating in international business.

We'll look more into the question of international business and the problems of the "stateless corporation" in a subsequent chapter. Suffice it to say that where personnel management might have been able to overlook the effects of world population trends in the past, it will become increasingly difficult in the future.

POPULATION AND HUMAN RESOURCES IN THE UNITED STATES

It is now clear that without an understanding of the major influences in world population and demographic factors generally, we are hardly able to intelligently interpret the changes in population trends in the United States, or for that matter, in any of the major industrialized nations with which American corporations are likely to have substantial interests.

The immediate effects of shifts in population we'll look at in a little more detail in subsequent chapters when we are analyzing labor markets of today and tomorrow.

The growth in numbers and percentages

In 1790, with four million inhabitants, the United States was mainly an agricultural nation. In the following 150 years it has become industrialized, urban, settled in the West, and by 1960 it had reached a population of 179.3 millions. During the sixties its population went over the 200-million mark, which made it one of the four largest nations in numbers of inhabitants.

Even more interesting than the absolute growth, which showed fully the effects of industrialization—low death rate and continued high birth rate—was the decline in the rate of growth as industrialization progressed. As shown in Table 8–2, this declining rate of increase began about 1860 and continued unabated until the decade of 1940–50, during which time it started upward again and continued through 1960, at which time it turned around once more.

TABLE 8–2

The rate of increase of population in the United States, 1860–1960

Period	Rate of change per decade
to 1860	30%
1860–1890	25%
1890–1910	20%
1910–1930	15%
1930–1940	7.5%
1940–1950	10%
1950–1960	18%

SOURCE: NICB "Studies in Enterprise and Social Progress" 1938 for figure prior to 1940. Figures since then U.S. Census.

The decades from 1940 to 1960 comprise a source of surprise to some of the forecasters, who had predicted the continued decline of the rate of population which had been demonstrated for 90 years following 1860. As late as 1947 it was a consensus of the experts that the early marriage boom precipitated by World War II would soon end, that persons with two children would not continue to enlarge their families, and it was forecast in 1947 that the population of the United States would gradually increase until 1990, when the country would have approximately 165 million inhabitants, and then start a gradual decline.[2] The astounding changes of

[2] P. K. Whelpton, *Forecasts of the Population of the United States* (Washington, D.C.: Bureau of the Census, 1947), p. 39.

the fifties and sixties proved the difficulties of forecasting, and perhaps the dangers of reducing these predictions to print. By 1970 the population was well in excess of 200 million.

The rate of increase for the decade 1950–60 reached a level not seen since the turn of the century. The explanation for this lies in a general high level of prosperity, early marriage, and the effects of the Korean War. That the rate has once more turned downward is perhaps justification for the basic nature of the trend, to which the two decades are merely an unusual exception.[3]

The decline of immigration

An important factor in the changed composition and growth of the American population lies in the decline of immigration as a source of increased population. In the years 1905 to 1914 about one million immigrants came to the United States each year. By 1920, 13 percent of the inhabitants of the United States were foreign born. By 1940 this had declined to 8.8 percent and has tapered off ever since. Thus, where the worker in the mine, mill, factory, or labor gang in 1920 was very likely to be a foreign born person, the worker of the sixties will be at least a second and more likely a third generation American. More a product of the American educational system, he acquired the values of his native land in America, and altered the character and quality of managerial practice required for his supervision. Through upward mobility tied closely to education, it became quite likely that the manager, the engineer, or the teacher were apt to be the children or grandchildren of immigrants.

Social structures in the United States were often formulated by immigration patterns as well. The largest percentage of immigrants and the earliest to arrive were from the United Kingdom. It was only natural then that the accumulation of property, status, and influence should be vested mainly in this group. They were followed next by immigrants from Germany, Italy, Austria-Hungary, and more recently Russia and Scandinavia.

The westward movement

In addition to the immigration changes which brought foreign inhabitants to America, another significant trend has been the movement of that population within the country. The general direction of this movement has been westward in a steady stream, which continues at an abated pace even today.

In 1860, 14 percent of all the people of the United States lived west of

---

[3] The decline by years was rapid after 1957, the highest year of the decade shown in Table 8–2. These are illustrated by three year figures: 1955—1.23%; 1956—1.15%; and 1957—1.10%.

the Mississippi. By 1890 this had risen to about 27 percent and advanced more slowly after that. By 1940 this reached 37 percent. The geographical center of population has moved steadily westward, despite the decline in the rate of increase since 1900. In the early days, this was a result of the Homestead Act, which provided free or low-cost lands to settlers. Most of those taking advantage of this free land were of native white stock, generally from the central and border states. The foreign immigrant for the most part remained in the eastern cities, seeking work as laborers. A few exceptions were those imported by large railroads and mining companies seeking cheap labor, but the percentage of population which was foreign born always remained lower in the West than the East.

The ease of transportation, coupled with unsatisfactory conditions in the eastern locations and the hope of better things in the West, were the major influences behind this migration of native Americans. This combination of transportation and the intangible effects of push and pull upon the people still has its effect, and the movement west, especially to the California area, is still strong.

The effect of the frontier, with its folklore and legend of gold, furs, rich farm lands, made its mark upon the entire character of the nation. As Frederick Jackson Turner wrote in 1893, "The free lands of the United States have been the most important single factor in explaining our development."[4] Known as the Turner thesis, this presence of the frontier had multiple effects upon America and its people. Liberalism was centered in the West, with western state constitutions being invariably more liberal than those of their eastern counterparts. New political parties arose, the demand for new lands and new opportunities for settlers called for better transportation. The West afforded a demand for eastern capital, and the typical settler was apt to bring much of his capital goods for farming with him. As a market, and as a drain upon eastern labor markets, it made its impact upon labor supply and wages in East and West.

The democratic ways of the frontier affected the political and social arrangement of the entire nation, breaking down caste and promoting a more egalitarian form of relationship between citizens.

In more recent times the growth of such cities as Los Angeles, San Diego, Phoenix, Denver, and the addition of the states of Hawaii and Alaska have moved the center of population ever farther westward.

Urbanization and the flight from the farm

As the westward movement declined after 1890, the trend toward clustering of the population in cities was made more apparent. From the

---

[4] Frederick J. Turner, *The Frontier in American History* (New York: Henry Holt and Company, 1920).

earliest days of the nation, an urbanization movement was underway, ameliorated by the movement to the frontier. This urbanization, since the turn of the century, has been the dominant feature of population movement in the United States. Whereas in 1860 only about a sixth of the population of the United States lived in cities of 8,000 or more, by 1940 this ratio was one out of two.

By 1968 a little over 10 million people lived on farms, which is but one person of 18. This figure was a drop from 15 million in 1960, with an estimated three quarters of a million persons per year leaving the farm during the sixties. This movement was caused by the mechanization and growth of the large farm, the application of technology and creative chemistry to agriculture, which produced a decline in income for the small farmer. It was accelerated by industrial growth which created a demand for labor. During the period 1960–68 the United States enjoyed one of the longest periods of uninterrupted prosperity in its history. As a result, the demand for persons who could operate machines, or be trained to do so, and for service occupations in the urban areas increased. Without a ready history of unemployment to diminish their enthusiasm, the younger generations in such states as West Virginia, North and South Dakota, and many of the intermountain states fled the farm. A rising level of education, which meant that over 55 million persons were entered in school or college, made this mobility easier. A 70 percent rise in college enrollments to over 6 million was projected by experts to rise to between 9 and 11 million enrolled in college by 1985.

This urbanization was especially notable among Negroes, whose population characteristics were among the most significant of the period of the sixties and seventies.

Major trends in Negro population

One of the more significant trends in population, evidenced by the civil disorder in the large cities of the nation during the sixties was that of Negro movement to the cities. A rapid increase in Negro population, their migration to the cities and to the North from the South, have made up the most characteristic trend. The Negro population facts seem to duplicate that of many of the underdeveloped nations mentioned earlier in this chapter. For many years the population of Negroes remained constant or declined. In 1790 ,for example, 20 percent of the population of the United States was Negro, in some states, such as South Carolina, making up a majority of the population of inhabitants. The percentage of population which was black declined through 1860, when it comprised 14 percent of the population, and finally declined to a level of 12.8 million or about 10 percent in 1940. This decline was a combination of two influences.

1. The rate of white immigrations from Europe was high during this

period and even though Negro population was increasing, it was not as fast as the rate of white immigration. With the decline of immigration to a level of around 450,000 by 1965 the influence of this addition of white inhabitants became less influential in population.

2. A rapid increase in the population of Negroes occurred following 1940, growing mainly out of a declining death rate, coupled with a continued high fertility rate among Negro women.

For more than 200 years the Negro in America in population trends adhered to that described earlier for underdeveloped or agricultural countries. A high fertility rate was combined with a high death rate, and the resultant stable population rate was close to that found in such agricultural nations as Uruguay or Argentina.

In 1900, the death rate among Negroes started a steady decline which is illustrated in Table 8–3.

TABLE 8–3
Death rates among Negroes in the United States per 1,000 population

Year	1900	1940	1965
Rate	25.0	13.6	9.6

SOURCE: Bureau of the Census.

By 1970 the death rate among Negroes in the United States was approximately the same as that for whites. Coupled with a continued high fertility rate, approximately double that of whites, the effect was an explosion of population. Because of the high birth rate, the age of the Negro population was significantly younger than whites, with 45 percent being under 18, and one out of every eight Americans being black in 1972.

The future possibilities indicate that this rapid rate of increase will not continue as the level of education among Negroes increases. Table 8–4 shows the relationships between the level of education attained and the number of children fostered.

TABLE 8–4
Relationship between education and number of children in Negroes

Educational level	Number of children
Elementary	3.0
High school	2.3
4 years of college	1.7
5 years of college	1.2

These figures for Negroes, comparable to similar figures for whites suggest a future decline in the birth rate and accordingly the rate of population increase among Negroes, once the transition from high birth-high death rate to a low birth-low death rate has been achieved.

The migration from the South. In 1910, 91 percent of the Negroes in the United States lived in the South, with only 27 percent of them residing in cities and urban areas. By 1966 the percentages had changed radically, and the percentage of Negroes residing in the South had dropped to 55 percent and the percentage living in cities had risen to 69 percent. This flow from the South was accompanied by a concentration in the larger cities. The rate of flow from South to North, and somewhat less to the West, is shown in the Table 8–5.

TABLE 8–5

Migration of Negroes from South to North in the United States, 1910–70 (in thousands)

1910–20	454
1920–30	749
1930–40	348
1940–50	1,597
1950–60	1,457
1960–70	1,113

SOURCE: U.S. Department of Commerce, Bureau of the Census for 1910–66, since then projected using rate of 125,000 per year estimate.

This influx into the large metropolitan centers, which declined through 1940, was accelerated by: demand for labor in wartime industry during the forties, the accelerated rate of mechanization in agriculture in the South, and high levels of employment since 1960.

It is now predicted that the concentration in the larger cities will continue, and that 98 percent of the growth of black population will be in these urban areas. White population growth at the same time has occurred in suburban areas, with actual decline in white population in urban areas. Over 60 percent of American Negroes live in the 12 largest cities, and the exodus of whites from these cities continues.[5]

Many of the problems which perplex employers and manpower experts find their roots in the bare facts presented in the trends in Negro population. Identification of these specific problems, and some alternative solutions, will be dealt with later in this book.

WHAT WILL TOMORROW'S POPULATION LOOK LIKE?

For the personnel manager with a human resources outlook, these major facets of population study become part of his background informa-

---

[5] *Report of the National Advisory Commission on Civil Disorders* (New York: Bantam Books, 1967) deals with the social and civil effects of this population trend.

tion which he uses in making manpower plans and projections. What are some of the important conclusions we might draw from population studies? For one thing, we might do some forecasting of the future growth and composition of the population. For another, we might see some policy guides for individual firm's manpower plans.

How many people in the future?

As was noted earlier in this chapter, the dangers of prediction are considerable, and in population the margins of error are rife. In 1969 President Nixon sent to the Congress a request for the establishment of a major program of population studies and control. In that message he estimated that there would be 300 million residents of the country by the year 2000. How is such a figure arrived at? Based upon the experience of some early failure to predict, population experts have now turned to stating several series of *assumptions* and making predictions in numbers for each of these assumptions. Usually these are assumptions about the number of children 1,000 women will bear during their lifetime.[6] Thus, in 1965 the predictions were as follows:

Prediction A: 3,350 children (about the 1960–63 period experience)
Prediction B: 3,100
Prediction C: 2,775
Prediction D: 2,450

Thus, the predicted range is from a high of 3.4 children down to 2.5 children, which, other things being equal, seems to be a reasonable range to experienced observers.

Table 8–6 shows the predictions for years through the year 2000.

TABLE 8–6

Predictions of the population of the United States using four assumptions, 1970 to 2000 A.D. (in millions)

Year	Prediction Level (levels of fertility)			
	A	*B*	*C*	*D*
1970	211	209	206	206
1980	252	245	236	233
1980	252	245	236	233
1990	301	288	271	161
2000	362	338	309	291

SOURCE: Statistical Abstract of the United States.

---

[6] Statistical Abstract of the United States (Washington, D.C.: U.S. Government Printing Office, 1965).

Two ways of casting figures for the future are that of projecting, or statistically extending the past into the future, and predicting, which starts with projecting and adjusts for other foreseeable changes and altering the figures as it is estimated it will affect outcomes. Keyfitz and Fleiger, using projections of the past and current data, favor the low or D assumption.[7] Each of the assumptions has its proponents. It would seem that the figures used by President Nixon were toward the lower assumptions, and in fact are exactly the average of the two lowest. Thus, a conservative, but not pessimistic, estimate of the population of the United States by decades, using the same method of estimating, would be as follows:

1970	206 million
1980	234.5 million
1990	266.5 million
2000	300 million

It might also be noted that predictions are that the world population will double the 1965 level by that time. The magnitude of the changes over the 30-year period ahead cannot be fully foreseen, but it may be noted that the following things will occur.

1. Almost one hundred million new residents of the United States will be added. This will create immense demand for food, clothing, housing, recreation, education, jobs, and governmental services.
2. Although land masses still exist, the accumulation of these people around the major urban areas is predictable. The growth of strip cities between New York and Washington, between Cleveland, Detroit, and Chicago, and the like, may be expected.
3. Whole new systems of transportation will be called for. More companies and organizations to service them will emerge and present companies will become larger in assets, profits, payrolls, and sales incomes.
4. The crowding of people together will bring more of the kinds of human relations problems that come simply from numbers and congestion.

These are but a few of the kinds of changes which can be foreseen, even without considering the impact of a doubled world population, a majority of them nonwhite, upon American life and economy.

The implications of these for the manager of human resources are numerous. It will require him to be broader in his estimates of possibilities, and encompass more parameters in his personnel planning.

---

[7] Nathan Keyfitz and Wilhelm Fleiger, *World Population* (Chicago: University of Chicago Press, 1968).

QUESTIONS AND PROBLEMS

1. Recent attention to ecology has produced many statements about the "population bomb." What does this really mean?
2. Would you agree with Malthus? Where would you go to make the best case that he was incorrect? That he was right?
3. "The major population burst will occur when people have their aspirations raised and start to make progress." Would you agree with this statement? Why?
4. Go to the library and find the rate of population growth in the United States since 1960. What are the implications of what you have found in the light of the Table 8–6?
5. Do you think the Turner thesis was proven true or false? Why?
6. Some have suggested that the solution to the plight of the Negro lies in jobs which will permit blacks to become employed middle class? Do you agree? How would population trends explain this?
7. How has the movement of blacks from South to North affected population figures?
8. What is your estimate of the population of the United States in the year 2000? How did you arrive at that estimate?
9. What would be the implications of a stable population upon economic conditions and personnel policies?
10. What were the major findings of the 1970 decenniel census?
11. Why is population important in personnel administration strategy?

THE CASE OF THE GLOOMY PARSON

Thomas Robert Malthus (1766–1834) was one of the original distinguished members of that group of early economists known as the "classical school" generally including Adam Smith, David Ricardo, and Malthus. Malthus is best known for his views on population, the original of which is set forth below. The persistence of his argument even today testifies to its insights.

As a case study, it does not fit the format of ordinary business case studies, yet it lends itself to the same analytical treatment by students of personnel and manpower policies. The proposed analytical method suggested here is that outlined in the preface. What are the facts? What are the key problems? Which one is preeminent and highest priority? What are its causes? What options are there for its solution? What action would you propose now and in the future?

PART I: RATIOS OF THE INCREASE OF POPULATION AND FOOD *

In an inquiry concerning the improvement of society, the mode of conducting the subject which naturally presents itself, is,

1. To investigate the causes that have hitherto impeded the progress of mankind towards happiness; and,
2. To examine the probability of the total or partial removal of these causes in future.

The principal object of the present essay is to examine the effects of one great cause intimately united with the very nature of man; which, though it has been constantly and powerfully operating since the commencement of society, has been little noticed by the writers who have treated this subject. The facts which establish the existence of this cause, have, indeed, been repeatedly stated and acknowledged; but its natural and necessary effects have been almost totally overlooked; though probably among these effects may be reckoned a very considerable portion of that vice and misery, and of that unequal distribution of the bounties of nature, which it has been the unceasing object of the enlightened philanthropist in all ages to correct.

The cause to which I allude, is the constant tendency in all animated life to increase beyond the nourishment prepared for it.

It is observed by Dr. Franklin, that there is no bound to the prolific nature of plants or animals, but what is made by their crowding and interfering with each other's means of subsistence. Were the face of the earth, he says, vacant of other plants, it might be gradually sowed and overspread with one kind only, as for instance with fennel: and were it empty of other inhabitants, it might in a few ages be replenished from one nation only, as for instance with Englishmen.

This is incontrovertibly true. Through the animal and vegetable kingdoms Nature has scattered the seeds of life abroad with the most profuse and liberal hand; but has been comparatively sparing in the room and the nourishment necessary to rear them. The germs of existence contained in this earth, if they could freely develop themselves, would fill millions of worlds in the course of a few thousand years. Necessity, that imperious, all-pervading law of nature, restrains them within the prescribed bounds. The race of plants and the race of animals shrink under this great restrictive law; and man cannot by any efforts of reason escape from it.

Population has this constant tendency to increase beyond the means of subsistence, and it is kept to its necessary level by these causes. The

---

* From T. R. Malthus, *An Essay on the Principle of Population* (Reeves and Turner, London, 1878, 8th ed.).

subject will, perhaps, be seen in a clearer light, if we endeavour to ascertain what would be the natural increase of population, if left to exert itself with perfect freedom; and what might be expected to be the rate of increase in the productions of the earth, under the most favourable circumstances of human industry.

The potential rate of increase of population

It will be allowed that no country has hitherto been known, where the manners were so pure and simple, and the means of subsistence so abundant that no check whatever has existed to early marriages from the difficulty of providing for a family, and that no waste of the human species has been occasioned by vicious customs, by towns, by unhealthy occupations, or too severe labour. Consequently in no state that we have yet known, has the power of population been left to exert itself with perfect freedom.

In the northern states of America, where the means of subsistence have been more ample, the manners of the people more pure, and the checks to early marriages fewer, than in any of the modern states of Europe, the population has been found to double itself, for above a century and a half successively, in less than twenty-five years. In the back settlements, where the sole employment is agriculture, and vicious customs and unwholesome occupations are little known, the population has been found to double itself in fifteen years. Even this extraordinary rate of increase is probably short in the utmost power of population. Sir William Petty supposes a doubling possible in so short a time as ten years.

But, to be perfectly sure that we are far within the truth, we will take the slowest of these rates of increase, a rate in which all concurring testimonies agree, and which has been repeatedly ascertained to be from procreation only.

It may safely be pronounced, therefore, that population, when unchecked, goes on doubling itself every twenty-five years, or increases in a geometrical ratio.

The potential rate of increase of food production

The rate according to which the productions of the earth may be supposed to increase, it will not be so easy to determine. Of this, however, we may be perfectly certain, that the ratio of their increase in a limited territory must be of a totally different nature from the ratio of the increase of population. A thousand millions are just as easily doubled every twenty-five years by the power of population as a thousand. But the food to support the increase from the greater number will by no means be obtained with the same facility. Man is necessarily confined in room. When acre has been added to acre till all the fertile land is occupied, the yearly increase of food must depend upon the melioration of the land already in possession. This is a fund, which, from the nature of all soils, instead of increasing, must be gradually diminishing. But population, could it be supplied with food, would go on with unexhausted vigour; and the increase of one period would furnish the power of a greater increase the next, and this without any limit.

From the accounts we have of China and Japan, it may be fairly doubted, whether the best-directed efforts of human industry could double the produce of these countries even once in any number of years. There are many parts of the globe, indeed, hitherto uncultivated, and almost unoccupied; but even in new colonies, a geometrical ratio increases with such extraordinary rapidity, that the advantage could not last long. If the United States of America continue increasing, which they certainly will do, though not with the same rapidity as formerly, the Indians will be driven further and further back into the country, till the whole race is ultimately exterminated, and the territory is incapable of further extension.

The science of agriculture has been much studied in England and Scotland; and there is still a great portion of uncultivated land in these countries. Let us consider at what rate the produce of this island might be supposed to increase under circumstances the most favourable to improvement.

If it be allowed that by the best possible policy, and great encouragements to agriculture, the average produce of the island could be doubled in the first twenty-five years, it will be allowing, probably, a greater increase than could with reason be expected.

In the next twenty-five years, it is impossible to suppose that the produce could be quadrupled. It would be contrary to all our knowledge of the properties of land. It must be evident to those who have the slightest acquaintance with agricultural subjects, that in proportion as cultivation extended, the additions that could yearly be made to the former average produce must be gradually and regularly diminishing. That we may be the better able to compare the increase of population and food, let us make a supposition, which, without pretending to accuracy, is clearly more favourable to the power of production in the earth, than any experience we have had of its qualities will warrant.

Let us suppose that the yearly additions which might be made to the former average produce, instead of decreasing, which they certainly would do, were to remain the same; and that the produce of this island might be increased every twenty-five years, by a quantity equal to what it at present produces. The most enthusiastic speculator cannot suppose a greater increase than this. In a few centuries it would make every acre of land in the island like a garden.

It may be fairly pronounced, therefore, that, considering the present average state of the earth, the means of subsistence, under circumstances the most favorable to human industry, could not possibly be made to increase faster than in an arithmetical ratio.

The potential rates of increase of population and food compared

The necessary effects of these two different rates of increase, when brought together, will be very striking. Let us call the population of this island eleven millions; and suppose the present produce equal to the easy support of such a number. In the first twenty-five years the population would be twenty-two millions, and the food being also doubled, the means of subsistence would be equal to this increase. In the next twenty-five years, the population would be forty-four millions, and the means of subsistence only equal to the support of thirty-three millions. In the next period the population would be eighty-eight millions, and the means of subsistence just equal to the support of half that number. And, at the conclusion of the first century, the population would be a hundred and seventy-six millions, and the means of subsistence only equal to the support of fifty-five millions, leaving a population of a hundred and twenty-one million totally unprovided for.

Taking the whole earth, instead of this island, emigration would of course be excluded; and, supposing the present population equal to a thousand millions, the human species would increase as the numbers 1, 2, 4, 8, 16, 32, 64, 128, 256, and subsistence as 1, 2, 3, 4, 5, 6, 7, 8, 9. In two centuries the population would be to the means of subsitsence as 256 to 9; in three centuries as 4096 to 13, and in two thousand years the difference would be almost incalculable.

In this supposition no limits whatever are placed to the produce of the earth. It may increase for ever and be greater than any assignable quantity; let still the power of population being in every period so much superior, the increase of human species can only be kept down to the level of the means of subsistence by the constant operation of the strong law of necessity, acting as a check upon the greater power.

PART II: OF THE GENERAL CHECKS TO POPULATION, AND THE MODE OF THEIR OPERATION

The ultimate check to population appears then to be a want of food, arising necessarily from the different ratios according to which population and food increase. But this ultimate check is never the immediate check, except in cases of actual famine.

The immediate check may be stated to consist all those customs, and all those diseases, which seem to be generated by a scarcity of the means of subsistence; and all those causes, independent of this scarcity, whether of a moral or physical nature, which tend prematurely to weaken and destroy the human frame.

These checks to population, which are constantly operating with more or less force in every society, and keep down the number to the level of the means of subsistence, may be classed under two general heads—(i) the preventitive, and (ii) the positive checks.

The preventive and positive checks described

(i) The preventive check, as far as it is voluntary, is peculiar to man, and arises from that distinctive superiority in his reasoning faculties, which enables him to calculate distant consequences. The checks to the indefinite increase of plants and irrational animals are all either positive, or, if preventive, involuntary. But man cannot look around him, and see the distress which frequently presses upon those who have large families; he cannot contemplate his present possessions or earnings, which he now nearly consumes himself, and calculate the amount of each share, when with very little addition they must be divided, perhaps, among seven or eight, without feeling a doubt whether, if he follow the bent of his inclinations, he may be able to support the offspring which he will probably bring into the world. In a state of equality, if such can exist, this would be the simple question. In the present state of society other considerations occur. Will he not lower his rank in life, and be obliged to give up in great measure his former habits? Does any mode of employment present itself by which he may reasonably hope to maintain a family? Will he not at any rate subject himself to greater difficulties, and more severe labour, than in his single state? Will he not be unable to transmit to his children the same advantages of education and improvement that he had himself possessed? Does he even feel secure that, should he have a large family, his utmost exertions can save them from rags and squalid poverty, and their consequent degradation in the community? And may he not be reduced to the grating necessity of forfeiting his independence, and of being obliged to the sparing hand of Charity for support?

These considerations are calculated to prevent, and certainly do prevent, a great number of persons in all civilised nations from pursuing the dictate of nature in an early attachment to one woman.

If this restraint does not produce vice, it is undoubtedly the least evil that can arise from the principle of population. Considered as a restraint on a strong natural inclination, it must be allowed to produce a certain degree of temporary unhappiness; but evidently slight, compared with the evils which result from any of the other checks to population; and merely of the same nature as many other sacrifices of temporary to permanent gratification, which it is the business of a moral agent continually to make.

When this restraint produces vice, the evils which follow are but too conspicuous. A promiscuous intercourse to such a degree as to prevent the birth of children, seems to lower, in the most marked manner, the dignity of human nature. It cannot be without its effect on men, and nothing can be more obvious than its tendency to degrade the female character, and to destroy all of its most amiable and distinguishing characteristics. Add to which, that among those unfortunate females, with which all great towns abound, more real distress and aggravated misery are, perhaps, to be found, than in any other department of human life.

When a general corruption of morals, with regard to the sex, pervades all the classes of society, its effects must necessarily be, to poison the springs of domestic happiness, to weaken conjugal and parental affection, and to lesson the united exertions and ardour of parents in the care and education of their children:—effects which cannot take place without a decided diminution of the general happiness and virtue of the society; particularly as the necessity of art in the accomplishment and conduct of intrigues, and in the concealment of their consequences necessarily leads to many other vices.

(ii) The positive checks to population are extremely various, and include every cause, whether arising from vice or misery, which in any degree contributes to shorten the natural duration of human life. Under this head, therefore, may be enumerated all unwholesome occupations, severe labour and exposure to the seasons, extreme poverty, bad nursing of children, great towns, excesses of all kinds, the whole train of common diseases and epidemics, wars, plague, and famine.

On examining these obstacles to the increase of population which I have classed under the heads of preventive and positive checks, it will appear that they are all resolvable into moral restraint, vice, and misery.

Of the preventive checks, the restraint from marriage which is not followed by irregular gratifications may properly be termed moral restraint.

Promiscuous intercourse, unnatural passions, violations of the marriage bed, and improper arts to conceal the consequences of irregular connexions, are preventive checks that clearly come under the head of vice.

Of the positive checks, those which appear to arise unavoidably from the laws of nature, may be called exclusively misery; and those which we obviously bring upon ourselves, such as wars, excesses, and many others which it would be in our power to avoid, are of a mixed nature. They are brought upon us by a vice, and their consequences are misery.

The mode of operation of preventive and positive checks

The sum of all these preventive and positive checks, taken together, forms the immediate check to population. In every country some of these checks are, with more or less force, in constant operation; yet, notwith-

standing their general prevalence, there are few states in which there is
not a constant effort in the popultion to increase beyond the means of
subsistence. This constant effort as constantly tends to subject the lower
classes of society to distress, and to prevent any great permanent
melioration of their condition.

These effects seem to be produced in the following manner. The constant effort towards population, which is found to act even in the most
vicious societies, increases the number of people before the means of subsistence are increased. The food, therefore, which before supported eleven
millions, must now be divided among eleven millions and a half. The poor
consequently must live much worse, and many of them be reduced to
severe distress. The number of labours also being above the proportion
of work in the market, the price of labour must tend to fall, while the
price of provisions would at the same time tend to rise. The labourer
therefore must do more work, to earn the same as he did before. During
this season of distress the discouragements to marriage and the difficulty
of rearing a family are so great, that the progress of population is retarded.
In the mean time, the cheapness of labour, the plenty of labourers, and
the necessity of an increased industry among them, encourage cultivators
to employ more labour upon their land, to turn up fresh soil, and to
manure and improve more completely what is already in tillage, till ultimately the means of subsistence may become in the same proportion to the
population, as at the period from which we set out. The situation of the
labourer being then again tolerably comfortable, the restraints to population are in some degree loosened; and, after a short period, the same
retrograde and progressive movements, with respect to happiness, are
repeated.

One principal reason why this oscillation has been less remarked, and
less decidedly confirmed by experience than might naturally be expected,
is, that the histories of mankind which we possess are, in general, histories
only of the higher classes. We have not many accounts that can be de-
pended upon, of the manners and customs of that part of mankind, where
these retrograde and progressive movements chiefly take place.

A circumstance which contributed to conceal this oscillation from common view, is the difference between the nominal and real price of labour.
It very rarely happens that the nominal price of labour universally falls;
but we well know that it frequently remains the same, while the nominal
price of provisions has been gradually rising. An increased number of
labours receiving the same money-wages will necessarily, by their competition, increase the money-price of corn. This is, in fact, a real fall in the
price of labour; and, during this period, the condition of the lower classes
of the community must be gradually growing worse. But the farmers and
capitalists are growing rich from the real cheapness of labour, and thus
the wages of labour, and consequently the condition of the lower classes

of society might have progressive and retrograde movements, though the price of labour might never nominally fall.

But without attempting to establish these progressive and retrograde movements in different countries, which would evidently require more minute histories than we possess, and which the progress of civilisation naturally tends to counteract, the following propositions are intended to be proved:—

1. Population is necessarily limited by the means of subsistence.
2. Population invariably increases where the means of subsistence increase, unless prevented by some very powerful and obvious checks.
3. These checks, and the checks which repress the superior power of population, and keep its effects on a level with the means of subsistence, are all resolvable into moral restraint, vice and misery.

chapter 9

THE LABOR MARKET—WHERE SUPPLY AND DEMAND MEET

THE HUMAN RESOURCES in a society include the whole population, but for purposes of economic planning and analysis we narrow it down to a smaller segment. From the total population we subtract people who aren't in the labor force at all, don't wish to be, or may never enter that work force. For example, we don't include residents of prisons, poor farms, mental institutions, schools, and retired people in the work force. Neither do we include the housewife, which is, of course, really insulting when we consider that she probably works longer and harder than other members of her household who may be included in the labor force.

The decision as to who should be included in the labor force is, of course, an arbitrary one, made necessary by practical demands for counting the membership in the labor force, observing changes, and predicting trends. In many cases people who actually make a contribution to output, and who supply their labor regularly, aren't included simply because it would be difficult to obtain an accurate count of their number. Children working casually in the home, or doing chores on their parents' farm without pay, may make a significant contribution to the work of the farm or home, but aren't included in the supply of labor. Volunteer workers aren't counted, for another. The reason is that nobody could estimate how many children work as compared with how many do nothing, or how many gray ladies work at helping the sick. Thus, it is easier to simply lump them into one category, "not included" in the labor supply. If they work over 15 hours a week in a family business, however, even if they aren't paid for that labor, they are included.

The quantity of labor available

One way of looking at the supply of human resources is the way in which the United States Department of Labor does it. They are the master scorekeepers on labor supply in the United States. In order to keep score and report changes such as gains or losses, they have adopted some common rules which they use every time. The labor force, they tell themselves, consists of the employed plus the unemployed. The unemployed are people who are not working, but are looking for work. If they are unemployed and don't care enough to want to find work or couldn't accept it if it were offered, then they are not in the work force. The measurement of the quantity of the work force usually takes place at a specific time, usually a one-week period, and the supply includes all persons who, during the reference week did any work for pay or profit, or worked at least 15 hours as an unpaid family worker for a family business. Also included are those who were absent from their regular work because of illness, bad weather, vacation, and the like. The unemployed segment includes those who are actively seeking work. "Actively seeking" means that they have registered at an employment office, written letters of application, applied at a factory gate, ran a "position desired" ad in the classified section of the newspaper, or took some other overt action to locate an employer.

The manner in which these figures are compiled would be more in the province of the labor economist than in the personnel man, and the figures are described in the materials of the United States Department of Labor. They are very complex, and are admittedly not perfectly accurate. They are based on samplings to determine the level of unemployment. The staff of the Bureau of Labor Statistics, which compiles these data, is far too small to actually count every working person and every unemployed person. The definitions themselves leave room for variation in quantity. People who have become discouraged and stopped actively seeking employment because they are convinced it is a fruitless task, for example, are not considered unemployed. Another variance comes in the people who would enter the work force and start actively searching for work if more attractive jobs were available. Housewives might not be considered unemployed if they learned that many attractive positions which they could fill were available at high pay. If such information became available to them, they would then enter the workforce, and might change from the category of "not in the labor force" to unemployed simply by starting to look for a job.

Thus, in a total population in the United States of over 200 million, after we subtract the housewives, school children, prison inmates, members of the armed services, we are left with 80 million in the labor force.

It is expected that by 1975 the labor force will total 88.7 million. Annual increases will be slightly below 1.5 millions per year after 1970.

The labor market

While these figures would represent the total amount of labor in all categories available for the entire United States, they could also be broken down according to the region or city in which they actually exist. Usually, labor economists don't use political and geographical definitions to define levels of supply for labor. Their breakdown is very suitable to treatment of labor as a commodity—they refer to the *labor market*. This is defined as a geographical area within which a person can change his job without changing his residence. This is Mr. Smith, who quits his position at Ford and joins General Motors five miles away, but doesn't have to move his home to do so; he merely drives in a different direction each morning, he hasn't left that particular labor market. If, on the other hand, he should move to Continental Oil Company in Houston, and thus be required to sell his house and move his family, he has changed jobs and labor markets.

Labor markets have a way of changing their boundaries, too. A large throughway is built and people can whiz along at 60 miles per hour from their home into a city, a trip which previously took several hours of tortuous traffic driving. The number of people who would consider accepting a position in a plant along the new throughway is greater than before it was built, and the margins of the labor market have been enlarged. In Ypsilanti, Michigan, for example, over 70 percent of the people working in the automobile plants there live in Wayne County, which includes Detroit, some 20 to 40 miles drive. The reason for this is a wide freeway between the cities.

The labor market for a management or professional person might be determined by the traveling distance in a modern motor car. The labor market for a domestic servant or waitress might be within the limits of a bus line. The supply of labor which enters an economy, that is, the segment of the human resources which will be available for formal employment, usually enters the work force in some labor market.

1. A person may enter the labor force from school.
2. A person may enter the labor force from the military.
3. Some will enter the work force from female pursuits, such as being a housewife and mother, or from other nonlabor market sources.

Figure 9–1 shows schematically how a total supply of available workforce might be pictured.[1]

---

[1] Gerard Carvallho, *Washtenaw County Market Characteristics* (Ann Arbor: Office of Research Administration, University of Michigan, 1965).

FIGURE 9–1

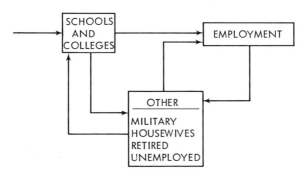

LIMITATIONS UPON SUPPLY OF LABOR

For a specific labor market, and for the economy as a whole, the supply of labor is dependent upon a number of causal variables. These variables are also affected by the supply of labor, and accordingly, predicting supply is a rather imprecise matter. The source of this imprecision lies in the factors which affect supply. These include the following:

1. *Demographic factors.* Population growth in absolute numbers may shape the available numbers of persons who can enter the work force. A rapidly growing population may result in a predominantly young population, most of whom will be enrolled in schools and not available for work. A rapidly declining rate of population growth may result in a population which tends toward a preponderance of older people, with a high level of retired and unemployable old people in the population. Only when population grows at a steady rate, a most unlikely condition, will the distribution be evenly spread among the age groups.

2. *Economic growth.* The rate of expansion in production may have an effect upon the supply of labor. How this growth rate is calculated is important. The rate of increase in per capita income or in production output, or corporate assets, or the rate of growth in personal disposable income could be used. Growth could also be measured as a rate which will provide full employment for all those who wish to work. Yet the desire to work may be affected by the rate of economic growth, which leads to some circularity in estimating and projecting supply. When the economy suffers a downturn in employment, and male family heads work reduced work weeks, there is a tendency for females in his household to seek work to supplement the declining income. This act of entering the labor market in search of employment by females who previously had not been searching adds to unemployment, thus accelerating the statistical rate of downturn. This means that projections of the size of the work force are closely allied to projections of economic growth, since one determines the other.

3. *Quality indicators of labor force participation.* If we were to picture the labor supply as a large bowl of beads from which available workers could be drawn, each identical with each other, we would be unrealistically describing the labor market. Rather than a single labor market there are thousands. Rather than one kind of worker, there are likewise thousands of occupations. Workers who have available skills to sell will be distinguished from others by a number of distinct characteristics: [2]

a) *Age.* The availability of youth between 16 and 21 without a completed high school education may be very different from the availability of computer experts between 25 and 40. While a surplus in the former may exactly match in number the deficit in the latter, this doesn't mean that the labor force is at a break even, since the untrained youth is not available for the vacant computer position.

b) *Education or training.* Machinists, pipefitters, electricians, and other skilled trades may be in short supply in a labor market where the overall level of unemployment and surplus labor among unskilled help runs in excess of 10 percent.

c) *Sex.* Since Title VII of the Equal Employment Opportunity Act was enacted, it has been against the law to discriminate for sex alone, but there are many positions where the work is limited by sex. Heavy manual work, dangerous or potentially hazardous work, or other special tasks which can only be done by one sex, but not the other, may create differences in supply. It is obvious that trained models for women's clothes could be in limited supply, and a surplus of interior linemen for the local professional football team would not solve the shortage by adding to the supply of labor.

The fact that units of labor supply are not identical means that not only are the places of residences apt to create distortion in the accurate depicting of labor supply for the whole society, but internal variances for these factors mentioned above plus many more could make the accurate description of labor supply a complex process. These comprise a limitation upon the actual supply of labor, as well as a limitation upon the measurement of that supply.

Overall projections of total growth, 1965–75

It has been estimated, based upon population projections and labor force participation rates for various age groups of men and women, that the total available supply of workers for the labor force will increase by some 12.5 million workers between 1960 and 1970, and will grow by another 7.5 million between 1970 and 1975. By 1975 it has been estimated there will be a total labor supply of 93 million workers in the United States.

---

[2] See the *Dictionary of Occupational Titles* published by the U.S. Department of Labor for detailed example.

Changes in the relative size of the work force can be illustrated by the statistics for the period 1950–75 as shown in Table 9–1.

From these data it is apparent that not only will the total supply of the labor force be changed in the future, but over this period of about one generation drastic changes in the structure of the work force will occur. The percentage of the total work force which is female will have increased for one thing. The employment patterns of women is referred to by statisticians as bimodal, that is, it has two peaks. Women ordinarily enter the work force in their teens, then retire from it to marry and raise a family. They then return again to the work force at age 35 to 40 and remain a part of the manpower pool until nearly retirement age. More detailed breakdowns of figures shows that the total work force will expand, even though the number of persons who remain out of the labor force because they are enrolled in school will increase greatly.

TABLE 9–1

Changes in the total labor force in the United States by age and sex, 1950–75 (in millions)

			Projected	
	1950	*1960*	*1970*	*1975*
Males over 14	46.1	49.6	56.3	60.9
Females over 14	18.6	73.0	29.4	32.1
Both sexes over 14	54.7	18.4	85.7	93.0

SOURCE: U.S. Department of Labor, Bureau of Labor Statistics, Special Labor Force Reports No. 14 and 24.

Another way of looking at the labor force is to note the change in age levels of those in the available labor force.

This addition of 20 million workers to the labor supply over 15 years is a net figure, which means that it is the difference between total inflow and total outflow. The labor supply can be pictured as in Figure 9–2 as a reservoir.

The central figure is the available labor supply. Into it are flowing constantly persons who enter the labor market from schools, from the military, from prior retirements such as for marriage or to raise families. Out of the labor force are withdrawn those who die, retire, enter military service, go to prison, and marry and become housewives, or return to school. The remaining level in the container in the middle is the labor supply. The pool also includes the unemployed.

Projections of the available labor force by age comprises an important planning source for the future. Government figures, displayed in Table 9–2 show the following projections which are already predictable between 1970 and 1975.

FIGURE 9–2

The input-output of the labor supply

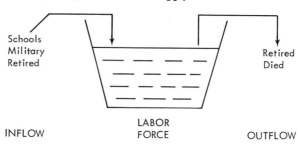

Schools
Military
Retired

INFLOW

LABOR
FORCE

Retired
Died

OUTFLOW

TABLE 9–2

Changes in the labor force by age, 1960–75 (in millions)

	Actual		*Projected*	
Age	*1950*	*1960*	*1970*	*1975*
14–24	13.3	13.6	19.8	21.7
25–34	15.1	15.0	16.7	20.8
35–44	14.1	16.8	16.5	16.2
45–64	19.1	24.1	29.1	30.5
Total	64.7	73.1	85.7	93.0

SOURCE: U.S. Department of Labor, Bureau of Labor Statistics, *Interim Revised Projections of U.S. Labor Force, 1965–75,* Special Labor Force Report No. 24.

1. A rapid rise in older and younger workers.
2. A shortage of manpower in the ages between 35 and 44.

For the corporate manpower planner, these trends have some important implications for such matters as management development, training, recruiting, placement, and compensation practices. Let's examine each of these trends in a little more detail.

The tidal wave of younger workers

One of the most significant, if somewhat imponderable, influences on labor supply will be in the age distribution. In the decade of the sixties workers under 25 will contribute about half the net increase in labor supply, and will number close to 20 million in 1970. Workers under 25 will comprise about 23 percent of the labor force, compared with less than 19 percent in 1960. The number of younger workers under 25 will rise, but not as fast during the 1970–75 period.

This comprises a potential problem. Many of the younger people are unprepared for work, since jobs today tend to call for more skill, and 30 percent of the young people entering the labor market will be dropouts, they have not completed high school. As many as 2.5 million are dropouts after the eighth grade, a condition which makes their likelihood of employment less. They are, furthermore, inexperienced, have less seniority, which, combined with lack of education, creates an even more serious problem. The decline of blue-collar jobs sharpens the problems. The rate of unemployment among teenagers, especially those of nonwhite background, who are also dropouts, is severe. Combined with a rising pride in color, an increased willingness to engage in confrontations and civil unrest, combines to provide the ingredients for a social explosion.

Even less calculable than the sheer weight of numbers of young people are the rapidly changing values which seem to have occurred in the young people. Sometimes known as the "generation gap," it is apparent that the aspirations of the new generations are different from those of their parents. The generations of the depression and World War II have often achieved their dreams of their youth and fail to understand that the succeeding generations each hope for improvements and gains over the past. Where the goals of the adult generation were materialistic, and were fought through unionization and increased education, the goals of the young are often antimaterialistic. They seem to seek goals which are centered in humanistic values. The Peace Corps of the sixties, and other occupations which provided an opportunity to serve others, such as teaching, government service, and health services became more attractive.

Still another important difference between the older and younger generation lies in their unwillingness to be submissive to authority as was the case in the past. The educational system taught them that the unexplained order was offensive, and that democratic values in which the governed, however young, should participate in the decisions which affect them, became more firmly rooted in the youth of the sixties. Campus riots, civil disobedience, and downright obstruction to capriciously administered institutions such as the colleges and universities occurred, not only in America but around the world. Estimating the effects of this egalitarian philosophy upon the quality of manpower for employment is difficult. It is safe to predict that supervisory and management styles will be more humanistic and participative.

The shortage of 35 to 44-year-olds

The changes in the age distribution of the supply of labor is of particular concern to those companies requiring the services of middle and top management. Typically these positions are filled with those in the 35 to 45 age group. However, the supply is projected to show an absolute decline in numbers in this age category by 1975. This reduced rate of supply is being made that much more acute by the increased demand resulting from the growth of major corporations and the increased demand for professional managers by governmental and other nonindustrial concerns.

This imbalance of supply and demand will produce higher prices for this talent and possibly the reduction in the qualifications required by employers. The individual firm faced with the problem of obtaining and protecting the best managerial talent it can get will be required to engage in more intensive recruiting. The corporate employer must also recognize that the tightness of the supply of this type of labor requires all employers to pay more for it. Pay can be interpreted to include the satisfaction of all the objectives of the manager, not only his monetary or material demands. Firms must recognize that unless new compensation techniques are devised they may be subject to piracy, which aggravates the shortage. A short-run approach suggests that the firm must protect its internal supply through improved compensation techniques and develop the ability to acquire the appropriate talent from outside the firm.

Still further predictable effects can be forecast from this shortage of managerial age group. More attention to the early identification of managerial potential may be expected. The long process of climbing the career ladder may be expected to change, in favor of early choice of persons to move into higher ranks and the accelerated growth and development of such people. Thus, it may be expected that with a decline in the 35–44-year-old group, management may be expected to reach down into the 25–35-year age group and accelerate the career progress of those identified. The advantage of doing this over promoting more persons over 45 lies in the length of service before the newly promoted manager at the younger age. Investment in managerial talent for younger persons can be accelerated economically if the time period for pay-back is 15 to 25 years longer service by the candidate.

The possibilities of general managers and senior executives under the age of 30 may seem heretical and perhaps foolhardy for those whose careers consisted of long periods of shelf sitting, but the statistics of manpower supply make it increasingly likely in the seventies.

Why early identification?

Early identification of management potential is the part of the manpower strategy that is designed to identify those men in the organization at a relatively early stage in their career who have the potential to be the top managers of the future and alter the supply situation by accelerated development. Men who are identified can be given special training and guidance to develop their potential. It is therefore an integral part of management development and manpower planning.

The policies, procedures, and methods that are used by different companies vary considerably, but the desirability of early identification is generally accepted by most companies.[3] Fifty out of 62 corporation presidents agreed that it was necessary to have a definite plan to identify and develop executives in advance of need, but there was little agreement on how it should be done, when in a person's career it should be done, and what special training the identified individuals should receive.

There is considerable disagreement on whether or not tests given early in a man's career can be used to predict top management potential. Standard Oil Co. (N.J.), AT&T, and Sears have reported good success, while General Electric has reported little if any success with tests. For example, Standard Oil reports that they can predict success over 70 percent of the time while GE reports that their predictors are right only 30 percent of the time. In fact, GE warns their supervisors in an internal publication that tests, especially personality tests, should be viewed with extreme caution in assessment of potential.

When, in a man's career, this identification should take place is also unsettled. One author indicates that it is not necessary or desirable to make this decision much before a man is 35. Studies have shown that a mans' traits and characteristics, as measured by tests, change considerably up until he becomes 30–35 and then remain relatively constant. However, Laurent of Standard Oil says that these critical characteristics and traits vary in a predictable way with age and can be corrected by developnig and applying proper age correction factors, thus making it possible to use tests for those at any age. But studies at GE strongly suggest that many who attain ultimate success in management at GE do not show their colors until well into their 30's.

Those who are identified as having top-management potential are usually given some kind of special training which is designed to broaden them for top management. This may take the form of a special training program, rotation to special job assignments, or working under outstanding managers in the company who have previously demonstrated an aptitude for developing executive ability in their subordinates. However, membership in this group is usually no guarantee of success. The manager of training at Ford Motor Co. said that "in planning developmental opportunities for those having both potential and willingness to make the special effort required, it should be understood clearly that the opportunities offered carry no promise of promotion, but merely the chance of preparing for promotion."[4]

Generalist or specialist first

The chairman of the board of Shell Oil feels that top managers should come from those individuals who have first excelled in some nonmanage-

---

[3] John R. Hinrichs, *High Talent Personnel* (New York: American Management Association, 1968).

[4] *Ibid.*

ment discipline. He argues that since no one can agree on a list of indispensable qualities necessary for top management, the only criteria is previous success in nonmanagement discipline.

Others argue that training a man as a generalist after he has been made a specialist results in an unnecessary delay. By the time he has distinguished himself as a functional specialist, he is probably in his middle years and in a fairly responsible position in his speciality. If men with general management talent can be spotted while still young, their whole careers can be shaped to broaden them for their future responsibilities. They can be helped to develop as "specialists" in general management.

Another argument against overspecialization before identification and training for upper management is that certain functional specialists such as engineers, accountants, and scientists develop work habits and patterns of thought which may be injurious to success as an executive. For example, studies have shown that engineers underestimate the importance of attitudes and tradition, they like the "lone wolf" approach, they are slow in making decisions, they avoid close personal relationships, and they are hostile to authority, traits which are not desirable for top management. However, engineers have been trained in handling problems objectively, an asset said to be vital for success as a manager. If identified early and not allowed to get "set in their ways," engineers can make excellent top managers, especially in a company that is technically oriented, and where an engineering background is desirable even in top management.

The Standard Oil (N.J.) method [5]

This company makes heavy use of tests given during the first ten years of an employee's experience to identify potential top managers. The proponents of this method argue that present performance may not be as good a predictor as tests since the jobs a man will hold will change as he advances, which will require different traits for success. For example, they argue that it has been found that there is no correlation between success as a salesman and success as a sales manager.

The test battery consists of an intelligence test, a temperament test, a management judgment test, a background survey, a management attitude test, and a self-performance report. The assumptions on which this method are based are as follows:

1. There are differences in personal characteristics of the more successful and less successful members of management.
2. These differences can be measured.
3. The chances are greater for a candidate's success if his personal

---

[5] H. Laurent, "Early Identification of Managers," *The Conference Board Record*, Vol. 24, No. 5 (May, 1963).

characteristics and background are more like those of the successful manager than like those of the less successful ones.

4. These characteristics can be measured early in a person's career.

This method is based on a study of 443 managers of Jersey who completed an eight-hour battery of tests in 1955. Various traits and characteristics of each manager were correlated with a success criterion, which consisted of job level, salary (after adjustment for age), and superior's performance ranking. Since the average age of the study group was 47, and there was found to be a relationship between age and some of the traits that were measured, a correction factor for age was developed so that the tests could be used on younger employees. The final result is a relationship between a candidate's weighted score on his measured traits and the probability that he would be in the top one third of the success criterion after a given period of time. For example, if a candidate scored in the top 20 percent, the probability he would be in the top one third of the success criterion is 0.76.

A follow-up study was made in 1960 on the original study group. The scores of each participant were compared with their performance in the stock option program, which is geared to the company's opinion of past and anticipated contribution. The results showed that the men who scored in the top 40 percent on the test had cornered almost the best stock option offerings. However, it was also found that 8 percent of those scoring in the bottom half of the test were also in the group that got the best stock option offerings.

An attempt was made to check the predictive validity of the tests by analyzing the results of a supervisory selection study made at one of the Jersey refineries in 1949. More than 500 first- and second-level supervisors took a battery of tests which were similar to those used to develop the current predictors. The results of the 1949 tests were correlated with various success criterion. It was found that the people who scored high on the 1949 tests had advanced much farther and more rapidly than those who scored low. It was also found that the number of promotions the high scorers had since 1949 is more closely related to the test scores than the criterion against which the test was validated.

The Jersey method is based on validation using the present employee or concurrent validity approach, which is said to be good only for a "first guess" about predictive validities. The traits and characteristics necessary to be successful in top-management jobs will probably change over time, and this change in turn will probably change the actual probabilities of success as determined by the tests. The validity check on the 1949 study suffers from the same problem.

The follow-up validation approach is the most rigorous. The tests are filed away unscored for 10 to 20 years and then the test results are compared with the degrees of management success of each participant. This should tend to minimize the number of "success" traits that change with time, and the effect that the predictors may have on actual success. This long wait is probably impractical since something is usually desired that can be used after a relatively short time.

As long as the tests have some validity and not too much emphasis is placed on them for early identification, they are probably useful as a supplemental tool. Jersey apparently realizes this and used the test results as a supplement to their other assessment methods.

The AT&T method [6]

This company uses what they call an assessment center to determine management potential. Although this method is primarily used as a management selection or promotion criterion, its proponents claim it is also good for identifying top-management potential in young employees.

Twelve candidates at a time are run through the assessment center where they take an in-basket test, participate in miniature business games and leaderless discussions, and take various paper and pencil tests. This takes a little over three days. A final report on each candidate is sent to his line manager, which contains among other things a judgment on whether he is (1) promotable now, (2) not eligible now but could qualify if some faults are remedied, and (3) doesn't have the qualifications and chances are not good for qualifying in the future.

Bray and Campbell of AT&T report that the assessment center ratings have shown good validity. A comparison of men promoted before the assessment center program began with those promoted after shows that twice as many men rated highly by the assessment center have demonstrated potential to advance beyond the first level of management as those not rated. They also report that 51 percent of those who were predicted to make middle management have made it, while only 14 percent of those predicted not to make middle management have made it.

This doesn't prove validity since, as Bray and Campbell report, the assessment center is rarely overruled, and that is what it proves. It's like saying that only men over 6 feet will be admitted to top management, and later finding that all the men in top management are indeed over 6 feet tall. A high assessment center rating seems to be itself a criterion for success, not a predictor of success. A good assessment center rating will do more for an employee's future than no rating. Cause and effect may be reversed. One also wonders what effect being rated as a failure by the assessment center has on an employee's later performance, since the candi-

---

[6] D. Bray and R. Campbell, Assessment Centers: An Aid in Management Selection," *Personnel Administration* (March-April 1967).

dates usually are given some indication of their rating after returning to the job.

The Sears method [7]

This method assumes that a cluster of psychological characteristics contribute to general executive competence that transcends the boundaries of specialized or nonspecialized assignments, and that psychological tests appear to be more effective predictors of long-run job progress than supervisory ratings. The present-employee method was used to validate the tests, which is based on tests given to executive failures and successes at Sears. Again it is difficult to determine if success is caused by or predicted by a high test score.

Gross says that none of Sears' management men have been promoted without first hurtling the tests. To be promoted you must look like the ideal Sears man, or at least look like him according to the tests.

The review board method [8]

Several companies, including Ford and General Mills, have what appears to be a very effective and sensible program for identifying young men who have the potential for top management. This program concentrates on finding these men before they become functional specialists and giving them, early in their career, the broadening experience necessary for top general management.

Once a year each senior manager, based upon supervisory recommendation, nominates to a review board an unlimited number of outstanding subordinates who must be under 35 and who have worked for the company for at least two years. These candidates must have demonstrated rapid learning, superior performance of new assignments, improvements made in operations within the young man's responsibility, a display of initiative as indicated by working on problems without being directed by the superior, a willingness to stretch himself to learn, on his own, more about other jobs, a broad perspective to appreciate the relationship of his own job to the total operation, and an aggressiveness suited to the occasion. Each nomination must be backed with concrete observations of superior performance that justify the superior's judgment, a personal history form, and a work record.

One such review board, which consists of the division general manager and several other top-division executives, screens the candidates and

---

[7] "Identifying Management Talent," *The Conference on the Executive Study,* Educational Testing Service, Princeton, 1961.

[8] R. Wikstrom, "Identifying Comers in Management," *Management Record,* Vol. 24, No. 3 (March, 1962).

divides them into groups based on age. The first group is under 28 and the number admitted is unlimited. The second group is between 28 and 30, the third group is between 30 and 32, and the fourth group is between 32 and 34. Membership in the second, third, and fourth groups is limited to 1 percent, 0.5 percent, and 0.3 percent of the number of people on the division salary payroll.

No one is "frozen out." A man can qualify one year and be dropped from the group the next year, or he can qualify at a later age even if he hadn't qualified earlier. Men not in the group are considered unfit only for general management, but can still rise very high in a functional specialty. Since membership in the early identification group is not a prerequisite for top management, those not identified early can still make it. However, embarrassing questions would be asked of supervisors who failed to recognize high potential. Promotions are based strictly on demonstrated performance and not on membership in the early identification group.

The program is not publicized and most men don't know they have been selected. No list is published. However, the program is not a closely guarded secret. If a man learns of it, the program is fully explained to him.

Although frequent job rotation for all young employees is a part of this company's manpower and management development policy, the early identification group members are rotated specifically to broaden their experience. In some cases job openings are created to provide the member with needed experience.

Advantages of the review board method

This program overcomes several of the difficulties inherent in other methods of early identification such as the reliance on tests, the "crown prince" problem, the "bottling up" of good people by a supervisor problem, and the delay caused by training a man as a specialist before he is trained as a generalist. In the review board program, the early identified individual must continuously prove himself on the basis of demonstrated performance over a long period of time in a variety of functional areas and in real-world situations. As one author puts it, there is little real danger attached to taking risks or making a wrong decision in a leaderless discussion, in-basket test, or a business games test. Behavior may be little more than a projection of the way the candidate would like to behave on his job if things were different, and may not reflect real behavior on the job.

One problem that can come up when individuals are identified as having top-management potential is the "crown prince" problem, which can be very disruptive. Individuals who have been singled out as something special on the basis of something less than proven on-the-job performance, and where they are known to one and all, have had difficulty in some cases in being accepted by line managers and coworkers. One company had a "star quarterback" program, which turned out poorly and finally had to be dropped. Apparently, the district managers among whom they were rotated to give them experience, didn't accept them. The managers gave them very little training and experience. The "star quarterbacks" also developed some arrogant attitudes, which didn't help.

The review board method avoids the "crown prince" problem since most members don't know they have been selected, or if they do know, they also know that membership is no guarantee of success, and that any display of arrogance could wash them out. Since membership is based on proven on-the-job performance, their acceptance by supervisors is also high.

The very real problem of a top performing subordinate being "frozen in" a current assignment by a supervisor is also overcome. The organizational and personal pressures on a typical supervisor in a large organization motivates him to keep his best men even if they might be of greater value elsewhere in the company, or they could be developed for top management. Since the typical supervisor is usually rated on the productivity of his department, he is usually reluctant to give up his best performing subordinates. This is good for the supervisor, but bad for the company and the individual subordinates whose development is being arrested.

In the review board program, when an outstanding man not earlier identified emerges, the supervisors for whom he worked will be asked to explain why they were not alert enough to spot him as a comer. Thus, the identification of potential top managment becomes one of the criterion upon which the supervisor is rated in addition to the productivity of his department. Also, the policy of frequent job rotation for all young employees should minimize the possibility of a given supervisor "bottling up" his most promising and higher producing subordinates.

QUESTIONS AND PROBLEMS

1. Take a sheet of paper and divide it into two columns, heading them: *In the labor force,* and *Out of the labor force.* What parts of the population should be listed in each?
2. Construct a hand-drawn map of the labor market in which you live. What are its special contours and how did they form?
3. How do we measure quality of the labor force? Can you think of some improvements and refinements to measuring this quality?
4. What effect would the women's liberation movement have on the labor market?
5. What are some of the effects of young people entering the labor market with different value systems than older workers presently in the labor force?
6. What would be the effects of an aging labor force?

7. List six ways in which high talent manpower has special significance in the labor market.

8. Identify the major methods used in early identification of managerial manpower. Next to each, note the favorable and unfavorable features of each from your viewpoint.

9. Investigate one of the methods and prepare a sample demonstration for the class of how it would look and feel to be assessed by one of these methods.

10. Do you think corporations in a free society should have lists of high talent manpower? What are the favorable features? Who might not like such a system and why?

11. Prepare a "role playing" skit in which a personnel manager is explaining to a worker why he was passed over for promotion to manager because he had never been to college. The man has done a good job and wants to be promoted.

THE CASE OF
SAM LEGG'S SPEECH

Godwin, assistant plant manager, creaked back in his swivel chair and lit a cigarette, apparently forgetting another lighted one laying on the edge of a book on the telephone table behind him. A book, *Techniques of Executive Control* by Erwin H. Schell, had apparently been subjected to the same abusive treatment before. A series of burnt spots pocked its bindings. Jake Doolan watched the forgotten butt as its faint blue thread of smoke turned brown from the burning dust jacket.

"Jake," Godwin ruminated, "I got us a couple of tickets to a dinner tonight and you're invited, at company expense."

Not having a night class that evening, Jake silently figured the advantages to his budget from the free dinner. From this he quickly subtracted the 35 cents he'd have to pay in fares on the Hudson and Manhattan railroad to Newark. He calculated a net profit of $2.65.

"This dinner," Godwin went on, "is part of your development as a manager. You see, the Executives Club of Jersey City has invited a speaker, and the company feels that you should begin to broaden your horizons by coming into contact with the stimulatin' experience of gettin' a broader perspective and all that crap."

Jake observed that the glossy stock of the dust jacket on Godwin's book must be fireproof because the cigarette had gone out.

"Yessir, management development is the key to succession of the high-potential management talent in the country," Godwin went on. "You see,

Jake, there's a real executive shortage in this country. The boys in the *big* jobs are all worryin' 18 hours a day." He leaned forward. "You know what about?"

"Their income tax?" Jake suggested.

"Well, yeah, but I mean executive development."

"You mean they want to be developed?"

"Oh, they're still learnin', as I am too . . . I keep Erwin Schell's book right here all the time . . . but I mean *you*."

"Oh come on, Mr. Godwin. The president and those people don't even know I'm alive."

"Don't be so sure. Like I said, they're worryin' plenty about who'll be *able* to take their place.

"How can that be, Mr. Godwin? Those people over in New York don't know anybody in the plant."

"Oh-ho! Don't fool yerself. They got replacement charts and info' on every man in management in this company!"

"I don't think they know *me*. They don't know what I can do. They don't know what I'd *like* to do. I don't think they even know what I do! And that goes for every one of us."

Godwin struck Jake with a gaze which Saint Peter might have fixed on Hitler as he stumbled up the top steps and pushed the door bell to the pearly gates.

"That just goes to show how much you young smart alecks know!" he roared. "And just to prove what I'm gettin' at, let me tell you whose gonna be the speaker at this dinner tonight." He leered triumphantly at Jake. "The guest speaker tonight is none other than Sam Legg, Assistant General Manager of the Commercial Products division of our company." Godwin lit another cigarette, forgetting temporarily the second one still parked on Erwin Schell's dust jacket.

"To top it off, my wise young friend," Godwin said, "I was called by *his* secretary personally and told that I would have two tickets waiting for me if I cared to attend, since the old man is out of town. Now, tell me, do they know us over here in the plant or don't they?"

Jake shrugged and debated whether to rescue Erwin Schell from oxidation by cigarette.

"Okay," he said, "I'll go."

Ignoring the triumphant smile on Godwin's face, which, he reflected, looked like a wrinkled cuspidor most when he smiled, he went back down into the plant. Big Viola was having another hassle with a mechanic and he spent twenty minutes breaking it up.

Sam Legg had snow white hair and a florid complexion, heightened somewhat by three double scotches which the program committee of the Executive Club of Jersey City had happily provided during the VIP reception before dinner. After several belches, Legg nibbled the crust off his fried chicken, mixed the peas with the whipped potatoes, lit a cigar, and took out his speech. It had been written by a four-eyed young Yale punk in public relations, and he decided to try to read it privately once before doing it out loud. "God, it's long," he thought.

He was about half way through his first reading when he heard his name and noted that the toastmaster was introducing him. Standing up, he laid the speech on the podium, took a shot from the water glass, and began.

Sam was no novice at speeches. When he was younger he'd taught public speaking at Colgate. For a time he'd imagine that he might stick with teaching. At that time, now 25 years past, he'd hoped to get out of public speaking and into teaching literature.

One fall afternoon, however, in the middle of a faculty meeting, he'd taken the floor on an issue in dispute by the faculty and in faultless prose, had demolished a dozen full professors on the other side of the room.

They'd naturally never forgive a junior instructor for this, and in March he was informed that his betters had voted against his reappointment. Having an offer to join the sales training department of Cosmic Can in his pocket and two babies at home, he convinced himself he didn't really give a damn. God, how fast that 25 years had shot by!

Mr. Moderator, Distinguished Guests, and members of the Jersey City Executive Club. These are troubled times. As a man said in the Hudson tube station tonight, "things are tough all over, even the subway is in a hole." (laughter) But seriously, Gentlemen, at the risk of being provocative—and you may feel perfectly free to disagree with me—I should like to take an unequivocal stand, it's always darkest before the dawn.

As we survey the glorious past of this last bastion of democracy in this greatest hope of all mankind—and I refer, of course, to our free enterprise scheme of things in democratic America—I think as hard-headed practical business men we've got to keep our eye on fundamental objectives. Let me define briefly what I mean by fundamental.

Fundamentalism is the root of our system—the hard-hitting, day by day things that all of us learn by experience.

Now you may ask—and rightly so—what pertinence does this all have in *my* business? The answer I would suggest lies in the basic integrity of the individual—in short—human relations!

The high regard which one man holds for another, and the regard which is reciprocally held, can result in a keen rapport between men of all rank. I can assure you that from my own company's experience—right here in Jersey City and in the 62 other locations in which our firm conducts its business untrammeled by the fetters of a Godless socialism—Gentlemen—and I say this in all sincerity—it's the only foundation stone for achieving the fundamentalism which we all agree are the true goals of the free enterprise capitalistic system as so ingeniously devised and preserved by the blood, sweat, and tears of our forefathers. (applause)

Legg slugged at the water glass and reflected that this young cornball in PR would have to quit laying it on so thick. Even for Jersey City! Legg went on,

Many will dispute this fundamental tenet of our beliefs, because they have lost the vision. They will not take a "Message to Garcia." They seek the decadent influence of cradle-to-grave security and hope to find their true security in the illusory warmth of conformity—our greatest threat to individualism. As William H. Whyte has put it, and I quote, "We worship a false scientism," close quote.

The result has been a decline in the moral tone and fiber of our very national character. The scandals which bear so greatly on us today are symptomatic of a more fundamental malaise.

In fundamentalism, as I've defined it here in these brief remarks, Gentlemen, I would suggest lies the best and brightest hope of the Western World if not the Universe! Don't think this is too imaginary, for the dream of today is the commonplace of tomorrow—and as a Chicagoan of some note once quoted, "Make no small plans—they lack the magic to stir men's souls."

And in conclusion, Gentlemen, I'd propose that indeed it is as ephemeral a thing as the soul that we are in mortal combat for with the forces of tyranny and demagoguery—whether they be in the halls of a communistic Kremlin or the halls of a corrupt and cynical power-hungry group in this country.

Now I'm not proposing we turn back the clock. Yet, unless the forces of freedom—and I might modestly add—fundamentalism prevail, America as we know it is doomed.

Yet, as I said in the beginning, my faith in freedom is unwavering and unbowed. In closing, let me say that I trust that in some small way this light of fundamentalism—stuck in the tinder of a few responsive breasts—is an unquenchable flame which may serve to kindle yet others. If I've done even that, I think I've served a purpose in these halting words here this evening. For, as the philosopher said, "It's better to light a single candle than to curse the dark." Thank you. (applause)

Taking another slug of water, Sam Legg heaved a quiet sigh of relief that another of the damn things was over. Amazing, how the clods loved it the more schmalz you put into it. He began the usual amenities for leave taking, thinking of the bar he intended to visit before catching the late Long Island train home.

Surging through the crowd like a tanker taking the waves, Godwin ran a sturdy interference to the speaker's platform. Jake trailed him like a dinghy.

As they surged to the speaker's table, Sam Legg began a fast mental shuffle to dredge up the name of the big burly fellow bearing down on him. Dammit, that face was familiar, and he knew he worked for Cosmic. Sam was certain he hadn't met the young fellow with him. Quickly he stuck out his hand toward the youngster.

"I'm Sam Legg," he said, "You're one of the Cosmic managers I haven't met."

"I'm Jake Doolan," Jake said.

"I've heard of you." Jake looked a little skeptical. "You're supervisor of Department 10, aren't you?" Legg dredged up from his photo-organization personnel chart a connection that clicked. From the pleased and surprised smile on young Jake's face he could see he'd scored a bull's-eye.

"How'd you like the speech?" he asked.

"It was a classic," Jake said. Legg glanced at him quickly to detect any signs of mockery. Jake's face was inscrutable. Here was a cool one. Better point him out over in New York as a comer. He studied the close-cropped hair, high cheek bones, wide eyes, steady stare, slim body, broad shoulders. A comer for sure. "Thanks, Doolan," he said, fixing the name in his mind with a repeat. He turned to Godwin and shook hands.

"It's been a real pleasure seeing you again, *Goodman.*"

chapter 10

UNEMPLOYMENT — A SPECIAL CASE IN SUPPLY AND DEMAND

WHAT IS UNEMPLOYMENT? Calvin Coolidge once was heard to state that "when large numbers of people cannot find work, the result is unemployment." This trite observation is often cited as an example of the simplistic approach to the complex subject of unemployment by the public, and indeed, many economists. The complexity of the issue is pointed up by the numerous ways in which unemployment is treated by various interested publics.

1. *The politician* treats it in one way. The existence of large segments of people without regular employment and income is hazardous to politicians, since each unemployed worker is a voter, and may cast his ballot in a way which evicts incumbents from office.

2. *Labor economists*, especially those in the U.S. Department of Labor, Bureau of Labor Statistics may treat unemployment as a technical statistical problem.

3. *Social workers* may see it as a form of social blight which leads to undesirable social deterioration, leading directly to crime, decline of the family, health hazards, slums, and class unrest.

4. A more modern look at unemployment is that of considering pros and cons, *unemployment as a behavioral (or skill deficiency)* problem which might be resolved by enlarging skill or education.

Let's look at each of these four aspects in turn.

I. UNEMPLOYMENT AS A POLITICAL ISSUE

One of the biggest problems for a politician in an election year is to find good *issues*. With a presidential election, numerous gubernatorial races, and hotly contested congressional contests in many states, it is reasonably accurate to suggest that this year is one of the prime times to observe examples for such a search. Many of the best issues will be economic in origin.

Since your hasty retreat to the dictionary might not produce a useful definition of "issue," perhaps this subject of such determined activity can be illustrated by defining it this way:

An issue is some catchy word, phrase, or idea around which candidates and parties can cluster their forces, embarrass their opponents, and make their own position stronger to prospective voters.

Two important points can be made about economic issues. The first is that, to be a good issue, it need not have complete validity in fact. Secondly, it is more often than not created by practical politicians who invade the field of economics in search of data—not the issue itself, but some raw material which can be shaped into one.

Over the years economics has always been a fertile ground for politicians' raids in search of the grist for issues. Wandering across the prosaic and somewhat complex territory of the economist, the politician seems to have unfailingly returned from such a trek with enough stuff to construct an icon that could serve as an issue.

Our country was founded, and the American Revolution (considered as a political occasion) was motivated by, the economic issue of fiscal policy—"taxation without representation." The tea tax, the tariff of abominations, and other levies by the Crown became more than a strain on taxpayers' budgets in the colonies. In the hands of politically minded men, they became "issues" that served political goals. Being identified as a free trader or a protectionist was once a political issue of some import. In 1836 you could commit political suicide by being on the wrong side of the fence in banking theory. Monetary theory in the 1890's led to the "cross of gold" as an issue in an election. Balanced budgets had a fairly respectable run as an issue, although the subject seems to have lost some of its potency in recent years.

In the early days of economics the term "political economy" was used to describe the close relationship which existed between politics and economics. In more modern times political science and economics have emerged as separate disciplines, although through the mechanics of issue creation the two remain inextricably tied together.

This isn't to suggest that economics is the only source of issues for politicians. Civil rights, states' rights, and foreign affairs are also present as issues. Nevertheless, economic issues seem to hit closest to home and accordingly have the best potential as a political issue—one that can switch votes and win or lose elections if not properly dealt with in electioneering. Prosperity, payrolls, prices, wages—all these are strongly personal, and for that reason are important to political parties.

Modern political machinery calls for two kinds of staff workers behind the scenes. The first and most apparent are the political people (the organizers, the managers, the contact men, the pulse takers, and the survey men). Behind them are the issues men (the speech writers, the experts, the intellectuals who produce ideas and create the issues). Today the economist is an important adjunct to the issue department of the campaign machine.

It becomes of more than economic significance when in July of an election year the Bureau of Labor Statistics announces that unemployment has fallen, as occurred in 1964. The announcement actually reported that employment has risen faster than the number of new entries into the labor force, and "recent improvements appear to have broken the 10-year uptrend in unemployment." This meant that in July of that year the unemployment rate in the United States had fallen below 5 percent for the first time in more than four years. The "recent improvements" alluded to by the Bureau were taken by many to mean the actions of the present Administration, most probably the tax cut, the retraining bill, area redevelopments, and the like. In short, unemployment figures "prove" the worth of the present Administration's policies and should lead every straight-thinking member of the electorate to vote for its reinstatement to office. By this train of logic, an economic statistic becomes a political issue.

Naturally, if labor statistics showed a rise in unemployment, the party *not* in office could use the economic statistics as an issue in the campaign to prove that the policies of the Administration were the root cause of the unsatisfactory condition, thus proving that a change is needed soon, this November preferably.

Since 1932 unemployment has become an emotional gong to be rung with resounding effects during a political campaign. Even when there is none, unemployment can be considered as a threat. The campaigns of 1944 and 1948, for example, used the threat of possible unemployment as an issue. From a purely economic viewpoint, we might note that our performance in the employment of our citizens hasn't been bad. Good or bad, however, keeping all of the variables in mind is mighty hard. The labor force has grown by some 21 million workers, including 16 million new jobs since 1946. Eight million veterans were absorbed into the labor force after 1945. Since 1940, 23 million people have migrated off the farm, and breadwinners and many of their wives in this group are now in the labor market, and for the most part employed. The number of working women has risen enormously: 2.3 million more now than in 1947, of which four tenths of a million are considered unemployed. Wages have risen as a percent of national income.

Naturally, such a swirling mass of variables doesn't lend itself to orderly and complete treatment when campaign time shows up. The trick is to oversimplify and not to be squeamish at putting down a tendency toward logic. Unemployment as economics is one thing; unemployment as an *issue* is another matter.

Unemployment as an issue is the deplorable condition in which the breadwinner of a family has his lifelong position struck out from under him by a mysterious specter called automation. This leads to poverty. (An annual income for his family is less than $3,000.)

The conclusion is that higher government spending or lower government spending, whichever is espoused by a party, will avert this condition. For the party in power seeking reelection, the issue becomes a matter of patching up enough economic evidence to show that the Administration has eliminated or reduced unemployment. The party seeking to "get in" has two choices. It may deny that unemployment has really been reduced, or declare, as Representative Thomas Curtis once did that such achievement is the result of the Administration "playing politics with the unemployment statistics to make the job picture better than it really is." Thus unemployment, when removed from the economic area and drafted into the province of political issue making, becomes a rubbery sort of mass which can be affected in these ways:

• *Definitions.* By changing the definitions of some key terms such as "unemployment" or "labor force," the number of unemployed changes in one direction or another.

• *Omission.* By failing to note certain facts which a complete search of causes would entail, the size and scope of unemployment is politically manipulable.

• *Non sequiturs.* By pointing to one fact and then to another, the assumption of cause and effect, which may not have the remotest logical connection, is perfectly legitimate in issue-building from economic data.

Perhaps the unique feature of the Labor Department's election year announcements of July employment and unemployment levels is that it stresses joblessness as "the difference between new jobs created and new entries into the labor market." It was this latter figure of new entries into the labor force that became the focus of Congressman Curtis' attention. Such a definition opens the possibilities that perhaps the causes of high unemployment, figured by present methods, lie more on those things that attract so many women, youngsters, and oldsters into the labor supply rather than in the job-eradicating measures such as mechanization, methods improvement, and automation. Mr. Curtis also suggested that it opened the door to defining things in such a way that the unemployment picture looks better now because the Labor Department has, "for political purposes,"deliberately doctored the figures, not by forgery, but by changing the way it defines "increases in the labor force."

Nobody has suggested that the Bureau of Labor Statistics would resort to outright falsification. A committee to investigate such matters found that labor statistics relating to unemployment were, for the most part, objectively prepared and presented, and that any discrepancies between the figures and the underlying facts were those growing out of sparse funds and simple technical impossibilities of being perfect in retaining pristine purity to such a complex phenomenon.[1] With more than 80 million people in the labor force it might be possible, by herculean effort, to determine exactly who is working and who isn't at any one time; but the costs of doing so would be so exorbitant that no possible useful purpose could be served that could approach the cost of finding out the actual facts.

The figures, then, are estimates. Unemployment is calculated by a complex procedure which has some 70 variables to be weighed. Samples which have a reasonable chance for error are the basis for most calculations for unemployment. These are checked for complete accuracy only when the decennial census of population is taken. Their accuracy for the nation as a whole has proven remarkably close, although for smaller labor markets within the whole, their accuracy varied from 59 percent too high to 30 percent too low.

TABLE 10–1
Employment and unemployment in the U.S. (in millions)

Year	Civilian Labor Force	Total Employed	Unemployed
1930	49.8	45.5	4.3
1935	52.9	42.3	10.6
1940	55.6	47.2	8.4
1945	53.8	52.8	1.0
1950	63.1	59.7	3.4
1955	65.8	62.9	2.9
1960	70.6	66.7	3.9
1961	71.6	66.8	4.8
1962	71.9	67.8	4.1
1963	73.0	68.8	4.2
1964	74.7	71.0	3.7

SOURCE: Manpower Report of the President, 1964, and U.S. Dept. of Labor.

Small wonder, then, that unemployment should provide a fertile source of issues as election time nears. Given a figure which is of vital interest to the voters, yet founded in large part upon expert but subjective judgments and technical but arbitrary definitions, it provides a natural backlog of justification for just about any position that anybody might want to take in attacking or justifying administration policies which affect jobs.

To the economists these estimates and definitions are both understand-

---

[1] President's Committee to Appraise Employment and Unemployment Statistics (Washington, D.C., 1962).

able and perfectly justified. To the layman and voter, whose main education in their use is acquired from partisan interpreters, the end result is a lowering of confidence in the objectivity of governmental employment statistics. This, perhaps, is the saddest aspect of unemployment—or any economic problem—being converted into a political issue. Having lost its virtue in the heat of the campaign, it cannot easily reacquire it when elections are done and the hard work of improving conditions in society remains to be achieved.

When converted into the never-never land of issues, unemployment has a remarkably simple explanation that it can't possibly attain when it is dealt with by mere economists. That explanation is *automation.* The sequence is beautiful in its simplicity. Unemployment is a serious problem that is caused by automation. Its result is poverty. This sequence has enough complexity for the campaign trail so that it gives the candidate an aura of sophistication, without requiring that he get into the economic complexities. Automation, for example, is not all bad—only when it causes unemployment. Poverty isn't caused by unemployment alone, but by being old, colored, or living in Appalachia. Presumably no one will ask if automation has caused the poverty of the hillbilly or any one of a host of other matters of cause and effect which would require some economic information and training to answer.

One of the nicest things about automation as an issue is that you don't really have to have a clear idea of what you are talking about to use it. It has the advantage of being a single cause to explain the single effect called unemployment. Any kind of cost reduction, methods improvement, new machine, or layoff fits the definition of automation when it is being dealt with as an issue.

Perhaps the clearest spokesmen on automation are the labor leaders. In one capacity union officials bargain with employers for their members. In another they act as political issue makers.

The labor press, which spends a certain amount of its column inches in discussing automation, often deals with automation as an issue rather than as an engineering or economic phenomenon.

A study of the content of 58 leading labor union periodicals over a four-year period by the University of Michigan showed that these periodicals reported in editorials or news stories, including the statements of labor leaders, 474 items on the subject of automation. The substance of these stories is as follows:

• Most labor leaders state that they recognize the economic benefits which can accrue to society through the judicious application of the principles of automation.

• They accept the inevitability of the expansion of automation, but wish to have its rate of introduction controlled to cushion the impact on workers.

• This means that federal intervention in the form of investigation, retraining of displaced workers, and public works expenditures to reduce unemployment is necessary.

The summary of these three recommendations is, of course, that automation adds up to a political matter and is therefore an issue. J. A. Bierne, head of the Communications Workers and a vice president of the AFL-CIO, was the leading spokesman for the labor movement on the subject. Of eight statements on the subject of automation, only two of these statements reported were suggestive of action by the employer. The majority espoused government investigation, creation of a federal bureau, and federal control of automation. Other spokesmen, such as Howard Coughlin of the Office Workers, Al Hayes of the Machinist Union, and other national figures, spoke on automation, in substance saying:

We have no intention of disputing automation and its introduction from an economic or engineering viewpoint. We concede its inevitability, and point to that irrevocable movement as the basis for further federal intervention into business and the labor-management relationship.

In short, this treatment of automation is political, and its major effect should be political—in this case the pursuance of Democratic party policy.

This is, of course, a far more sophisticated approach than mere opposition to automation and identification with the Luddite posture which might evolve from a purely economic analysis of automation's effect upon union membership. From a labor leader's viewpoint, the major result of automation being halted would be the loss of an issue for political issue making.

Contrasted with this is the posture of the unions when dealing with employers in their capacity as bargainers for their members. Here they can readily accept the realities of cost reduction and job protection which come from keeping the employer competitive.

The fact that automation has never been clearly defined, nor its actual effect spelled out in any definitive studies, can readily be brushed aside when the political wars are to be fought.

In the construction of issues from economic data, it is readily apparent that the Liberal and Democratic political groups have a clear superiority in using economics to their advantage. The trilogy of Automation-Unemployment-Poverty comprise a Democratic argument rather than a Republican or conservative one. Representative Curtis, challenging Labor Department statistics and conclusions from them, is defensive and plays into the hands of the Democratic issue makers. No person of good will, including a politically ambitious person, can appear to be in favor of unemployment or poverty. This gives the liberal politician the advantage if he is the creator of the issues, since some unwary conservative may play on liberal ground and slip into the error of favoring these evils—or appearing to do so.

Notably lacking in the position of American conservatives is a posture half as good as the issue adopted by the Conservatives in England with vast success to date: "Vote Conservative and raise your standard of living." This has the value of being affirmative, of being economic in nature, personal in effect on voters, yet sufficiently vague that it cannot be successfully attacked. As an economically based issue it ascribes the readily apparent good times to governmental policies which allow private firms alone to do the job of providing silk stockings to working girls as well as the Queen. Tired cliches about the virtues of private enterprise, and the mystic nature of profits, certainly lack in luster as issues and merely indicate the paucity of economic advice available to the American conservatives.

II. UNEMPLOYMENT AS A TECHNICAL STATISTICAL PROBLEM

It is not uncommon to read in the business or financial section of your newspaper that "unemployment has remained stable at 3.7 percent" or has gone up or down from previous months. Apart from the political tremors, or the effect that such an announcement has upon businessmen expectation and planning, what does this actually represent in economic and human terms?

The construction of unemployment statistics

Because the final number is watched so closely by so many key people in government and industry, it is noteworthy to review the procedures by which the figure is developed. A small group of economists in the U.S. Department of Labor, relying upon data compiled from around the nation by a larger group of information gatherers actually are responsible for preparing the final figure which is issued to the public. Several important facts about this collection procedure are worthy of note, and for the company personnel man who may advise his management upon labor market data, a more extensive knowledge of the methods of estimating unemployment is necessary in order to use it effectively.

Perhaps the most important fact about periodically taken samples of unemployment is that they are not intended to be perfectly accurate. Not that the economists for the Bureau of Labor Statistics so pretend.

In a free society—one which has a free labor market—the power of compulsion is not available to government statisticians. For this reason they must play a kind of detective game to figure out the level of employment and unemployment. No law compels people to register monthly with a government agency. Yet, the power of an unemployment check permits the agency giving it to register certain kinds of information, and this is useful in estimating unemployment. At the same time, it leaves a large margin for error, especially among the people who might be unemployed but aren't eligible for an unemployment check.

The difficulties of estimating unemployment are well known to those who compile and release the figures. As the handbook used by the experts has stated:

The term unemployed encompasses a variety of meanings. It may describe a condition—that of not being at work; an activity—that of seeking work; an attitude—that of desiring a job under certain conditions; and a need—that of needing a job. The term has other connotations and various shadings and combinations. For example, should a definition of unemployed include individuals who do not have a job and who are not looking for a job but who would accept a job under certain conditions? Is a person unemployed who is in need of a job but because of home responsibilities is unable to look for or to accept a job? Should only those persons be counted as unemployed who are without jobs but who are breadwinners of their family? Obviously, the definition used determines the resultant count.[2]

The composition of the labor force is reported monthly in the *Monthly Report on the Labor Force* and includes figures on both the employed and the unemployed, which combined make up the labor force, or the aggregate supply of labor. Because of the importance of these figures to policy and behavior of employers and citizens, it is necessary that these estimates be made.

The estimated nature of the unemployment and employment figures means that while they are fairly accurate on a national basis, they are less apt to provide accurate figures on the variations between regions or local labor markets. For this reason the employer or manpower planner for the corporation must understand the shortcomings of the method. If he were, for example, to generalize about the Detroit or San Francisco labor market based upon national figures he might be falling into a serious error.

For company and individual employer manpower planning, the use of national unemployment and employment figures must be tempered with added information about his own local labor markets before action is taken upon the facts.

The decennial census as a check

Although the estimates of unemployment are prepared and released monthly in the *Monthly Report on the Labor Force* (MRLF), the only full scale, meticulously accurate count of employed and unemployed is

---

[2] U.S. Department of Labor, Bureau of Employment Security, *Handbook on Estimating Unemployment*, Handbook Series BES No. R–185 (Washington, D.C., March, 1960), p. 1.

known when the decennial census of the entire population of the United States is taken by the Bureau of the Census. Started in 1870, the Census included a count of the "gainful workers" in the country, which led to many inaccuracies in the calculation of the labor force. In 1940 the first accurate count of the labor market was taken, and has been taken again in 1950 and 1960 and 1970.

The household survey

The data contained in the MRLF is based upon a monthly field survey of a scientifically selected sample of households throughout the country. Currently about 35,000 households are visited and polled. Originally conducted and reported by the Bureau of the Census, the MRLF since 1959 has been published by the Bureau of Labor Statistics of the U.S. Department of Labor.

This scientific sample is constructed on a nationwide basis, and is not considered nor intended to be perfectly reliable for local labor market studies.

This scientific sample begins with a definition of unemployment which is used in all samples. It is based upon the activity of the individual in question during the sample week, usually that week of the month which includes the 12th of the month. The status of a person is based upon his labor force activity during the previous week. If he did any work at all for pay or profit he was considered as at work, and employed. If not at work, but seeking work, he was considered as unemployed. He might also be considered at work if he was attached to the labor force during the week, but for such reasons as illness, being on strike, or on vacation was off the job. If he had prospects for employment, say within 30 days, he is nonetheless unemployed.[3]

Since seeking work is the gist of being unemployed, this is defined as making any effort to get a job or establish a business or profession. This could include registration at an employment office, being on call from a personnel department, or a union hiring hall, or listed on a professional register. It also includes such activities as meeting with employers in person or by phone, placing or answering ads, writing letters of application, or working without pay to get experience or training.

Relating the unemployment insurance system

Since the thirties, the U.S. Department of Labor and the states have operated a national network of employment service offices. The Social Security Act created the unemployment system, to provide income for per-

---

[3] *Ibid.*

sons who have lost their jobs, and who have contributed through payroll deductions to unemployment funds while they were employed. The employment service and unemployment insurance systems are often physically combined into a single office to cover a local labor market.

The unemployment system, being designed to pay benefits to unemployed, provides the first basis for the estimating of unemployment. Since there is a tangible reason to come in and register for an unemployment compensation check, this office comprises the first platform upon which unemployment estimating is done. If the man out of work is covered by the act, and has worked in the past and is eligible for payments, he must register to collect. At the same time he becomes a statistic. Much is known about him in this faceless condition. He has worked, but is not now doing so. He would be willing to accept a job and has tried to get one (the office is the same for registering to find work as for collecting a check for not having work). In the words of the experts, the MRLF and UI definitions of unemployed are identical in basic conditions.

This first count in estimating unemployment is referred to as the first *building block* of three such buildings blocks.[4] When you lose your job, you register for another, pick up an unemployment insurance check, and you are counted among the unemployed.

The second building block attempts to estimate the number of unemployed who are not covered by the law, and thus never show up at the office to be counted.

The third building block is made up of those who have never been employed, and therefore aren't registered, or have reentered after a long stay away from the labor market and are not registered.

Let's look at each of the blocks in brief form.

Building block 1. These figures estimate how many unemployed there are by counting noses at the unemployment security office. They include the following categories of unemployed:

a. The insured unemployed, those reporting having been out of work for at least one week. It often includes people who were partially employed and meet a kind of income test.

b. Unemployment exhaustees are those people who have been unemployed so long that they have exhausted all of their rights to further compensation under the law. Even though they do not come in for checks, through sampling estimations they are approximated.

c. Unemployed disqualified are persons who aren't eligible to receive checks but are able and available for work.

d. Delayed filers and "never filers" are the fourth part of the first building block. Although small, some persons eligible drop out of the labor force involuntarily and don't apply for benefits due to illness, ignorance

---

[4] *Ibid.*

of rights, and other reasons. Such people are estimated in numbers through a standard formula developed out of past experience.[5]

These four together comprise the hard data of the most important of the blocks for estimating unemployment.

Building block 2. Unemployment among noncovered workers. Certain kinds of employers are not covered by the act, and cannot register for checks. Such industries as small industry, nonprofit institutions, domestic employment, self-employed, and unpaid family workers, agricultural workers, and state and local government workers are in this category. From time to time coverage of new groups is achieved through expansion of benefits to them, but in every case the estimation of the number of unemployed in this category is based upon standard ratios developed from past experience. Studies over several years in numerous labor markets have shown that such ratios are reasonably consistent, and MRFL data is provided to those making the estimates to calculate this building block.

Building block 3. New entrants and reentrants include such unregistered persons as those entering the labor force from school who haven't enrolled in the employment office, dropouts who have not applied at the employment service for work, women who have reentered the labor force after a period of many years being out of the market, and others who have been out of the labor market but have returned without registering. This figure naturally rises most sharply in June each year when school ends. In total it runs in the range of 600,000 to 700,000 persons who enter the labor market monthly and don't find work immediately. In June, when the peak period occurs, over 1.5 million workers enter the labor market and generally add about 1.0 million to the unemployed that month. Here, too, the estimation is based upon detailed studies in specific labor markets over time to estimate standard ratios allowing for seasonal variation.

After these three building blocks have been completed, the experienced eye of the professional applies judgment factors for a typical situation such as a major strike, large movements of workers into or out of an area, or other important and specific influences which might affect the estimate.

Adding these three blocks, as tempered by on-the-spot observation, unemployment is estimated and reported.

Summary—the unemployed as a part of the labor supply

In periods of high employment, the unemployed comprise a readily available source of labor only in some special sense. For the most part they are unemployed in prosperity for some reason. They have extremely low skills, are too old, have physical or apparent neuropsychiatric defects, or

---

[5] The formula is $D (7.5-50u)tI$ and is based upon estimating nonfilers from past ratios of unemployed to nonfilers, related to time lapse, and number of initial claims in the estimating office.

don't find some kind of culture bias which has been equated to a credential for employment.

In periods of higher levels of unemployment, say over 5 percent, there are available skilled and qualified workers who can be hired if employers have positions for them. The environment of the labor market in such periods is radically different, yet the impact of a population of unemployed has significant character in a society which tends to judge the entire system by how well it can take care of its own without too much want, misery, or unhappiness.

III. THE SOCIAL CONSEQUENCES OF UNEMPLOYMENT

Having treated unemployment as a political problem, and a technical problem of estimation, we may note another characteristic which bears upon manpower quality. In brief, unemployment and the low income related to it comprise the breeding ground for many of the facts of social disintegration in our society.

The family

Reports before the special senate committee on unemployment problems in 1960 point up some of the effects upon the family.[6] Nine out of ten workers in the United States are members of families, almost equally divided between families with one wage earner and families with more than one wage earner.

The effects of unemployment are drastic for all three categories. The loss of wage payments is supplemented at about 50 percent of the average weekly wage through unemployment insurance. When this is exhausted and unemployment continues, the family must fall back on other sources of income, traditionally onto welfare administered by the city or county. Before this welfare stage is arrived at the family must deplete other resources it has acquired in order to be eligible. In 1958 this exhaustion of benefits occurred in about two thirds of the unemployed. Other members of the family may be employed (in 45 percent of the cases this is so), which means a stepping down of the scale of living rather than absolute stoppage. In other cases members of the family not previously working, find work. The mother finds domestic or waitress work when her husband exhausts his benefits.

After such stepping-down methods of adjusting to lower income have been exhausted, studies show that family savings and investments and insurance policies are a source of income during stress. About 44 percent

---

[6] Hearings, Special Senate Committee on Unemployment Problems (Washington, D.C.: U.S. Government Printing Office, 1960).

of the unemployed heads of families reported that they had some savings which they used in an emergency, according to a Michigan study. These are further supplemented by reductions in buying, borrowing from friends, relatives, or associations; deferring payment of bills; and reduced quality of purchases in essentials. Some move to cheaper quarters, permit repossession of durables to reduce time payments, and economize in other ways. The major areas of deferred expenditures are clothing, recreation, community activities, food, insurance, housing, and postponement of medical and dental work.

The effects are a steady decline in the quality of family life, and even reemployment does not solve them quickly since accumulated costs of repayment and deferred health an other costs must be caught up with.

The effects upon the social order

Continuous or chronic unemployment has its major immediate impact on the family, making it unstable and erratic. In some instances it had been found advantageous for the father to leave in order to enlarge welfare income. Family life becomes disorganized as the traditional authority of the breadwinner declines. Children in such homes leave school at earlier ages than in higher or steady income family homes. Juvenile delinquency is high. The rate of index crimes (major crimes such as assault, rape) in areas of high unemployment such as the big city ghetto is 35 times that in white, middle-class areas where the unemployment rate is minimal. Most of these crimes are against persons rather than property. Despite police coverage that runs 14 times as high as in the white areas, the crime rates remain higher in the ghetto and high unemployment areas.[7]

Deficient diets from low income lead to health problems, substantially greater in areas of high unemployment than where low unemployment prevails. One report shows that 30 percent of the families with incomes under $2,000 show chronic health problems compared with 7 percent of families with more than $7,000 per annum. Yet the likelihood of treatment is lessened by lower income levels.

The attention which is currently being paid to "law and order" focuses attention upon those areas where causes of lawbreaking and disorder emerge. They are a product of a disorganized and shaky family structure, living in a chaotic and trouble-riddled social environment. Law and order is learned at an early age in a stable home with ample amenities, and a breadwinner who commands respect for his role.

Unemployment as a breeder of disorder, riots, and social decay is apparent.

---

[7] *Report of the National Advisory Commission on Civil Disorder* (Washington, D.C.: U.S. Government Printing Office, 1968), chap. 8.

IV. UNEMPLOYMENT CONSIDERED AS A SKILL DEFICIENCY

One of the major tenets of faith during the sixties was that one of the major causes of unemployment was a drying up of jobs for the unskilled. The thesis presented by eminent economists, popular writers, and government officials was that automation had so profoundly affected the nature of work that those without at least a high school diploma could not possibly manipulate the dials, read the meters, and push the buttons in the modern Sunday Supplement factory. Economist Charles Killingsworth was identified as the major proponent of this viewpoint, called a "structural" theory of unemployment, as were a majority of government economists and policy makers.[8] Educators and educational associations perpetuated this thesis in radio spot commercials against dropping out of school, telling the youngsters—and everyone else, including many employment managers—that "people without high school diplomas can't do the work of the modern factory or office." While their prescriptions were to *stay in school,* it was often considered to be for the wrong reasons by those who saw the problem as a demand shortage rather than structural in cause.

This automation revolution of making ordinary human endowments untouched by education useless and unemployable was spelled out clearly in the Clark Committee hearing in 1964. Leon Greenberg of the United States Department of Labor suggested that we should prepare to anticipate 11 percent unemployment or 9 million unemployed by 1970 if past trends continued.[9] Mr. A. J. Jaffe in the same hearings, stated that "rising productivity—another way of describing automation—would eliminate 4,000 jobs a week." Mr. John Snyder, a corporation president, suggested that this figure was too low and his own estimates are that automation would produce 40,000 jobs eliminated each week.[10]

Herbert E. Striner of the W.E. Upjohn Institute for Employment Research, Walter P. Reuther, President of the United Automobile Workers Union, and Issac L. Auerbach, President of the International Federation for Information Processing, were in substantial agreement with the structural thesis, and tended to agree that education and retraining were the solutions. Criticism of our vocational educational system, and emphasis upon the need for upgrading those unemployed through retraining were common elements in prescriptive advice.[11]

In 1964 this was a most plausible conclusion based upon projections into the future from the statistics of the past.

---

[8] *The Manpower Revolution—Its Policy Consequences,* excerpts from senate hearings before the Clark Subcommittee, Garth Magnum ed. (Doubleday Anchor Books, 1965).

[9] *Ibid.,* p. 46.

[10] *Ibid.,* p. 56.

[11] *Ibid.,* p. 57–87.

TABLE 10–2

Unemployment and education for males 18 and over—April, 1950 to March, 1962

| | Unemployment rates | |
Years of school completed	1950	1962
0 to 7	8.4%	9.2%
8	6.6	7.5
9 to 11	6.9	7.8
12	4.6	4.8
13 to 15	4.1	4.0
16 or more	2.2	1.4
All Groups	6.2	6.0

SOURCE: Clark Subcommittee.

A study of the table shows that the less education one had, the more likely one would be unemployed. The gist of the structural unemployment case lay in the elimination of jobs through automation. This was because automation raised the skill requirements for working at all, and left behind those without enough skills.

Are higher skills really necessary?

Edwin L. Dale, Washington correspondent for the New York Times, took an opposing viewpoint in an article in New Republic the same year. It was his assertion that "unemployment will decline in the years ahead and that two or three years from now the great huzzah over automation and 'structural unemployment' will be over and forgotten." Since, as a prophet, the journalistic Mr. Dale proved far more correct than his more academically based opponents, we might note his reasoning.[12] He called upon three case studies to illustrate his point.

The first was the experience of the United States during World War II. Because of huge budget deficits aggregate demand expanded rapidly. Not only did full employment come quickly after a decade of unemployment, but employers quickly learned to train the unemployable. Some 11 million workers were recruited in war plants and outproduced the world.

The second example was that of Germany in 1948. Aggregate demand was high and unemployment was not only not known, but illiterate and unskilled workers were drafted and recruited from Spain, Sicily, Turkey, and Greece. This, in spite of the fact that the rate of automation has been faster in Germany than in this country. Despite these, because of high level demand there is still a great shortage of labor in Germany today.

The third example is that of West Virginia from 1946 to 1953, a period in which automation in the coal mines was proceeding rapidly. Yet the

[12] Edwin L. Dale, "The Great Unemployment Fallacy," cited in *The Battle Against Unemployment*, A. Okun, ed. (Norton, New York, 1965).

rate of unemployment did not become distressingly high because the level of demand in the economy as a whole remained high, and unemployed workers moved.

If the demand is high enough, the levels of skills of the unemployed or of the new entries into the labor force is irrelevant.[13]

If, indeed, no structural unemployment existed, then the problem seen by the Clark Subcommittee witnesses, which became a focal point of much public policy was worthless, or at best a small flip in the right direction for a trend which would have occurred amply without it.

Others pointed out that the table showing the rise of unemployment among the lower levels of education could also be explained by an explosion of population among teenagers during the period.

The proponents of the demand rise theory of solving unemployment relied upon a more classic explanation of the expansion of demand to create a derived demand for labor, which would in turn create purchasing power, and so on. It relies upon the dynamics of a capitalist and market system to correct itself, and government's role is less to provide guaranteed income, or deal with a nonexistent structural problem, but to make policies which accelerate demand.

The Clark Subcommittee devoted some time to hearing witnesses who made the case for aggregate demand, and included Walter W. Heller, then chairman of the Council of Economic Advisors, who refuted the structural arguments, and especially those of Professor Killingsworth, in some detail. Professor Otto Eckstein of Harvard likewise emphasized the growth aspects of preventing unemployment, along with Leon H. Keyserling, former chairman of the Council of Economic Advisors.

In retrospect, the deficit years following the escalation of the Vietnam War had the effect predicted by Dale, Heller, Keyserling, and Eckstein. The economy grew, aggregate demand expanded, and unemployment fell.

Yet for many corporations the lasting lesson which persisted long after the debate was over was the fallacious continuation of selection policies which placed a high premium on education and automatically excluded by policy of the employer those whose educational level was considered too low. The riots of the middle and late sixties by blacks prompted programs to reduce these credentials, but nonetheless they remained in both business and government. Man made, personnel administration department implemented, they provided a wholly false barrier to employment. It aided in the creation of an artificial restriction of the supply of many workers, and at the same time numerous jobs were left unfilled.

It brought into focus the possibility of a credentials revolution which lies ahead in the seventies, and a need for a whole new look at "quality" in manpower.

---

[13] *Ibid.*, p. 39.

QUESTIONS AND PROBLEMS

1. Find out the rate of unemployment in your city and county for the past year and at the present time. What is its composition?

2. Interview some person who lived and was in the labor force during the great depression of 1932. Report on his observations to the class. Do you think such impressions have had an effect upon present day policy? How?

3. What are the four major viewpoints upon unemployment? Explain each.

4. What are the major arguments against automation? Does it cause unemployment?

5. Describe and diagram how unemployment levels are estimated. What improvements in the system could you suggest if you were commissioner of Labor Statistics?

6. Interview the head of the local branch of the State Unemployment Service. What does he do? What are his major problems? What is the most difficult issue facing his office today?

7. Interview an unemployed worker. How has unemployment affected his life style? His family? (Tape it and play it back to the class if he is willing.) What does he see for the future?

8. Unemployment is a skill deficiency. Discuss this statement.

9. What effects does the going wage rate have upon unemployment? Does a minimum wage law create unemployment as some have suggested?

10. How do political considerations affect the definition of unemployment and affect the measures taken to correct it?

11. Why is it important that government unemployment statistics be scientifically and accurately cast?

THE CASE OF THE SAN FRANCISCO FEDERAL EMPLOYMENT PROGRAM *

San Francisco and Washington, D.C. offer useful comparisons and contrasts in their approaches to employing the disadvantaged in the federal Civil Service. Like Washington, San Francisco is primarily a "paper" city though as a "capital" of private enterprise rather than a federal or state capital. Again, in contrast to the federal city with its diverse, *ad hoc,* and unrelated efforts on behalf of Civil Service employment for the disadvan-

---

* G. Mangum and L. Glenn, *Employing the Disadvantaged in the Federal Civil Service* (Ann Arbor, Mich.: Institute of Labor and Industrial Relations, 1969). Reproduced by permission of Garth Mangum.

taged, San Francisco emerged with a single, coherent, and largely successful program which has already had national impact. While the numbers involved have been few, the San Francisco experience provides a better model of what can be accomplished in more normal labor markets than Washington's, given adequate political commitment.

The coherence of the San Francisco program is even more surprising in that it began on a crash basis in response to a series of political accidents and a civil crisis. The experiment began at a time when a strict hiring freeze bound most federal agencies, and when personnel cielings for all agencies were expected to be lowered rather than raised. Yet almost overnight, startled regional Civil Service Commission administrators found themselves casting aside the hallowed merit system and hiring more than 1,300 hard-core men and women "off-the streets" without benefit of examination, either assembled or unassembled. Within two years, not only were significant numbers of disadvantaged persons employed, but three important concepts all relevant to the private as well as public hiring of the disadvantaged had been tested.

The first was the "hire now—train on-the-job" concept. The federal government had been advocating this practice in the private sector, but had not asked its own agencies to sample the same medicine. While many federal administrators had little patience with the "merit systems" employed by private industry, few had viewed their own merit system as a barrier to the employment of the disadvantaged. A crack appeared in that barrier in San Francisco and a sizable number of the city's disadvantaged were placed in federal jobs. However, the merit system was not bypassed altogether. Most of the disadvantaged workers in the program were given training on the job and, to become permanent employees, had to qualify for their positions within a year.

The second concept tested was the validity of the examination process as it applied to low-grade entry jobs. A job performance comparison was made between those who entered the San Francisco Post Office outside the merit system and a control group of those who entered through regular Civil Service appointments with results favorable to the former. As has been mentioned before, the Civil Service Commission is now considering just such a proposal from the D.C. government. In San Francisco, the experiment has been in operation for almost two years.

Perhaps the most instructive aspect of the San Francisco experience was the role played by political power in overcoming seemingly insuperable obstacles. Civil Service Commission regulations, agency reluctance, hiring freezes, and personnel ceilings fell by the wayside when the President of the United States, in answer to an embattled mayor's plea, put the weight of his office behind the San Francisco program. In this respect, the federal government is not much different from private industry. Successful job development programs in the private sector depend on the direct involvement of company presidents and the bypassing of personnel departments and traditional hiring policies. The appeal in the case of San Francisco was not made to the Civil Service Commission or to the personnel department of federal agencies, but to the President of the United States. Without his approval, the program would never have been started.

HOW IT HAPPENED

The San Francisco program now has a long, bureaucratic title: "Training Upgrading for Newly-Appointed Civil Service Employees in the San Francisco Bay Area." In the beginning, there was no title and no comprehensive plan; there was only a mandate to put people to work as fast as possible. Six factors helped bring about the mandate: (1) the nature of the San Francisco job market; (2) San Francisco's inability to receive what it considered to be its fair share of poverty and manpower funds; (3) a riot in the Hunter's Point area of the city; (4) the Mayor's plea to the President of the United States; (5) the appointment of a noncareer federal administrator to the chairmanship of a Presidential Task Force; and (6) the endorsement of the White House.

The skills in active demand in San Francisco reflect a shift from the relatively balanced industrial/commercial pattern of a decade ago to that of a 'headquarters' city. New industrial starts have almost disappeared; in fact, there appears to have been a net loss of some 20,000 industrial jobs since 1960. If, therefore, San Francisco's unemployed expect to find jobs within the city, channels must be opened into the white-collar world of finance, trade, services, real estate, insurance, and government. Nearly one fifth of San Francisco's 500,000 workers are employed by government; 30,000, or 6 percent of them, by the federal government. The proportion is small relative to Washington; yet federal employment is an obvious "port of entry" to the white-collar world for a group so much the concern of current national policy.

However, as San Francisco's largest single source of employment, the record of various levels of the government in hiring the disadvantaged had not been impressive. Black leaders had described the city's Civil Service as a "white ghetto," and the State of California could boast of few positive efforts to bring members of minority groups into nonsubsidized employment. The federal government's record was no more adequate.

Following the Hunter's Point riot, however, the federal government was given the chance to set an example.

Residents of Oakland, California often complained about living in the shadow of one of the world's most famous cities. In the distorted world of poverty, however, the situation was reversed. Since the Watts riot in Los Angeles, Oakland had been considered "hot"; and federal funds had poured into the city at a rate greater than its size warranted. San Francisco's poverty warriors looked enviously across the Bay as an MDTA skills center was erected, an Economic Development Administration program launched, and poverty funds supplemented by grants from the Ford Foundation. San Francisco, which had no skills center and did not qualify for EDA, felt it had been discriminated against by both the federal government and the foundations. San Francisco's Neighborhood Youth Corps and MDTA on-the-job training allotments had been less than those of Oakland, even though San Francisco had nearly twice the population.

The crowning blow came in 1966 when, because of a cutback in MDTA funds, the State of California decided to invest the majority of its MDTA institutional funds in the existing skills centers. This meant that Los Angeles and Oakland, both with skills centers, would receive most of the State's MDTA funds. San Francisco and other cities would have to suffer the consequences. Rumblings were heard from the mayor and poverty officials, but they didn't reach a crescendo until September 18, 1966, when a riot erupted in Hunter's Point, one of San Francisco's most deprived and segregated neighborhoods.

After all the federal worry about Oakland, and perhaps partially because of it, a riot broke out in "safe" San Francisco. As riots go, it was rather mild, but it did serve to focus attention on the needs of the city and brought the mayor out fighting for a program to help ease the plight of the city's poor. It brought about the establishment of new organizations in tht Hunter's Point area, one of which was the Young Men for Action—a group which would have a good deal to tell federal executives about the merit system and the poor.

The Mayor ventured into the ghetto area during the riot and was hooted down whenever he attempted to speak. He returned to his office and made his appeal via television. He castigated labor and management for discriminatory employment policies, and called on the entire community to join in a program to find jobs for San Francisco's poor. He then sent a telegram to the President of the United States in which he demanded that cuts in San Francisco's MDTA allotment be restored, and asked the President for full federal assistance during San Francisco's emergency. The mayor then established a "Job Center" close to City Hall and asked all San Francisco employers to phone their job orders into the Center, acting on his conviction that the causes of the riot could only be attacked successfully by an immediate full-scale hunt for jobs which would take rioters off the streets and place them in productive employment.

At first glance, the task force appointed by the President in response to the mayor's request did not appear promising. Its membership was almost identical with that of the Federal Executive Board; that is, regional directors of the major federal agencies in the San Francisco Bay area.

Over the years, the role of the FEB had been to serve as an information exchange between top regional administrators. Although it had conducted a few studies of government programs in Oakland and San Francisco, it had never engaged in an action program of any kind, nor did it consider itself an action-oriented group.

Despite the similarity in membership, the task force proved to be quite different from the FEB. The President appointed as chairman of the task force the regional director of the Office of Economic Opportunity, a non-career federal administrator who took his job literally and refused to consider the merit system and other traditional practices as sacrosanct.

To the surprise of the regional administrators who made up the body of the task force, the chairman announced that the first order of business would be to canvass all federal agencies operating in the area, to effect actual hiring of persons in distressed areas on a substantial scale. What about Civil Service regulations, hiring freezes, budget restrictions? The chairman brushed these considerations aside. With White House backing, all obstacles could be overcome. Despite scepticism about hiring ghetto-bred youth right off the streets into federal agencies, a federal employment program for the disadvantaged was to be put into operation immediately.

At the second meeting of the task force, the chairman invited the Young Men for Action from Hunter's Point to talk to the federal officials. This group was formed during the Hunter's Point riot to act as peacemakers. Now that the riot was over, they wanted to tell the Establishment what it was like to live in a ghetto, and what they believed would cure the ills of their neighborhood. Most were school dropouts, many had arrest records, a few had convictions, and all had been through at least one government training or work experience program.

Their message was simple: "We need jobs." They told the task force that they were tired of training programs that lead nowhere, NYC programs that paid substandard wages, and promises from both private and public employers. They asked the federal officials to give preference to the poor over "hippies" and other "white dropouts" who score well on examinations. They bluntly told the regional administrators, including the regional director of the Civil Service Commission, that the examinations given for most entry level federal jobs bore no relationship to the work required by the job.

With the experience fresh in the minds of task force members, the chairman pointed out that the San Francisco Chamber of Commerce had responded to the mayor's plea by pledging 2,000 jobs for the poor of the city. Could the federal establishment do less? As it turned out, most of the 2,000 jobs pledged by the Chamber never materialized, while 1,000 placements were made in federal agencies. Nevertheless, the argument served its purpose at the time, and the task force went to work on a crash program for the employment of the disadvantaged in federal agencies.

A President's Committee on Manpower team which had been working on coordination of manpower programs in the San Francisco Bay area for five months prior to the Hunter's Point riot, was assigned the job of working out the details of the program. The Civil Service Commission agreed to lend personnel to the PCOM team during the course of its assignment. Regional directors contacted their Washington offices for hiring authority, and the chairman presented his program to the White House.

The proposal submitted by the task force to the White House was not the standard plea for more training funds or work experience programs. Rather, it was a proposal that called on federal agencies to provide direct employment for the disadvantaged citizens of San Francisco.

The nature of the job market made a breakthrough in white-collar employment in government imperative. The fact that San Francisco had been shortchanged in its manpower and poverty funds, and that the so-called "safe" city had suffered a riot, made it possible for the mayor to demand, not request, special federal efforts in behalf of the city. Finally, because San Francisco was in a state of emergency, it was necessary to adopt a plan which could be put into effect immediately, and which would be a visible sign of positive action to the residents of the city's ghettos. For all these reasons, the White House backed the proposal and saw to it that hiring authorities and job slots were made available.

The importance of the White House endorsement cannot be overestimated. There was no doubt of the Civil Service Commission's opposition to the program nor to the reluctance of most federal agencies to participate. Without the endorsement of the White House, the proposal would have been quickly shelved. One year later, when the Federal Executive Board proposed an extension of the program under the Concentrated Employment Program, the Civil Service Commission turned down the proposal for 500 Schedule A positions in the San Francisco Post Office, even before it was formally submitted. With San Francisco's riot a year-old memory, the heat was off, and there was no pressure on the Commission to continue the program. Without the personal intervention of the Postmaster General, the San Francisco experiment would have died.

THE PROGRAM

The San Francisco Federal Employment Program can be divided into two phases: the President's task force phase, and the Concentrated Employment Program phase. The first is the "cut-and-paste" program which was put together in an emergency to help ease tensions in the city. The second, which is still in operation, is a much smaller and more carefully planned version of the first.

Following the Hunter's Point riot, the immediate goal of the President's task force was to place as many disadvantaged workers in federal jobs as possible. In the beginning, little thought was given to the training of these workers, or to any supportive services which might help them succeed on the job. The first order of business was to achieve the authority to hire; the second, to canvass the federal agencies for job orders; and the third, to develop a mechanism to insure the referral of the hard-core to the job openings. A total of 1,000 disadvantaged workers were placed in jobs through 700-hour appointments, and NTE (Not to Exceed) one-year appointments. All major agencies, with the exception of the Department of Labor, participated in the program.

Unfortunately, no records were kept on the approximately 500 people who were placed more or less at random with various federal agencies. The remainder were placed *en bloc* with the Post Office so that reasonably good data are available on their experience. Because the local Post Office register had been exhausted, the Civil Service Commission granted the San Francisco Post Office 500 NTE one-year appointments. The men and women who filled these positions were told that they must qualify by Civil Service examination within the year or be separated. They were also required to take the examination once every 90 days, or until qualified.

An experimental and demonstration project was funded by the Labor Department to help the new Post Office employees pass the Civil Service examination. Classes were held five days a week for two hours a day at the work site coinciding with the various reporting times of the employees. No time was allowed from the employees' regularly-assigned duties; thus, all students were faced with at least a ten-hour day. The trainees were taught simple arithmetic up to and including algebra. They were also taught communications skills.

Because the task force phase of the San Francisco Federal Employment Program evolved out of a crash effort to respond to a crisis in the ghetto, there were many deficiencies.

1. Initial attendance at most of the classes was sporadic. This resulted from scheduling classes for trainees either prior to or after eight hours of employment. A later shift of classes to a "swing" period during regular work hours resulted in a substantial improvement in class attendance.

2. The lack of supportive services affected the program adversely.

3. The lack of pretraining orientation program for trainees, as well as for Post Office supervisors, contributed to a higher than necessary dropout rate.

4. Inadequate records were kept to make a detailed job performance comparison between those who entered the federal service outside the merit system and those who received competitive appointments.

Despite these deficiencies, the program proved to be a successful one. In January, 1967, prior to the commencement of the classes, an examination was given in which 273 of the 500 employees took part. Only 13 passed the examination. Approximately one month after classes began, 243 trainees took the examination, and 92 qualified. A total of 513 employees received training under the MDTA portion of the program. Of these, 416 took the examination and 263 passed. Less than $60,000, or an average of $235 per success, was spent on the program. In addition, 230 of the original 500 employees found other employment, at least in part, as a result of the training they received while employed by the Post Office.

At the end of the year, a comparison was made between the experience of 489 of the disadvantaged persons hired without regard to selection standards and a control group of 103 selected from the regular Civil Service register to work together in the same occupations. The results are shown in Exhibits A and B.

The retention rate did not differ significantly for the two groups, nor did the extent to which the two groups of women were either terminated by their supervisors or simply abandoned their positions. However, the proportion of men terminated or who abandoned their jobs was twice as high for the disadvantaged group as for the controls. As might be expected these tended to be concentrated among the younger, single males with the least education. Within the experimental group of both men and women, those with arrest records had substantially poorer retention and performance records. The performance of the experimental group was clearly worse than that of the control group. However, the experimental group was younger, blacker, less educated, less experienced, and from more disadvantaged backgrounds; while no special provisions had been made to prepare them or their supervisors in any way to shield them from normal pressures and discipline in the workplace. Observers therefore concluded that the fact that over two thirds of even the group receiving the very lowest test scores still performed adequately on the job was more significant than the fact that they had not done so well as the less disadvantaged. One comment is particularly relevant to the theme of this paper.

The distinction we are making between the success of the Control Group and the achievement of the Experimental Group is essentially that between the concepts of "selection" and "utilization." If the primary concern is *to select* the best available, the register is the place to go. But if we accept the responsibility *to utilize* segments of the labor force who heretofore would not have been considered, we see that many of these persons can perform satisfactorily in socially useful jobs.[14]

Because of the success of the task force program, the sponsor of the San Francisco Concentrated Employment Program enlisted the aid of the

---

[14] Report prepared for the U.S. Civil Service Commission by David Futransky and Donald Wagner, "On the Job Follow-up of Postal Clerks Hired in San Francisco without Employment Tests," Standards Division, Bureau of Policies and Standards (July, 1968) (mimeographed).

EXHIBIT A

Employment status after one year

	Experimental (N=489)		Control (N=103)	
	Men (N=216)	Women (N=273)	Men (N=57)	Women (N=46)
Still employed	38%	71%	42%	65%
Terminated/abandoned job ...	29	13	14	15
Voluntary resignation	21	12	33	11
Other	12	4	11	9
Total	100%	100%	100%	100%
Still employed	57%		52%	

SOURCE: Report prepared for the U.S. Civil Service Commission by David Futransky and Donald Wagner, "On the Job Follow-Up of Postal Clerks Hired in San Francisco without Employment Tests," Standards Division, Bureau of Policies and Standards (July, 1968) (mimeographed).

Federal Board in developing jobs for CEP enrollees in federal agencies. A contract was signed with a private consultant to aid the FEB in this job development effort. As part of this program, the FEB proposed a continuation of the Post Office program, only this time under far more controlled conditions. These included:

1. The creation of 500 Schedule A positions in the San Francisco Post Office for enrollees of the San Francisco CEP.

2. That no priority be given to employees in these positions for advancement to permanent postal positions.

3. That a full complement of 500 be maintained during the period of the project.

4. That such appointments not exceed one year without the permission

EXHIBIT B

Performance as rated by supervisors

	Experimental		Control	
	Men (N=48)	Women (N=138)	Men (N=12)	Women (N=25)
Adequate or better	50%	80%	83%	100%
Poor	50	20	17	—
Total	100%	100%	100%	100%
Percent adequate or better	72%		95%	

SOURCE: "On the Job Follow-Up of Postal Clerks Hired in San Francisco without Employment Tests," *op. cit.*

of the Civil Service Commission and the Post Office, and that such permission be granted only if the enrollee had qualified for a permanent position and had reasonable expectation of being called in the near future.

5. That basic education and preparation for examination taking be part of the project.

6. That follow-up and data collection already built into the CEP be used as a source of information to evaluate the project.

7. That priority for entry into these positions be given to disadvantaged veterans.

8. That such employees had to take the Civil Service examination at least once every 90 days to remain employed.

The proposal was prepared in October, 1967 but was not approved until February, 1968—and then only for 200 positions. Top level officials of the Post Office Department worked closely with the FEB, the Employment Service, and the CEP staff to assure that all details of the program would be carefully worked out. All enrollees would receive a two-week orientation course before reporting for duty. While at the Orientation Center, they would receive a medical examination and could arrange for legal aid or child care services, if needed. In addition, a follow-up coach would be assigned to each enrollee.

Hiring began in March, 1968, building up to 181 in September; 96 of them male and 85 female. Of the remaining 19, 11 failed to report for duty after having been assigned through the CEP, four resigned for personal reasons, two resigned to enter military service, and two were disqualified for medical reasons.

By ethnic grouping, the total complement was:

Negro	96
Spanish surname	47
Chinese	23
Indian (American)	3
Other	12
Total	181

Because of the careful planning and preparation that went into the CEP phase of the program, the preliminary results were even more encouraging than the results of the task force phase. Of the two groups who had taken the examination by September, 1968, a total of 41 of 50 in the first group, and 31 of 39 in the second group, had already passed the examination. Thus, 71 of the first 89 enrollees to take the examination had qualified for permanent positions in the postal service.

Equally encouraging was the comparative statistical analysis maintained by the Post Office between CEP enrollees and regular merit system employees. For the first 14 weeks of the program, comparative statistics reflected the following:

	CEP enrollees	Merit System employees
Turnover rate	8.0%	12.0
Sick leave usage	1.0	1.6
Annual leave usage	0.0	0.4
Separated employees (average number of weeks worked)	7.0	2.5

In the earlier experiment, the disadvantaged, in addition to poorer performance, had tended to make greater use of sick leave and annual leave, perhaps because they felt less secure. In the later phase, the CEP enrollees apparently performed better in each category than their merit system counterparts, perhaps because of better orientation and training of employees and supervisors. While this performance does not necessarily challenge the validity of the Civil Service testing process for such entry level jobs, it does indicate that handicaps can be overcome. It leaves little doubt that many persons not able to compete successfully on regular examinations can become satisfactory and productive civil servants.

Group discussion question

What implications do you see for government hiring policy? For industry?

chapter 11

THE CORPORATION AND
TWO REVOLUTIONS

THERE WERE two revolutions, begun and carried on simultaneously in the sixties and into the seventies, each with strong impact on personnel policies and practices. The first of these was the black revolution, which was materialistic in nature. The left-behind black, Mexican American, or Indian excluded from the labor market by credentials he couldn't meet coming from his social milieu, became militant in demanding pay, jobs, and the things which those two would produce, such as housing, food, and luxuries. His main objective was economic.[1] The second revolution was that of the young white intellectual. His was an antimaterialist revolution. Despite frantic efforts of corporations to convince him to join up, many of the better young people from middle-class backgrounds rejected business as a life's work.

These two revolutions are complex in causes and difficult to comprehend, but the key to personnel strategy in the face of them both swirls around the question of credentials. It is their credentials which keep the blacks from being employable, and it is their credentials which makes the middle-class educated white youth desirable. In this chapter and the one which follows we'll examine the political economic aspects of each of these revolutions, and their implications for personnel strategy.

THE RISING BLACK REVOLUTION

During the latter days of the Eisenhower administration and continuing through the Kennedy, Johnson, and Nixon administrations, blacks all over America had arisen from their former state of toleration of their lot to one of active revolt.

[1] Herbert Northrup and Richard L. Rowan, *The Negro Employment Opportunity* (Ann Arbor: Bureau of Industrial Relations, University of Michigan, 1965).

229

In 1963 riots involving blacks and whites occurred in Birmingham, Savannah, Cambridge, Maryland, Chicago, and Philadelphia. Mobs battled with each other and with the police. White retaliation came in the form of bombing, including a black church where four young black girls were killed while attending Sunday School. In 1964 the revolution continued at a fever-pitch with riots that shocked the nation in Harlem, Brooklyn, and Rochester, New York. It was in the latter city that the National Guard was required to be called in. Philadelphia underwent two nights of rioting following the arrest of a black woman for insulting two policemen.

In 1965 the mixture of black and white civil rights workers in Selma, Alabama produced retaliation by the police. A white clergyman and a Detroit housewife, active in civil rights in that city, were slain. The most serious of the riots up to that time, and a model for many of the others to follow, occurred in Watts, a section of Los Angeles, a confrontation between police and blacks. This led to three days of burning and looting which was finally stopped by the National Guard. Thirty-four persons were killed, hundreds more were injured, and nearly 4,000 persons were arrested. Snipers were reported active, and damage to property was reported at $35 million. As the nation's worst riots since the Detroit riots of 1943, they shocked the nation.

1966 produced further eruptions in Watts in May, followed by a riot with fire-bombing, looting, and rock-throwing in Chicago which required 4,200 National Guardsmen to be put down. Three died and hundreds were injured. A week later in Hough, a section of Cleveland, a riot erupted in which four were killed. Sniping was reported, and it was stated that instigators had been present, fanning the flames of discord. Forty-three major and minor disorders of the black communities of the nation were reported for 1966.

In 1967 the rioting began on the campuses of southern universities for blacks and extended to Tampa and Atlanta with riots following confrontation between blacks and police. In July of 1967 the major riot of the year to date occurred in Newark, New Jersey. An arrest of a cab driver produced a mob of blacks around the police station where molotov cocktails were thrown. For several nights after, the central ward became a battleground with reports of snipers, heavy damage to businesses and homes due to fire producing 23 deaths; two whites and 21 blacks. Property damage came to an estimated $10 million. The disorders spread to neighboring cities of Jersey City, Elizabeth, New Brunswick, and Plainfield, where a policeman was stamped to death by a mob of blacks. The worst lay still ahead for 1967.

In Detroit on Twelfth Street, early one Sunday morning in July, a conflict between police and blacks accelerated and raced across many square miles of Detroit. Forty-three people died before the Michigan

National Guard, bolstered by a regiment of federal paratroopers, restored order. Fire fighters were fired upon by snipers as they fought the conflagration. More than 7,000 persons were arrested, looting was rampant, and insurance losses or property damages were finally estimated at $32 million.[2]

In 1968 violence erupted once more following the assassination of Dr. Martin Luther King. The capital of the United States became the focal point of the worst of early riots but violence was not limited to the nation's capital. Block after block of slums in Washington, Pittsburgh, Chicago, and Baltimore were burned out. Other incidents occurred in Oakland, Nashville, Tallahassee, Richmond, Topeka, Buffalo, Battle Creek, and a dozen other cities. Retail stores were hit especially hard and only a few blocks from the White House rioters rolled "F" Street, selectively looting jewelry, radio-television shops, and men's wear stores.

By 1969 the police were ready with new methods to cope with the riots of the years before, but the tactics had changed. By this time the movement had gone to activists movements on the part of Black Panthers, Blackstone Rangers, and some of the more militant black groups. In Cleveland a group known to be militantly aggressive was involved in a night-long shooting spree with the Cleveland police in what was described as "a shoot-out in Cleveland." The general focus of most rioting during the year on the part of blacks extended to the campuses where armed students took over a dormitory at Cornell University and black activist movements arose on hundreds of campuses around the country. During the summer the number of disturbances continued to rise even though the number of fatalities declined. Property damage continued high and it was evident that the black militant movement was not about to expire of its own accord.

The causes of a riot

The basic process of a riot has been described by the Kerner Commission. An accumulation of grievances in a black community builds up, growing out of poor job opportunities, bad housing, inability to move from bad housing even when employed, frustrated aspirations of many members of the black community, and a sense of rage over an inability to affect change.[3] This generates the pressure for an explosion of violence to follow.

This is usually triggered by a specific incident involving the police and a single group or small group of blacks who moan that a real offense or injustice is done by the police. Such incidents are often trivial by them-

---

[2] *Report of the National Advisory Commission on Civil Disorders* (New York: Bantum Books, Inc., 1968).

[3] Editors of Fortune, *The Negro and The City* (New York Life Books, 1968).

selves, but coupled with the underlying frustration and discontent they rapidly become the starting point of riots and revolutionary activity. The next stage is violence and disorder, which produces property damage, multiple injuries, arrests, and heightened tension in the city. Violence normally occurs where the conditions are congested, people are in the streets, and traffic flow is dense. It tends to occur in the evening when people are not at work, often on weekends,[4] and very frequently when the temperature is high and the undesirable conditions of the ghetto are more apparent. Violence mounts as word spreads, more youngsters gravitate to the scene, and minor crowds turn first to looting and then to property damage and finally to personal injury.

These are the bare facts. What do they imply for a manager in a modern business? What do they imply for him as an employer of a large segment of the population? What are the alternatives for business policy in the face of this urban crisis which has been partially outlined above?

A number of possible alternatives for the business firm and its personnel policies present themselves.[5] They include the following:

Alternative 1. *Do nothing.* If a problem will go away when ignored, there is little sense in a company exercising effort, energy, and the expenditure of funds to solve it. Population figures, however, plus a rising pride in race in the black youth of the cities, indicates that the problem of the black revolution won't go away but rather will be aggravated.

Population studies have shown that the rate of increase among the population of blacks is nearly twice that of whites. One estimate shows that the number of blacks under the age of 15 is sufficiently high that they make up about one youngster in six in the United States. A majority come from a ghetto home with no male head of the family. A rising tide of numbers, a rising level of aspiration, an increased pride in race, and an easy willingness to engage in revolution and a rising skill in doing so indicate this problem will not respond successfully to this alternative.

Alternative 2. *Insist on law and order.* The teaching of law and order is not customarily done best by riot troops nor by squirting a youngster in the eye with a can of mace. Ordinarily it is learned in a stable home from parents who have respect for the values of law and order. The deterioration of black family life undoubtedly accounts for the loss of respect for law and order. This deterioration is a direct function of the high levels of unemployment and underemployment in these communities.

Alternative 3. *Let the government handle it.* Some managers might long for a simple solution such as passing the entire problem back to the federal or state government or perhaps the local police force or human

---

[4] *Report of the National Advisory Commission on Civil Disorders.*

[5] George S. Odiorne, *Green Power, The Corporation and the Urban Crisis* (Pitman, New York, 1969).

relations commissioner. The major limitation of this solution is the high taxation that would be required to support the massive program which would be necessary. Manpower programs, economic opportunity programs, and the like have an exorbitant cost per person and the amount needed would soon run beyond the tax toleration of the population at large. In addition to this, the government itself is having serious problems implementing its own equal employment opportunity program in the face of civil service laws which require that the merit system be protected and that "testing as usual" go on.

Alternative 4. *Use raw force through riot control.* The major limitation upon the amount of force we can let police use on citizens is nearly reached under the present circumstances. The major limitation of this alternative is that the use of direct force breeds a diversion of the militancy into the guerilla warfare. The requirements for a guerilla warfare in a modern American city with its high percentage of blacks are very high.[6] The needed ideology, such as black power, is readily apparent, a ready availability of targets, and above all the presence of a large dissatisfied population into which a major strike force could fade back after making a guerilla hit is readily available in most ghettos. In addition to this, the effects of morale upon troops, especially black troops is an imponderable. Of interest too would be the watering down of the effectiveness of the armed forces if required to carry on such an extensive internal warfare against their own people.

Alternative 5. *Business could hire the rioters and train them.* The experience of World War II in which 13 million previously unemployed and untrained persons were inducted and trained to work in war factories, with spectacular results, demonstrates that industry and business has the capacity to train and hire them. Not only would this alternative be faster and cheaper than any other, but it would eliminate many undesirable side effects of the other alternatives. Unless the slum dwellers and ghetto residents are given a job, trained, and helped to start or take over businesses and enjoy the benefits of the free enterprise system, their violent opposition to it is most apt to continue. It is up to private business, those who would preserve the system because they own it or run it, to give those who do not—the poor—a stake in our society.

There are massive opportunities for *business* as well if it solves the problem: higher profits, a great growth, and a stable society in which orderly, legitimate business can prosper.

Black people today represent a market segment that spends $30 billion and includes 23 million consumers. The population and buying power of the blacks is rising. By providing them with jobs, the corporation adds

---

[6] Peter Paret and John W. Shy, *Guerillas in the Sixties* (New York: Praeger Paper Backs, 1962).

to their buying power. The rise in black population from 1960 to 1966 was a 42.2 percent increase which compares with the growth of 8.6 percent of the white population in the same period of time. If the future growth of cities resembles the past, it is entirely possible that 35 percent of the population of the cities will be black by 1985. At present the income of blacks is about equal to 55 percent of that of whites. While the income and purchasing power of both groups is increasing, there are some distinct economic advantages of looking to the black market. Its importance is illustrated by the percentage of customers it comprises in major urban centers where retail statistics show that they frequently comprise a distinctively higher percentage of the customers in the downtown store.

The size of the Negro market could be substantially increased in the future, not only in numbers which appears inevitable, but in incomes if unemployment and poverty were eliminated through a comprehensive job program. For example, if the differential between black and white per capita income were cut in half, the other market would come to about $7 billion per year. If the gap between the two races' income were closed by 1985, the added purchasing power would range from a probable $45 billion to a possible high of $52 billion annually.

The basic point here isn't an especially esoteric one. The economic rise of the black man comprises a kind of economic revolution certainly equal to other major economic efforts that we have seen such as the space program, health, education, and welfare programs, or perhaps even the equivalent of a small war. To the point of the urban crisis this economic growth would have the effect of restoring the family through the infusion of payrolls into the areas which presently don't have them.

It entails using the vast productive and distribution capacity of the private enterprise system as a solution to the urban problem.[7] This naturally entails some rethinking of past practices and personnel selection procedures which in part are a cause of the present unemployability of the blacks. The credential which excludes the black is not designed to exclude him merely because of the color of his skin. It merely has that effect in the preponderance of cases. By changing its employment policies, the corporation is recognizing that black employment and black consumption must go on concurrently and that the creation of consumers is identical with the process of employment of workers.

Confronted with a materialist revolution, the solution is calculable. Make blacks employees, thus consumers, and members of the middle class. This will end the revolution. Yet another exists, that of the young people.

---

[7] Joseph Schumpeter, *Capitalism, Socialism, and Democracy* (New York: Harper and Brothers, 1942).

THE ANTIMATERIALIST REVOLUTION

Concurrently with the black revolution was a youth rebellion. Its goals were diametrically opposite those of the blacks; rather than wanting more of the material things of life, they desired less. Born of parents raised during the depression, they were an enigma to the elder generation. Oldsters, raised in a time of depression in the thirties, had seen the effects of massive unemployment, of austerity and hunger. For them a steady income, a house, car, and radio were the goal. Following their emergence from World War II their dreams were realized. Not only a house in the city, with two cars in the garage, but a house in the country, a vacation in Europe, color TV, and luxuries which far exceeded their youthful dreams fell upon them. Their children lived in a world of comfort, freedom from want, and "all the things we didn't have when we were growing up."

The educational systems, taught by college and university graduates, went beyond the rudimentary teaching of fundamentals and taught a life style which extolled permissiveness, participation, and social awareness. The combination of the two produced a generation which sought "more," not in the Gompers sense of even more material things, but idealistic in character.

It left the colleges and their stuffy and humorless administrations baffled and irrelevant. As this work force emerged from the colleges into jobs, it produced a generation gap between old and young which accentuated the customary differences between order givers and order takers. For the corporation it presented an entire new range of personnel problems.

1. At the very time when ethnological change was occurring rapidly, when staff departments were increasing and credentials demanded more college graduates, the college graduates themselves were concluding that corporations were not suitable sites for a life's work.

2. The emphasis upon college recruiting, the early identification of high-talent manpower, and the high-pressure search methods for the more intelligent young people occurred concurrently with the withdrawal of many of the best from the supply of their own volition.

3. The effect of this upon the starting salaries created great stress within the firms, as older and more experienced employees found themselves working for equal—sometimes inferior—wages to the beginners.

4. Tensions between the Young Turks and Crown Princes and the older generation of employees, perhaps with less education but vastly more experience, mounted steadily.

5. A shortage of 35–45 year olds and the tendency to promote man-

agers quickly at younger ages accentuated this tension between the generations.

Affecting almost all of the younger generation, even those not sympathetic to the SDS and similar radical student groups, the problems of hiring and managing the younger generation were a direct product of this youth rebellion.[8]

The intellectual and the corporation *

Not long ago the *Michigan Daily*, a rather elegant and highly regarded student-newspaper around Ann Arbor, featured an article maintaining that corporations and the best students were incompatible. One of the editors, subsequently a winner of a Rhodes Scholarship, had recently returned from a gathering sponsored by several large corporations. Chief executives of these firms were apparently trying to convince a selected group of college students that business really isn't a bad career. Apparently this able student was not convinced. The story, a well-worded kick in the shins for corporations, pointed out that essentially corporations were far too interested in making profits. In the process, they make cars that kill people, pollute the air, and generally act in ways with which students have little sympathy.

Among the many lessons we might learn from this report, and the conference it discussed, the most prominent would be that liberal student-editors have preconceptions seldom changed by information, and certainly not by meeting company presidents. But, more seriously, many corporations find that they are not attracting as many good students as they would like, although they are hiring more college graduates than ever before, and more college students are electing business as a major course of study than ever before. Ford, for example, hired some 2,000 graduates in 1966 compared with 500 in 1960. The problem isn't simply one of filling jobs, however: corporations apparently want to be loved by the young. This is often compounded by the fact that children of executives are not entering business, but choose the professions, the arts, teaching, or public service.

In a campaign that the New York *Times* has labelled "The College Kids don't love us anymore—the story of an overpublicized disenchantment" a frontal attack has been mounted. It has all of the vigor, imagination, and lack of insight of a well-tooled advertising campaign aimed squarely at a rather dim-witted target. If the object of this program were

----

[8] The *Journal of the Academy of Political Science*, Columbia University (Summer, 1969) devoted an entire issue to the shades of student involvement, with reference to historical patterns, and especially the Columbia University riots of 1968.

* Adapted from an article by the author originally printed in *Michigan Quarterly Review*, Vol. VIII, No. 2 (April, 1969), pp. 87–95. Reproduced by permission.

indeed the video bemused idiot who makes Beverly Hillbillies a top entertainment show, the results might be felicitous. Unfortunately, it comes out as another instance of management talking to itself.

Marketing Insights, a magazine published by Advertising Publications, Inc., goes to 29,000 students and 6,400 instructors of marketing in 1,463 colleges and universities, a group not exactly needing a change of attitude. The apparent results can hardly be expected to meet the needs of the top executives who pick up the tab for this grand sales-pitch. In fact, we suspect that maybe the marketing experts have missed a basic tenet of their own trade: sell your product to prospective customers not to your own copywriters. Most students of business, engineering, and law are sufficiently convinced already that business is a pretty good site for a career. The liberal arts, journalism, the psychology, sociology, and economics student is perhaps a more germane target.

Time Inc., in 1966, devoted full-page ads monthly to persuading college students that business is OK for them. Motorola, Chrysler, and many other firms diverted presidential time to the campaign. Bob Galvin, dynamic young Motorola president, made a campus tour to bandy words with youthful business critics on the campuses of Harvard, Michigan State, Cornell, and the like.

General Electric, never bashful about stating their interests without ambiguity to the public it wishes to influence, bought ads in campus newspapers stating realistically: "Let's face it, the Peace Corps isn't for everyone." The recruiters for the Peace Corps would be the first to admit this. Nor is General Electric for everyone, apparently. Perhaps the realization that this poor match works two ways, that the heart of the problem is a matter of fitting interested people into suitable jobs, rather than of being loved-more-than-VISTA, would solve many of the imagined problems the company executives are trying to alleviate by their campaign to win today's involved generation of college students over to corporate life.

The Peace Corps, sit-ins, teach-ins, demonstrations, and the rise of the new left on campus indicates a healthy shift away from the quiet generation of the fifties, or the beat generation of the late forties. Only a tiny fraction of today's activists are genuine radicals. By tapping issues with wide popular support—civil rights, the war, the alienation of man from society, and so forth—the new left has filled the needs of their ideological group, without exposing the ideology. But student activists are clearly a minority on most campuses. Their groups include many of the better students, and in adopting the causes of the movement, they incidentally reveal a great bias against corporations and the profit system.

Where did these youthful critics get their biases against business as a career for themselves? In many instances, they are children of the middle class: executives, managers, and professional staffers in corporations.

They learned it at home. They watched dear old dad come tooling home most nights—except when he was on the road—too tired to be jovial or interesting. His best energies drained, his cleverest talk expended in the exciting world of the market, all he sought was a refuge where talk was turned off, where the ragged nerves were mended, and the empty reserves were rebuilt for the next day's fray. The kids never saw him in the ring at his best, only in the dressing room cut and bleeding, his behavior boring and occasionally truculent. Given a paternal figure who can carry his zest and moxie into the home environment, and transmit to his family the same energy and brains he dished out to peers and competitors all day long, there is no great hostility to business— even among the sons of Willie Loman.

The most ambitious college kids, the ones who seek business eagerly today, are the sons of laborers, or lower clerks, or civil servants, who see in a diploma a route upward. Unlike the sons of executives, they have seen the stresses that come from low pay, the coming home with dirty hands, the insecurity in working for a living. The offspring and their parents set higher levels for themselves. The laborer's son who can get a master's in accounting may probably not duplicate the occupational trauma of his father, but can join the upward-mobile group, who see business as a vehicle for escaping the lower middle classes forever. Being a laborer is clearly less satisfactory than being a manager or professional, and children brought up in the workman's home are hungry for better things.

To the youngster who hopes to move out of the tenement or small development-home into the upper middle class, the possibility of corporate employment is a prize to be sought eagerly. To psychologist Robert McMurry, long experienced in selection of managers, the solution is simple. *Find the guy who is hungry* is McMurry's realistic answer. The kid who doesn't need the job won't try harder; he may not even want to try at all. Maturity, McMurry states, is a matter of not being dependent, and the kid who hasn't scrambled for his position is less apt to put out when the chips are really down. Having gotten things the easy way, he still longs for something better, and sees little challenge in simply holding his own.

Sons of entrepreneurs are often, to their parents' dismay, uninterested in the business the old man has carved out, but want to spend life doing something else. Here lies much of the discontent of executives over the failure of better students to love the corporation. It is being rejected by its own progeny. The answer probably lies in the large corps of hungry applicants who hope to scramble up the corporate pyramid, and have few compunctions about selling out their personality in the process. They'll sell their right to free thinking in a tenement for the comfortable middle-class life of corporation manager or professional employee.

We may simply dispose of these recent self-flagellations by executives. They might well quietly desist from this wave of apologetics, at which they are patently inept, and get back to running their firms, and making profits. Executives are notably poor propagandists, and might do much better to stick to the things in which they excel. Not only have they exaggerated the problems of students not being attracted to business, but their attempts to alleviate the problem of parental guilt by talking to students personally borders on bathos.

Do corporations really need intellectuals? Perhaps we should distinguish between people of higher intelligence and "intellectuals." The intellectual today seems to be any person who is chronically critical. Intellectuals were once considered people who lived by their brains. Today the term intellectual is synonymous with "intelligent critic." This shouldn't mean that critics are necessarily harmful, nor should we further assume that all criticism is intellectual, although the term has come to have almost this definition of late. The chronic griper, the carper, the nit-picker, and the rebel who draws himself up short of bombs and guns are often included among the intellectuals. Perhaps we might define the modern intellectual as the person who is a conscientious objector to something or other, usually an existing system. If in fact he isn't the brightest individual and may be even dull, he may still be among the intellectuals of the sixties. A further characteristic is that he is respectful of platonic argument, and expects that others should be also. No collective bargainer who throws his power, influence, or strength into the argument, he gains his leverage from his willingness to object in oral or written form, expecting that this objection will be listened to for its moral content alone. The strength of the intellectual is the weight and credence placed upon his arguments by the hearer and not by his boycotts or force. Because he is almost always a moralist, his fervor and conviction give him importance, which cannot be ignored, regardless of his numbers or influence in worldly affairs.

If the ranks of intellectuals contain a few of lesser intelligence, the current definition of "intellectual"—which is perhaps more accurately described as "moralist"—does for the most part include persons above the average intelligence. It does not, however, automatically include all intelligent persons.

The campus intellectual indeed qualifies as being both intelligent and critical. And, of course, he is critical of business. He is opposed to profit and the profit motive. This is not merely a resistance to capitalism, and an attendant embrace of socialism or communism. In fact, he also attacks the "morbidity of profits" in the "emergence of modified-market principles in Russia and East Europe," known there as Libermanism. He views Russian economic planning and the American search for profits with the same distaste. To him, the motive for profit supplants the enjoyment and realities of life. He is apt to applaud Keynes' opinion that the love of money is "a somewhat disgusting morbidity, one of those semicriminal, semipathological propensities which one hands over with a shudder to the specialists in mental disease." Such views are perhaps more emotional than intellectual, but they nevertheless characterize the young intellectuals of the sixties and seventies.

Recently in the *Wall Street Journal*, Roger Rapoport reported the troubles Michigan State University encountered in its recruitment of National Merit Scholars, a vigorous campaign bringing 560 National Merit Scholars to East Lansing. Harvard, second best, caught only 425. But this intellectual èlite initiated and manned most of the dissent in East Lansing in the past few years. They picketed Vice President Humphrey, published a critical newspaper, and documented their own university's embroilment with the CIA in Vietnam. Again, brains seemed to lead to antiprofit behavior.

Intense competition in high school probably also contributes. National Merit Scholars are customarily those who have racked up the highest grades in high school in science and in accelerated math, in which they scoop the field on the National Merit Scholar Examinations. They work under an ungodly pressure in these two areas to prove that they are off-spring of superior parents and teachers. But once on campus, free of parents and teachers, they exploded into the new left and activist move-ment. Their first point of rebellion was often a resistance to soap and water. The second was to bite the hand that fed them. They denounced the auto companies and oil firms, while unfailingly cashing the checks sent by fathers who toil as middle managers and executives in the ranks of these outmoded institutions.

Perhaps this can explain the rather shoddy ideology of the new left. The campus radical of the thirties would be aghast at this unwashed, undisciplined, and obscure-minded crop. Where he would spend his nights mimeographing blasts for the trade unions, or the committee for the Spanish Civil War, his modern counterpart is an ideological illiterate. His fervor is at its best when he opposes something—Vietnam, auto-mobiles, autocratic management, and profits—which permits him to draw himself up majestically this side of suggesting anything constructive. When pressed for affirmatives, he falls back on platitudes: "Well, all I can say is unless these problems are solved, we cannot survive." Two verbalizations culminating in a dangling generalization are his stock in trade.

Not without a useful function in society, the critic, the gadfly, the questioner, and the doubter keep our civilization from pomposity, inflexi-bility, and complacency. The role of the serious critic becomes ever harder, and the dissenter today finds that he as well as his dissent is attacked. The price he pays for his moral posture—misguided or not—

is high in terms of personal comfort, and the comforts of neighborliness and gregariousness outside his group.

Do corporations need intellectuals? The answer is an emphatic "yea." It needs them outside of its own walls. It needs them off its own pay-rolls. It needs them free of its own golden handcuffs. The answer is also negative. It doesn't need them inside the corporate office. It doesn't need them on the salary and bonus rolls. It doesn't need them on the cadet-trainee roster. Such a setting would water them down, debilitate their critical powers, and diminish their voice to a pale bleat. They also make poor employees. The only value of the critic to the corporation lies in his independence, his ambiguous status. If the executives and staffers can figure out just where he fits in their hierarchy his value is gone; they have him pegged.

A corporation does better to invite in outsiders occasionally, gulp manfully, and invite them to blast away. Many of the things the executives will hear won't be pleasant, nor will they always be fair. The critic can't always understand why things have emerged as they have. He won't be able to see the inevitability of the decision. All he'll see is the absurd, the venal, the hurtful, and will point them up indignantly. As a mirror image, even a fun-house distortion of the truth, the critic makes his mark.

But among the intelligent nonintellectuals, corporations find their most valuable people. Skilled barbarians are not without their use. In fact, the corporation has become increasingly dependent upon brainy persons, but can still get along nicely without intellectuals of the moral-ist stripe on the payroll. On the other hand, the moralist and inde-pendent intellectual, located in editorial office, in university classroom, and in consulting office, is perfectly compatible and provides a useful service to the corporation, simply because of his intellectuality and his independence.

In fact, if corporations can dispose of the question of conformity and criticism, they will find that their recruiters have somewhat overstated their needs for intelligent people, let alone intellectuals. Reach out and pick a corporation—say the largest—General Motors. Its chairman, Mr. Roche, never went to college. The chief engineer of one of its largest divisions never went to college. Ninety percent of its 16,000 first-line supervisors are not college graduates. Eighty percent of its semiskilled factory employees have less than a high school education—they are dropouts. On the other hand, General Motors also employs many thou-sands of college graduates, and their General Motors Institute is an engineering school accredited to graduate schools around the world. In short, corporations both require higher education and can get along well without it. Many large corporations seek college graduates and many do not. The average IQ of executives is about 104, and the average

IQ of engineers and scientists is about 130, both working for the same organization.

For more than four decades now, a small band of sociologists, led by Lloyd Warner of Michigan State University, have analyzed the qualities that make the successful corporation executive.

Their first conclusion is that ability counts more than social background. The second is that a college education is now practically a necessity. Over 75 percent of today's corporate executives attended college and almost 20 percent had postgraduate education. The bulk of some 8,000 top managers graduated from a handful of colleges—including Yale, Harvard, Princeton, Illinois, Michigan, Chicago, Minnesota, California, Stanford, North Carolina, Texas, and New York University.

Yet the managers of tomorrow may not spring from the same roots as those of today. Forces are at work that may soon alter the portrait of the corporate manager, educated 40 years ago. Men who achieved power in the business world during the twenties were living in a very different world. For one thing, many more people are going to college today, and with backgrounds often different from the students of a generation ago. In 1928, for example, only eight percent of the sons of laborers went to college; in 1960, 34 percent. This "upward mobility" is especially important beyond the bachelor's degree.

Recently at The University of Michigan, we asked 105 company recruiters to identify the strongest and weakest candidates for managerial positions from among those interviewed. Those graduating with master's degrees rated nine to one better than the bachelor's candidates. Sons of laborers rated lower on the B.S. level, but equally at the M.A. level. The recruiters found the laborer's son less attractive at the B.S. level, not primarily because of his background, but because he lacked the requisite "maturity, poise, personality, and appearance." The advanced degree, which more and more students are acquiring, seems a clear avenue to higher levels of management.

A favorite game of business students is to pick the academic course most likely to lead to the top. Every time a controller steps into the presidency of a large firm, as happened recently in the automobile business, students are sure to rush into accounting classes. Actually, of course, there is no one route up the ladder, and managers are just as likely to enter the executive suite from a side door.

Engineers who reach the top at an early age attribute their accomplishment to the engineering mind they acquired at "good old Tech." Accountants, by and large, believe they can get to the top by entering a CPA firm and going into corporate life through the controller's route. Some very prominent firms are headed by lawyers who reached the top in their companies after having first acted as corporate counsels.

The electronics industry has its share of scientists who parlayed the brain power they applied to the creation of company products into the chief executive position. In at least two of the larger electronic firms, RCA and Westinghouse, the chief executive came in at the top from a large management-consulting firm that had advised the corporation. In some companies, the sales department has proved the best route; in others, the manufacturing department.

What, then, leads to success in business? Does a formula actually exist?

First we might consider the Horatio Alger model for success—a formula which became popular in the latter half of the 19th century. The typical Alger hero was a poor, uneducated youngster who, by dedicating himself to the aims of his betters and adopting the basic virtues of the 19th-century American morality, was able to rise through the ranks.

The Alger-hero's success was measured by the steepness of his ascent. There was always a tremendous contrast between his humble origins and his final arrival among the tuxedos and evening gowns. The plucky shoeshine boy could eventually establish his own dynasty. Thus, the institutions of property and family were happily linked with equalitarian democracy.

Much of America's economic growth can indeed be attributed to family solidarity, which still contributes something to the image of success. But little similarity remains between Algers' formula and modern requirements for success in the business world. The owner-manager is a dying breed, and family ownership of corporations is increasingly rare. The new corporate managers soon found it neither natural nor appropriate to imitate the old-time family-capitalists.

Managerial success became associated more and more with the performance of the corporation itself, and less with the old symbols of family capitalism—such as wearing an opera cape or having a chauffeur. The job became its own measure of success and high pay. Large but functional offices, expense accounts, a company plane, and a company lodge became the symbols of success. The shoeshine boy now worked his way through the Massachusetts Institute of Technology or the Wharton School; the rich but kindly gentlemen in the hansom now became the company recruiter who offered him a job at $750 a month in an interview at the campus placement office. Once employed, his ascent through the organization was unrelated to his appreciation of fine wines.

Thus, the new model for executive success became more complex and more diverse with the decline of family capitalism and the emergence of the managerial society. Joseph Schumpeter, perhaps the best theoretician of the new capitalism, emphasized the *productive* aspects of our new economic system as it emerged. He felt that productivity, engendered by the businessman's innovation, would bring continuous economic growth. This in itself drastically altered the picture of the business leader. The creative leader must now adapt his own particular personal qualities to the situation and to his followers.

Do corporations have anything for intelligent people? The idea that corporations are so monolithic and uniform that they need a single kind of employee is obviously out of touch with the realities of corporate life. Some corporate jobs, despite automation and the computer, are still routine and repetitive. Other jobs call for great problem-solving skills and technical knowledge. A few call for higher levels of invention and innovation, and the introduction of change. All of these can be attractive to different populations, and the matter is more one of effective placement than of hiring college graduates for every vacancy.

Staffing Routine Jobs. Automation, mechanization, and instrumentation have gone far toward eliminating monotony, but not completely. Approximately 25 million persons work for a living doing repetitive, simple tasks. They keep mechanical processing equipment fed; they turn knobs and press buttons in well-defined patterns; they wire and solder, and assemble small parts—jobs for which the mentally retarded have proven adequate. As data-processing has mechanized paperwork, the number of machine-paced clerical jobs has increased; and, as Leonard Rico has shown, a mechanized office is like a factory. Coffee-breaks are tightly scheduled, absenteeism becomes a more serious matter, and human performance is paced by the computer. "Dull world? Never for me," declares Robert O. Anderson, chairman of the Atlantic Richmond Company, speaking of his corporate work. But Mr. Anderson is not confronted with ten years of sitting eight hours a day twirling dials on a console for an alcohol plant, or feeding tops into a machine filling quarts of oil. The danger is not that persons of lesser intelligence will be bored by simple work, but that corporations will "overhire" engineers and accountants and expect them to find zest where none is to be found. Such placements cause college recruits to leave their first job after a few months, so reports the College Placement Council.

The corporation offers the intelligent person more in its market research, operations research, industrial engineering, labor relations, and human relations—among the most fascinating jobs in business. Genuine wisdom is often called for, and the rewards are high. Making decisions and solving problems, where the effects of the choices soon become apparent—sometimes painfully so—makes for interesting and challenging work. But the interest and challenge stay keen only so long as some novelty remains and new skills can be developed and applied. Short bursts of intelligence amid long drills of routine are the usual demands upon the intelligent person, who may succumb to the lure of the routine and become apathetic and lose his edge, and his value to himself and to the corporation.

But we frequently overlook the opportunities for problem solving in many of the skilled jobs and craft. In their haste to push children into the middle class, parents often downgrade the intelligence required of the machinist, tool-and-die maker, plumber, or millwright because getting one's hands dirty is socially less acceptable than wearing a white collar. The carpenter, the mason, the bricklayer, and even the truck driver, often finds the satisfaction of problem solving in his work, although with *things* rather than concepts, which our culture tends to value higher. Many a bored clerk or computer programmer might have spent creative years building homes, or machines, or the things that make up our standard of living, using both his brains and his hands.

Opportunities for genuine innovation are relatively rare in corporations. Innovative ability is coupled with the authority to make changes only at the top of the firm, except for few staff positions. And even with these, the individual effect is concealed under a welter of procedures, approvals, and controls necessary to hold the organization together.

These jobs are not open to beginners, nor to all who seek them arduously, unless they start their own business and elect themselves president. Here, the innovation is that of creating *an organization* where none or little existed. The excitement of building a group of people into a joint endeavor is the main satisfaction for many in management, as statements of chief executives in *Time Magazine* show. The absolute satisfaction of being top man is one that makes the hours, the frustrations, the disappointments, and the guilt at failure seem trivial by comparison. The pleasure is sufficiently great to block out the truth that not everyone lower down in the organization enjoys the same heady sensations. General managers in divisionalized firms, sales managers of autonomous territories, and plant managers of geographically separated plants often find the same kinds of satisfaction in their work, as in the military, the company commander of infantry separated from the tight control of regiment and battalion. Each has freedom to express himself through building an organization and using it to achieve objectives largely of his own choosing.

Being a staff *systems maker* has many of the same kinds of satisfaction in handling matters logically, collecting facts, relating them into meaningful wholes, and lending order to potential chaos. The accountant, the engineer, the personnel manager, the lawyer, the public-relations programmer, the traffic manager, and the purchasing agent have such opportunities for innovative intelligence. Changing an accounting system may substantially affect the lives and behavior of thousands. The personnel man who generates policies for hiring, training, appraisal, promotion, and payment can see tangible improvements in orderliness and achievement from his application of intelligence.

The things that concern the campus intellectual seldom receive more than flickering attention from the corporation man who is engrossed in innovation and solving problems. He seldom asks the overall purpose of the firm, or how it may conflict with other values. The simple pursuit of goals to which one has made commitments to a senior whose opinion he respects is far stronger than generalized sentimental values received from the outside. Making bathtubs, or cereal, or selling life insurance is only a means to more generalized values, which the tightly focussed application of intelligence toward specific goals tends to play down. Yesterday's campus radical finds that beating Chrysler to the market with a new kind of Ford is enough of a challenge without assuming larger sentimental responsibilities. This is both the genius and the weakness of corporations in attracting and using intelligent people. They may become so preoccupied with immediate targets that they lose sight of social values, and are in turn denounced by the next generation of campus radicals. The disengaged critic, not caught in the heady game of chasing objectives for the firm, not finding his abilities used and challenged, merely sees the venal and the invidious, without understanding its devotees' enthusiasm for corporate endeavors.

Intelligent people enjoy the application of their intelligence, and the skills they have acquired. They will continue to utilize them with enjoyment until they have perfected them. And corporations evidently provide such opportunities. Most people who work for corporations enjoy their work, as the surveys show, and people at higher levels find their work more satisfying than those lower down. The higher levels also find more frustrations in their work. A study by Gurin Veroff and Feld showed that 35 percent of college graduates are "very satisfied" with their jobs, and another 41 percent were "satisfied." Among the highly satisfied were more college graduates than high-school or grade-school people. Evidently the corporations can satisfy the intelligent ego.

What, then, should the presidents say in their gigantic sales-pitch to the campus critics? Perhaps they should first examine their policies to make sure that their internal practices do not repell the college grad while they are persuading him on the pages of *Time*. Here are some suggestions:

1. *Don't overhire.* The present tendency to collect engineers, accountants, and other college-trained persons for every staff and managerial job is a costly error. Nothing repels the young graduate engineer more than a job that could be done by a high school graduate. If the company has no job for his abilities, don't hire him.
2. *Provide opportunities to feel adequate.* In placing intelligent people, give them challenges that tax intelligence but permit success. The firms most successful in employing brains, including AT&T,

General Motors, and Ford, have found that the challenge of a real job, with results expected, is more effective than a babying through a series of "experiences" that train but never test.

3. *Set objectives early.* Before the highly intelligent person is hired at all, define for him the results expected—not merely the activities. These should be specific, complete, and under the control of the individual. If learning new things is part of the early objectives, state this as a program. If the results are to be in production, or in revenue, or in tasks to be achieved, spell these out before the final offer. The objectives should be tough and should induce a certain amount of creative uncertainty in the individual as to whether he can measure up.

4. *Arrange for constant feedback of success or failure.* As he works, he should be able to measure his progress toward the goals set. He should gain constant knowledge of what a good job and a bad job is, and thus measure his own successes and failures while he is working at the job. This can be supplemented by the usual periodic reviews with a boss or counselor, if they are additive of the many small targets he has been seeking along the way.

5. *Make all systems work to rewarding excellence.* Supplant "automatic" salary increases with rewards for performance—in salary, bonus, or promotion. Both performance and satisfaction in it will be greater.

6. *Let him sort himself out.* Intelligent people will find different levels of achievement and effort. Some will seek out the innovative levels; others will settle for a comfortable shelf where the innovation is minimal. Make clear that the lower levels are those of routine —which must be well done, however trivial—and the highest levels are those of problem solving and innovation. Watch for indications of ability to function at the next higher level. The person will probably determine his own level by criteria other than intelligence, such as willingness to pay the price. Forcing people beyond their depth too early can lead to failure.

The experience of professional football teams in using college talent provides a lesson for the employers of intelligence. Some of the more highly-touted stars never get off the bench because they never get responsible assignments. Some recruits well down in the draft turn out to be stars because they have been at the right place at the right time. Almost uniformly, they all want to play. Perhaps the intelligent college graduate today is just expressing a desire to be where the action is. As a Peace Corps volunteer, or a second lieutenant of Marines, he finds it. If the puzzled company presidents can arrange their policies and placement procedures so that the recruits get where the action is, they can give up their new campaign. The answer lies inside the firms, not outside. Perhaps that is the place for the chairman of the board to look first.

QUESTIONS AND PROBLEMS

1. What would you say were the major differences between the Yippies of the seventies and the Black Panthers? What likenesses?

2. Describe the conditions which seem to exist as a precondition to an urban population engaging in violent riots.

3. Interview an officer of a local minority group organization, such as NAACP, Urban League, etc., and determine his opinion as to whether or not such conditions exist in his community.

4. "The Government itself is so firmly insistent upon maintaining the merit system of appointments that it is in fact discriminatory against minorities." Would you agree or disagree? What are the two sides of the case?

5. Review the history of industry hiring "unqualified employees" during the manpower shortages of World War II. What would be the conclusion you might draw about hiring unemployables today? Has anything changed? Have such changes been sufficiently large to change the credentials required for employability?

6. What are some of the tensions you could picture between the young turks and the old guard in employee ranks in a firm?

7. Would you agree with McMurry's statement that the best managers of the future will be those who are "hungry?"

8. What difference does it make for personnel practices whether or not a firm emphasizes educational background in promoting managers?

9. "Overhiring is a common form of misplacement of newly hired people." Could you think of some examples where this might have happened in your experience?

10. What kind of program would you suggest for a firm to make the work inside the company attractive to intellectuals?

11. Prepare role playing assignments showing how an interview might look in which the following situation occurs: a personnel manager for a large corporation must tell a middle aged man that he is to be passed over for promotion because he did not obtain a college degree. He has been an excellent performer, and has completed all but eight credits for his degree. Assign the roles and direct the skit. What could be learned from this?

THE NU BANK CASE

After his discharge from the Navy in August, 1960, Jonathan Cox Tweed, III, applied for a job in the credit department of the Nu Bank, one of the larger banks of Central City, an important Midwestern financial center. During his initial interview with the personnel director, Mr. Reynard, Jonathan was told that the bank had a formal training program and that soon the credit department would begin its program, which consisted of lectures, case studies, and outside assignments. Later in the day, Jonathan talked with several of the younger loan officers, who explained the internal workings of the bank. All expressed enthusiasm for their work and loyalty to the bank. Moreover, they assured him that he would be happy if he accepted the job. In the final interview, Mr. Reynard told Jonathan that the bank's training program was one of the best in the country. Two weeks later, Jonathan began his new job with enthusiasm and high expectations.

Prior to his new employment, Jonathan had served a three-year hitch as a navy supply officer aboard the U.S.S. Gut Bucket in the Atlantic. His resumé showed that he was graduated from Stanford University in 1954 with honors in Classical Studies. Between graduation and his naval duty, Jonathan had worked for one of the largest commercial banks on Wall Street. While with this bank, he had completed the six-month advanced training program for college graduates, done special work as an installment loan representative, compiled a constructive critique of the bank's advanced training program, and spent about six months in the credit department. The critique of the training program was done in conjunction with three contemporaries and at the request of a personal friend, who was a senior member of the top-management group. The credit department training program was to last approximately two and a half years and consisted of many special lectures and classes, case studies, and on-the-job assistance from the department head or one of his assistants. The areas covered were statement analysis, working capital loans, secured loans, term loans, finance company loans, and foreign loans. However, before Jonathan could complete the entire program he began his naval career at Newport.

The credit department at the Nu Bank consisted of Assistant Vice President I. M. Rock, two elderly senior clerks who assisted Mr. Rock, and Miss Medulla, who supervised training and credit analysis. She had nearly 20 years of analytical experience. There were 12 senior analysts and 12 junior analysts, all of whom were located in the same large work area as Mr. Rock and his staff.

As an introduction to the department, A.V.P. Rock told Jonathan that he could expect an accelerated tour in the department since he had previous training.

MR. ROCK: I expect that within about two and a half years you should be moving across to the platform since your training time will be less than for most of the boys. As a starter, why don't you begin spreading statements, and then after a couple of weeks we'll move you to analysis.

JONATHAN: Fine. Where will I sit?

After agreeing upon this program, Jonathan was introduced to each member of the department and anyone who happened to be visiting it at that time.

That afternoon Jonathan was told how to spread a statement according to the bank's established system. Within several days he had memorized the 60-odd marking lines and knew reasonably well what went where. For the next three months Jonathan marked statements. Frequently, however, much of his time was spent reading the department's copy of THE WALL STREET JOURNAL, for this was the slack season and there were few statements to mark. On several occasions during this period he asked Mr. Rock when he was scheduled to begin his analytical training. To this Mr. Rock usually replied, "As soon as Miss Medulla has a free moment she'll explain the procedure to you and the two other new boys."

Several weeks later when looking for work, Jonathan was told to go over to the supervisor's desk as she wanted to talk with him. The ensuing conversation revolved around the spreading procedure and future plans for analytical training. Beginning the following Monday, Jonathan and the other two newcomers would start the analytical phase of their training.

On Monday, when the three trainees gathered around Miss Medulla's desk, she greeted them and said, "Why don't you have some coffee first?" After the coffee break, Miss Medulla told the trainees she could not talk to them.

MISS MEDULLA: I can't talk to you now since I've just been given a rush analysis to do. Go back to your spreading and I'll call you when I get a free moment.

Towards the end of the week the trainees were summoned over to her desk for a preliminary introduction to analysis.

MISS MEDULLA: The Nu Bank has a very high set of standards with regard to whom we extend credit. We just don't make loans to anyone wanting credit. Also, our analysis follows a definite format. You can begin your training by reading through these five files. Pay particular attention to the analyses, and I expect that most of your questions will answer themselves.

The reading period lasted three weeks, and then there was another conference. At this time, each trainee was given an analysis to do. One of the other trainees protested, "But where do we begin? Aren't you going to explain the analysis to us?" To this Miss Medulla replied, "No, here we believe in the 'sink or swim' approach. Besides, you can learn more from your mistakes than my telling you how to do it."

Jonathan wrote the analysis in general conformance to the prescribed method, but there were overtones of his previous training. Miss Medulla, after reading the analysis, made the following comments.

"Jonathan, here we always refer to the acid test, not 'cash, securities, and receivables to current liabilities.' Also, we never refer to a firm's liquidity as such, but rather it's 'margin of creditors' protection.' Why have you omitted the receivables to days' sales ratio?"

At this point, he began to question her as to why such language must be used when everybody knew the meaning of his statements and why such ratios were to be included when they were insignificantly small. In this conversation, he cited his past experience and the method of his former employer as a basis for his work and decisions. Miss Medulla concluded the conversation by saying, "Well, we do it differently here, and I don't want you to question my reasons."

Much perplexed and concerned about this situation, Jonathan returned to his desk and rewrote the analysis. He was bothered by the need to use only certain phrases. He also was puzzled as to just what to include in future analyses. At the same time, the other two trainees were struggling with their respective assignments, for neither had any prior training, nor any formal education in accounting, although both were taking accounting courses at night school.

As a supplement to his training, Jonathan was enrolled in the N.C.O. correspondence course. He protested by saying that he had completed a more comprehensive course elsewhere and that the N.C.O. course was merely repetitious. His arguments did not prevail, and Mr. Rock mailed his enrollment. Other members of the department sympathized.

Scott Drake: The course is an absolute waste of time, but you'd better do what 'The Rock' wants. It's really designed for high school graduates, but C'est la guerre! Here are my answers. Go ahead and use them; no one who has taken this course ever did any work.

Throughout the next month an acute tension built up between Miss Medulla and Jonathan. He felt that if the basic philosophy behind the bank's approach had been explained, he would have been able to see why certain things were done and that this knowledge would make his work more meaningful. With the approach of the rush season in mid-February the situation was much the same; however, prior to this time Jonathan had been told by one of the senior clerks not to challenge the authority of Miss Medulla.

JONATHAN: I only want to know why I am doing things the way I am told to do them. After all, should not the training program be informative, as well as instructive?

In April at the peak of the rush season, Jonathan was assigned to the finance company desk. He was delighted to be assigned permanently to one area, but at the same time he had misgivings since he had had no training in finance company analyses. Subsequently, he expressed his concern to Miss Medulla, but she told him not to worry since he would surely learn the job in due time. However, this did not satisfy him.

JONATHAN: Well, then what's the primary purpose of the credit department? Is it not to provide analytical service to the loan officers, as well as train the future officers of the bank?

MISS MEDULLA: I don't know. My job is to see that the analyses are written, and written the way the department wants them.

JONATHAN: In that case, wouldn't it be wise to have a booklet describing the aim of the department and the why and wherefores of our work? Wouldn't this reduce your training burden?

MISS MEDULLA: Certainly not! We don't want anything written, for that implies permanency.

JONATHAN: But . . . .

MISS MEDULLA: Jonathan! Don't challenge me. I'll do my job the way I see fit!

Shortly thereafter Jonathan submitted his resignation, which was not well received by Mr. Rock. When asked why he was resigning, Jonathan said, "I want a broader background." To this Mr. Rock replied, "Why don't you go to night school?"

JONATHAN: I am, but under the circumstances I can get more for my money by going to school full time. Why doesn't the bank reimburse us for our night schooling; the other banks do.

At the termination interview, Mr. Reynard talked to Jonathan about the chances of the Twins winning the pennant and his future plans.

Group discussion question

What problems do you see here? What solutions?

PART III

The service and control outputs of the personnel department

RESEARCH IS one kind of output for personnel departments, service is another. We'll deal with the major services and controls produced by the personnel department for line, staff, and executive departments in this section. Services and controls fit well into the management by objectives framework, even though they are often intangible and nonhardware. Such outputs can be described in unit terms. It includes placements, classes, reports, records, and cases completed. It includes such outputs as are customarily produced in employment, training, and other managerial services such as benefits, food services, blood banks, and suggestion awards.

The remaining section of the book which follows will be devoted to other forms of output: the advice kinds of outputs.

chapter 12

THE CREDENTIALS REVOLUTION – SELECTION BY OBJECTIVES

WHEN GRANDFATHER was discharged from the army in 1918 the chances were that he could find a job without having more than a grammar school education. In many occupations, primarily day laborer, he could indeed find employment if he could physically handle the job, and mark an X on the payroll next to his name. Large numbers of workers were foreign born and in many instances illiterate in both their native language and in English.

At the upper levels of education a small percentage of the population had college degrees. These were ordinarily from middle and upper classes, were more likely to be children of professional persons, or other managerial or wealthy parents. Not only because they had such education, but because they had been reared with the assumption of positions comparable to their parents, they tended to move rather quickly to the top in their social standing and economic holdings. As the corporation emerged as the dominant form of economic organization, this led to the emergence of a new kind of tycoon. He was the individual who managed that which he did not own, but wielded more power than the lords and leaders of individual holdings of the past ever dreamed of. The system of selection which ranked people from top manager (the elite) down through the common laborer in the process adopted many of the credentials which had been used for joining the membership of the landed aristocracy in Europe, or the upper middle class in the 19th century America.

By 1955 numerous scientific studies of the occupational and personal backgrounds of the dominant business leaders showed that two major types emerged:

1. The birth elite, whose ascendency was based upon a form of family capitalism. America's large corporations were for the most part not in this category, but a number of dramatic examples, including Ford Motor Company, and most big-city retail stores were in the hands of a birth elite.

2. The managerial elite was more apt to be comprised of men whose mobility was more important to their rise than their lineage. It was this second category which is most important in studying today's problems in selection criteria.[1]

While the effects of the selection procedures for managerial ranks were well researched for the 8,500 leading corporate chief executives, it was less well understood how this policy for choice of the top leaders affected lesser ranks. Yet the effect was direct and closely related in a causal fashion.

The manner in which the top executives were selected determined the mobility of younger men through the hierarchy, and functioned to determine who would start at the bottom of the ladder and even be excluded from employment altogether in the corporation.

The evolution of the corporate selection system was an evolving process which led to severe difficulties in the seventies both inside the corporation and in the society around it. Having begun with an adopted assumption from an earlier time when the birth elite were destined for the top ranks, the criteria for selection of a managerial elite evolved with the tacit assumption built into policy and procedure that the same criteria for the former would serve for the latter. This criteria development came about through the growth of employment officers and personnel managers, the rising use of psychological testing for selection, and the adaptation of all of these influences toward perpetuating or creating the same kinds of people in managerial elite as populated the leadership posts in the birth elite. Education of itself was primary, and the construction and validation of psychological tests was systematically, if unconsciously, biased in favor of the educated with values and manners of the birth elite.

In recent years the rising trend toward emphasizing what a person produces rather than what he has been in the past has been slow in arriving, and resisted at every step.

---

[1] The major sources of data in this and following discussions of Executive Mobility are drawn from W. Lloyd Warner and James Abegglen, *Big Business Leaders in America* (New York, 1955), and Warner and Abegglen, *Occupational Mobility in American Business and Industry 1929–1952* (Minneapolis, 1955). Also, Eugene E. Jennings, *The Mobile Executive* (Ann Arbor, Michigan: Bureau of Industrial Relations, University of Michigan, 1968).

The criteria for defining successful managers

During the decade of the sixties, the author conducted a continuing research study into the criteria which present managers in American industry (with some small samples from foreign managers) use to identify the difference between excellence in management and unsatisfactory performance in management. The procedures of the investigation were briefly as follows. Groups of managers attending executive development programs at universities and associations (a bias in favor of successful firms) were asked to make free response on a questionnaire with two headings:

Column 1	*Column 2*
In this column please list a few characteristic words or phrases which best describe and explain why successful managers are successful.	In this column please list a few characteristic words or phrases which best describe and explain why unsuccessful managers are unsuccessful.

The responses, without further suggestions from the researcher were classified, and it was discovered that they could be grouped into four major categories.

1. Personal preference explanations: Words or phrases such as likable, friendly, warm, human, compatible, and the like were classified here.

2. Psychological properties of the individual: This included words which could sensibly be considered to be traits which were relatively fixed, changeable only by therapy, surgery, or similar traumatic occurrence to the individual. They included such words as initiative, drive, intelligence, loyalty, aptitude for figures, and the like.

3. The behavioral or skill explanation: In this category were placed those words or phrases which describe specific behaviors, using B. F. Skinner's definition of behavior as "activity which can be seen or measured." This would include personal skills such as reading, writing, speaking, and also the complex chaning of behaviors into managerial skills such as organizing, planning, and controlling.

4. Background kinds of explanation. These included words which described the successful man's education, perhaps with details about major areas of study, grades, college or university attended, and other things which would ordinarily be historical to the man and perhaps his ancestors.

As the following table shows, the total of all responses indicates the following about present methods of selection.

1. Overt use of background and degrees as a selection criteria comprises 11 percent among the sample of middle managers polled.

2. Personality or other psychological properties comprised 27 percent of the criteria suggested by the managers.

3. Skills and behavior exhibited comprised 42 percent of the criteria suggested by the managers.

4. Personal preference adjectives were displayed less frequently but comprised 5 percent. This may in part be attributable to a reluctance to state such criteria, or to the fact that often they are unconscious with the person who holds them most deeply.

TABLE 12–1
Explanation of managerial success and failure by American managers during the 1960's

Proposed Criteria	Number of Respondents	Responses	Percent of Responses
Personality	990	3051	27%
Background	580	1243	11
Skills	1410	4746	42
Goals-results	530	1605	15
Personal preference	140	575	5
Total	3650	11,300	100%

Perhaps the most significant finding was the relatively small percentage of managers who define goals-setting and achieving results against those goals as significant criteria for executive success or failure.

Interpretation of these data must take into consideration this unconscious bias. Yet we might note that background seems to be stated as equal to results achieved in success. We might also observe that both the psychological properties stated as essential in the successful and absent in the unsuccessful are strongly biased in favor of the college graduate who is also a middle class person. It might also be charged that the listing of skills, such as communication skills, organizing skills, decision-making skills, is part of the curriculum objectives of colleges of business and engineering, and the skills are the substance of many company management development courses.

The credentials revolution, it is suggested, will drastically alter many of our standards for joining the managerial elite. In the process of making such changes, we will also affect the criteria for employability at the lowest levels of education and social origin. How would such a system operate?

SELECTION BY OBJECTIVES *

The foreman of a gang of lumberjacks was being solicited for a job by a rather spindly-looking little man. The giant gang-boss scoffed: "Why, this work would kill you. Just to show you what I mean, why don't you take this ax and go chop down that giant fir?"

Despite the grins of the regular crew, the little man approached the tree and with a quick flurry of blows had the giant conifer on the ground. The grins turned to whistles of awe, and the foreman's voice took on a tone of respect.

"Holy Mackeral, fella, that's great! Where did you learn to chop down trees like that?"

"I worked on the Sahara forest job."

"Forest? I thought the Sahara was a desert."

"*Now* it is."

This tale might be an illustration of how selection by objectives would look in the lumbering business. No personality tests, no aptitude tests, little concern about degrees held. Just a good record of having achieved good results in the past and an on-the-spot demonstration of some of the key behavior which might be required on the job ahead.

The entire matter of employment methods is under serious fire from a number of quarters, and perhaps a new approach to the selection of persons for employment, or for promotion—which is really internal selection—is indicated.

What's wrong with present selection methods?

The major shortcomings of present-day selection methods seem to fall into these major categories.

Techniques are mainly for low level workers. Since Hugo Munsterberg and others about 60 years ago seriously undertook the study of employment testing, the major emphasis has been upon the selection of workers.[2] The problems of early identification of high-talent manpower, and the techniques for hiring and promoting managers, engineers, and staff persons are different and at this stage very problematical.[3]

---

[2] Hugo Munsterberg, *Psychology of Industrial Efficiency* (Boston: Houghton Mifflin, 1913).

[3] Joseph Dooher and Elizabeth Mauting, *Selection of Management Personnel* (New York: American Management Association, 1957), Vol. 1. Thomas A. Mahoney, Thomas H. Jerdee, and Allen N. Nash, *The Identification of Management Potential* (Dubuque: Wm. C. Brown, Co., 1961).

* Adapted from an article of the same title by G. S. Odiorne and E. L. Miller, originally published in *Management of Personnel Quarterly* (Fall, 1966). Used by permission.

Psychological testing has come under serious fire. From within the profession and from outside, numerous attacks have been leveled at psychological tests.[4] They comprise an invasion of privacy, some hold. They have logical improprieties, say others. They breed conformity, say still others. Whatever the merits of these charges, the effect nonetheless has been to cast a cloud over their use in selection. A small fringe of charlatans promising psychological miracles in a manner akin to the snake oil peddlers of old have not done much to clarify the issues.

The civil rights laws have shaken many long-accepted practices. The civil rights law of 1964 has shaken traditional employment practices seriously.[5] Not only are racial guidelines to hiring barred, but women are protected from discrimination in hiring and promotion because of sex.

The mad rush is to college graduates. Despite a rapidly rising curve of enrollments in the colleges, the rush at the exit door of the institutions of higher learning is greater.[6] Surely one of the most bizarre and absurd fads ever to sweep industry, the clamor to collect degree holders for every white collar position shows no sign of abatement. There is apparently little inkling of manpower planning to identify which job requires a degree and which one doesn't.

While all of these shortcomings could be expanded at length, and the list itself lengthened, they comprise typical evidence of the illness that presently besets the hiring and promotion process.

This chapter outlines a *new approach* to the selection process. It makes a quick tour of the four major methods now being used in selection, then turns to a more detailed explanation of a new—or fifth—approach to selection. The purpose isn't to deny the value of the four, but to place them in a new perspective and improve the effectiveness with which they are used.

The proposal is based on experiments done in industrial and governmental organizations in applying the system of management by objectives to the selection process. The method described here thus becomes *Selection by Objectives.*

The approach presumes that the first step in management is to establish objectives and to obtain commitments in advance to seek them.[7] It also presumes that the person who has achieved objectives consistently in the

---

[4] William H. Whyte, Jr., *The Organization Man* (New York: Simon and Schuster, 1956).

[5] Howard C. Lockwood, "Critical Problems in Achieving Equal Employment Opportunity," *Personnel Psychology*, XIX (Spring, 1966), pp. 3–10. A. G. Bayroff, "Test Technology and Equal Employment Opportunity," *Personnel Psychology*, XIX (Spring, 1966), pp. 35–39.

[6] John S. Fielden, "The Right Young People for Business," *Harvard Business Review*, XLIV (March-April, 1966), pp. 76–83.

[7] George S. Odiorne, *Management by Objectives* (New York: Pitman Publishing Corp., 1965). Edward C. Schleh, *Management by Results* (New York: McGraw-Hill Book Co., 1961).

past is more likely to achieve them in new situations. It is further proposed that these selection criteria have primacy over testing, hunch, behavioral inventories, or background. Thus, the major purpose of selection procedures should be to uncover evidences of achievements against objectives in the past.

/ Personnel staffing decisions are gambles in much the same way that a decision to bet on a particular horse is a gamble. Both decisions are based on predictions of performance among alternative choices. Predictions of the future are estimates or expectations based upon observations of past and present achievements and the known or assumed relationship between these observations and future wants.[8] For the horseplayer, prediction of the outcome of a race might be based in part on such variables as ancestry of the horse, performance in previous outings, current times, and physical condition of the horse and the jockey. For the manager involved in personnel staffing decisions, the prediction of a candidate's performance will be based upon observations of variables believed to be associated with or determinative of the desired level of future performance. In either case, the horseplayer or the manager is seeking to identify the winner. Needless to say, there are many poor choices and many disappointed people.

Employment managers and supervisors have always concerned themselves with trying to identify the best man for the job. Typically the supervisor makes his decision based upon his ability to size-up a man. In far too many instances, this method has led to failure and unsatisfactory performance. Errors in personnel staffing decisions can be costly mistakes. For the individual poorly placed, his inability to perform his work competently, and the consequent prospect of reprimand or dismissal can lead to his frustration and possible personal bodily harm. For the company, mistakes in personnel staffing decisions frequently lead to increased expense to the business in terms of recruiting, selection, training, and production. Although major stages in the development of a scientific approach to selection are well-known, the objectives-results approach—tried experimentally by the authors (and on a tentative and sometimes unconscious basis in many places)—has not to their knowledge been consciously described. Such a description of the Fifth Approach is the purpose of this article.

The four approaches to selection now in use

The systems of selection used to date have fallen into four major categories, described here in summary form. These selection techniques are based upon the major presumptions of the person applying them.

---

[8] Marvin D. Dunnette and Wayne K. Kirchner, *Psychology Applied to Industry* (New York: Appleton-Century-Crofts, 1965).

1. The personal preference method. This is still the most commonly-used method, even when disguised by the apparatus of science; the hunch of the manager, his biases, or his likes and dislikes determine the selection of employees.

2. The occupational characteristics approach. Earliest of the scientifically based methods, this method applied aptitude measurements to applicants, and allowed one to attempt to predict success on the job.

3. The behavioral approach. Another scientific approach to selection of employees was that of identifying behavior patterns out of the past, and predicting that such behavior (as demonstrated in tests or verified through resumé and reference checks) would continue into the future. With these results matched against job requirements, success could be predicted.

4. The background approach. The fourth method is evidenced most strongly in the career pattern studies of Warner and Abblegen, and evidenced by the search for college graduates in campus recruiting. It presumes that successful managers and professionals can best be selected by studying the careers of the already successful, and hiring those who best seem to duplicate them.

The fifth approach. What is suggested here is that a new approach is now possible, synthesizing the useful features of the others plus an important new addition, a new point of origin for selection. Because it proposes to supplant the others, and in fact has proven more successful where applied, a brief review of each of the former four methods is in order.

The personal preference method. The proprietary right of an owner to make the decisions about who shall be hired and who shall not be hired to work in his business grows out of the property rights of ownership. If the small merchant or manufacturer decides to hire only members of his own lodge, church, or family, there are few constraints upon his doing so. Title VII of the Civil Rights Act of 1964, if applicable to him, theoretically limits his exercise of this right in the public interest. Clearly he cannot flout the law openly, but his preference may lead him to the creation of standards which make the law ineffective while serving his preferential biases. The administration of the law in future years may corner him in these subterfuges, although at present the strong voluntary compliance aspects of the law can leave him relatively untouched. Since many of his biases are unconscious—and hotly denied if pointed out—they are difficult to eradicate from outside the firm. Kahn's studies of the employment of Jews,[9] and the open challenging of tests in the Motorola decision on the basis of their "culture biased"

---

[9] Robert Kahn *et al.*, *Discrimination Without Prejudice* (Institute for Social Research Center, University of Michigan) (Ann Arbor, 1964).

aspects illustrate the tacit application of how bias might be used or alleged.

These personal preferences originate in the emotions and sentiments of the employer and extend from hiring alumni to Zulus simply because the employer feels the way he does about the people he wants around.

The internal characteristics approach. Since psychologists are usually the only professionals qualified to devise and validate tests of psychological characteristics, it is not surprising that testing of various kinds has all of the strengths and limitations of psychology itself as a science. In recent years, this approach has come under fire for a variety of reasons. Writers of a moralist type have written with great fervor about the invasion of privacy which attends testing. By selecting questions out of the body of extensive test batteries, congressional committees and critical writers have generated righteous wrath. "Did you ever want to kill your father?" for example, reads poorly when it becomes a headline in a Washington newspaper. Martin Gross, Vance Packard, and others have attacked the indignities which occur when psychologists pry.[10] Other criticisms have come from within the profession itself. Logical improprieties in testing are often discussed in professional journals. Still other critics have been behavioral scientists who have queried the scientific propriety of some testing methods.[11] As a result, it is now forbidden in government agencies to use personality tests upon job applicants, and this ban has recently been extended to government contractors by letter sent to all such contractors. Not totally banned, the list of limits placed upon their use has been sufficiently complicated that the actual effect will be a falling off of this kind of testing.

Two families of tests. The purpose here isn't to outline the varieties of tests and their advantages and disadvantages; the aim is to outline only the objectives of tests which comprise the "inward characteristics" approach to selection. Achievement tests would not fall into this approach, since they measure demonstrable behavior being observed, but two others do: aptitude and personality tests.

Aptitude tests. Because of the magnitude of the wastes and losses in selection there has arisen a more and more insistent demand to reduce errors in staffing decisions. It is this necessity that has given rise to aptitude prediction by means of testing. At the present, various kinds of psychological tests are the chief means for making aptitude prognosis.

Testing in all applied sciences is performed on the basis of samples, and human aptitude testing is not essentially different from the applica-

---

[10] Vance Packard, *The Pyramid Climbers* (New York: McGraw-Hill Book Co., 1962), pp. 279–85. Martin Gross, *The Brain Watchers* (New York: Random House, 1962).

[11] Harry Levinson, "The Psychologist in Industry," *Harvard Business Review,* XXXVII (September-October, 1959), pp. 93–99.

tion of tests in other sciences. The thing sampled in aptitude tests is, in most cases, human behavior. Specifically, a psychological test is the measurement of some phase of a carefully chosen sample of an individual's behavior from which extrapolations and inferences are made. Measuring differences among people through the use of psychological tests has made a signal advance to understanding and predicting human behavior.

In its simplest terms, aptitude testing rests on a correlational relationship between a normally distributed predictor variable (which may or may not be related to the skills and abilities required on the job) on the one hand, and another normally distributed measure of satisfactory performance on the other hand.[12] The simple matching task is to eliminate, on the basis of the relatively inexpensive predictor variable, those individuals with little likelihood of success on the job—obviously an easy task in theory but beset by complexities in practice.

The conception of specialized aptitudes and the desirability of having tests of behavior which will indicate in advance latent capacity has its roots in ancient history. Over 23 hundred years ago, Plato proposed a series of tests for the guardians of his ideal republic. His proposal was realized in the United States Army mental tests of World War I.

The use of tests to measure aptitudes didn't receive much interest until the late 19th century when a number of psychologists became interested in mental testing and the psychology of individual differences.[13] The tests of the early aptitude psychologists were largely individual tests. This approach changed with the advent of World War I. Based on the pioneering work of A. S. Otis, a set of tests which not only could be administered to a large number of subjects at the same time but could be scored by semi-mechanical means appeared on the scene.[14] Nearly 2 million army recruits were tested, and aptitude testing on a group basis was born.

Following rapidly upon the heels of the spectacular accomplishment of psychological testing in the army, industry picked up the cue that tests could be effectively used in employment and personnel work. The individual worker came to be considered a conglomerate of traits that could be measured by tests. It did not matter whether these traits were regarded as innate or acquired. What mattered from the employer's viewpoint was that tests could be utilized in the selection and job placement of workers. The result of this hasty and ill-advised exploitation of an approach really useful in its own field was temporary failure and disillusionment. Quite naturally, a distinct reaction against aptitude testing set in.

---

[12] Mason Haire, "Psychological Problems Relevant to Business and Industry," *Psychological Bulletin,* LVI (May, 1959), pp. 174–75.

[13] Anne Anastasi, *Psychological Testing* (New York: MacMillan Co., 1954), pp. 8–18.

[14] Clark Hull, *Aptitude Testing* (New York: World Book Co., 1928), pp. 16–19.

The road back from almost complete denial of aptitude testing in industry has been paved with both successes and failures. Today, aptitude testing is finding ever-increasing use in American industry. Aptitude testing has proven to be helpful in staffing decisions involving clerical personnel, salesmen, and certain other industrial occupations; however, in that area where effective prediction is most desperately needed—in managerial selection—aptitude testing has met with only limited success.[15]

One of the most telling criticisms of aptitude testing is that made by Hull in 1928.[16] He suggested that something in the neighborhood of .50 might be a practical limit for validities of tests. Nothing in the history of selection testing has radically revised this figure after almost 40 years. Nevertheless, the quest goes on—to develop tests which can efficiently estimate or forecast aptitudes and success on the job from test scores.

Personality tests. Success on the job is not solely determined by ability; it is also attributable in part to the personality and interest of the worker. Aptitude tests are not tests of motivation and interest; consequently, something else is needed to measure these dimensions of the worker. Not only is the supervisor interested in finding out whether the worker *can do* the job, he is also interested in determining whether he *will do* the job. It is to this question that personality and interest inventories in the industrial setting are addressed.

The instruments used to assess the "will do" side in prediction come in all shapes and sizes. Some of these devices are simple inventories, others are based on specific personality or motivational theories. Some seek to measure those aspects of the personality called temperament traits. Still others are projective in design and are intended for "global assessments" of personality.[17]

These instruments are impressive in their diversity and approach. However, notwithstanding their multiplicity of technique and design, the history of personality and interest measurements in industrial selection has been something less than spectacular. Much of the variety in approaches to the measurement of personality stems from the desire to overcome the deficiencies in existing tests and the fact that the relationship between the predictor variable and the criteria are infinitely complex and dynamic.

Many of the tests presently used in assessment, particularly in the

---

[15] Robert M. Guion, *Personnel Testing* (New York: McGraw-Hill Book Co., 1965), pp. 469–71.

[16] Hull, *op. cit.*

[17] Five widely used inventories are:
1. California Psychological Inventory
2. Gordon Personal Profile
3. Guilford-Zimmerman Temperament Survey
4. Minnesota Multiphasic Personality Inventory
5. Thurston Temperament Schedule

selection of managers, are general personality tests which have not been validated for managerial performance but rather for the identification of particular personality traits. The relevance of these traits or characteristics to successful performance on the job frequently comes about because of some intuitive judgment as to the type of man one would like to have. Relatively few attempts have been made to forecast accurately the demands placed on the applicant once he is in the organization. Thus, it seems that we may be playing Russian Roulette with the future of the enterprise by attempting to select managers through screening devices which in effect merely assure us that all those admitted to managerial ranks are alike. Fortunately, this is not the problem for the organization today as it might be in the future. At present, the validities of personality tests are low enough so that the consistent use of any of the personality tests will allow enough people to slip by that the organization will be protected against poor judgment about the qualities it thinks it is selecting.

What is needed by management with regard to its personnel staffing is apparently a heterogeneous supply of human resources from which individuals can be selected to fill a variety of specific but unpredictable needs. Thus, the problem with personality tests is much more than that of overcoming distortion due to faking, presenting an idealized concept of oneself rather than a realistic self-appraisal, and a lack of self-insight. The basic issue is ability to predict the future with an extremely high level of probability. This clairvoyance will be a long time in coming.[18]

The behavioral or skills approach. A third approach to selection has been through tests which are less concerned with inner qualities, or inferences about such qualities. Behavior—activity which can be seen or measured—has been the subject of measurement and observation in this cluster of selection devices. In its simplest form, it was the test applied to the itinerant craftsman who wandered from town to town in the early part of the century. The boss of the machine shop would simply give him a piece of metal and a drawing and tell him to "make this." If he made the piece to precise specifications, did it quickly, with few errors, he was hired. The achievement test of typing skill was to place the applicant in front of a typewriter and have her type. Her work was timed, checked for errors, and if she performed well she was hired.

The use of such tests—which aren't any more psychological than the height and weight of the applicant are psychological—are still used, and are extremely useful screening devices. There has been an attempt to extend such testing to selection of managerial applicants, or candidates

---

[18] As Guion has commented concerning personality measurement: "the available measures have generally been developed for clinical and counseling purposes rather than for selection, they are too subjective, and the evidence of their value is too weak."

for sales, professional, or technical positions. Perhaps the most comprehensive plan for this approach is that of Robert N. McMurry, whose pattern interview program,[19] coupled with tests and full dress exploration of behavior histories, is widely used by many firms.

Actually a combination of personality, aptitude, and behavior history approaches, McMurry's system hypothesizes that the prediction of what a man will do in future assignments is already written in the record of his past behavior. Determinism is the underlying assumption here. If a man has been a job hopper in the past (has held five jobs in the past five years), he will probably be a job hopper in the future. The goal of the pattern interview then is to probe intensively into the resumé, filling in each gap to uncover "patterns" of behavior. It is presumed that these patterns will persist into the future.

The McMurry system, which has been widely adopted and copied by firms and by a corps of consultants who have developed similar plans, delves into attitudes by eliciting verbal reactions to the conditions of past employment. An applicant who states that most of his past employers have been incompetent, unpleasant, or otherwise deficient may be predicted to adopt similar verbal responses about the new employer after the initial period of adjustment is over. Further, one may predict such things as leadership, creativity, and maturity by asking questions which get at past behavior from which reasonable inferences can be made. Table 12–2 shows how such questions might be devised in this behavioral approach to managerial selection.

TABLE 12–2
Using verbal responses to obtain predictors of future attitudes or capacities

Trait	Question which will highlight the trait
Creativity	Has the applicant ever created anything?
Leadership	Has he ever led anything?
Loyalty	Does he speak well for former employers, school, parents, and associates?
Maturity	Has he been dependent upon others? He he destroyed things which were his responsibility? Has his behavior been excessively oriented toward pleasurable activities?

The assumptions in this line of questioning are that people's behavior doesn't change, or that it may be costly to change it. Such being true, the time to find the undesirable behavior patterns in applicants is when they are still applicants. One might even hire persons with less than desirable behavior patterns, knowing what the defects are and allowing for them.

[19] Robert N. McMurry, "Validating the Patterned Interview," *Personnel*, XXIII (January, 1947), pp. 263–72.

Clearly more scientific than some of the more esoteric methods of personality and aptitude testing, McMurry's system nonetheless shares the limitation that it is deterministic, and is more apt to achieve conformity in hiring than any other outcome.

The distinctive feature of this approach is that it presumes that a *pattern of behavior* is the key ingredient in hiring. Reference checks, intensive attention to past behavior, and the reports of past observers about the behavior of individuals, are coupled with the hardest possible probing into every aspect of the applicant's past results in order to create an extensive dossier which gives the interviewer the equivalent of many years of personal acquaintanceship with the applicant. The interview, which is vital in this approach, may be nondirective when it will manipulate the individual into revealing things he might not otherwise divulge. Telephone checks of former employers are larded with probing questions to strip aside the amenities which former employers customarily drape over people they've fired.

The method's most important shortcoming, although it comes closer than many other approaches, is that it deals mainly with behavior and not with the effects of that behavior in results.

The background approach to selection.   One of the fastest rising in popularity, the background approach has resulted in a dramatic rise in campus recruiting in recent years. In fact, much of the pressure upon the campus recruiting process has grown out of an unstated and sometimes unconscious assumption that a college degree is needed for most managerial and staff positions. There are some interesting assumptions here.

1. It is assumed that the person who has a degree learned something in college. It is further assumed that this learning is something which he will carry to his first and subsequent positions. It is further assumed that the learning will convert into behavior on the job, and the behavior in turn will produce results that could not be produced by the noncollege graduate.

2. Much of the drive to garner diploma-holders was caused by studies which show that 75 percent of the present crop of chief executives of the largest firms are college graduates. The studies of Warner, Abegglen, and others, it is held, comprise predictors of the promotability of college graduates.[20] To some extent, this has become describable by the favorite cliché of the psychologists—"a self-fulfilling prophecy." Companies which presume that only college graduates can do managerial work enact policies which permit only college graduates to become managers. As a result, over time their ranks become filled with college graduate man-

---

[20] W. Lloyd Warner and James C. Abegglen, *Occupational Mobility in American Business and Industry* (Minneapolis: University of Minnesota Press, 1955), pp. 95–97.

agers. As an example, one utility company for many years recruited at colleges, limiting interviews to those in the upper brackets of their class in grades. Later they found that only high mark students succeeded.[21]

Where are the soft spots?

• There are many studies which show that the most successful automobile dealers, real estate men, and successful small-business operators are not college men.[22]

• The two largest firms in the country in sales and profit have diametrically opposed policies with respect to the promotion of college men into managerial positions. In AT&T the college man enjoys a distinct edge. In General Motors, where results are primary guides to internal selection, a vast majority of managers are not college graduates, including at this writing the president. GM *has* an extensive college recruiting program; however, its assumptions are different from some of its corporate counterparts. GM assumes when it hires a college graduate that he will demonstrate what he has learned once he is on the job, and that this learning will be verified by the results he achieves rather than by the degree he acquired before joining the firm. (Ford, number two in manufacturing industries, shares GM's pattern of selecting managers.)

• The background approach has the limitations of all the single-cause approaches to selection. It examines a single variable (academic degree) and generalizes this as a predictor. In fact, some combinations of degrees are automatic guarantees of rapid rise in the large corporation. The man with a BS degree from Massachusetts Institute of Technology and an MBA from Harvard, for example, may never have to really work again. His rise to the general management post is assured. Admittedly, he has already, as a youth, gone through several screens that many fail to survive, but his subsequent progress will not be measured by his results-achieved until he reaches a crucial position in the firm. Who would dare to give him a bad appraisal? He might remember it when he gets on top. His salary progress will be swift in order that the jump need not be too great when he arrives at the top.

(The suggestion here isn't that background is not useful information, but rather that as a single predictor is has the limitations of all single-cause explanations for multiple-cause outcomes. Meanwhile, this approach to selection gains momentum. The average cost of recruiting an MBA at Michigan in 1966 was $2,100. This doesn't include any of the cost of education, merely the cost of moving the inexperienced graduate from classroom to his first office. After he arrived he received an average

---

[21] Frederick R. Kappel, "From the World of College to the World of Work," *Bell Telephone Magazine* (Spring, 1962).
[22] Warner and Abegglen, *loc. cit.*

monthly pay of $750, with a range running up to $2,000 for certain rare types in the upper reaches of academic grade achievement.[23] What this is doing in salary administration inside these firms staggers the imagination. The average monthly salary in 1966 was some 30 percent above that offered three years ago.

The fifth approach

An objectives-results approach doesn't presume to displace all of the presently-used methods. It merely subsumes them to other criteria and shapes the plan for selection in somewhat different terms.

It starts with statements of job objectives for the job being filled, rather than with job descriptions which have been oriented toward skills, experience, and man-requirements. The method turns secondly to a measurement of the candidates' results on past jobs.

The approach breaks these objectives down into three major categories of objectives, and uses the selection process to uncover predictors in the individual's history which would point up probabilities of his operating at each of the three levels. The presumption in this selection of managers is that routine duties are a *must* requirement and that movement into the higher levels is demonstrated by problem-solving results and, most especially, by innovative or change-making abilities. [A special and somewhat temporary kind of objective will be learning-objectives, in which the candidate must complete a learning or training program in order to bring himself up to the minimum (regular) requirements of the position for which he is applying.]

These duties comprise an ascending scale of excellence in management achievement, and the tools of selection should be designed to identify these objectives in the job and to uncover, in the candidate's results on past jobs, predictors of these kinds of results for the future.

Defining the objectives. This fifth approach to selection starts with a

FIGURE 12–1

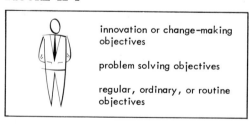

innovation or change-making objectives

problem solving objectives

regular, ordinary, or routine objectives

[23] Arthur S. Hann, *Salary Summary of Job Offers and Acceptances to Date Spring, 1966* (Graduate School of Business Administration) (Ann Arbor: University of Michigan, June, 1966).

TABLE 12–3
Sample job objectives for general foreman—manufacturing

Objectives	Indicative past achievements
1. To aid in selection of foremen for production	Has he ever picked a foreman, or does he have some firm ideas on what a foreman's functions should be?
2. Train foremen on the plant floor	Does he know the foreman's major objectives and functions? Has he ever broken in a new one? How many? Have any of them been subsequently released? Promoted?
3. Production quantity	What departments has he led? What were the output requirements? Did the department meet them? Exceed them? What occurred during his tenure in office in terms of levels of output? What did he do which might have affected output?
4. Quality	What was the reject rate when he started? What direction did it go? How did he get along with the inspectors? quality manager? What techniques for improvement did he use?
5. Cost control	What cost results did he achieve? How did his prime costs vary? His indirect labor? Indirect materials? Direct materials? Direct labor? Did he use any cost reduction methods such as work simplification? What were the effects? Has he submitted any improvement ideas in costs?
6. Employee relations	What was the turnover rate when he assumed charge? Did it change? Grievance rates? Absenteeism? Any special methods used or introduced? Were any attitude surveys done in his area, and with what effect?

clarification of the objectives of regular or routine duties, of the problems to be solved, and of the innovations sought. The first step in the fifth approach calls for a change in the job requisitioning procedures. For a typical position in which a job applicant might be considered, the employment manager or recruiter—or the manager himself if he is to do his own hiring—constructs a roster of job objectives, broken into the major categories. A sample description of the objectives for a general foreman (manufacturing) is shown in Table 12–3. From this guide it is seen that this position has more regular duties than it has problem-solving or innovative duties. These could be broken out as selection criteria. Other positions might emphasize the requirements of problem solving.

Table 12–4 shows the objectives for a systems engineer. This list of objectives, constructed by a group of 100 managers in systems engineering laboratories, could inspire an entirely different approach to selection from the traditional method. Here is an example of a different approach to selection, based on this set of objectives. Acme System Company is

TABLE 12–4

List of typical functions and results criteria for a systems engineer

Function	Result criteria
1. Interprets organization objectives when laying out project	Upon receiving tasks, projects, or assignments must develop working plans and approaches to achieve them which requires interpretation of sponsor's objectives.
2. Checking progress for compliance	Must check with superior or customer to determine whether direction and rate of progress are satisfactory. Has few if any complaints that he is checking back too often (being too dependent) or too infrequently, thus getting off the track too far.
3. Making stop-or-proceed decisions	Makes decisions on work whether to proceed a course of study or action or to drop that course and try another. Generally gets concurrence of customer or superior. Should run into occasional blank wall if he is really experimenting.
4. System engineering skill	Applies laws and principles of systems to the solution of specific problems in the project. Has well stocked memory for principles, has access to many more, and learns new ones quickly. Manipulates memories into new and original mixes.
5. Visual display of concepts	Devises, plans, and executes visual displays (drawings, sketches, working models, breadboards, etc.) of the underlying concepts.
6. Communicating ideas	Clarifies ideas, converts them into the language of the receiver, transmits them effectively, gets feedback to assure understanding: includes report writing and technical manuals.
7. Adherence to policy	Stays customarily within accepted and promulgated guides to technical action in that firm, the industry, the lab, unless overriding reasons dictate otherwise.

Others rated highly important included self-development activity, and introduction of new ideas.

recruiting people for engineering posts to fulfill a long-run contract. It also hopes that out of this group will emerge some managers for the future. Some tangible effects might alter the selection procedure:

1. Despite the common nature of many of the activities, this work will be primarily innovative or problem solving. All job information sought in interview should aim at reaching a conclusion about such results achieved by the candidate in the past.

2. Certain kinds of objectives cannot be expected from new hires directly from college. In the objectives shown in Table 12–4, those which could be expected of the beginner are handled apart from those which would be required of the experienced professional who might be expected to start in immediately and achieve most of his objectives.

3. The inquiry about the candidate should aim at uncovering how his

past results in each of these areas indicate probable achievements of similar results in the future. Such questions as the following might be used.

Objective	Line of questioning
To apply laws and principles of systems engineering to specific problems in a project	Courses taken? Grades? Do they apply here? Special research done? List of past projects? Key issues in technical field? Does he see any interdisciplinary approaches? Is he mathematically sound?
To interpret objectives for technical projects.	What projects has he designed experiments for? How has he decided on working plans and approaches?

It is apparent that the one conducting the interview and making umpire-like judgments as to past achievements in terms of results must be conversant with the objective of the man's job. The specifics of the question aren't of major concern here, but rather that the interviewer be seeking evidence of results in both kind and amount. The short illustration presented above demonstrates that the end product of selection by objectives comes from a different look at the work the man is expected to do when he is hired.

When objectives are set for the first time. Before a company can select by objectives, it must establish what the objectives for the position being filled actually are. The statements of the systems engineer's functions had to be constructed for this study since they did not exist in the firm at the time of the study. The statements of responsibilities were hammered out in small conference groups with the managers of these engineers. Only those statements which over 90 percent of the managers felt were of above average significance for the jobs of the systems engineers in that lab were included. Others were specifically reflected by the majority. (Community and civic activities, training technicians, and delegation to technicians were rated as of little or no significance.) While one may deplore the standards set by the managers in some areas, it must be realized that this is the climate into which the new engineers are going to be hired.

The same step can be taken elsewhere, partially by asking the present encumbents what they think their objectives are, but more importantly, by asking the manager of the position to clarify the objectives for that position. It is he who will administer salaries, appraise for the annual performance report, coach, and recommend promotions.

Predicting success on the basis of results. Once job objectives are in hand, all selection methods should focus on uncovering result-getting activity in the history of the applicant. If the accustomed way of thinking about hiring suggests "Why, we're doing that right now," please read on. Most application forms or proposed resumé forms do not demand specific statements of results achieved. Take the case of the government agency which was stymied by its selection problem because it found so many people at the higher levels had resumés including such information as the following: /

1956–59: Director of Underground Utilization of Overhead Manpower, Department of Midair Coordination and Development. GS-15
Had full responsibility for coordination and implementation of all liaison missions of this service base. Reported directly to the deputy chief of staff-coordination. Base operated with 6,000 military and civilian personnel, and annual budget $32 million.

Such nonsense implies that the applicant is the sole leader of 6,000 men, spending $30 million yearly, and it surrounds him with an aura of responsibility. The agency required that resumés be written to include answers to the question:

What did you actually achieve during that period; give year by year summaries. Who could we talk with to verify these achievements? How many of them were attributable to your efforts, how many were jointly performed with others?

The replies were matched with some intensive looks at the vacant positions to see what the objectives and criteria were for the persons being hired. The result was a drastic change in the way selections were made, and while it is still early to be certain, preliminary reports indicate a sharpening of performance in the newly placed persons.

Another example occurred in a firm which was seeking a college grad trainee for a marketing management position. One of the prime candidates was labelled as having "leadership" because he was president of the student council in college. At the urging of the writers, the firm probed a little deeper along these lines:

During your year as president what did the council do? What condition was the treasury in when you took over? When you left? Did you finish any projects which would make a lasting effect on student life? Who could we talk to that would know best what the achievements of the council were under your leadership?

This intensive line of questioning elicited from the young man himself the fact that the year had been marked with constant trouble growing out of his inability to handle the officers and get programs going. He had been selected "on my good looks, I guess, and the coeds make up a big part of the vote." The very king-pin criterium of the selection decision proved to be the weakest link.

Job applicants have increasingly recognized the values of listing accomplishments on their resumés rather than claiming attributes or positions which emit golden glows. Some personnel men have shied away from the use of such information because "Most people will dress it up, and you can't really tell whether the interviewee was responsible, or just went along for the ride."

The same cautious skepticism is needed in evaluating accomplishments and results as is needed in statements of responsibilities, personality, or background. How can one overcome the tendency of applicants to paint an over-rosy picture? Ask specifically how much of the achievements listed are genuinely attributable to their own efforts and how much were shared with others. For example, the following question has produced some candid responses in interviews observed and reported:

Your record shows some fine achievements in this past job. Now many of us do things jointly with others. What *percentage* of this achievement would you say is directly attributable to you or your subordinates?

Now, you note that these achievements are partially shared with Mr. A, the controller. You estimate that . . . .% of this is rightly attributable to you and your organization. Do you think that Mr. A would agree with your estimate of that percentage?

The only reason, generally, a candid and honestly-held estimate may be withheld is that the applicant doesn't know, is deluding himself, or is lying. Verification procedures, reference checks, and telephone reference chats substantiate the information. Rather than checking such matters as initiative, drive, personality, and the like, the interviewer restates the achievements the applicant has claimed and simply asks the informant, "Would you agree that the achievements he has stated for his performance in your company are accurate? If not, how did they differ?"

Private good and public weal—a conclusion

Hiring and promotion policy and practice badly need an overhaul. The perpetuation of our firms, and the observance of public interest through equitable selection are at stake. We have learned from all of our past experiences. Selection by objectives won't guarantee success, but may help us improve our averages. It may also stem the onrushing trend toward hiring overqualified people and ease the job opportunities for the present unemployables. It is a method of rewarding excellence rather than conformity or social class of origin.

QUESTIONS AND PROBLEMS

1. Why did the college graduate have an advantage in obtaining higher level positions in the early part of this century?
2. If most presidents are college men, how could the case be made that col-

lege degrees are not necessarily the cause of leadership performance? How could an opposite case be made?

3. "While you are in college, you should try to learn something useful?" What are the pros and cons for this statement?

4. If a company believes that psychological properties are the most important criteria for executive success, what affect will this have upon promotion, selection, and hiring of men for the future?

5. Colleges should teach young people to live the examined life, and to think. They can learn the specific skills once they have chosen a life career. Do you agree? Why?

6. What personal preferences do *you* have for choosing people to be leaders, or peers? How do you prevent such biases from affecting the health and performance of your organization?

7. Outline a pattern interview of skills and interview four acquaintances to determine which of them would best fit a selection problem: that of choosing a roommate.

8. Do you think that a patterned interview would work in choosing a husband or wife? Why or why not?

9. What is the first step in selection by objectives?

10. Prepare a set of objectives for a student leader, such as president of a club. What interview questions would you want to ask to determine who was most likely to succeed in that post?

11. Visit a local employer and ask for a summary of his selection procedures. Classify his procedures according to the five possibilities suggested in this chapter and report on what his model of selection is.

PARAGON PULP & PAPER COMPANY, LTD. CASE *

"Sure, we'll be glad to give you all the information you want on our personnel selection method. Why don't you talk to Bill Gilroy first, though. He's our office manager and the man who does the actual interviewing and evaluation."

John Humphrey was the manager of the newest of the Paragon Pulp & Paper Company's two Vancouver plants. The plant, which he had designed and now supervised, had been completed in the summer of 1956, and produced a heavy duty kraft stock for use in making paper boxes and containers.

---

* Copyright, 1958, by the University of Alberta.

All names, places and dates are disguised. Cases are prepared for educational purposes. They typically represent actual administrative problems and situations, but not necessarily the most effective methods of dealing with such matters.

Paragon Pulp & Paper maintained a standard personnel selection method at each of its plants. This method had been worked out by a management consulting firm, together with the company's industrial relations vice president, a former Austrian who held degrees in psychology and law. Company management attributed a considerable portion of the company's low turnover rate, among the lowest in the industry, to its personnel selection method. Both John Humphrey and Bill Gilroy also felt that their success in attaining an efficient level of production six months ahead of schedule was due in large part to this method.

The formal paperwork required by this method of selecting plant personnel was comprised of three main parts: an application form, Exhibit A, a test of reasoning ability called Progressive Matrices (1938), and a patterned interview form, Exhibit B. Evaluations resulting from these three sources and face-to-face contact were recorded on a summary form contained in Exhibit C. Bill Gilroy, office manager, had spent three days at a course given by the management consulting firm to instruct potential users in the administration, application, and evaluation of this series of selection method.

The functions of the overall system, in Bill Gilroy's opinion, were (1) to determine, insofar as possible, an applicant's reasoning power, personal compatability, and stability, and (2) on the basis of the final summary, to permit selection of the proper men for jobs in the plant.

Each step in the process served as a screening, which started when an applicant obtained an application form from the office receptionist and continued until a man had successfully completed the required one-month probationary period in the plant. This latter final screening was spelled out in the company's union agreement, the relevant article of which is contained in Exhibit D.

"You'd be surprised," said Bill Gilroy in describing the first screening, "but we've had people come in for a job who are obviously drunk. We don't waste much time in dealing with them. Similarly, we'll get applicants who might be what I call miscast—their social tendencies might be bad. This is the type that says in a loud voice to our receptionist, 'Get me the big boss—I don't want to speak to the office manager.' Finally, there are the one-armed, the cripples, the paraplegics, and so on. The physical requirements of the jobs we have to offer are beyond the abilities of this latter group. In most of these cases, I go out to the man and tell him at the present, there are no openings, but leave his name—we'll call him, he needn't call us—you know the routine."

The next step in the process required the filling out of the standard application form. Bill said,

We're looking for several things here, some general and some specific. As an example of the former, take the way a man fills out the form. You can tell if a man's careless and sloppy, or if he's ambitious enough to take a little care when he fills in the form. Basically, the application form gives me a brief look at the man before the interview. Take his date of birth—this gives me an idea of what job he can hold. What about his residence? If it's a fashionable address what's he doing here? How long has he lived in the same place? This gives you an idea as to a man's stability. Of course, if he has been working in the construction field, I expect him to have moved around a lot. What kind of earnings does a man expect? If he wants $2.50 an hour, why? I'm going to offer him $1.26.

Another thing I check for in the application form is the number of children a man has. If he's got too many, he's out. You can't support six or seven kids in Vancouver on monthly wages of $250, but a man's not going to make any more than that when he starts with us. So he just couldn't do it without some other income; unrest and trouble would eventually result. I also find out in the interview what type of car a man has, because where we are, just outside the city, you really need a car. Of course, a man doesn't have to have a car, but it helps. To get back to the application form, I want to know how much education a man has had. We're not looking for men with university degrees, either. I've found that if a man with a degree applies for a job in our plant, getting that degree was probably the last constructive thing he did in his life. But if a man has been to trade school, or a business school, that's O.K.

Then I take a look at a man's extracurricular activities, if any, and especially at any offices he might have held. This gives you an idea of a man's initiative, and willingness, and desire to lead. Similarly, as far as a man's military service goes, I look for a man who was promoted—indicating some ambition. I begin to wonder about the man who went in and came out a private—professional privates, they call them.

Finally, I look at a man's record of employment on the back of the application form, especially the last five years. There are eight spaces, and if a man says that's not enough for five years (unless he's been in construction work), we don't want him. We seldom bother to check a man's references if it involves anything more than a phone call.

The next step in the selection procedure was the Progressive Matrices test. This test on which there was no time limit, was comprised of 5 sections of 12 problems each.

Each section was progressively more difficult than the previous one. The test was designed to compare people with respect to their capacities for observation and clear thinking. It was "a test of a person's capacity at the time of the test to apprehend meaningless figures presented for his observation, see the relations between them, conceive the nature of the figure completing each system of relations presented, and by doing so, develop a systematic method of reasoning."

The scoring of this test involved two steps. First, each of the five sections was graded from 0 to 12, depending on the number right. Secondly, the five separate scores were added together to attain a final score. This score was then related to a scale divided into five parts, I, II, III, IV, and V, I representing the highest bracket, III the average, and V the lowest. In addition, each score, whether I, II, etc., was given a "stability" rating, determined by a man's separate scores on the five parts. For example, the normal distribution for a total score equivalent to a III for a man aged 45 would be progressive scores on the five parts of 10, 8, 7, 7, 3. A man whose separate scores deviated from these norms by more than two in any one case (for example 10, 9, 4, 4, 3) was thereby considered erratic.

Bill Gilroy commented,

We don't want the erratic type, and people can be erratic whether they're brilliant or not. Almost every time I've hired somebody whose Matrices' test result on two individual sections or more was off by more than two from the norm, thereby indicating he was erratic, there's been trouble. One example is a man whose test results showed him to be erratic—I hired him and found out later he was an alcoholic, a highly excitable type. Another man, who was a fork truck driver in the plant, all of a sudden blew up at the plant superintendent one day, and we had to let him go. The funny thing is, though, he'd formed a social club among some of the fellows in the plant that collapsed when he left.

Basically, with this test we're looking for men who can reason. Anyone below a score of Grade III is automatically out—with rare exceptions—and we fell flat on our face in every case. One good example involves a young woman who came to Vancouver from Edmonton, with her six-month old child. She told me she'd left her husband, who was 20 to 25 years older than she and who wasn't taking good care of her. She really needed a job. Even though she was Grade IV on the Matrices test, I gave her a job plus an advance in wages. She told me she felt she hadn't done her best on the test, so a couple of weeks later I let her take it again and she barely made Grade III. Then she started being absent for sickness—either she was sick or the child was sick. Well, we reserve to let a person go if their absentee rate indicates that the work is adversely affecting their health, so I called her in and pointed that out to her. She was O.K. for two or three weeks, but then it was the same old story, so the plant supervisors were forced to release her.

I've found that people who score Grade III on the Matrices test are the workers, while people with Grade II have the top jobs. Some of the men in Grade III appear stupid in the interview as a defense mechanism, but I've found this type often makes a good routine worker. Of course, you can't equate reasoning power alone with ambition and the desire to take responsibility.

We will take people with a score of Grade I, subject to their having the right background. They're too mentally active for the type of job we have here—they tend to ask questions that aren't necessary to get the job done. We have one man in that category. Similarly, because of our seniority clause, we're cutting down on the number of Grade II's we take. We can, if the senior man is not qualified to take the responsibility, jump him. We haven't had much trouble with this situation, however, because usually an unqualified, although senior, man will refuse the promotion.

The next step in the screening process for a job applicant involved the patterned interview conducted by Bill Gilroy, using the form shown in Exhibit B. The interview ordinarily took 20 to 30 minutes, unless, as

Bill said, "a man was frightened, reticent, or opposed." Each man, before the actual interview started, was assured that he did not have to answer any questions he did not want to. Bill felt, however, that any man who did not want to answer all questions directly was leaving himself open to indirect questioning to determine the necessary information. He said:

In the interview I look for quite a few things, as you can see from the form. The main thing the questions bring out is a man's stability, and as far as his personal compatability goes, I get a good idea of that by the way he conducts himself in the interview, and then of course there's the 30-day probationary period on the job. I'm always thinking of the summary sheet (Exhibit C) as I go along.

A man has to prove himself in the interview. If the man is obviously trying to gain sympathy from me, say, by telling me about his aches and pains, I usually don't want him. This type of thing will carry over to the job. One question I think is pretty important is the one, 'When did you have your last drink?' Typically a man will hesitate a moment, and then remember the beer he had a few nights ago, and then he might mention the drink he had at his birthday party, or something like that. But when a man says, 'I had my last drink at 2 o'clock on such and such a day and year,' watch out! The man, 99 out of 100 times, is, or was, a confirmed alcoholic. Any man that can tell you to the minute the last time he had a drink is the worst risk from the alcoholic point of view.

I deliberately hired two alcoholics not long ago. When they're sober, they'll work twice as hard as any one around them—to punish themselves. You can't put them on the line, because when they're out there will be a hole. Maintenance, stores, etc., are O.K. for this type. One of the two I hired had been a major league pitcher, and had owned his own furniture manufacturing outfit. I thought he'd be able to transfer his knowledge, but he couldn't do it; the job was too broad for him.

Another thing I definitely look for is the man who is accident-prone. That's the only way I can think of saying it, but I don't like the expression. I check on health, car accidents, and the last accident on their former jobs. Of course, a man with too many accidents tries to hide it, but it usually always comes out.

I also look for a smooth domestic life. It's almost a prerequisite. I like to see a good healthy home life, too. For one thing, with poor health in the family, a man usually needs extra money. As far as our plant goes, we have voluntary medical service insurance with the cost carried by the workers, but no hospitalization insurance. Vancouver, the city, that is, has a plan that helps out there.

We have some fringe benefits, but don't forget this plant is still growing and right now we can't afford to commit ourselves to these expenditures. Take our wage spread—from a base rate of $1.26 up to $1.83. That $1.26 might be a little low, but we deliberately tried to start low in anticipation of union demands.

Notice the questions about an applicant's financial situation. Here I'm looking for the man in the middle. You'd be surprised how many people come in here and tell me about the farm their father left them, from which they might be earning $5,000 a year. It's not hard to predict that these people aren't going to be the steadiest workers in the world. They just aren't hungry. On the other hand, we can't take people who are too hungry, with too many mouths to feed, as I mentioned before.

Single girls on their own are especially bad. It's typical of them to say, in answer to my question as to how much they need a month, 'Oh, I can live on a $100 a month.' Then when I ask them about the payments on the coat they're wearing, and their car, rent, and so on, they'll say 'Oh, gosh, guess I can't live on a $100.' Eventually, they realize it will be tough for them to live on the wages that we pay.

The final step in the selection process required Bill Gilroy to fill out the Selection & Evaluation Summary form, as shown in Exhibit C. Bill filled out this form from information and opinions he obtained from the application form, the Matrices test, and the patterned interview. Applicants were rated "Outstanding," "Good," "Marginal," or "Poor" in comparison with men actually working in the plant, and not against any outside standard. Bill explained that the ideal applicant would have a series of checkmarks distributed between the first three categories—from "Outstanding" to "Marginal." "We don't want a man with too many 'Poor' checks," Bill said, "but neither do we want a man who is the opposite—too outstanding. It just wouldn't work out."

I first used this method, back in '56, when we were just starting up. Another fellow from the company was helping me. Then last year, when we added a second shift, the other fellow and I had to hire another 60 men, and we had over 300 applicants. Ordinarily, though, I'd say we reject about 65 percent of the people who apply for jobs. Right now, we're back to one shift, so we've got a backlog of men with experience on our seniority list that aren't working right now. The last six months, we've had about one or two applicants a month.

Even though on two occasions we needed a lot of men in a relatively short time, I can think of only one instance where we hired a man who didn't pass through the selection procedure, and that was due to coincidence. A foreman called me up and said he needed a man on the line right away and at the same time, a fellow was outside just starting to fill out his application form. He was out in the plant before the ink was dry.

There are some men in the plant now that I wouldn't hire today. They're chiefly the ones in the 45–60 age bracket. They're able to reason, but they are not as alert physically as they should be. Older men sometimes lack that certain something that is necessary on production jobs requiring continual judgment.

What we try to do, if possible, is give these men 'prestige' jobs, though we have only a few. One example is our first-aid man. Although he's on a low paying job, he gets a bonus—10¢ an hour—for his first-aid job. He's between the devil and the deep blue sea, which is where we want him. You see, we have a 4-cent spread between rates, and if this man were promoted up one notch, he realizes he'd probably lose the 10 cent bonus—in other words he'd be out 6 cents. So he's happy right where he is.

Sometimes you have people who hunger for authority. We occasionally put a man on the safety committee to satisfy this hunger. The union's the same way—they provide positions that have the prestige and authority.

The important thing is to keep the plant operating efficiently, and if it is not operating, all this red tape and all our records are meaningless. We are attempting to keep it going as efficiently as possible. The plant is the be-all and end-all.

EXHIBIT A

APPLICATION FOR EMPLOYMENT

Date_____

Name_____   Home Tel. No._____

Present address_____
No.   Street   City   Province   How long have you lived there?_____

Previous address_____
No.   Street   City   Province   How long did you live there?_____

Position applied for?_____   Earnings expected $_____

PERSONAL

Sex: ☐ M, ☐ F; Date of birth_____19____   ☐ Single,   ☐ Married,   ☐ Separated   No. children_____Their ages____

Height____ft____in. Weight_____lbs.   ☐ Engaged,   ☐ Widowed,   ☐ Divorced   No. other dependents____Ages____

Are you a Can. citizen? ☐ Yes, ☐ No   Date of marriage_____   U. I. C. No._____

Do you: ☐ Own your home? ☐ Rent? ☐ Live with relatives? ☐ Board? ☐ Stay with friends? Other_____

(If you rent) What monthly rent do you pay? $_____Do you own your furniture? ☐ Yes, ☐ No

Is your wife employed? ☐ No, ☐ Yes, part time, ☐ Yes, full time; What kind of work?_____Her earnings $_____per____

Do you carry life insurance? ☐ No, ☐ Yes; Amount $_____

What physical defects do you have?_____

In case of emergency, notify_____
Name   Address   Phone

EDUCATION

Type of School	Name and Address of School	Courses Majored in	Check Last Year Completed				Graduate? Give Degrees	Last Year Attended
Elementary			5	6	7	8	☐ Yes, ☐ No	19
High School			1	2	3	4	☐ Yes, ☐ No	19
University			1	2	3	4		19
University			1	2	3	4		19
Post Graduate School			1	2	3	4		19
Business or Trade School			1	2	3	4		19
Corresp. or Night School			1	2	3	4		19

Scholastic standing in H. S.?_____ In University?_____

EXTRACURRICULAR ACTIVITIES (athletics, clubs, etc.)
(Do not include military, racial, religious, or nationality groups)

In high school_____   In college_____

Offices held_____   Offices held_____

MILITARY SERVICE

Have you had Military Service? ☐ Yes, ☐ No; (If yes) Date enlisted_____ 19____

Which Service?_____What branch of that Service?_____Starting Rank_____

Date of discharge_____19____Rank at discharge_____

WORK HISTORY

List below the names of all your employers, beginning with the most recent: a. Employer's Name b. Business address	Kind of Business	Time Employed From Mo. Yr.	To Mo. Yr.	Nature of Work	Starting Salary	Salary at Leaving	Reasons for Leaving	Name of Immediate Superior
1. a. b.								Name Title
2. a. b.								Name Title
3. a. b.								Name Title
4. a. b.								Name Title
5. a. b.								Name Title
6. a. b.								Name Title
7. a. b.								Name Title
8. a. b.								Name Title

Indicate by number———————any of the above employers whom you do not wish us to contact. Why:————————————

References (Not former employers or relatives)

	Address	Phone Number
1.		
2.		
3.		

Are there any other experiences, skills, or qualifications which you feel would especially fit you for work with our Company?————————

If your application is considered favorably, on what date will you be available for work?——————— 19——— Signature——————————

APPLICANT SHOULD NOT WRITE BELOW THIS LINE

Comments——————————

Interviewer:—————

EXHIBIT B

PATTERNED INTERVIEW
(Short Form)

Name_____ Sex: ☐ M, ☐ F; Date of Birth_____ Soc. Sec. No._____

Address_____

SUMMARY

Rating: [1] [2] [3] [4] Comments:_____
In making final rating, be sure to consider applicant's stability, industry, perseverance, loyalty, ability

to get along with others, self-reliance, leadership, maturity, motivation; also, domestic situation and health.

Interviewer:_____ Job Considered for:_____ Date____

Why are you applying for work in this Company?_____
Is his underlying reason a desire for prestige, security, or earnings?

If you were hired, how long
would it take you to get to work?_____How would you do it?_____
Is there anything undesirable here?

WORK EXPERIENCE. Cover all positions. This information is very important. Interviewer should record last position first. Every month since leaving school should be accounted for. Note military service in work record in continuity with jobs held since that time.

	LAST OR PRESENT POSITION	NEXT TO LAST POSITION	SECOND FROM LAST POSITION
Name of Company			
Address			
Dates of employment	From To	From To	From To
		Do these dates check with his application?	
Nature of work			
		Will his previous experience be helpful on this job?	
Starting salary			
Salary at leaving			
Was anything especially liked about the job?	Has he made good work progress?		General or merit increases?
		Has he been happy and contented in his work?	
Was there anything especially disliked?			
	Were his dislikes justified?		Is he chronically dissatisfied?
Reasons for leaving			
		Are his reasons for leaving reasonable and consistent?	

OTHER POSITIONS

Name of Company	Type of Work	Salary	Date Started	Date Left	Reasons for Leaving
	Has he stayed in one line of work for the most part?				
	Has he gotten along well on his jobs?				
	Are his attitudes toward his employers loyal?				
	Was he interested in creative work? In work requiring activity?				
	Has he improved himself and his position?				

EXHIBIT B (continued)

How much unemployment
compensation have you drawn?_____ When?_____ Why?_____
Does he depend on himself?

How many weeks have you been
unemployed in the past five years?_____ How did you spend this time?_____
Did conditions in his occupation justify this time? Did he use his time profitably?

What accidents have
you had in recent years?_____
Is he "accident-prone"? Any disabilities which will interfere with his work?

SCHOOLING

How far did you go in school?   Grade: 1 2 3 4 5 6 7 8   High School: 1 2 3 4   College: 1 2 3 4   Date of leaving school_____
Is his schooling adequate for the job?

If you did not graduate from
high school or college, why not?_____ Who paid for your schooling?_____
Are his reasons for not finishing sound?   Self-reliant?

What special training have you taken?_____
Will this be helpful? Indications of perseverance? Industry?

Extracurricular activities (exclude military,   What offices did you
racial, religious, nationality groups)_____ hold in these groups?_____
Did he get along well with others?   Indications of leadership?

FAMILY BACKGROUND	FINANCIAL SITUATION	DOMESTIC AND SOCIAL SITUATION
Father Mother living?_____ living?_____ Normal background?	Own home: $_____ Mortgage: $_____ Stability?	Single?_____ Engaged?_____
Father's occupation_____	Rent House: $_____ Apt.: $_____	Married?_____ When?_____
Average earnings_____	Live with friends: $_____ Relatives: $_____	Widowed?_____ Divorced?_____
Number of brothers or sisters older_____ Younger____ Has he been babied?	Own Number of furniture_____ Rooms_____	Ages of children_____ Motivation?
Financial aid to family_____	Cost of living per month $_____ Realistic?	How do you and your wife get along?_____ Maturity?
Leisure time activities_____ Habits of Industry?	Any current debts?_____ Mature financially?	Recreation_____ Maturity?
Summer vacations_____ Did he keep busy?	Wages ever garnisheed?_____	Hobbies_____ Will these help?
Church activities_____ (Do not ask what church)	Borrow from small loan agency?_____ Judgment?	Entertain at home?_____ Get along well with others?
Group activities_____ (Exclude military, racial, religious,	Savings on Net last job $____ Worth $____	Group activities_____ (Exclude military, racial, religious, nationality groups)
and nationality groups)	Wife Her employed?____ earnings: $____ Effect on motivation?	When did you have last drink?_____ Sensible?
Positions of leadership_____ Leader?	Other income $_____	What types of people rub you the wrong way?_____ Bias?
How old when fully self-supporting?_____ Self-reliant?	Life Accident insurance $____ insurance $____ Is he provident?	Ever arrested?_____ Charges_____ Immaturity?

HEALTH

What serious illnesses, operations,
or accidents did you have as a child?_____
Has he retained any infantile personality traits due to childhood illnesses?

What illnesses, operations, or
accidents have you had in recent years?_____
Are his illnesses legitimate rather than indicating a desire to "enjoy ill health"?

How much time have you lost from
work because of illness during past year?_____
Will he be able to do the job?

Does anyone in your home suffer ill health?_____
Are his wife, children, or family relatively healthy?

Do you suffer from:
☐ Poor Eyesight
☐ Rupture
☐ Rheumatism
☐ Asthma
☐ Heart Trouble
☐ Diabetes
☐ Ulcers
☐ Hay Fever
☐ Flat Feet
☐ Nervousness

ADDITIONAL INFORMATION:_____
_____
_____
_____

EXHIBIT C
Selection and valuation summary

Applicant's Name _____ Date _____ 19 ___.

Position Applied for _____ Job Class _____

Rating on Each Factor	Out-standing	Good	Mar-ginal	Poor

"CAN DO" FACTORS

Rating on Each Factor	Out-standing	Good	Mar-ginal	Poor
Appearance, manners				
Availability for this work				
Education, as required by this job				
Intelligence, ability to learn, solve problems				
Experience in this field				
Knowledge of the product				
Physical condition, health, energy				

CHARACTER TRAITS (Basic Habits)

"WILL DO" FACTORS

	Out-standing	Good	Mar-ginal	Poor
STABILITY; maintaining same jobs and interests				
INDUSTRY; willingness to work				
PERSERVERANCE; finishing what he starts . .				
ABILITY to get along with people				
LOYALTY; identifying with employer				
SELF-RELIANCE; standing on own feet, making own decisions				
LEADERSHIP				

MOTIVATION

	Out-standing	Good	Mar-ginal	Poor
INTEREST in this work				
ECONOMIC NEED				
NEED FOR RECOGNITION; personal status . . .				
NEED TO EXCEL				
NEED TO SERVE				
NEED TO ACQUIRE				

DEGREE OF EMOTIONAL MATURITY

	Out-standing	Good	Mar-ginal	Poor
Freedom from dependence				
Regard for consequences				
Capacity for self-discipline				
Freedom from selfishness				
Freedom from show-off tendencies				
Freedom from pleasure-mindedness				
Freedom from destructive tendencies				
Freedom from wishful thinking				

Important: Do not add or average these factors in making the Over-all Rating. Match the qualifications of the applicant against the requirements of the particular position for which he is being considered.

Strong Points for This Position _____

_____

Weak Points for This Position _____

_____

Over-all Rating: [1] [2] [3] [4]   Recommendation to Employ: [ ] Yes [ ] No   Rating by_____

EXHIBIT D
Paragon Pulp & Paper Company Limited
Article VIII—Seniority

Section 1:
The Company recognizes the principle of seniority, competency considered. In the application of seniority, it shall be determined firstly, by department, and secondly, by plant. Notwithstanding anything to the contrary contained in this Agreement, it shall be mutually agreed that all employees are hired on probation, the probationary period to continue for thirty (30) calendar days during which time they are to be considered temporary workers only. Upon completion of the probationary period, they shall be regarded as regular employees, and shall then be entitled to Seniority, dated from the day on which they entered the Company's employ.

Section 2:
(*a*) Promotions shall be based on departmental seniority, competency considered, but must follow the lines of progression from job to job within the department.
(*b*) Any employee shall have the right to refuse promotion. However, in no case can departmental seniority be used to bypass any position in the line.
(*c*) Job openings will be held open for twenty-four (24) hours, during which time the employee eligible for promotion must make his intention known, as promotion may involve a change from swing shift to third shift and vice versa. In the event the eligible employee for the promotion refuses, other employees in the same category will be approached in order of their departmental seniority. Should no one in that category accept, the employees in next lower category of the department shall be approached in a similar manner. Should no one in the department accept the promotion, in such event the job will be posted for forty-eight (48) hours and in such case employees in other departments will be considered according to their plant seniority.
An employee who has entered a department in this manner shall be eligible for further progress in the new line of progression, subject only to longer departmental seniorities of other employees in the same bracket into which he has entered.

Section 3:
In the event of reduction of forces, the last person hired shall be the first released, subject to provisions as outlined in Section 1. The employees retained on the payroll will have the right to retain their jobs according to their departmental seniority. Those with insufficient departmental seniority to retain their jobs shall return to the job(s) previously held in the department and in such case replace anyone holding such job with less departmental seniority. Those with insufficient departmental seniority to remain in the department will take the jobs opened up by those laid off. In case of reestablishment of forces, those "demoted" shall have first claim on their previously held jobs and in such event jobs will not be posted.

Section 4:
The Committee and the Company shall meet whenever necessary to discuss the basis of departments for seniority purposes.

Section 5:
It is hereby agreed that, when rehiring, all employees laid off due to a seasonal shutdown or reduction in the working forces will be notified by telegram at least seven (7) days before restart of operations and they shall be rehired in the order of their plant seniority, provided that they reply to the telegram in the affirmative within ninety-six (96) hours of the telegram's being sent out,

and appear for work not later than the end of the above-stated seven (7) day period. However, employees resident in Alberta, Saskatchewan, or the Yukon Territory will be given one (1) additional day's time for reporting and any employee resident in any other Canadian Province or the United States will receive two (2) additional days' time for reporting. It is agreed that all employees shall, upon returning to employment within the required number of days of being notified by the Company, retain all seniority rights. It shall be the employees' responsibility to keep the Company informed of their address during lay-off.

Section 6:
It is agreed when hiring new employees, returned men with suitable qualifications shall have preference.

Section 7:
Any employee who is absent without leave for a period of more than three (3) consecutive working days, who cannot show just reason for such absence, shall forfeit all seniority rights. This shall not interfere with the Company's right to discharge for proper cause.

Section 8:
The Company shall supply to the bargaining agent, a complete seniority list every three (3) months. Said seniority list shall be immediately brought up to date in the event of a reduction of the working forces.

Section 9:
Weekend workers and others not desirous or available for regular employment will be regarded as casual employees, and will not accrue seniority.

Section 10:
Employees leaving the bargaining unit to assume supervisory duties shall, in the event of returning to the bargaining unit, retain that seniority which they held, at the time of leaving the bargaining unit.

chapter 13

COMPENSATION
BY OBJECTIVES

THE PAYCHECK has many meanings. To the person receiving it the paycheck is a basic income, from which he pays his bills, feeds the kids, buys his clothes, car, and house. For the society around him it represents an indicator, when lumped together, of economic health. For the economists it is the bit which adds together to become national income, personal disposable income, and the like. For the marketing department it becomes purchasing power which can be diverted into his coffers. For the paymaster it is a specific calculation which must be made weekly.

From the management viewpoint it likewise has many connotations. It is a cost of doing business, labor cost. Added to materials, supplies, and administration expense, it comprises total cost of goods sold. For the management, too, it is a measure of value of the employees' contribution. It also is a means of stimulating persons to excel.

Given all of these various viewpoints of the paycheck, how does the personnel manager view it? What are the requirements of a good system of wage and salary administration?

THE OUTPUTS OF A COMPENSATION PLAN

A survey of the literature of compensation shows that two dominant goals seem to be important in compensation programs; they should produce *equity*, and they should produce *competitive position*. While there are, of course, many others—some of which can be considered as subordinates of these two major outputs—we'll look first at these goals.

Equity

Equitable compensation means that the pay received by an individual worker will stand a comparison test with other workers or managers inside the firm, and also with others outside the firm. It means that the worker's pay in one department doing identical work with a worker in another department will be the same. It will produce paychecks which reduce the discontent from comparison when one worker notes that another gets more pay than he; the system which is equitable will have a rational explanation to explain that difference. The janitor will know that he gets less than the machinist, but he also knows the factors and their application through which the differences were calculated, and while he may not like the fact that he gets less, he can explain it to himself. This is, of course, simple where the skill levels differ, but it must also work to produce the same result where the jobs are different both in the kinds of activities carried out and in their worth—even though apparent similarity in skills is called for.

Competitive compensation

Competitive compensation means that the company pays enough to attract adequate or better than adequate candidates for new positions. It means that they are making the pay attractive enough to a sufficient number of qualified candidates that the positions needed to operate at all levels will be found. It also means that those already on the payroll when making comparisons of their own pay with that of persons doing similar work in other firms, won't be attracted away by higher wages or salaries.

Beyond these two major outputs, some of the criteria by which compensation plans can be evaluated might include any or all of the following:

a) The plan is based upon full information about the objectives (output requirements) and man requirements of each position of the job holder.

b) Job objectives will be described in writing using some uniform patterns of inquiry to assure that the same questions relevant to uncovering worth are uncovered by systematic study.

c) A uniform system of evaluation of the described positions against an objective scale or measurement yardstick will be used and applied.

d) Positions will be classified in such a way that the employee will know where he stands with respect to certain families of positions in the firm, and how well he is doing while he is working.

e) Money amounts paid for each position will correspond closely to the objective classifications of position worked out under job evaluation.

f) The persons being paid will recognize the fairness of the system, both in design and administration.

g) The average level of compensation for employees in each level or grade will be consciously known and controlled by the company, related closely to his contribution to company goals, and a policy about relationship with competing employers will be consciously chosen.

h) The average level of compensation will be responsive to changes in the cost of living, or changes in the value of money in the outside world.

i) Each individual will be paid within a price range from low to high, and the basis for upward movement of pay within a single job will be rooted in job performance.

j) Higher level persons will be paid more than lower level persons, and promotions are accompanied by pay increases.

k) Nonwage and salary compensation will be as consciously planned as cash payments, and be consistent with monetary pay.

OTHER OUTPUTS OF A SOUND SYSTEM OF WAGE AND SALARY ADMINISTRATION

In addition to the two dominant outputs described above, there are some further outputs which management should expect from its salary administration program.

Control of labor costs

In the decade of the seventies the control of labor costs, relating wages and salaries to productivities, may be the crucial difference between company or organization success or failure. For the corporation it may be the difference between profit and loss. For firms whose work is received in bids and estimates, predictability of labor costs is an essential ingredient. For the hospital the control and justification of labor costs may be necessary to work equitably under medicare programs. Whether unionized or nonunionized, the firm which permits the vagaries of the labor market to whipsaw its labor costs constantly upward makes a costly if not disastrous mistake. This means that the prelude to good labor cost accounting and cost control is to build stability and control into such costs through establishment of evaluation and pricing of positions on a scientific basis.

Motivational effects

In some countries money in the form of wages is paid for such nonjob related facts as number of dependents, political connections, nepotism, or other reasons not related to job performance and contribution to the objectives of the firm. A properly constructed job evaluation system, however, should result in a system which rewards excellence, high output, high contribution to objectives; and to withholding such rewards from those whose contribution is lower. The use of ordinary pay, including pay raises for incentive effect, is an essential of good salary administration.

How can such a system be constructed and installed?

PROCEDURES FOR WAGE AND SALARY DETERMINATION

The traditional system of job evaluation and compensation administration varies in detail from company to company, but the essential elements limited to achieving equity and competitiveness are similar. They attempt to achieve the criteria listed above by following a systematic process in estimating worth of work and pay levels. The distinctive feature of Salary Administration by Objectives is shown graphically in Figure 13–1, and has six major phases.

1. Rudimentary determination

The starting point for wage and salary administration is when more than a single employee is hired. They might start comparing their pay, and noting what the other fellow does to get the sum of money he receives for doing it. Actually, wage and salary administration would be most unlikely in an organization with less than 50 employees, unless it were a small subunit of a larger one. The small independent retail store, for example, probably would use a kind of intuitive and guesstimate system. The owner scouts around with other employers, or the Chamber of Commerce, and finds out what other employers in his category are paying. He makes his scale comparable. Often for small employers trade associations have standard scales which they publish.

In larger organizations, the necessity to compare different jobs requires finding a standard scale that provides internal equity and keeps the company competitive.

Using objectives as the base point.   Where in customary methods of job evaluation the beginning point for grasping the managerial job is to study the *activities* contained in the job, the basic difference in salary administration by objectives lies in a new point of departure.

Where the conventional salary administration procedure calls for "job descriptions" salary administration by objectives begins by a clear definition of job objectives (outputs) which will be required of the job encumbent for the coming year.

FIGURE 13–1
Salary administration by objectives

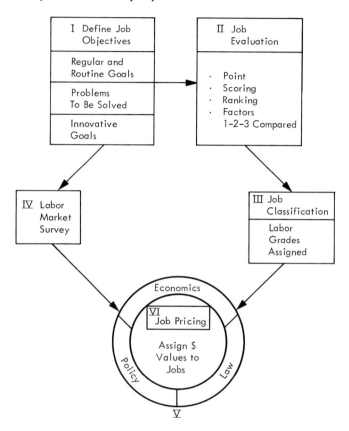

The job objectives are stated in terms of three major categories of objectives:

a) *Regular, recurring objectives,* describing in summary form that output which will be required for a related period of time.
b) *Sample statements of problems* which can be foreseen in the position which it will be a responsibility of the encumbent to solve.
c) Possible *areas of innovation and improvement,* including statements of condition which would exist if the innovative projects were well done.

Figure 13–2 shows a sample objectives statement for an assembly foreman.

While such job objectives will not always be the same from year to year, for purposes of job evaluation, the coming year is taken as a *repre-*

FIGURE 13–2

NAME_____   DEPT._____

ROUTINE OBJECTIVES
(FOREMAN)

Indicators

Outputs per Shift	P	R	O
1. First Runs OK's	___	___	___
2. Cripples	___	___	___
3. Total	___	___	___

KEYS

WATCH THESE KEYS: 1 + 2 = 3

	P	R	O
4. Crew size	___	___	___
5. Material Lead (Hr.)	___	___	___
6. Operator Mistakes	___	___	___
7. Housekeeping Score	___	___	___
8. Reportable Accidents	___	___	___
9. Ind. Material Costs	___	___	___
10. Scrap Costs per Unit	___	___	___
11. Reports Files			
· Daily	___	___	___
· Weekly	___	___	___
12. Special Instructions			
· Daily	___	___	___
· Weekly	___	___	___
13. Employee Training			
(In hours per week)			
· New	___	___	___
· Problem	___	___	___
· Flexi.	___	___	___
14.	___	___	___

*P —Pessimistic
R—Realistic
O—Optimistic

sentative and accurate sample of the outputs which can be expected of the job encumbent. This requires that objectives stated be those actually facing the job encumbent for that year, and be specific and not generalized—be outputs and not activities.

The first information to be gathered about the position takes the form of a *job objectives* questionnaire to be provided the worker in which he will provide data about the *outputs required* to be used in evaluation. Such data gathering is more than simply asking the workers or job encumbent for a narrative description. It has specific questions about output for a specific time period, and not in boxes to be checked, or scales to be rated by intuition. This is often done through an interview, in which the interviewer has a guide chart of objectives which he must complete. If done in an office, time may be saved, but if done on the job itself the analyst can see conditions as they exist. An example of such a job objectives form is shown in Figure 13–3. This is a composite of several such forms in use in industry, and aims at eliciting all of the necessary information, without being overly complex. The additional feature here lies in starting with *specific job output objectives.*

The end result is a description of the objectives of each evaluation, much of it originating with the worker, reviewed for factual accuracy and concurrence by his supervisor. The final job objectives statement is one which has been edited, agreed to by superior and subordinate, and is a thumbnail picture of the output requirements of each position, without irrelevancies, but complete enough to move to the next step evaluation of basic man requirements. It should be noted that it is the job output expected and not the worker being evaluated here.

2. Job evaluation methods

The next step in the process, after objectives are written, is to determine the relative worth among the jobs which have been described. This consists of matching job objectives against certain measuring sticks or yardsticks. Then list and evaluate detailed and accurate information about the actual activities being performed, or, as one pioneer in job evaluation E.O. Griffenhagen put it, "learn all that is practical to learn regarding the duties of each position in the service." [1] One way of doing this would be a description of the objectives and man requirements of *every* position in the organization, a process which would be extremely expensive in large organizations and not wholly useful. More practical is the process of selecting representative sample jobs:

---

[1] *Handbook of Business Administration* (New York: American Management Association, 1931).

FIGURE 13–3

Relation of worksheets for applying job evaluation by objectives (illustrative only)

Job objectives—year 1973—   Man requirement statement
    foreman—assy.   (Refer to job objectives statements)

Output per period *of time*	*Indicator level*			I *Regular responsibilities* (*require these amounts*)		*Points*			
	P	*R*	*O*						
1. Regular objectives for output				1. Education required	1	2	3	4	5
				2. Experience need	1	2	3	4	5
Units *per* shift				3. Responsibility for:					
Crew *per* shift size				(*a*) Safety of others	1	2	3	4	5
				4. Work of others	1	2	3	4	5
Accident frequency per mon.				5. Physical demand	1	2	3	4	5
				6. Mental and visual demand etc.	1	2	3	4	5
Grievances (step 1) per mon.									
2. etc.									

P = Pessimistic level
R = Realistic level
O = Optimistic level

Beginning with bench-mark jobs. This begins by listing all of the jobs in a single department, and defining objectives for all of them. From this, select a few "bench-mark" jobs which are wholly distinct and common to several departments. These bench-mark jobs can be enlarged in number until representative sample positions for the entire plant or industry have been chosen. This is judgment work, and entails the opinions of foremen, managers, and perhaps, on wage jobs, even union stewards. Other jobs which are similar in kind will later be slotted into the job classes. The time saving here can be illustrated by the results obtained in the Southern California Aircraft Industry in World War II in which only 28 key jobs were selected as representing the range of difficulty and work requirements for the entire industry.[2]

Advantages of starting with objectives. The organization which begins job evaluation with complete definition of job objectives has an advantage over those doing job evaluation without them.

1. Without objectives clearly stated, the basis for pay systems lies in casual observations, narrative descriptions of activities, and subjective judgments.

2. The employee may not fully know what proper activities are in his

---

[2] C. W. Lytle, *Job Evaluation Methods* (New York: Ronald Press, 1946), p. 133.

job until after he and his boss have agreed upon their purpose. Without clear objectives, the employee is not a reliable informant.

3. Objectives provide hard criteria and clear-cut differences in contribution expected, and make subsequent performance review more precise.

4. In selecting bench-mark jobs, objectives statements make the choice of such key jobs more responsive to organization needs.

5. Objectives statements clarifying organization status and function, where, in their absence, general job descriptions of activities *conceal* differences.

Once *job objectives* are clear, the bench-mark jobs chosen, then job evaluation can proceed.

Three major methods are presently used in evaluating jobs to spell out levels of relative importance: ranking, point scoring systems, and the factor comparison method.

Ranking jobs. This is simply a sorting system in which the judgments of experienced and responsible managers are pooled to array jobs in families or groups according to importance. It could be simply laying the finished job descriptions on a table (or up a set of stairs) and deciding that the janitor is worth less (lower in pay) than the secretary, and the time keeper the same as the secretary. The various jobs are thus *ranked* with reference to one another, but not against an objective or neutral scale. In effect, the manager of a committee sits down with the job descriptions and answers this question: If we were to try to decide how to sort these jobs into ten pay grade levels, which would be lowest, which would be highest, and how would all of the rest fit into that division?

The advantages here lie in simplicity. No scales or measuring instruments are needed, no job grade systems are predetermined. The disadvantages lie in the fact that it is wholly based upon subjective judgment, and thus less defensible if questioned by the employees or the union.

Point systems. Under one of the many point scoring systems each of the factors included in the job description are assigned points according to a standardized scale. Table 13–1 illustrates in summary form how points might be displayed against which each position will be evaluated. The positions with the highest points will end up in higher labor grades than those with lower points.

The key elements in using the point scoring system lies in three major measurement variables as shown in Figure 13–4.

Down the left margin are the factors which have been selected as important in evaluating the position. Across the top are the degrees to which these factors might apply. This grid is fleshed out with specifically assigned weights. For example, in Figure 13–5 we see a summary evaluation guide for evaluating jobs on a point scoring system.

TABLE 13–1

Labor grade	Key job title	Points
1	Janitor	410
2	Laborer, elevator operator	490
3	Machine operator	570
4	Packer	635
5	Helper, machinist	705
6	Junior electrician	770
7	Fireman, boiler	840
8	Truck driver, warehouseman	895
etc.		

FIGURE 13–4

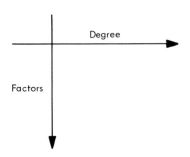

Thus, the evaluation person or committee must decide on a specific job, such as office supervisor, how many points within the permissible range of degrees are required for each factor, such as basic knowledge, or complexity and judgment. *For each factor,* then, another table must be constructed which defines the meaning of each degree. Table 13–2 shows what such a subordinate table would look like. Note that the total number of points possible is identical with that on the master table in Figure 13–5. This additional table gives you the basis for calculating the points and to what degree the position demands practical experience of its holder.

FIGURE 13–5

Factors	Degree ⟶	1	2	3	4	5	6	7
	1. Basic Knowledge	15	30	45	60	75	100	
	2. Practical Experience	20	40	60	80	100	125	150
	3. Complexity & Judgment	15	30	45	60	80	100	125
	4. Initiative	5	10	20	40	60	80	
	5. Error Prevention	5	10	20	40	60	80	
	6. Contacts with Others	5	10	20	40	60	80	
	7. Confidential Data	5	10	15	20	25		
	8. Att. to Functional Detail	5	10	15	20	25		
	9. Job Conditions	5	10	15	20	25		
Super. Only	10. Character of Supervision	5	10	20	40	60	80	
	11. Scope of Supervision	5	10	20	40	60	80	

The end result of this assessment and evaluation is that it is possible to assign a definite point total to every position evaluated.

FIGURE 13–6
Table for calculating points on Factor 2, practical experience

FACTOR 2. **PRACTICAL EXPERIENCE**

DEGREE	YEARS	POINTS
1	¼	20
2	1	40
3	3	60
4	5	80
5	7	100
6	10	125
7	OVER 10	150

1. Previous experience on related work, either with present or other company

Plus

2. Time needed to learn job in question.

Factor comparison method. A further method of evaluating jobs is known as the factor comparison method. This is often used in technical, managerial, and professional kinds of jobs. It assumes that the same factors may not be present in every job, and the job description and factors included in it are determined as part of the job evaluation. The major difference here is that the weights among factors can change or be assigned in evaluation, where in a point scoring system they remain constant for all levels.

Whether you use one or another of the three evaluation systems, all require two major tools:

a) A description of the jobs being evaluated (in outputs).

b) Some kind of measuring scale or system to weigh the relative worth of the jobs compared one with another.

3. Assigning jobs to labor grades

After the evaluation and point determination are made, the array of all jobs can be prepared. This could be done simply by totaling up those with the highest point scores and making them the highest labor grades, and so on downward. However, the removal of pay matters from human judgment cannot be this easily done, and the ranking of jobs is more than a totaling and listing, but is a check on the evaluation system itself.

Reduction in job grades. One of the benefits of job evaluation is the reduction in the number of distinct jobs which are carried on the rolls of the company. By choosing bench-mark jobs, and classifying jobs into grades, a company can reduce the number of distinct jobs to the number of rates of pay included in the grade system. The end result of this grouping of jobs is that jobs which are close together in difficulty and complexity will get similar pay, by falling within a group of jobs, all of which receive that grade. Table 13–2 shows one sample job grade chart, based upon points for salary groups.

There are in this case 20 labor grades (or groups as they are identified in the table) which include every employee below corporate officer rank in a national corporation. Thus, a middle management staff person might have 410 points and fall into grade 14. He would also find in this grade all other employees between 398–420 points.

TABLE 13–2
Table of job grades with points (points for salary groups)

Group	Points	Group	Points
1	Up to 121	11	329–351
2	122–144	12	352–374
3	145–167	13	375–397
4	168–190	14	398–420
5	191–213	15	421–443
6	214–236	16	444–466
7	237–259	17	467–489
8	260–282	18	490–512
9	283–305	19	513–535
10	306–328	20	536–558

4. Doing labor market surveys

With the production of the labor grades, the process of internal equity can be approximated, and the relative worth of jobs established systematically. This, however, does not assure competitiveness among different employers, nor assure an employer that his wages and salaries are high enough to attract good people, nor so much higher than the going rate that he is paying an unnecessary premium for labor. The essential steps in determining market prices for labor in a specific labor market should include the following:

a) The surveying company must have carefully drawn descriptions of its own jobs, and not seek comparisons based upon job titles alone.

b) It should select companies which are in the same labor markets, and the segment of employers sampled should be neither too narrow nor too wide. This need not be a complete survey, but rather a carefully chosen sample. Michigan Bell Telephone, for example, must survey all of those cities in Michigan in which it hires employees. Detroit Edison, on the other hand, will survey only major firms in Southeastern Michigan in which it operates.

c) Visitation to cooperating companies in the beginning, later followed by letters or telephone calls, is safest to assure comparability of responses.

d) Preparation of some working instruments for such a survey would include a survey worksheet to list the data collected from each company. This data should include more than simply wages paid, but should include fringe benefits such as vacations paid, paid holidays, special benefits plans such as paid life, hospitalization, and other benefits. If the positions being surveyed have been evaluated under a formal job evaluation plan, this might facilitate comparison.

e) The completed product of such a survey should provide the basis for the analyst to prepare a general wage and salary level for the labor market. This could be in the form shown in Figure 13–7. The numbers on the left vertical scale represent amounts paid for various levels of worth. The horizontal scale shows the surveying company's labor grades.

FIGURE 13–7

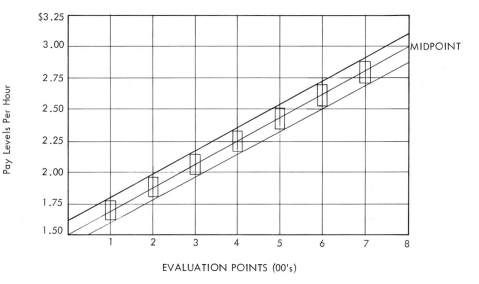

EVALUATION POINTS (00's)

5. Policy

By plotting your own company's jobs against the community picture of how other employers are paying for similar work, a policy decision can be made about pay levels. For the company which is determined to be among the highest, it gears its average pay curve along the top line of the ascending curve. For the firm which intends to stay with the average, the rates paid aim at adhering to the midpoint line. For those who for internal reasons determine to pay less than others, the diagram provides a basis for establishing its rates in relationship to the community.

6. Pricing

The end result is a series of job prices for all the jobs in the firm. Ordinarily they would be arranged in a series which could be illustrated in Figure 13–8.

FIGURE 13–8

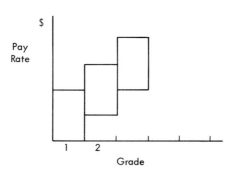

This is, of course, a segment of a whole job pricing chart, but it illustrates the principle. It should be noted that the bottom of labor grade 2 is below the top of labor grade 1. (The distance from the bottom to the top of a single labor grade is called the *range*.) The basis upon which an employee moves upward within his labor grade is merit, or performance review, based upon his superior's estimates of his performance on that job for a specific period of time.

CAN EXECUTIVES BE PAID WHAT THEY'RE WORTH? *

To pay an executive what he's worth, a company must resolve the three dilemmas that currently limit proper compensation. Just how much is an executive worth? It usually depends on whom you ask. Anyone who has attended a stockholders' meeting is aware of the inherent conflicts between the corporate managers and the so-called owners. No aspect of corporate life is more loaded with economic, social, political, and administrative implications than the question of executive pay levels. For example, most companies wrestle with problems like these:

■ When is an executive overpaid?

■ Should an executive be paid according to different criteria than lower-level employees are?

■ How can executive pay become part of corporate strategy?

---

* Adapted from an article by the author originally printed in *Business Management* magazine. Copyright 1966 by *Business Management*. Used by permission.

■ To what extent are executive pay levels determined by public needs and interests?

■ Is there a discernible relationship between the level of executive salaries and the profits accruing to stockholders?

■ How large must executive salaries be to provide corporations with vigorous and skillful leadership?

■ How do tax laws affect executive pay practices?

"There are only three problems in executive compensation," a member of a board of directors of a large corporation said recently. "The first is internal dissension, the second is litigation, and the third is public criticism." These three factors provide a useful framework for an examination of the problem.

Resolve internal inequities

In large companies, executive salaries are scaled downward from the salary of the chief executive. Surveys of certain kinds of companies show that if the president gets $100,000, the vice president in charge of sales will get about $70,000, the vice president of manufacturing or research, $55,000, the vice president of engineering, $45,000, and the vice president of personnel, $35,000. If the president refuses to accept a raise, he may compress salaries at the bottom levels of the scale, especially if there are six or seven levels between the top executive and the first-line manager.[3]

The problems don't end here, however. Psychologist Jay Otis of Western Reserve University, who specializes in salary administration problems, points out that within each department or division, pay scales are likewise cued to the remuneration of the chief officer of the department.

Consider the sales vice president who gets $70,000 per year, and the vice president of manufacturing who gets $55,000. In their respective departments, the salaries of their subordinates will tend to slope downward from their own pay levels. Thus, the manufacturing vice president may have reporting to him the manager of a substantial manufacturing plant who will earn, say $20,000 per year, while a regional sales manager who doesn't even report directly to the sales vice president may get as much as the plant manager, though he has less responsibility and certainly fewer people to supervise. This arrangement extends down through the organization so that the plant manager's secretary is paid less than the sales manager's secretary simply because the salaries are arranged around different clusters.

Admittedly, a rational salary administration system would eliminate

[3] Recent evidence shows a narrowing of these differences: Arch Patton, "What is Experience Worth?" *Business Horizons,* Vol. 11, No. 5 (October, 1968), pp. 31–40.

such inequities at the lower levels of the corporate hierarchy. But, in practice, the salaries usually cluster under the department's top man, and this may create internal dissension within the company.

The problem could be resolved to a considerable extent, however, if agreement could be reached on a definition of the term "executive." Some authorities take the view that an executive is someone who formulates plans, reviews the work of others, and integrates the demands of various groups within a business enterprise. Others would classify in the executive category anyone who has professional, managerial, or technical status and makes important decisions bearing on profits. This definition would encompass such individuals as researchers and corporate counsel. Milton Rock, a management consultant, recently endorsed the latter view in a talk before the Montreal Personnel Association.

Dean Charles Abbott of the University of Virginia Graduate School of Business has proposed still another definition. He concludes that the executive is someone who acts in a way that gives him a unique role in the company and in society. He is the paid risk bearer, which is different from being a paid administrator (who is, in reality, a high-level employee). The administrator is an expert solely responsible for the professional quality of his advice. The executive must make decisions, guide their implementation, and bear responsibility for the results.

The risk taker must be compensated for his risk-assuming role, which was formerly incumbent on the owner. In the large company, then, individuals below the rank of division general manager cannot be classed as true executives, according to Abbott's definition. A division general manager may be the lowest ranking official who makes decisions directly bearing on corporate profits.

Under this concept, a designer for General Motors, for example, is responsible for the quality of his work, which is vital to the future of the business. But only the company president, the executive committee, and the managers of Chevrolet, Buick, Oldsmobile, and other GM divisions decide which alternative design will be chosen and put into production.

Salary policy for the executive group is quite distinct from that for engineers, market research experts, and others. All the latter are vital employees, but their salaries can be arrived at by standard procedures. Determining the salary of a vital employee is a matter of viewing his particular job against a set of factors that apply to all jobs—his grade classification, the condition of the labor market at the time, the funds available for salaries, and so on.

It is pointless to follow this standard procedure in determining the remuneration of risk bearers, because their functions are unique. The executive must be paid for the results he obtains in terms of profit and growth.

Let's consider the president of a small manufacturing company. Under his management, the company makes a profit of $1 million on $10 million in sales and an investment of $5 million. The president's aggregate compensation is $95,000 a year, though the company has only 500 employees. The competing companies in his field are doing one quarter as well in terms of profit and return on investment.

Now let us compare this company president with the top executive of a company in a different field with annual sales of $300 million and earnings of $3 million on an investment of $150 million; he gets only $80,000.

If we applied the standard job evaluation procedures to both executives, the president of the first company would be considered overpaid. Yet the president of the large company may not be worth his pay, while the president of the small company may actually be underpaid considering the results he is achieving in his own firm.

Or take two division managers of one large corporation. General manager A runs a highly profitable small division which earns 15 percent on sales. General manager B runs a division with 10 times as many employees, a bigger investment, and a sales volume 15 times as large. Yet his absolute profit is only twice that of the small division, and his rate of profit 90 percent lower.

Obviously, we must consider other factors as well in determining the relative remuneration of the two executives in this instance. Is one man cruising along in a soft job where any manager of average ability could make money because of trade advantages, patent position, or windfall profits? Is the manager whose division shows a lower rate of profits faced with extraordinary problems of competition, costs, declining markets, or other obstacles that would overwhelm a person of ordinary caliber, problems which he, through special ability, has partly overcome and, as a consequence, has succeeded in preventing them from causing sizable losses?

It is evident, therefore, that no simple formula can be applied in rewarding individuals for generating profits.

Resolve legal problems

Corporation and tax laws provide ample opportunities for legal troubles when a company, especially one with a board heavily dominated by its officers, appears to be self-serving in its compensation policies.

As a rule, the stockholder is a fairly passive animal when it comes to suing his company or its officers for excessive compensation. The stockholder is willing to be treated simply as a recipient of the "wages of capital" and only asks for a fair shake. When dividends are not forthcoming, the stockholders may unite into a militant, but for the most part, ineffectual organization which badgers management at annual meetings.

It is only infrequently that stockholders' ire results in a lawsuit against management.

More often the dissatisfied stockholders simply sell their holdings and buy another stock that is paying a higher return. The thought seldom crosses their minds that they have bought anything more than an equity on earnings.

Another kind of litigation that might confront management is a suit in the tax courts by the Internal Revenue Service. Such suits are brought by the IRS against corporations who don't abide by rulings on executive compensation.

The most important legal restraints, however, are those affecting possible tax loopholes for executives. High salaries obviously provide little incentive if a sizable proportion of them has to be remitted to the tax collector. Accordingly, corporations are continuously devising executive compensation plans designed to mitigate the tax burden. One answer to the problem is deferred compensation. Here, part of the executive's compensation is held back until he retires, when his income will be smaller and subject to a lower rate of taxation.[4]

Stock option plans permit executives to buy company shares at a price below the going market price as of a certain date. Since the executive is granted several years in which to pick up his options, he can often wait until a propitious time arises to buy. Or he may buy the shares and hold them until he can sell them at a sizable profit. Either way, provided he holds the shares for three years or longer, he pays a capital gains tax instead of the steeper ordinary income tax. At the same time, he has a powerful incentive to make the company prosper so that the value of his stock will increase and he can sell it at a profit. Recent changes in tax law, however, have reduced the time period over which options may be exercised, thus making this form of compensation less attractive than it was before the new law was passed.

Resolve public criticism

Public criticism is another important factor influencing the compensation of executives. It is mainly directed at the practice of granting top managers large bonuses over and above their high salaries. Typical labor union newspapers usually make a point of comparing hefty executive bonuses with the pay of workers. Such comparisons are especially popular at a time when contracts are being negotiated.

Recently, the Railroad Brotherhoods protested that during the past year, while jobs of workers had been eliminated, the number of executive

---

[4] For a complete discussion of varying needs of executives, see George Foote, "The Executive's Compensation and his Career Cycle," *Business Horizons*, Vol. 8, No. 1 (Spring, 1965), pp. 35–42.

positions on Class I railroads, paying over $25,000 annually, had sharply increased. And in 1963 the *Detroit Free Press* headlined two stories: a statement by an auto company official that further wage increases for workers were considered inflationary and a report that large bonuses had been distributed to officers of the same company. Such stories impress the public, but how valid are the objections to the managerial bonuses?

The real test is whether the stockholders, the workers, and the public profit or suffer because of such bonuses. Few General Motors stockholders, for example, complain because 12 percent of profits, after deducting 6 percent of net capital, may be placed in a bonus pool and distributed to key officials on the bonus roll. The progress sharing plan of American Motors extended the sharing of profits down to assembly-line workers, an innovation that made executive bonuses much more palatable.

Perhaps arguments for rewarding such intangibles as leadership can never be fully communicated to the general public. Thus, public criticism can be expected to continue. The true test is whether the policy makers in Congress and the executive branch of the government will have the insight and the pertinent facts to refrain from reducing everyone's rewards to one common denominator.

Some psychologists maintain that people seek other rewards besides money. However, I haven't been able to get those same psychologists to expound their theories at a management conference for less than a $200 fee. As one wag put it, in motivating people, "money beats whatever comes second best by a substantial margin."

For more than two decades now it has been fashionable to proclaim the death of economic man and to kick the corpse for good measure. Experience with executive compensation indicates, however, that there is still some life left in the old boy.

QUESTIONS AND PROBLEMS

1. A matter of constant debate is how important money received is to the employee. How would you rate it?

2. What makes equity such an important issue?

3. Should a university pay wages and salaries scientifically calculated to be competitive? What else could make up for money?

4. Give three examples of how whipsaw could work.

5. At what point in the salary administration system do we prepare job objectives for the position? Why are they inserted at this point?

6. What is the difference between a job description and job objectives?

7. What are the three systems for evaluating jobs? What are the advantages and disadvantages of each?

8. Why would the factor of experience merit 150 points where unsatisfactory working conditions earn 25 points?

9. Refer to Table 13–2. If a man went from 214 points to 232 points because his job was enlarged, would he get a raise? How would you justify this?

10. What is the difference in payment philosophy between executives and workers?

11. What can happen if you allow your executive compensation system to fall into disarray?

AMBERGRIS ELECTRONICS
AND SPACE COMPANY CASE

Ambergris Electronics and Space Company had been in technologically based business for many years. A line of radio products had been the basis of the business for many years, to which there had been added a new division in 1960 to enter the rapidly growing computer field. Although the company never intended to compete with IBM or Honeywell, or the other giants, they saw some great potential in peripheral equipment, and in the industry generally. By 1965 they had assumed a recognizable position in the field, although profits had not yet appeared after five years of steady growth. 1965 proved to be a somewhat more troublesome year. With the advent of time sharing, the company found itself involved in some fairly expensive development efforts which ate seriously into profits of the whole company.

Despite a steady rise of earnings in the consumer electronics division, especially through acquisition of parts and units from Japan, the losses in computer related products ate up almost all of the profits for the entire company, and a dividend being passed was a distinct possibility.

Upon orders from the top, a moratorium upon salary increases was ordered, and the salary administrator was required to administer the ruling. The ruling had not been put in writing, but the president was most emphatic:

"You recognize that we don't want to set this down in print, but I can assure you that no raises should be given this year, unless a man moves to a higher position, or his job content changes and he gets a raise on the basis of classification."

When the general manager of the radio products division was appraised of this decision, he was furious. "How in heck can I keep my best engineers when you cut off the raises at the very time when they are doing better than anybody in our business. They should not be penalized for the errors in judgment up above, nor for conditions of the marketing and technology in a line which they have no connection with. We should pay them for performance. If we don't, we will lose the best men, and then where will we be? We will lose on the very items that are keeping us from financial disaster."

Despite the plausibility of his argument, which all conceded, the impending storm when dividends were passed would make such a move impossible, the president declared.

"I don't intend to sit here and be critical of my bosses on the board, but I can tell you that they are apt to overlook fine distinctions such as yours, and crawl my frame for overall results. I simply can't present a budget with raises in it."

The general manager retreated at this, and after some several days of thinking called in the divisional personnel manager.

I have some ways of finding some funds for increases for my key people, but I'm worried about the mechanics and technicians who have done such a fine job for us in the past years. Some higher priced men are leaving and I'll replace them with some new and lower priced men and use the differences in salaries for the remainder on a selective basis. I can do this without giving details upstairs. I want you to go over our classification system which we use for hourly rated employees very, very carefully. I want you to find the weak spots in that classification manual so that we can raise the pay of certain selected classifications by enlarging the points accorded to each of those classes.

Come back with a plan, telling me how, within the existing classification manual, you can get some raises for our key people in mechanical and technician spots through reclassification of those jobs. When you have such a plan, come back and see me personally. I don't want anyone but your eyes and mine to see the plan until after it is accomplished.

The personnel manager slipped the classification manual into his briefcase and took it home with him that night. He saw that it would take 50 points addition to a specific job in order to get a man a raise. He then sat down to work out a general strategy for inflating the point scores of selected jobs.

APPENDIX I: AMBERGRIS JOB CLASSIFICATION MANUAL

Job evaluation schedule

Factors evaluated	Degrees of value to job (showing maximum point values per degree)				
	1st	2nd	3rd	4th	5th
1. Educational requirements	10	20	30	40	50
2. Experience and knowledge of essential details..	20	40	60	80	100
3. Individual judgment required	25	50	75	100	125
4. Manual skill	15	30	45	60	75
5. Phyiscal effort	5	10	15	20	25
6. Mental and visual attention	10	20	30	40	50
7. Exposure to personal hazards	15	30	45	60	75
8. Responsibility for safety of others	20	40	60	80	100
9. Seriousness of mistakes (not including personal hazards)	15	30	45	60	75
10. Supervision of others (leadership requirements)	30	60	90	120	150
11. Public contacts (customer relations)	25	50	75	100	125
12. Working conditions	5	10	15	20	25
Total	195	390	585	780	975

Factor 1: Educational requirements

First degree—0 to 10 points. Must be able to read, write, speak, and understand English; follow simple instructions and perform routine operations of simple character. Equivalent to six or more years of common school education.

Second degree—10 to 20 points. Must be able to perform routine operations of moderate complexity and variety based on more detailed instructions. Equivalent to about two years of high school.

Third degree—20 to 30 points. Must be able to perform semiroutine operations of considerable complexity and variety where standard methods of procedure are available. Equivalent to four years of high school, or two years of high school plus two years apprenticeship or trade school training, or common school graduate plus four years apprenticeship or trade school training.

Fourth degree—30 to 40 points. Must be able to understand technical or commercial problems and perform a wide variety of nonroutine work where only general methods of procedure are available. Equivalent to high school plus at least two years trade school, commercial, technical school training.

Fifth degree—40 to 50 points. Must be able to understand advanced technical or professional problems and perform nonroutine duties of considerable complexity and variety, frequently without standard methods of procedure. Equivalent to high school education plus extensive training in special branch of knowledge, such as engineering, law, economics, accounting, business, or personnel administration, etc.

Factor 2: Practical experience and knowledge of essential details

First degree—0 to 20 points. Not over six months previous experience necessary.

Second degree—20 to 40 points. Work of comparatively simple nature, usually requiring one to two years to learn and coordinate all necessary details of work routine and company organization, policies, and procedures applicable to job.

Third degree—40 to 60 points. Work of moderately complex nature, usually requiring two to five years in related work to learn and coordinate all necessary details to work routine and company organization, policies, and procedures applicable to job.

Fourth degree—60 to 80 points. Work of considerable complexity and variety, usually requiring five to seven years in related work to learn and coordinate all necessary details of work routine and company organization, policies and procedures applicable to job.

Fifth degree—80 to 100 points. Work of high complexity and varied nature, usually requiring more than seven years in related work to learn and coordinate all necessary details of work routine and company organization policies, and procedures applicable to job.

Factor 3: Individual judgment required

This factor gives consideration to the need for ability for original conception, independent action, or exercise of judgment.

First degree—0 to 25 points. No independent decisions required. Employee is told what to do and his work is subject to close supervision by higher ranking employee.

Second degree—25 to 50 points. Needs to exercise minor judgment in the making of relatively unimportant decisions. Employee performs only that work which he has been instructed to do, subject to frequent checking by higher ranking employee.

Third degree—50 to 75 points. Needs to exercise considerable judgment in making important decisions within the limitations of standard practice or procedure. Employee performs work which he has been instructed to do, which is reviewed from time to time by higher ranking employee.

Fourth degree—75 to 100 points. Needs to possess mature analytical ability and judgment in making independent decisions, planning courses of action, and performing work where only general methods of procedure are available. Employee works under general instructions and his work is reviewed or checked fairly frequently by higher ranking employee.

Fifth degree—100 to 125 points. Needs to possess keen analytical ability and judgment in making important decisions, supervising complicated procedures, and performing work predominantly intellectual and varied in character, for which there are no standard methods or procedure, and whose output produced or result accomplished cannot be standardized in relation to a given period of time. Employee works under general instructions only and results are reviewed infrequently by high ranking employee.

Factor 4: Manual skill and dexterity

First degree—0 to 15 points. Work requires practically no manual skill.

Second degree—15 to 30 points. Requires use of hand tools, instruments, or devices with moderate skill and dexterity; or the operation of moderately complex machinery or equipment.

Third degree—30 to 45 points. Requires considerable skill and dexterity in the use of hand tools, instruments, or devices; or the use of shop tools to dismantle and repair equipment of moderate complexity; or requires the operation of complex machinery or equipment.

Fourth degree—45 to 60 points. Work requires high grade mechanical skill such as machine tool operations working to close tolerances; or the repair, assembly, and adjustments of complicated machinery or very delicate equipment; or requires skill in the execution of artistic designs, mechanical drawings, etc.

Fifth degree—60 to 75 points. Work requires highest grade of mechanical skill and dexterity and extremely fine and accurate workmanship such as that performed by highly developed craftsmen; or requires outstanding talent in the execution of artistic designs, etc.

Factor 5: Physical effort

First degree—0 to 5 points. Work requires a minimum of physical effort.

Second degree—5 to 10 points. Minimum physical effort required most of time. Moderate exertion required occasionally.

Third degree—10 to 15 points. Work requires almost continuous physical activity but usually not of strenuous nature.

Fourth degree—15 to 20 points. Work requires continuous physical activity of a moderately fatiguing nature. Occasionally may require unusual strenuous activity.

Fifth degree—20 to 25 points. Major portion of work requires such strenuous activity that employee of average physique cannot continue it to normal age of retirement.

Factor 6: Mental and visual attention

First degree—0 to 10 points. Work is practically automatic routine requiring minimum mental and visual effort.

Second degree—10 to 20 points. Frequent mental or visual attention required but not of a fatiguing nature.

Third degree—20 to 30 points. Continuous mental or visual attention required accompanied by moderate fatigue.

Fourth degree—30 to 40 points. Work requires unusual mental concentration or close visual attention usually resulting in noticeable fatigue by the end of the day.

Fifth degree—40 to 50 points. Work requires concentrated and exacting mental effort subject to numerous distractions or continuous visual attention which is practically certain to result in considerable mental or visual fatigue by the end of the day.

Factor 7: Personal hazards

First degree—0 to 15 points. Minimum probability of accident at all times. Accidents likely to be of minor consequences.

Second degree—15 to 30 points. Minimum probability of accident most of time. Occasionally exposed to moderate hazards. In rare cases, accident may be serious.

Third degree—30 to 45 points. Major portion of time engaged in moderately hazardous work. Carelessness may cause serious injury.

Fourth degree—45 to 60 points. Major portion of time engaged in moderately hazardous work. Occasionally exposed to unusual hazards. Moderate extra premium required for life or accident insurance.

Fifth degree—60 to 75 points. Major portion of time engaged in unusually hazardous work. Very high extra premium required for life or accident insurance.

Factor 8: Responsibility for safety of others

First degree—0 to 20 points. Minimum responsibility at all times for safety of others.

Second degree—20 to 40 points. Only reasonable care in own work required to insure safety of others. Injuries likely to be of minor nature.

Third degree—40 to 60 points. Safety of others may be endangered at times; but observance of standard precautions and reasonable care should insure safe operation.

Fourth degree—60 to 80 points. Frequently engaged in performing or directing moderately hazardous work where safety of others is directly dependent on employee's carefulness. Accidents may result in serious injury to small groups.

Fifth degree—80 to 100 points. Considerable portion of time engaged in performing or directing unusually hazardous work where safety of others depends on employee's careful planning and clear thinking. Accidents may be of most serious nature and involve considerable numbers.

Factor 9: Seriousness of mistakes (not including personal hazards)

First degree—0 to 15 points. Mistakes likely to be of minor consequence, merely involving wasted effort of employee and expense of doing work over again; or it may involve minor spoilage of materials. Likely to be due to carelessness.

Second degree—15 to 30 points. Mistakes may involve wasted effort of small group of employees or considerable loss due to spoilage of materials; or may cause minor interruption of service. Likely to be due to carelessness.

Third degree—30 to 45 points. Mistakes in the preparation of reports, computations, or designs; and mistakes in construction, operation, maintenance, or inspection may cause moderate financial loss and/or small interruption of service. May be caused by inability to cope with unusual conditions.

Fourth degree—45 to 60 points. Mistakes in the preparation of reports, computations, or designs and mistakes in construction, operation, maintenance, or inspection may cause extensive financial loss and/or intensive interruption of service. May be caused by inability to cope with unusual conditions.

Fifth degree—60 to 75 points. Mistakes in the preparation of reports, computations, or designs and mistakes in construction, operation, maintenance, or inspection may cause very heavy financial loss and/or very widespread interruption of service. May be caused by inability to cope with unusual conditions.

Factor 10: Supervision of others (leadership requirements)

First degree—0 to 30 points. Does not direct work of other employees.

Second degree—30 to 60 points. Directs work of one or two employees of lower grade assisting on the same job.

Third degree—60 to 90 points. Supervises small group of employees engaged in routine work while performing similar work himself. Personnel problems, training of employees, and planning of work are comparatively simple.

Fourth degree—90 to 120 points. Devotes practically full time to the supervision of a relatively small group of employees engaged in routine work. Employee training comparatively simple. Considerable ability required in handling personnel problems and planning work.

Fifth degree—120 to 150 points. Devotes full time to the supervision of a relatively large group of employees engaged in routine work or a small group of employees engaged in nonroutine or very important work. Requires outstanding ability in handling personnel problems, training of employees, and planning of work.

Factor 11: Public contacts (customer relations)

First degree—0 to 25 points. Work requires no contact with customers, contractors, or the general public.

Second degree—25 to 50 points. Requires frequent superficial contacts with the general public or contacts incidental to work performed on the customer's premises.

Third degree—50 to 75 points. Work requires business correspondence, telephone contacts, or personal interviews with customers, contractors, or the general public on matters of minor importance but not including adjustment of complaints.

Fourth degree—75 to 100 points. Work requires business correspondence, telephone contacts, or personal interviews with customers, contractors, or the general public on matters of moderate importance including adjustment of minor complaints.

Fifth degree—100 to 125 points. Work requires business correspondence, telephone contacts, or personal interviews with customers, contractors, or the general public on matters of major importance including adjustment of important complaints.

Factor 12: Working conditions

First degree—0 to 5 points. Indoor work in clean, well-lighted, heated, and ventilated surroundings.

Second degree—5 to 10 points. Average indoor conditions with no features which disturb the well-being of the employee.

Third degree—10 to 15 points. Work having some disagreeable element which is not continuous such as heat, cold, dust, noise, or vibration, or occasional outdoor work in inclement weather.

Fourth degree—15 to 20 points. Work having some disagreeable element which is continuous such as heat, cold, noise, or vibration, or outdoor work continuing without interruption in all kinds of weather.

Fifth degree—20 to 25 points: Work involving exposure to some form of occupational disease serious enough, if contracted, to cause partial disability.

Group study questions

1. What changes in factors and degrees would you propose to achieve the general manager's instructions?
2. Could his purpose be achieved by any other means?
3. What would you advise the personnel manager to do?

chapter 14

SAFETY MANAGEMENT — USING THE SYSTEMS APPROACH

A LAMENTABLE but hard fact of industrial life is that a number of people are injured, crippled, or killed in the course of their employment and industry each year.

It may be predicted that some 14,000 workers will be killed in occupational accidents, and as high as 2 million will suffer varying degrees of injury in a single year. While this rate of accidents has not gone up in proportion to the size of the labor force, in certain industries where the hazards are greatest (e.g., construction, heavy manufacturing, and where lifting and handling of heavy objects or materials is involved), the rate continues to be appallingly high. Ordinarily the management in control of the safety programs is centered in the personnel administration department, and the attainment of safe working conditions and an accident-free work force are becoming increasingly important objectives.

The facets of occupational safety, health, and hygiene appear to be growing and include not only injuries to life and limb, which occur through unsafe actions and conditions on the job, but have been enlarged to include excessive noise at work, radiation hazards where the peaceful use of atomic energy has moved into ordinary operations of the plant, and new forms of materials which can adversely affect the health of the employee.

Beyond these traditional threats to employee health and safety, companies are becoming increasingly aware of the importance of constructive action to preserve emotional health. Although approaches to diagnoses or treatments of problem cases are not all alike, there are basically two different ways of organizing mental health services in a company: (1) to place a trained psychologist on the staff; and (2) to integrate the mental health activity into the total employee relations program with occasional assistance from a psychiatrically oriented professional as its director.

Beyond this, an increasing concern has also been shown for the physical, mental, and social health of executives as evidenced by the increase in funded medical and mental health examinations of these people.

A SYSTEMS APPROACH TO SAFETY MANAGEMENT

In France, at the end of the 19th century, when the manufacture of explosives was expanded rapidly to meet the demands of the armies of Europe, the French government applied a remarkable effective Systems Approach to the management of safety in explosives manufacture. It was made a matter of law that the chief executive of the explosives manufacturing company and his family have their place of residence in the geographic center of such operations. The purpose of this rather startling move was to assure that the senior executive's attentions would be pointed toward safety in operations. The effects were startling, and many of the conventional reasons given for the inevitability of accidents in hazardous occupations were found to be missing under such circumstances.

The systems approach to safety management begins, then, with the engineering of the product, the process, and the equipment upon which the work will be done; and it extends to the layout of the workplace, the flow of work between the machines, the handling of materials, and the policies which guide the company in its safety. Ordinarily, such systems approaches are part of the responsibility of the engineering and research and development departments of the company and not made the responsibility of the personnel administration department.

Nevertheless, the personnel administration department has an important role to play in the application of systems approaches to industrial safety. These include some of the following responsibilities:

I. Establishment of indicator systems

Perhaps the basic step in the establishment of a safety system is an adequate system of measurement of the effect of total operations and systems upon the safety, health, and welfare of employees at work. Accident statistics are an essential factor for a total safety effort on a systems basis. They provide a means of comparison with governmental and private industrial organizations who themselves collect and promulgate such figures; they provide a basis for measuring changes in accident levels within a single company and therefore show the negative or positive effects of various safety programs; they provide a measure of effectiveness which can be related to monetary expenditures and can create the basis for a cost effectiveness program as part of the systematic approach to accident prevention.[1]

Two of the more widely used indicators are the following:

$$\text{Injury severity rate} = \frac{\text{Number of days lost} \times 1{,}000{,}000}{\text{Number of manhours worked}}$$

$$\text{Injury frequency rate} = \frac{\text{Number of disabling injuries} \times 1{,}000{,}000}{\text{Number of manhours worked}}$$

Further additional indicators might include the number of reportable injuries, the level of activity in the plant versus office or physician's office or first aid stations.

Still another indicator which is easily obtainable in a personnel administration department is the effect upon workman's compensation claims, on temporary disability insurance rates, and on the costs of lost time production chargeable to accident rates.

II. An effective reporting system

The second major tool of the systems approach is an adequate managerial reporting system from which statistics required in the above indicator are developed. Such accident reports should be prepared immediately by the supervisor of the man involved, and it should be sufficiently clear that the major systems causes of the accident will be defined in writing and be made available for analysis. Such a procedure will have some benefits of a preventative educational nature for the supervisor who is required to complete the report.

Ordinarily, the collection of accident report data should include at least the following kinds of information:

Name of employee.
Location and organizational unit.
Sex, age, and occupation.
Time and place of the reported accident.
Narrative description of the events leading up to the accident itself.
A report of the injury itself with respect to extent and injury suffered.
Specific work being done at time of injury.
Tools, equipment, and physical apparatus involved in the injury.
Effect of unsafe condition on the equipment or facilities.
Description of unsafe actions taken by the injured.
Description of unsafe action taken by another person resulting in the injury to the victim.

---

[1] H. W. Heinrich, *Industrial Accident Prevention* (4th ed.: New York: McGraw-Hill, 1959).

Condition of safeguards which were provided.
Damage to materials or equipment attending the accident.
Days lost.
Statement of action taken to prevent similar accident.
Signature of the investigator.
Approval and review of the report form.

III. Development of safety management procedures

An essential ingredient in a systems approach is that there be an orderly system of organization, communication, and follow-up on each individual accident and on evidence of a statistical nature when accident frequency and severity rates show an upward movement. In the event that such a movement is not going in a favorable direction, it should be considered a matter of concern for the safety management organization. In many large companies there is an increasing tendency toward the use of safety committees involving the highest level obtainable of those individuals who are on an interdepartmental level. This committee is responsible for the preparation of indicators, the measurement of indicators on a regular basis, and the consideration of the problems when they emerge in the form of those indicators that have moved in the wrong direction. Such a committee should also have responsibilities for making recommendations for engineering and developmental changes; for recommending expenditures related to employee health, safety, and accident prevention; and for insuring overall evaluation of performance of the entire plant for safety.

In many companies, including the food industry, departmental committees under foreman leadership can bring forth a strong motivational effect in bringing about employee participation and employee safety. They also have a valuable function for safety training, for getting widespread publicity for safety programs, for obtaining willing compliance with safety regulations, and for on-the-job instruction in safety policies and decisions. In Hercules Powder Company for many years, all engineering changes, drawings, and proposed facilities developments have had to be approved by a director of safety before they were released for budgetary approval.

IV. Effective use of supervision in managing for safety

In those organizations where safety records have been achieved for a long period of time with remarkable success, it has appeared almost inescapably that effective supervision has been an important part of the safety system. Under such a system, any performance appraisal to be filed on any supervisor should include a record of his safety performance against specific indicators such as frequency, severity, and reportable accidents. Such an appraisal should be given weight on equal par with production and quality as it is in organizations such as DuPont. The effects of a bad safety record or failure to enforce safety regulations could result in a diminishing of salary increase, bonus, promotability, and other benefits which could recruit the supervisor to a higher position if he were effective in all facets of his job.

V. The role of employee and supervisory training in safety management

To the extent that industrial accidents occur through unsafe actions of employees resulting in injuries either to themselves or to fellow employees, there is no underestimating the importance of training programs in the achievement of satisfactory levels of low accidents or accident-free operation.

A. Job instruction training for the workers. Apart from the beneficial effects of cost, production, and quality, the effects of the job instruction training of new workers being conducted on a new systematic basis cannot be overemphasized. In World War II the JIT programs under the war industry training programs proved the beneficial effects of a well-organized program of job induction. Under such a system, each job is systematically defined in terms of specific steps marking *key points* which should be highlighted in any job. Safety, under such a condition, is always a key point, pointing up the hazards and also highlighting the correct manner of performing the job.

B. Supervisor training. The importance of supervision and the role of the general foreman in achieving accident-free operations is often established in the development of supervisors from their early days as supervisory personnel. The recognition that accidents follow a sequence which is a combination of unsafe conditions and actions that lead to injuries, requires that supervision be prepared to recognize such unsafe conditions and to remedy them by overcoming unsafe actions through training or on-the-job coaching, and proper discipline.

C. A professional safety director. Because the systems approach to safety requires organization, communication, and control, a full-time professional safety director is an essential systematic element. In smaller plants this is often combined, and a dual-function job, such as safety and training director, is devised. (In even smaller plants, such a responsibility becomes the function of the personnel manager.) In any event, this person serves in a staff capacity to assure that:

the accident reports are being completed.

the training be adequately done as each new employee enters the firm.

the supervision is being adequately trained and evaluated upon safety performance.

the supervisor be designed to serve as a staff executive director of the Safety Policy Committee.

Such a position requires an active, competent manager, a condition normally not found in too many companies. In those firms where safety programs have taken on vitality and have achieved outstanding results, there is almost always a strong and capable individual who occupies the safety director position.

SAFETY PROBLEM SOLVING—BY OBJECTIVES

Having organized for safety management, there remains a major facet of safety management, which in practice probably accounts for the majority of the effort and effectiveness of a safety program—the solving of problems and preventing potential problems. Using the systems approach in such problem solving requires that the following conditions exist:

1. An indicator system which can generate data early enough to show that a problem is present. This means two ingredients: definition of ideal conditions, and definition of actual conditions.

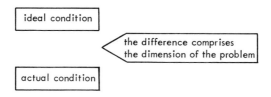

2. An alert attention to variation, or indicators that a problem has begun.[2]

Special category occupational hazards

In the old saying "a good day's work never killed anybody" lies an important omission. A good day's work in the uranium industry could lead to lung cancer because of radiation. Working in a cotton mill could lead to chronic bronchitis and emphysema. Other materials, including asbestos, talc, berryllium, laundry soap, enzymes, sugar cane fiber, or hot lead fumes, could lead to occupational diseases. These are in addition to the more widespread hazards from unsafe machines, tools, equipment, or physical factors in the job environment. After several thousands of years of digging ditches, men are killed every year by cave-ins of trenches and ditches on construction sites.

---

[2] G. S. Odiorne, *Management Decisions By Objectives* (Englewood Cliffs, New Jersey: Prentice-Hall, 1969).

Safety in the office

Because of the rise in the proportion of the work force which is engaged in office types of occupations, it may safely be predicted that accidents in the office may be a matter of increasing concern in the future. For one thing, they can be as severe and costly as production accidents, in part because they are not expected. One study of 8,000 insurance company office employees, and of more than a million office workers in 3,000 California companies provides some insight into the growing scope of this safety problem.[3]

Injury rates are highest here among new employees and transfers, both being unfamiliar with their new surroundings. Rates of female office workers are somewhat higher than for males in the office. Falls comprise the most frequent source of injury, followed by strains from overexertion, striking against objects such as desk drawers left open, or standing up suddenly to find that the top file drawer immediately overhead is sharp and painful. Next in order of frequency are the injuries which come from falling objects, such as typewriters and office machines slipping off desks or being caught between pieces of equipment or between machines. Machine injuries are another category.

Given this problem, some remedial measures include the following major steps which can be included in the company safety system. (1) Orientation of new employees on proper operating methods with emphasis upon safety to self and others. (2) Setting purchasing standards for design and care of equipment. (3) Approval and involvement of safety experts in the layout of offices, stairways, electrical outlets, lighting, ventilation, and choice of fluid such as reproduction liquids. (4) Supervisory briefings and attention to safety hazards should be considered a standard part of the curricula for office management training. Establishing standards for safety and noting any changes in levels would, of course, be the first step. This basic requirement sets the stage for problem solving by objectives when a difficulty appears.

In one large office a number of complaints by female operatives of regular duplicating equipment went unnoticed until the complaints reached a higher level. By this time it was discovered that the fluid used caused skin blemishes when used often. Secretaries, clerks, and typists who used the equipment were victims of a near epidemic before the problem was noted and corrective action taken. The final event which triggered action was when three girls resigned in one week and attributed their departure to the damage to their hands from the liquid.

---

[3] Thomas Powers, "Office Safety," *National Safety News*, Vol. 98, No. 4 (October, 1968), pp. 45–50.

A simple reporting system for occupational hazard and injuries in the office permits the establishment of norms, and of variations in the norm.

Noise at work as a problem

In the factory of 40 years ago the existence of noise was tolerated and accepted as normal. Workers and managers alike realized that the noise level was high, but tolerance could be developed, without realizing that long-run effects could be damaging and costly. Perhaps the factor which has done most to make the toleration decrease on the part of management has been a rising level of compensation claims which have been upheld for hearing loss or diminution. One report states that this cost in the future could be one of the leading items of cost for workmen's compensation. The Noise Research Center is reported as listing 4.5 million workers employed in areas of high noise, and if only 10 percent file claims for hearing loss, which is medically probable, they will collect an estimated $250 million. Studies have shown that the man who works in a high noise area is 22 percent more likely to wear a hearing aid later in life to understand normal conversation.

High levels of noise are usually defined at 85 decibels continuously for a shift, a figure which is startling to experts since a study by the American Industrial Hygiene Association indicates that 50 percent of the machines used in industry have a level above 90 decibels, and the general noise level in over 50 percent of the plants in operation today is above the 85 decibel level.[4]

The major control function here is centered in the safety engineering function, although the medical and safety staff have responsibility as well. Where it is suspected that decibel levels are beyond the safety level, which can be checked by standard measurement instruments, the employees in these areas should be subjected to periodic audiometer tests. Where any evidence of hearing loss can be determined, ear protection devices and sound cutting devices on machines should be programmed.

Industrial mental health

Perhaps even more significant than any other single problem in the safety area is that of employee mental health. It has been estimated that one out of ten persons will be admitted to a hospital for treatment of a serious mental illness in his lifetime. The fact that such illness can be considered compensable through workman's disability insurance has been established in the courts. In one automobile company a worker named James Carter was pressed by his foreman to follow a work pro-

---

[4] "The Growing Industrial Battle Against Dangerous Decibels," *Dun's Review and Modern Industry*, Vol. 8, No. 6 (June, 1963), pp. 45–49.

cedure on hub cap processing. Because he couldn't keep up, using the company method, he fell behind. When he varied his method to catch up, he was reprimanded. He became disturbed and was admitted to a mental hospital for treatment of a psychosis. After four months he was released and applied for workman's compensation, and was awarded several thousand dollars damages. This ruling was contested and subsequently upheld, even though Mr. Carter had a previous history of psychiatric treatment for illnesses. The court found that the illness emerged from the work and was a responsibility of the employer on whose premises it occurred.[5]

Because of these, and the wide-spread prevalence of mental illness, companies are including more mental health considerations in their employee health and safety programs. While psychoses are less often found than lesser conditions of neurosis or unsatisfactory behavior, the range of mental health extends from complete breakdown to unusual behavior normally identified as the "problem employee." Alcoholism, absenteeism, and tardiness are now considered by some experts to be evidences of unsatisfactory responses by very human employees to stimuli in the work environment and are mental health problems. Argyris has suggested that the forms of organization themselves are guilty of creating passive and dependent employees, which in turn creates apathetic and hostile employees.[6]

Two basic approaches seem to be in favor among those companies which have attacked the problem through an organized mental health program. (1) Place a trained psychiatrist on the staff of the personnel department or medical staff. He is empowered to range throughout the company and identify problem areas, based upon his own practice inside the plant. He may make recommendations about placement, hiring, working conditions, work assignments, job content, and supervisory practices to avert mental health problems. (2) A second approach is to integrate the mental health program into the overall company health program with a psychiatrically oriented internist (MD) as its director. As used in the Equitable Life Assurance Society, the latter approach has greater acceptance among employees who will visit a medical doctor where they might be reluctant to visit a "head shrinker."

Generally, the mental health program involves support from top management, a close working relationship with the personnel department, a high sense of confidentiality about its work, and cooperative relationships with local mental health facilities for referrals. The emphasis in most successful employee mental health programs would seem to be an emphasis upon mental health, rather than mental illness.[7]

---

[5] *Carter v. General Motors.*

[6] Chris Argyris, *Personality and Organization* (New York: Harper and Row, 1954).

[7] "What a Mental Health Program Can Do," *Employee Relations Bulletin,* Report No. 863, July 3, 1963, pp. 1–5.

A movement having great significance for industrial mental health is that sometimes described as Reality Therapy. The method here is the avoidance of the terminology of mental illness (neurotic, psychotic, schizophrenic) and emphasis upon responsibility. As one leading figure has stated it: [8]

"The term irresponsible is much more precise, indicating that our job is to help him become responsible so that he will be able to satisfy his needs as himself."

The purpose of such therapy is to help the patient and point out the reality of what the patient is doing now, not to search with him for the "why" that he will always grasp in the effort not to change. The patient is given an objective of behavior change—from irresponsible to responsible —and when he has achieved this he is cured.

These alternatives, the use of Freudian psychiatry or the reality therapy method, are a management choice when it establishes and funds the mental health program.

Executive health programs

The economic importance of executives to their firm makes executive mental and physical health especially significant in the total health program of the firm. Studies of the results of executive physical exams show that by and large executives are healthier than the population at large. In one study of results from 5,000 examinations, over 66 percent were normal, with overweight being the most ordinary deviation from the norm. Up to 40 percent had health worries which were unwarranted. Such diseases as hypertension, ulcers, and cardiac conditions were found to be no more prevalent among executives than among skilled workers.[9]

As with other health problems, indicators are required, which would seem to point in the direction of executive physical examination programs as a necessary first stage.

COMMITMENT—THE MISSING INGREDIENT IN SAFETY

One of the most important points about industrial safety is that without commitment of individuals to achieving certain objectives, and a clear statement of the criteria which would be met if the goal were successfully attained, no change in the present condition will occur. The plain facts about accidents are that they occur because nobody cares enough to eradicate them. They *care* somewhat, enough to spend a sizable sum of money for programs and staff, posters, and prizes, but not enough to trade off the indicators showing prediction and volume for safety.

---

[8] Wm. Glasser, M.D., *Reality Therapy* (New York: Harper and Row, 1965), p. 15.
[9] George B. Dowling, M.D., "Health of the Nation's Management," *Manage,* Vol. 15, No. 8 (June–July, 1963), pp. 52–57.

Using the commitment approach means consideration of all of the matters noted in this chapter, which is certainly not exhaustive. It also means that the top manager and his subordinates decide upon a level of safety which they intend to achieve on a reality basis, choice of some indicators to measure progress. Without such commitment, safety programs become forms of lip service and the inevitable effect of governmental regulation of internal operational practices will follow.

QUESTIONS AND PROBLEMS

1. Considering the volume of fatalities and injuries in occupational accidents, how do you account for the lack of excitement about it? Why aren't people outraged?
2. In what ways can a poorly designed workplace, product, or process comprise a safety hazard?
3. What kinds of indicators might you devise for the following occupations: Milk delivery man, IBM sorter operation, secretary, ski patrol supervisor, drill press operator, college dean?
4. Design a useful and complete but brief safety reporting system for an organization of your acquaintance.
5. How could safety committees have a beneficial effect in reducing accidents and injuries in an organization?
6. How would you state the regular or ongoing objectives of the safety staff head?
7. Find in your own area of operation, school, home office, a safety problem and state it in the terms of present desired conditions as described in this chapter.
8. Are there any special category problems which would make your ordinary place of daily functioning different? What are they? What should be done to avert any ill effects from them?
9. Obtain a meter for measuring decibel levels and rate the noise level in decibels for a number of ordinary locations around you: between classes, in dining halls, in dormitories, or in office work area. How do they compare with the decibel level suggested as maximum for safety?
10. Discuss the ideal of "alcoholism is a disease." What does this imply for its management?
11. Would you recommend a compulsory company policy of mental health exams for executives? Of compulsory physical exams? Why or why not?

DON'T TOUCH THE EMERGENCY BUTTON CASE

Adam Bacon, who was a graduate of a school of social work, decided that industrial supervision, and especially personnel work, was a worthwhile field since he had a way with people. He was delighted when he was chosen after two years of varied assignments as plant safety director in a fairly large plant. He felt that he could help people and protect them. As he got under way, he was appalled at the safety practices in the plant and conducted rigid inspection and made stern reports on supervisors who flagrantly violated safety rules.

One day he was riding on the elevator from the seventh to the first floor in the presence of several high executives. As the elevator passed the sixth floor, one of the executives noticed the company president standing outside the glass window of the elevator. One of the executives leaned over and almost shouted to Adam, "Stop the elevator, there's the boss." Adam knew that the elevator could be stopped only by pushing the "emergency" button. He also noted that the elevator had eight people in it, and that a small plaque on the control board said clearly,

NEVER push the emergency button with more than three people aboard the elevator.

1. What should Adam do?
2. Why?

THE NEW LIGHTS

For several months the design department manager had planned to have new lights installed over all the drafting boards. His budget was approved, and he had rough-sketched the layout for the contractor. On Friday afternoon he called the contractor in and showed him the set-up of the design room. The contractor agreed to work his crew overtime and have them all installed by Monday morning before work. When the crew left on Friday, the old drop cords were still there; when they came back Monday, the new fluorescents with modern reflectors were installed.

Much to the manager's surprise there were no comments of approbation. A number of old hands looked at the new lights in surprise and went about their work sullenly. During the morning the manager noticed around drafting boards a number of huddles which broke up when he looked at them. Before noon a number of the draftsmen were wearing home-made caps or eyeshades from paper and drafting tape. At noon one of the draftsmen who wore glasses said he had a severe headache and wanted to go home. He said that he thought the new lights caused it. The manager scoffed at this. He explained that over 500 companies had installed these same lights in drafting rooms without trouble. By this time several others gathered around and complained bitterly about the lights. Among them were several of his more mature and best men. The manager having placed a hurried call to the contractor during lunch hour, the lights were checked with meters and found perfectly normal. Three more men reported ill with headaches; and relations with the men, much to the manager's surprise, indicated that they were sore at him for putting in the lights.

1. What caused the men to rebel at the new lights?
2. What should the manager do?
3. What might he have done to prevent this minor furor?
4. Is there some sort of principle which the manager could follow in such situations?
5. What kinds of recognition did the men seem to be seeking?

THE CASE OF THE
NEEDED BUTT CANS

When Cosmic Foods moved from its old building downtown into its new glass and steel headquarters, everyone was delighted with the comfortable new quarters, much admired for their beauty and architectural style. One phase of life in the new quarters was less satisfying, however. The office manager decreed that, in order to maintain the cleanliness of the new building, smoking would be permitted in private offices and in cafeteria and lounge areas only. It caused surprisingly little stir, however, since everyone promptly ignored the rule. Elevator courts were often littered with cigarette butts, match papers, and similar debris. It soon became customary simply to drop the butt on the floor and step on it when walking along the hall. The office manager brought it up at a management meeting. "Our rules aren't being enforced," he said. "As a result, the floors are littered with butts and matches, which is terrible in this beautiful new building." Mike Hodson, a grizzled veteran, made a suggestion. "Why don't you put butt cans in the elevators and courts and along the corridors? Then they won't have to use the floor." The office manager was aghast: "But then we'll be inviting them to defy the rule against smoking. It would be an open invitation."

"That's easy," Mike said: "Eliminate the rule. Then enforce a rule about putting butts in butt cans."

1. What can be said for the office manager's position?
2. What is the argument in favor of Mike's position?
    (Huddle into buzz groups and work up your statement for a class debate.)

chapter 15

TRAINING BY OBJECTIVES

OVER THE YEARS at conventions of training directors, the perennial favorite among topics has been that dealing with the question: "How can we evaluate training?" Despite a plethora of proposals, the level of dissatisfaction among the audience has been customarily high. Why should it be so difficult to evaluate this function, especially in the light of the amounts of money which are devoted to it, and the significance it plays in the personnel administration function?

THE IMPORTANCE OF TRAINING

In the world in which the policy "hire qualified people" is being replaced with "hire—then qualify people for their jobs," the role of the training director and the contribution of the training department will be heightened considerably. The concepts of investment being applied to human capital, and the new developments in human asset accounting may well produce insights which will place a real economic value upon training efforts.

TRAINING BY OBJECTIVES

The greatest value of these economic measures, such as human assets accounting, is that they permit *tangible criteria* for the evaluation of training effort. Yet, this is but the first step in managing the training function of personnel by objectives. What else is involved:

1. A new definition of training is emerging from innovations in teaching. Under the heading of *behavioral technology*, training means "changing behavior." Training should shape behavior of individuals to some predetermined goal, the goal to be determined by the needs of the organization, organizational objectives, or the individual himself. Thus, if no behavior change occurs, then no success can be attributed to the

330

training effort. If it occurs, but is invisible, it must be considered to be an invisible result.

2. The training goal is always a subgoal of some larger goal, and not an end in itself. The company which needs a kind of behavior to achieve an organizational goal, trains for that purpose.

3. The evaluation of training effectiveness then is the achievement of behavior change which was predetermined and defined in advance of the release of the effort.

Since 1960 the field of training has been subject to considerable attention, unmatched since the early days of World War II. The emphasis upon manpower development as a method of eradicating unemployment, the demand for more technically trained persons for high technology businesses, the decentralization of firms, earlier retirements, shorter work weeks for many public servants such as policemen and firemen, and the development of numerous new forms of training have combined to produce a training revolution.

It became apparent early in the 1960's that unemployment at levels above 4 percent were becoming unacceptable, and politically explosive. It became further apparent that unemployment could be socially explosive as the civil rights movement turned from passive into active means. Riots in the cities were quickly attributed to unemployment and poverty in the ghettos, and the cause of the poverty and unemployment was attached equally firmly to lack of skills. The solution adopted for all of it was more training.

This produced a drastic change in training objectives. In management development and management training, learning theory has become the slave and instrument of economics. In this chapter we'll look at these two influences in that order, first economics of training, and then applied learning theory. These will then be integrated into an approach to training.

For most managers of training, the second—learning theory—has all too often been the master plan around which training is prepared, planned, and presented. This doesn't mean that training has been wrong, but rather that it has often misguided itself by asking the wrong questions: "Which form of training should be applied to work best?" has often been answered in favor of the most effective form, from the viewpoint of learning theory, rather than whether or not the training was designed to serve a specific end purpose, to achieve a needed objective.[1]

While the economics of the training programs are probably easier to figure out in the corporation, where profit is a form of economic discipline which is easy to understand, the same limiting conditions exist

---

[1] For a more complete exposition, see George S. Odiorne, *Training by Objectives* (New York: Macmillan, 1970).

in nonprofit organizations and government. As Mr. McNamara and the recent trend toward program budgeting (PPBS) in government has pointed up, there is an economic dimension to public service which sets the limiting conditions upon activity in that sector as well. Thus, this is for corporate and governmental trainers and management development experts.

Is there a theoretical justification for this arrangement of priorities— economic first, then learning theory? Clearly this adopts the assumption that intention, goals, and objectives determine the *effectiveness* of the means used. The motive for the training becomes a matter of some moment when we consider it from such a viewpoint. The firm has a charter, which justifies all of its objectives. The government agency has a limiting condition which comes to the same conclusion in many cases. The motive for government to train people, however, is less clear, and the forms of training and applied learning theory will not be centered in its limiting condition, even though they cannot be ignored. Political scientists have often chosen power as the major motive. Senator Fulbright proposes that a genius of our system is an ability to start with man as he actually exists rather than as he should be. The major realities he proposes are the goals of profit in economic matters and ambition in governmental and political life.

The sixties have seen a rather close alliance between the ambitions of politicians and the profit of economic institutions. Unemployment, poverty, and unenemployment have become issues in politics as well as matters of direct concern to corporations. In fact, it may be necessary to his survival as a trainer to do so continuously. It is becoming reasonably apparent by now that industrial training has a poor record of survival when the earnings of the business decline. When profits disappear, so does the training department in many cases. While this can be explained in part by the limited vision of the general manager, this can't be a complete explanation. It is also possible that much of the training being done is prosperity based, and under intense economic scrutiny comes out looking like so much purposeless nonsense. The time to turn an economic light onto training is before the crisis of survival of training (and trainers) is at hand. As a result, we may eliminate a lot of the pretentious nonsense which some of the more experimental schools of social scientists have been selling to trainers. *Learning theory and psychology can tell us how to teach. Economic analysis can tell us whether or not we should train at all!*

THE FUTURE DEMAND FOR TRAINING IS HIGH

Labor market statistics are all in favor of the training function being an important one in the future. The work of the trainer is an important one to the firm, and should be accorded status and function in keeping with it. Let's look at the big training jobs that lie ahead for our profession during the coming decade:

1. The induction training of 26 million people will be required simply to get new persons on the jobs to replace those leaving the labor force in the next decade.

2. The training of 6 million new skilled craftsmen to replace those retiring, as well as training present men in new crafts, will have to be done.

3. The upgrading of an additional 3 to 4 million managerial people faces us. One report states that 30 percent of the present managers will be replaced during this decade, and another 20 percent will move into lateral positions requiring new skills. The average age of company presidents is 59, and the average age of their assistants is slightly higher.

4. Job content is changing rapidly which means much retraining must be done to keep abreast of these changes.

5. The urban crisis of the sixties has highlighted the explosive potential of two societies: one white, educated, and employed; the other black, uneducated, and unemployed. Retraining is a key remedy here.

The total cost of such training in all its forms for on-the-job training has been estimated at around $30 billion annually. In the face of such a challenge the training professional has every reason to be optimistic about the economic potential of his field both as a career site and as a professional challenge.

Where does the economics of this field find its roots?

INVESTMENT IN HUMAN CAPITAL AS A BASE POINT

The president of the American Economic Association has pointed up the necessity for a new look at on-the-job training. In his presidential address in 1961, Professor Schultz has said: "Although it is obvious that people acquire useful skills and knowledge, it is not obvious that these skills and knowledge are a form of capital, that this capital is part of a deliberate investment that has grown in Western societies at a faster rate than conventional (nonhuman) capital, and that its growth may well be the most distinctive feature of the economic system."

This provocative idea has had a sizable impact on the thinking of others since it was stated. Some have concluded from this view of investment that companies should therefore never fire anybody! Others have concluded that since the tax man and the accountants' procedures don't accommodate themselves to this kind of thinking, then it really isn't an investment at all. J.K. Galbraith points out that since companies don't hold title to the men (since Lincoln freed the slaves), then government training must take over.

Roger Vuaridel points up quite reasonably that only part of the investment in educational expenditures has tangible effects, but we should not overlook the intangible effects which have benefits as well. While the tangible effects of education, such as more productivity, can be equated to producers' goods, it may well be the intangible ones (better citizens) which have greatest impact.

For one thing, education is good for the whole economy, as many studies have shown. In agriculture, for example, the higher educational level of farmers through land-grant colleges has been credited with much of the improved agricultural productivity which characterized this country from 1940 to 1960. Southern economists have studied the effects of human capital investments upon the economic health of the region.

The training director has an important argument to present to potential trainees in the studies showing that great personal benefits come from being trained that are denied the untrained. David and Morgan estimate that investment in education by the individual pays 4 to 6 percent return, as figured on a national basis. Professor Hansen reports that the return to individuals from schooling as private beneficiaries actually exceeds the social return.

Yet, far too few training directors have shown any awareness of this important economic facet of their work, that it does indeed add to the capital of the firm in the form of investment in human capital, and guide their efforts to accelerate this growth.

How does one begin?

Here's a worksheet to make a quick economic classification of your training programs:

Part I. Estimated total costs:
    a) Direct expense (paid out) .... _____
    b) Indirect (staff salaries, space, etc.) .... _____
    c) Participant salaries .... _____
        Total cost of program .... =========
Part II. Economic classification: (state as percentage of above $)
    a) Profit improvement training: (1 year period)
        1. Sales: increase volumes;
           cut selling costs .... _____%
        2. Manufacturing: cut costs .... _____%
        3. Service: lower unit costs .... _____%
        4. Staff: improve program,
           lower budget expense .... _____%   _____%
    b) Added human working capital .... _____%
    c) Investment in human capital .... _____%
    d) Fails to fit any economic classification .... _____%

This worksheet can help you classify your training costs into economic categories. It has two major sections: Part I, identify the major segments of costs; Part II, by percentage identify how much of that cost would be classified into (*a*) profit improvement, (*b*) human working capital, and (*c*) investment in human capital. Here's how this is done.

a) Profit objectives as a take-off point

The reason so many training departments find themselves come upon hard times, even when it is apparent that they are necessary and will continue to be in the future, often lies in the specific economic relation they hold to *their* organization. (Not all organizations are profit making, but all are economic in part.) The training function is not necessarily an organization of *reform*, but it is an organization of *change*. Of all the personnel and industrial relations functions, the training function alone has the function of being *change agent*. (The failure of many especially created change agent programs is probably explainable in their failure to adopt and be consistent with the training staff role.)

What is the economic take-off point for training? The diagram in Figure 15–1 spells out economic objectives for different parts of the firm.

FIGURE 15–1
Economic measures of organization performance

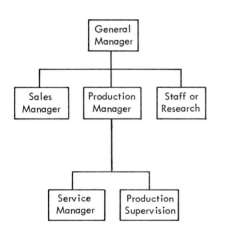

Results measured in terms of:

Profit: The surplus of revenue over expense. May be measured as a total, rate of return on investment, return on earnings, or upon equity.

Budget and Program: Did the department complete its program and stay within its budget?

Costs: Did it produce the right goods at specified unit cost, quality?

Contribution to Profit· Based on sales revenue minus cost of goods sold minus selling cost.

Units Produced· As compared with standard estimates, PERT, or learning curve.

The above diagram represents the different kinds of economic measures of organization performance. Each organization unit has a unique economic characteristic. Thus, the general manager level is the lowest possible level at which "profit producing training" is of immediate importance, since it is the lowest level which has responsibility for profit. It is the lowest level which controls *both* revenue and expense. Sales personnel are contributors to profit through the control of two variables under their control: sales volume and selling expense. (The combination of these is "contribution to profit.")

The manufacturing manager is primarily measured by cost of goods sold, with side conditions of quality, delivery, and the like. His subordinates in manufacturing or service supervision are measured by units produced as compared with certain engineered or historical standards.

Training or change programs which unqualifiedly purport to "improve productivity" are naive in many respects. They aren't attuned to the economic end measurements nor the specific language of the firm in its economic division of labor.

Sales training programs should produce new volume or cut selling expense. Manufacturing management courses should aim primarily at cost reduction. Little else is significant in this branch of the business. Manufacturing supervision courses or programs should increase units produced against standards, reduce scrap, eliminate accidents, downtime on machines, or prevent machine damage.

Service supervision should provide units of service at standard costs or below.

It should be noted that all of these kinds of training objectives are profit centered, and probably will pay off for the firm within the immediate accounting period. Such training should be classified as *profit improvement training*.

Is all training in this category? No, this is merely the take-off point and basic program for training which is economically oriented. Two other economic kinds of training are possible.

b) Training as addition to human working capital

A second major economic classification of training are those from which the results can be converted into relatively short time, but not within the one-year period in which profits are ordinarily measured. Periods from 1 to 3 years' return on the costs of training would include such training. Training expenses for such purposes as training understudies for people going on vacation, understudies for managers who will retire in a couple of years, training to have backstops for key personnel, or prior training for planned expansion of plant or sales force would be expense which would not contribute to profit during the immediate accounting period at hand, yet would be a sound economic expense for the firm since it would enhance profit and pay back the costs within a 1 to 3-year period. Such training expenses are in the same category as inventories and receivables.

c) Training as capital budgeting

The third category of training is that which falls into the economic category as major replacements or additions to plant, and take several years (up to 10) to return their cash outlay. These include such programs as sending executives to Harvard, rotation of junior executives through various departments in preparation for key jobs many years hence, upgrading workers in key crafts, and many other executive and managerial development programs upon which immediate cash return in this accounting period cannot be predicted.

CAPITAL BUDGETING FOR INVESTMENT IN HUMAN CAPITAL

Having thus classified our training plans and programs of how each will ultimately contribute to the profit of the firm, we'll probably discover that we've created some new problems in handling the long-range human investment portion of the budgets. To adequately prepare and sell such expenses the training director must be prepared to answer these four questions as they apply to his training programs for the forthcoming year:

1. Demand for funds

How much money in total will we need for expenditure in long-range investment in human capital during the coming period? The need here will be weighed against the prospective profitability of the alternative possibilities which are available. Shall we send three executives to executive development schools, and rotate six others, at a cost of $25,000, *or* should we run 40 weeks of education for 300 foremen in political action for supervision at the same cost? Should we make young Mr. X assistant to the president for training purposes for two years at $25,000, *or* should we conduct a cadet training school for 15 college recruits at the same cost? The answers to such questions of investment alternatives must always be based on a comparison of alternative profitable uses. It also competes with demands for capital for physical equipment, for research, and must have some basis for screening alternative uses.

2. Supply of funds

Unlike the competing demands for capital funds for conventional training, investments are never—to my knowledge—in business raised through conventional capital raising methods. Usually such capital comes out of operating income before it goes through profit—or reinvested earnings channels. In many instances it may come through depreciation allowances which are automatically reinvested in the business. Perhaps one of the needs of business in the future will be for the setting aside of allowances.

GUIDES FOR CONSTRUCTION OF TRAINER'S OBJECTIVE STATEMENTS

When the training manager or members of his staff prepare to establish training objectives, they will find that a convenient kind of classification system of preparation of objectives statements for training can simplify their preparation of such statements.

As shown in Figure 15–2, these three classes of objectives comprise an ascending scale of excellence in training administration.

FIGURE 15–2

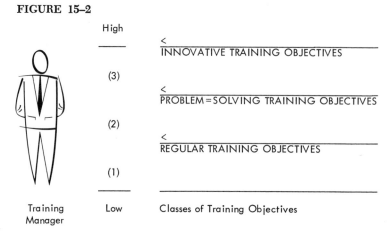

1. The minimum requirement for training departments is that they should conduct the *regular* recurring, or routine kind of objectives in training. These might include such training objectives as induction training for new employees, foreman training for new foremen, new product training for salesmen, or sales system training for new retail employees. These objectives should be based upon realistic figures drawn from history (the same quarter last year, for example) and should provide for such trade-off objectives as measures of numbers of trainees, hours of training, cost per trainee, time required for trainee to come up to standard levels of performance, and similar statistical indications of performance for the training department. These should be reality based and should include a range of possible outcomes including the highest and lowest possible outcomes permissible, plus a reality base from history. Such data establish a general base for administration of training, and comprise the minimum standards of performance for the training manager.

The training manager who performs all of his regular objectives within past limits is entitled to the same job for the same pay for another year. Excellence for manager of training is performing problem-solving training or introducing innovative forms of training.

2. The second category, and one which comprises the major kind of goals for trainers is *problem-solving objectives*. The manager of training whose department is finding and solving human behavior problems through applied training skills is worth more than the training department which merely performs last year's courses as before. This is a never ending process, for this year's problem analysis and course designed to alleviate the problem becomes next year's standard or recurring course in many instances.

The manager of training who sees problems that really exist and solves them through training is of a higher level of excellence. This area of training is often the major point of emphasis in the system approach to training.

3. *Innovative goals* comprise the highest level of excellence for the training manager and his staff. Innovation can take the form of objectives of special training projects which have as their purpose the achievements of breakthrough to new higher levels of excellence through added kinds of behavior, new techniques to improve the quality or cut the cost of training, or assure that the effects of training can be more certainly achieved.

Innovation goes beyond problem solving, for it assumes higher levels of achievement than problem solving, which often does nothing more than restore the status quo through eradicating causes of deviations from norms.

The difference between problem solving and innovation in training can be illustrated by the following case. The training manager, in addition to conducting regular courses, discovers that because of new orders and new products quality control is slipping in a plant. He conducts a new course in statistical quality control for all operating managers. The quality of the product is improved, that is, it is restored to previously former high levels. The problem is solved.

In another plant the submission rate of new ideas to the suggestion plan has reached a new level. The training manager, desiring to see it go even higher in order that even greater breakthrough to high levels of creative suggestion can be reached, plans and presents a work simplification course which teaches systematic skills in innovative behavior to managers and operators. As a result the plant moves beyond the highest expectation of anyone involved. The added earnings are a result of sharpening the creative behavior of many people, and are based upon some new forms of training.

Nobody had decided that a problem existed; in fact, they were well satisfied that the suggestion system performance of the people was excellent. Yet the trainer saw an opportunity to exploit the latent creativity of the people and moved the organization performance to higher levels than imagined feasible. This would illustrate an innovative goal.

Innovation might also include new forms of training technique to improve existing programs, even when the present programs seem to be working quite satisfactorily. Some examples of this would include such objectives as these:

Preparation of an instructor briefing guide

The application of video tape to conference leader skill training

The use of programmed texts in retail clerical training where it had not been used before.

Simplification and increased effectiveness of supervisory chalk talks on selling unwanted jobs to cut the time needed.

Reducing the paperwork without losing essential control in the tuition refund plan for employee outside courses.

The goal-setting procedure

About one quarter before the beginning of a new training year every staff member of the training department is required to set forth his objectives, using the three major categories involved. These objectives are discussed individually with the manager of the training department, and final training plan for the year fixed in almost final form. The training staff then meets a couple of weeks prior to the beginning of the budget or training year, and each staff member presents his training plans for the coming year. Jurisdictional conflicts are discussed, and areas of possible collaboration on objectives are discussed, as shown in Figure 15–3.

FIGURE 15–3

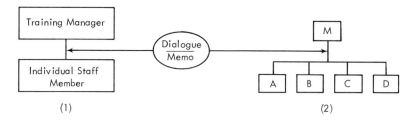

The first step is a *dialogue confirmed by a memo* (1) between the manager of training and his departmental members. This dialogue and memo comprises a commitment by each staff member to deliver on his regular goals, to try to solve certain problems, and, hopefully, to conceive innovations. (2) The staff meeting is the final commitment of all members of the team to their plan for the year.

The follow up. Clearly stated objectives comprise the basis for regular review during the year. Perhaps quarterly staff meetings, with reports of results achieved against objective stated with reasons for exceptions, will serve to keep progress moving. At the end of the year the goal-setting progress is repeated, except that last year's plans are reviewed, differences in achievement from stated goals are discussed, and the new goals for the forthcoming year are once more presented and discussed.

The achievement of results against objectives comprise the review and follow-up process. Since they are in writing there should be no disagreement as to the content of the objectives. If conditions change during the year, knock-out discussion confirmed by change memos is permissible if mutually agreed upon. These can be covered in quarterly review sessions as well as individual discussions between the manager and staff.

The staff member should also feel perfectly free to discuss the possibility of knocking out inappropriate goals when conditions change during the year in such a way that goals which looked sensible at the start prove no longer sensible or feasible. The purpose is not to set up a punishment system, but to gain a commitment system for every staff member. The training manager summarizes the goals and these comprise his commitment to his boss.

Despite the nonpunitive nature of goals, they can be used for performance appraisal of staff members, for such purposes as raises, promotions, coaching, self-development, and the training of trainers. It also provides some insights for the manager into which trainer can best complete the tough new jobs, and is a form of organization planning, managerial control, and departmental planning. It also has numerous motivational effects upon staff performance and includes the major communications vehicle for departmental operation.

Classifying training needs according to objectives

It should be noted here that much prior discussion of training needs has centered around problem-solving goals. While it is true that training should solve problems, it is also true that this does not satisfy the total requirements of training departments. The term "training need" has been treated in the literature in the past as being a single unified item of concern. Usually this has been limited to problem solving.

Problem-solving objectives merely restore normality, and training should do more than merely solve problems. It should serve as a change agent, to improve the already satisfactory, to make breakthroughs to newer levels of performance, and to have improving and innovating effects in the organization through enlarging and altering behavior of people in the organization.

Thus, the use of the term "training need" should be dropped and the term *training objective* substituted for it. These training objectives or goals are statements of the behavior change hoped for as a result of training.

Thus, training needs—or objectives—should be classified into three major categories at the time choices and decisions are being made about activities being planned and resources being allocated. These three as outlined here include:

1. Regular training objectives
2. Problem solving training objectives
3. Innovative or change-making training objectives

All such goals and objectives are not isolated from the real world, but are a product of an environment or context. Identifying and analyzing this context becomes the first step in identifying training objectives.

TRAINING AS A FORCE FOR CHANGE

Because training in the systems approach means moving toward an objective from some previous position, this can be called *training by objectives*. It also means that training achieves objectives or should attempt to do so. This is a kind of discipline which liberates training from the many kinds of activities which it could become bogged down in, and makes it purposeful, meaningful, economic, and possible to evaluate. The most important training objectives are those which solve problems and introduce change. The best way to achieve this is to define a behavioral objective you intend to achieve through training, and when the training is complete check to see if you have reached it.

What is a problem?

Professor Herbert Simon has made an immense contribution to the science of decision making and problem solving in his small book *The New Science of Management Decisions* published in 1960.[2] A computer man, Simon worked many years attempting to simulate on the computer the thought processes of the human mind. As a result of this research he has proposed a definition of a problem which is systematic. It suggests that a problem is a *deviation from some standard*. This implies that there are two dimensions to a problem, the present level and the desired level (or standard). If you don't know where you are, then you can't know what your problem is, or even if you have one. If you know where you

---

[2] Herbert A. Simon, *The New Science of Management Decision* (New York: Harper and Row, 1960).

are and like it there, you don't have a problem. If you know where you are and wish you were elsewhere (at another objective), then you have the distance to travel to get there, which comprises the problem. It's easy to see why this would fit a computer analyst's mode of thought. The computer, in making management decisions, is essentially a user of *comparison*. There is no need, however, for you to be a computer, since the computer is merely simulating what you do when you think clearly.[3]

In an earlier book, this writer spelled out some further extensions of that definition, proposing that a "problem is a deviation from a standard, important enough to be solved, and to which somebody will be committed to a solution."

Simon's definition of a problem, many suggest, is too limiting. The problem which is merely a variance from a standard leaves much undone in terms of achieving new goals. Management expert Joseph Juran has proposed that "breakthrough" to newer and higher levels of excellence, heretofore thought beyond the realm of the possible, is a more germane concern. Peter Drucker adds that managers should be more concerned with exploiting opportunities than merely solving problems. The distinction can be useful at the same time it exploits the systematic and logical methods of systems analysis proposed by Simon. This is done by dividing problems as objectives for training purposes into two major categories.

1. Problem objectives which restore the status quo. These are problems which are caused by some change which has produced a deviation from a norm, important enough for somebody to think the variance is important enough to close up. Somebody then is made responsible for closing the gap.

2. Innovative or breakthrough objectives which move the present level to new levels of excellence. The use of objectives is similar to plain problem solving; define the present level, then choose a new desired level. This new sought-after level of behavior becomes the training objective.

If the difference between the two kinds of objectives seems subtle, their differences in results are gross. The training program which merely restores the status quo never improves things, it merely prevents them from getting worse. Innovative and breakthrough objectives make quantum leaps in performance even though the present level is considered satisfactory.

If this kind of specific definition of a problem seems to be a trifle esoteric, we should hasten to note that actually it is a great timesaver in the end. All too often the average person, asked to define a problem, will respond by stating its *cause*, rather than specifying the problem exactly.

---

[3] G. S. Odiorne, *Management Decision Making by Objectives* (Englewood Cliffs, N.J.: Prentice-Hall, Inc., 1969).

"*What is your training problem?*"

"Motivation of workers."

"*What problem does that cause?*"

"Our people don't come in on Monday."

Thus, at the first question he indicates that the problem as he originally stated it isn't the problem, but the cause of the problem, which is apparently absenteeism. What the exact level of Monday absenteeism may be, and what a desirable or objective level might be, is not stated. To innovate, we ask: "What condition would exist if the training were successful?" These answers would be required before an effective statement of the training objective could be made. It would also be needed if the effect of training were to be evaluated later.

Specific definition of a behavior change objective requires that present level and desired levels be defined. In training, the differences between the two comprises the objective of training, sometimes called the "training need."

Task analysis means defining present and desired behavior of a specific population of trainees, in other words, it means a very detailed and specific spelling out in behavioral terms of the present behavior and the desired behavior. This analysis applies to either problem solving or innovative training. Let's use the example of a trainer who wants to do a task analysis upon a proposed course which will improve the delegation skills of some middle managers.

A MODEL FOR TASK ANALYSIS—USING A SYSTEMS APPROACH

1. Name the behavior change:

To increase managerial delegation to subordinates.

2. Nature and size of the group to be trained:

a) Nature and size of the group: about 30 middle managers ranging in age from 30 to 55, most having college degrees, usually in engineering, chemistry, or business administration, often accounting or finance.

b) Prior training or coaching: little if any, except for some possible outside reading. Several have taken management courses in colleges, but this has been at least seven years ago. Few, if any, have been coached by their superiors.

c) Situational facts: strongly technical business, frequent changes due to product short run, technical obsolescence of product. Must work frequently with nontechnical personnel such as pipefitters, millwrights, and the like.

3. Present level or condition:

a) Supervisors are often seen (ratio delay study shows 50 percent frequency of occurrence) doing work themselves while their subordinates are standing by, or doing other work.

b) Few, if any, coaching and instructing actions by the supervisors are observed. Subordinates never seem to be instructed in procedures which are repetitive, and which supervisors perform for them.

c) Supervisors often omit reports and other administrative requirements of their job. Fifty percent of supervisory reports are late. Supervisors report themselves too busy to prepare reports, and do them at home or on Saturday.

4. Desired condition:

a) Supervisors should be observed in less than 10 percent of observations doing work of technicians and mechanics, and then for instruction only.

b) Supervisors should be seen engaged in coaching workers in procedures which are repetitive, using Job Instruction Training technique for teaching. At other times should be supervising and directing, not doing.

c) All supervisory reports should be prepared on the operating day scheduled, and only emergency reports at home.

5. What would be the favorable end operational results if the training were successful?:

Productivity would increase and down time between production runs reduced 50 percent. Turnover among skilled people would be reduced 20 percent. Amount of actual work done by technicians would increase, freeing supervisory time by 50 percent. All supervisory reports would be in on the day prescribed, making administrative decisions and upward reporting more timely by 20 percent.

6. What indicators could you use to determine changes from present level to desired level?:

a) Do ratio delay studies of activities of supervisors and not percentage of time engaged in technical work part of job descriptions of lower ranking persons.

b) Do ratio delays study of supervisor (same study) and note percentage of time being spent in teaching, coaching, or JIT.

c) Count frequency of late reports from supervisors as percent of total report due by day.

d) Count frequency of delays in outgoing higher level reports, and show percentage delayed due to late supervisory reports.

Presuming that you had previously analyzed the situation behaviorally to determine that the cause of the behavior you are studying was not in the situation itself, nor simply a matter of enforcement, but had concluded that they didn't *know how*, or can't do it, your task analysis prepares the stage for breaking the training down into steps with criteria of achievement for each. As we noted earlier, this appears to be a training objective because it involves the behavior of people (the supervisor) which is caused by lack of knowledge, insufficient skills, wrong knowledge, or insufficient information.

In a more narrative style this would read somewhat as follows:

Most of our supervisors were hired from college with emphasis upon technical education for plant supervision, and accounting or finance for the office and administrative tasks. After a tour of duty in technical engineering or staff accounting work, they are promoted to supervisory positions. In the past we have done little to prepare them for the change in duties from technical expert to supervision of others. Their experience in this has been rewarding when they excelled at technical matters, and this has often been the reason for their promotion—technical excellence. It is not surprising that they continue to pursue the very things which led to their immediate success, promotion into management.

We find, however, that they cling to technical work, rather than teaching technical work to others, and doing the supervisory planning and administrative work which is necessary in their departments, and this leads to two ill effects. The first is that they usurp all of the technical work in the departments while the aids and assistants stand around watching. This has produced some quits among technicians and mechanics who feel that they are not being well employed. The second effect is that the necessary work of reporting, and doing similar managerial tasks are being left undone.

Not an uncommon story. What is the value of the task analysis and what are the key ingredients, and how is this task analysis used?

1. It described in specific, quantitative terms, in places where that is possible, what the present behavior consists of (part III).

2. It described the desired behavior in terms of quantitative differences and the quantification of the behavior change problems comes out something like this:

a) A reduction of 40 percent observed instances of supervisors working.

b) More observable instances of coaching and training would be going on. This rate of observations would be a declining curve, since the early evidence of coaching would permit tapering off and permitting the subordinates to be working independently once they have been trained. This could be described as a learning curve rate of observation.

ACTION TRAINING TECHNIQUES

Over the 20 years since the end of World War II, the race has been on to discover new and novel techniques of teaching managers and employees. Conference and discussion methods were probably the first breakthrough from straight lectures—or even worse—papers read by executives. The trend was undoubtedly needed, and may well have prevented training from being inundated under a great wave of boredom. Whatever else might be said about special methods of presentation which are akin to the theatre, unless the class is willing to stay through the whole session, and pay reasonable attention to the proceedings in the room, the chances of affecting any behavior change are diminished.

Despite the ever-present possibility that training can become a form of managerial entertainment on the company premises, there are volumes to be spoken in favor of such devices for presenting instruction as role play, management games, incident processes, and the like. The major virtue can be summarized in the common element which runs through all of them. The unifying thread in all of them is that they require some simulated behavior on the part of the trainee, and that it affords him some feedback on the effects of that behavior from both the trainer and his peers.

We will now move from the behavioral objectives uncovered in the task analysis, and scrutinize the optional kinds of training which might affect job behavior through a planned effort.

What is action training?

To make action training effective there are certain essential ingredients in the training session itself. This may be in a class, or might just as well be in a coaching session between a single trainer and single trainee. The key ingredients are these:

1. The desired terminal behavior of the trainee has been specifically defined.
2. His present level of behavior and performance are specified.
3. Through task analysis the specific behavior changes needed have been clearly defined.
4. During the training session he engages in some *action* such as talking, writing, walking, conferring, and the like.
5. The action which he engages in *simulates* the behavior sought back on the job.

6. The course of change in behavior is comprised of some orderly progression of small steps.
7. At each stage of training he obtains feedback which makes it known to him whether his action is successful or unsuccessful.
8. The learning is under the control of the instructor.
9. A summary evaluation, measuring actual outcome with stated objectives, is possible.

The forms which action training take include most of the major innovations in training such as role play, certain uses of case studies, management games, incident process, in basket, as well as practice sessions and workshops. The range of these applications is wide, and grows steadily.

If you understand the basics of action training, development of new forms to fit the training need is easily done.

The essentials of action training are illustrated in Figure 15–4, and show the time stages and the important ingredients of the flow in which the training is presented to the trainee. This isn't necessarily the way in which the trainer plans his action training, however. The first step is identifying the terminal behavior sought, although it appears as the final outcome on the action training diagram shown below.

FIGURE 15–4

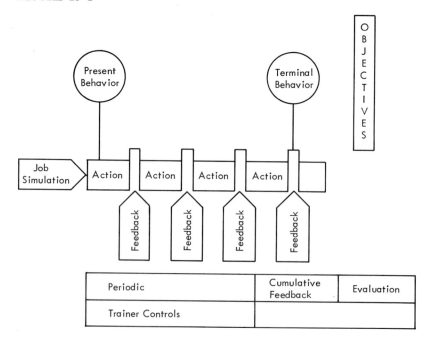

The forms of action training

The specific forms of action training break down into different kinds of simulation. The common element is that all of them simulate the situation in which the trainee must operate in the real world, and require him to behave in a way that he might behave back in that environment if he were to apply the new behavioral skills desired.

Simulation doesn't necessarily mean faithful, complete, and accurate reproduction of all details of the job. Completeness of simulation could only be achieved by taking the man right back to the department, the people, the machines, the problems, the pressures of the real job. Adding to details doesn't necessarily add to the certainty of behavior change. Plausible resemblance in important details is more desirable than exhaustive attention to little detailed touches. The overdoing of reality usually leads only to "cuteness" in the exercises.

These things become clearer as we look at some examples which illustrate the alternative methods of action training which are often used. These methods, all simulation of life, include:

Role playing   Management games
Case studies (with variation)   Demonstrations

Sticking with these main families of action training methods permits us to use variations of them in profusion, and to master a few key tools rather than becoming over-involved in making choices among too many specific techniques.

EVALUATION OF TRAINING EFFECTIVENESS

Being systematic in evaluation doesn't mean that you throw out old methods of testing; you merely supplement them by having a more firm set of criteria in mind. The systems approach suggests that the criteria for measuring training effectiveness is the set of objectives which you started out to achieve.

The futility of ordinary testing

One of the more fruitless activities of the customary classroom teaching is the folklore that somehow testing is a necessary part of the learning process. The teacher lectures to the students, assigns readings, and periodically sits the class before a blue book, away from books and notes, and tests his ability to reproduce verbally or in writing what his memory and reading skill have produced as a residue. Where the course consists of certain skills such as performing an experiment, he may actually perform such an experiment in the presence of the instructor. The vast majority of tests, however, are required demonstrations of verbal (oral or written) behavior, which may or may not reflect itself into some visible and productive behavior at a later time outside the classroom environment.

While this may serve many useful purposes in the school and college, it serves far fewer useful purposes in management training. The standard variations of verbal behavior testing, essay questions, true false, multiple choice, comparison, definition, and the like, when applied to a subject such as human relations is most unlikely to prove anything more than the student's ability to recognize certain written symbols dealing with the language of human relations. Since human relations or other managerial training is most apt to be a complex kind of behavior, or repertory of behaviors, success on the verbal or pencil and paper test can hardly be described as proof of learning, or a measurement of the degree of learning.

The systems approach to evaluation of training starts with a definition of behavior change objectives sought through a conscious development effort. This definition then remains a yardstick for measurement throughout the course, and achievement against the stated goals is the measure of success. All other forms of evaluation measure the internal character of activity itself, not the effectiveness of training.

BEHAVIOR AND ITS CONSEQUENCES

One of the procedural hitches which can occur in evaluating the effect of a training effort is that of sorting out behavior change from the results which that behavior produced. This can be illustrated in the following Figure 15–5 in which there is shown three separate ingredients of the behavior change process.

A training program (2) is conducted which is designed to change the behavior of the trainee from old behavior (1) to new behavior (3). As a result of the course or training effort the new behavior actually ensues. This new behavior affects something else in the environment (4) of the trainee when he behaves that way.

FIGURE 15–5

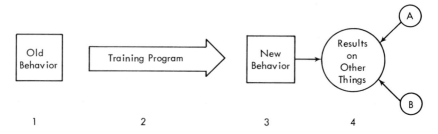

We note that it was the fourth effect that was desired before we started, that's why we organized and planned and executed the training effort. Yet, a limitation on the evaluation of training effectiveness lies in the possible existence of other forces (A) and (B) which might have occurred at the same time, or in concurrence with the training. Thus, the effect can't be wholly nor accurately ascribed to the training unless we can be certain that no other influences were at work. For example, if we conduct a cost reduction course for foremen and costs go down, we can't assume that it was wholly due to the training. It might have been due to better purchasing, longer runs in production, an easier product to make, better engineering, or a change in suppliers. Neither could we call the course in cost reduction a failure if after the course costs *rose*. They might have risen for any of the reasons which are cited above or other influences at work. It might also be true that costs went up but would have risen more if the cost reduction course hadn't been conducted, and the skill brought back to the job and applied.

From Figure 15–5 we might reasonably conclude that the best way of evaluating training would be to confine the evaluation to items 1, 2, and 3. Evaluations of item 4 might well be done, but if the first three have been used and proven effective, then 4 must be used cautiously. Perhaps it can give insights into whether or not the course objectives were properly designed; but even here there are many limitations.

If a course defines its intentions as changing specific old behavior to specific new behavior and this change actually occurs, the training must be considered successful. The evaluation of training is limited to assessing or measuring as accurately as possible how much of the desired (objective) behavior was actually attained and applied; first in the class, and secondly back on the job.

If training actually changed behavior in the class, then it must be considered a training success from the class standpoint and instruction technique standpoint. If it fails to convert back to the job, then the analysis of system support of that behavior may be at fault, and not the training but the prior planning and task analysis is probably at fault.

QUESTIONS AND PROBLEMS

1. Why would top management which is profit oriented be more receptive to "behavioral technology" than to simply "training"?
2. What has happened to training during the sixties was defined by one expert as "The Training Revolution." Outline the features of the changes which took place which might justify that label.
3. What is the relationship between the economics of the firm and the psychology of learning theory when it comes to training?
4. "Training is a fad and will die like the others." How would you rebut this statement?

5. Into what economic classification would you put a college education?
6. Where should the objectives for a training program come from? Where should the need be centered?
7. Why is training designed to innovate or change the character of an organization considered to be of a higher order than routine conduct of courses?
8. Briefly describe the procedure through which a training manager and his boss arrive at agreement about the objectives of the training department for a coming year.
9. You are coach for a little league football team. You find that the blocking is weak. The kids don't watch their targets; they let their legs get out of place; their bodies are not poised to hit the would-be tackler; and they jump too early or too late. Define a task analysis statement to teach blocking.
10. What are the various forms of action training? What are the key ingredients in each of them?
11. Select one of the forms of action training and prepare a sample session showing how it would work in a real training session.

CHRIS OUTERBRIDGES' CONTROL SYSTEM

Chris Outerbridges was a very self-disciplined man. He was fastidious in his appearance, physically in superior condition, and had his time tightly organized. He dictated letters on a portable dictaphone while driving his car to work. He used control charts and planning tools very well. His secretary was a happy, charming girl in her late teens. She worked very hard and energetically when the work piled up. When there was a low work load, she often engaged in small talk, joked, and was easy going. Mr. Outerbridges was very concerned over the latter behavior. He often lectured her on "making your own tasks" and stressed the importance of promptness, neatness, and industry.

1. What advice would you give Mr. Outerbridges?
2. What advice would you give his secretary?

THE CASE OF THE
UNDISCOVERED GENIUS

You have a young mathematician working in a research project for which you are director. He is brilliant in his mathematical work but causes some problems with his personal behavior. He dresses sloppily, is careless about getting in on time, and often works all hours of the night when he gets involved in a project. He is very sharp with others who are lower than himself on the IQ scale and is willing to show the sharp side of his tongue to anyone who disagrees with him. With other professionals whom he respects for their intelligence and competence he is warm, courteous, and cooperative. One day in a conversation the subject comes around to supervisory openings, and he indicates that he would like to be considered for promotion to project director if such a position opens up.

1. What would you tell him?
2. Why?

THE TUITION REFUND
PLAN REQUEST

Your company has a plan whereby it will refund tuition paid out for education which will benefit the company. The decision as to whether or not a course will benefit the firm is usually left to the supervisor, who indicates his approval by signing the request form. The standards for benefit are rather loose, and you have generally interpreted them rather liberally. For example, you approved a machinist who wanted to study for an engineering degree at night; and many engineers are studying for MBA degrees. You once turned down a millwright who wanted to take a course in dental mechanics because he stated that it was to prepare himself for going into business for himself. More recently you have received a request to approve a law degree program at night. The applicant tells you that despite the fact that he is now an inspector, he would like to get a law degree and move to company headquarters as a counsel. You have heard from one of his friends that he wants to set up his own law office. He is an excellent employee.

1. What would you like to learn during an interview?
2. Suppose you learn that he really does intend to leave after he gets the degree? Might you be able to persuade him to stay?
3. What action plan do you suggest?

THE UNCLEAR
ENGINEERING SCHEDULE

You are an engineer for an automobile supplier. At the beginning of each model year in the auto industry your company gets orders, which include specifications for tooling a final product performance. You barely get under way before the changes start coming in. You sometimes get them from your boss, sometimes from the planning department, and occasionally directly from the customer, calling to make verbal changes in orders. The steady flow of changes is making you very uncertain and is affecting your performance in technical matters. You lack confidence in committing yourself along a line of development, since you are afraid that it will change before you get anything accomplished.

1. What is the root cause of your problem?
2. What plans might work in alleviating your problem?
3. What action plan would solve your problem?

THE CASE OF THE
DANGEROUS POOL

The manager of a large motel was proud of an olympic size swimming pool, but he found that it was something of a headache to the management. For one thing, he found that people who weren't guests in the motel wanted to use the pool, and this required that it be policed, which added to the expense. For another thing, he discovered that lots of guests wanted to go swimming at odd hours. Late-arriving guests would often scoot out for a midnight dip and oftentimes alone. This came to the attention of his insurance company, which warned him to do something about it. Further, a few early risers would always get up with the crack of dawn for a brisk dip. He posted the hours when the pool was open and the hours of duty of the life guard, but it had no effect. He doesn't want to get too tough with paying guests, but he is worried. He asks you for some advice.

1. How might you control the unauthorized guests?
2. How might you eliminate late night swims?
3. How could you eliminate the early morning dips?

THE SPEECH THAT
SHOULDN'T HAVE BEEN MADE

The sales force at Grand Old Insurance Co. had been unionized for over 15 years. During that time it had expanded, and the management felt that, if an election were held in 1967, the union would be ousted. After several strategy conferences, the personnel manager expressed such an opinion to several salesmen. This apparently started something, for shortly afterward a group of members petitioned the NLRB for a decertification, and an election was ordered for June. The order was written in April, and both management and the union started campaigns to persuade the salesmen to vote "nay" or "yea" to continued unionization. Jim Black, the personnel manager, set up a score-card system and every two days asked each sales manager to estimate how the vote would probably come out in *his* area.

The score-card showed steady gains for management, until two days before the election Jim's cards showed 75 percent against union, 20 percent for it, and 5 percent undecided. He showed this to the company president. The president became very excited. "I think we should try for a unanimous vote," he said. "I will make a speech tomorrow and win them over. After all, they're salesmen and will appreciate a good sales pitch."

The next day he assembled all the salesmen in the auditorium and gave a one-hour pitch against the union. The next day the election was held. The union won 70 percent to 30 percent.

1. What could have gone wrong here?
2. Is confidence in the speaker significant in the effectiveness of the speaking process?
3. What can Jim do now?

HOW CAN I MOTIVATE MY ENGINEERS?

Mr. Billings was chief engineer and was unhappy with one aspect of his engineers' performance; they didn't get reports in on time. This was a chronic condition. He wrote memos, made talks, and coached people. No improvement followed. One day the company built a new building, and the engineering department moved to different quarters. There were private offices for engineers directing projects; and a large amount of new equipment for dictating, typing, writing, and working privately was acquired and installed in engineering. After several months Mr. Billings noted, to his surprise, that almost all of the reports were now coming in on time. He hadn't made a speech nor written a memo for several months. "I can't figure out how to motivate people," he confessed to a friend.

1. What could have brought about the behavior change?
2. Which explanation do you think is most significant?
3. What are some things Mr. Billings should avoid doing?
4. Are there any things he should do that he isn't doing?

A TALE OF FIVE MANAGERS

A pharmaceutical and medical supply manufacturer had a factory in Pennsylvania with five major department heads and a plant manager. The company had an efficiency rating system for managers which was filled out by the plant manager for his subordinates. On the first rating turned in Mr. Adams was rated "superior," and Mr. Evans was rated "unsatisfactory." The others were rated "average." The plant manager was promoted to another division, and his successor came from outside the firm. He rated Mr. Evans as the "superior" manager and stated that Mr. Adams was "incompetent" and should be fired. The other three he rated as "average" and recommended that they be kept in their present positions. Eight months later he accepted a position with another company, and a third plant manager was brought in from the southern plant. On his rating he stated that both Evans and Adams were "superior" and that the other three were "incompetent" and should be fired.

1. How could these different ratings be explained?
2. What should be done about the management?
3. How might you change the rating system, based upon your scanty knowledge of its operation?

THE UP AND DOWN
REGIONAL MANAGER

Jerry Trotter had started as a machinist in the Kansas City plant and had worked his way up through the ranks to the position of plant manager. Under his leadership in seven years the KC plant had become the best plant in the territory. Based on this performance he was promoted to eastern regional manager of factories. Unfortunately, things didn't go well in the plants under his supervision. Many of the managers complained about his bad judgment and the way in which he tried to run things about which he wasn't well informed. Finally the vice president in charge of manufacturing told Jerry he was being demoted and assigned as plant manager of one of the eastern plants—one which was in deep trouble on many counts. Jerry jumped in and straightened out the sick plant quicker than anyone could have hoped for. After three years he was once more promoted to regional manager of manufacturing, and this time he was an instant success. He made his region the best in the company.

1. What could be the explanation for Jerry's success the second time, where he had failed the first time?
2. What lessons might we learn from this?

THE CASE OF THE
PASSED OVER STAFF MAN

Glen Harrison had been a loyal member of the staff team at division headquarters for many years without having distinguished himself. He was in almost every day, although on good summer days he was known to skip out early to play golf. Golf was his ruling vice, and he would seldom work overtime or on Saturday, since he loved the game and tried to get in a game every night and 36 holes on Saturday. He always won the company tournament. When he was about 55 he had a slight stroke and had to cut down. About that time he got a new boss. The new boss reviewed his past performance records, went to the general manager, and asked permission to discharge Glen. The manager was sympathetic but firmly refused. "After all, Glen is an oldtimer here; and, besides, I would hate to see us lose our best golfer." The boss was grimly aloof from Glen from then on. Each year he passed Glen over on raises while others got regular increases. In order to please the new boss Glen began working harder than he ever had worked in his life. It was to no avail. At age 63 he still had not received a raise for nine years. "Next year I'm really going to dig in and work my head off," Glen said to a friend. "I want to get one more raise before I retire."

1. What are the chances of Glen's plan working?
2. What should Glen do?
3. What is the major thing wrong in the situation?
4. How could it be corrected? List several options and choose one which you think would be best.

PART IV

Advice as an output
of the personnel
administration department

THE FINAL, and perhaps most significant, part of the personnel administration department is the advice it produces. It produces it formally in memoranda and talks, it produces it casually in comments and remarks, and it proffers it under the day to day stresses of operation. Having a consistent pattern of advice, and understanding the significance of that output to the firm and to the personnel department, is a key to status and function as a personnel manager. The most prestigeful personnel men are those whose outputs of advice are recognized, sought out, and applied. In this part of the book we deal with advice in such areas as conflict resolution, managerial styles, employee and managerial motivation, employee discipline, and communication.

chapter 16

RESOLVING
ORGANIZATIONAL CONFLICT

AMONG THE MORE persistent kinds of advice which is produced by the personnel administration department is that related to conflict resolution. The issues of labor management relations, of bad morale, of conflict and fights within the organization, and of the stress-laden kinds of human relations which occur when people disagree, seem to be considered squarely within the province of personnel management. If, indeed, any single area of business activity seems to be an almost exclusive province of personnel, it is human conflict. What many executives refer to as "personnel problems" could be included under the heading of disagreements between humans.

What is the objective in conflict resolution?

Like parents, managers often presume that things are at their most satisfactory level when everything is quiet. People are often selected because of their "reasonable" nature. They are promoted because they are bland, that is, nobody opposes their promotion. This is often a result of scrupulously avoiding conflicts which sometimes produces enemies, who in turn can block advancement.

Having objectives in mind when proffering advice in the area of conflict resolution is vital. Without clearly defined objectives, the advice tends wholly toward silence and compliance to one another in the organization. This reflects itself in almost every key policy area of personnel management.

The selection of people tends toward reasonable people who never engage in disputes.

Training centers heavily upon "human relations" and harmony in behavior.

The promotion of people tends to favor the quiet and compliant person.

The rewards of pay and bonus, if this policy pervades the organization, will be withheld from people who are identified by such words as "contentious" or perhaps hostile.

Coaching is apt to center around somber discussions between bosses and subordinates which take up the matters of past hostilities and combative behaviors.

While such an objective certainly tends to produce quiet, the advice giver, the trainer, the policy level personnel manager has a larger imperative in shaping the general tenor of his advice in the conflict between humans.

The principle objective in handling organizational conflict is not conflict elimination, but conflict resolution.

The difference here is not a subtle one, but a large one. It implies that conflict is not only not wholly undesirable, but upon occasions may be desirable. On the other hand, it does not encourage conflict for its own sake. The management of conflict resolution entails a kind of discriminatory behavior in organization, complex, civilized, and in the management of it, full knowledge of the advantages and disadvantages of the variety of human conflict.

THE POISONS OF CORPORATE INFIGHTING *

Executive brawling can wreck a company's morale

"There's nothing wrong with a good fight," said a general manager recently. "It clears the air, stirs up vitality, and shows that the organization is alert." His organization showed the results of such thinking: the quality-control people were engaged in a vendetta with manufacturing, in the course of which huge quantities of goods—probably in perfectly good condition—were being held up for rechecking; the production people were coolly slipping goods past inspection without checking them properly; the chief engineer and the plant manager had not spoken a civil word to each other in months; the controller was whispering poisonous little words about everyone into the boss's ear; the purchasing man was using his power of signature to hold up requisitions of his enemies while speeding through orders for his friends.

In recent years, this illusion about the virtues of a "good fight" have spread widely with the new trend toward a "tougher line" in labor relations and the decline of "happiness" as a method of management. But

---

* Adapted from an article by the author originally printed in *Dun's Review and Modern Industry* (February, 1964). Copyright 1964 by Dun & Bradstreet Publications Corporation. Used by permission.

while it is true that in the past industry often went too far in the direction of making everybody on the payroll happy, it is a mistake to assume flatly that politicking, infighting, and open hostility does a company any good.

What kinds of fighting are mischievous and should be eliminated in management ranks? The dangerous kinds of managerial squabbles can be classified in six categories: (1) the boss-created-and-supported fights, (2) fights created by the excessive selfishness of one or two men, (3) battles generated by sincere but petty administrators, (4) those created by the organization structure itself, (5) fights that are enlarged by the pigheadedness of a few, (6) excessive rebelliousness for the sake of being rebellious.

Probably the most malignant kind of fighting in management is that which is actually generated and fed by the boss. Usually he is an insecure kind of man who is afraid that if all of his subordinates were to join together, they might discover some major weakness that will expose him to their pooled strength. The best way of keeping himself from being thus attacked, he senses, is to generate and feed internal cliques, thereby keeping his managers so busy attacking each other that they will not turn on him. It may be, for example, that he plays his management committee against his board of directors, creating for himself the role of interpreter.

In one Midwestern firm, for example, the president always reported any management resistance to board proposals back to board members, with sufficient adverse slant to incense them against the lesser officers. He then reported critical comments by the board about the officers back to the subordinates verbatim, without softening them. The result: the board was riled, and the officers were sullen. A management consultant called in to suggest remedies suggested that more officers be placed on the board, thus weakening the power of the middleman. This was done, naturally, over the strong opposition of the president. The problem resolved itself shortly.

In another variety of boss-created fight, a president took up the system of reporting back to subordinate executives the critical remarks of other officers made to him privately. "The controller," he might say, "tells me that your plant just can't stay inside a budget." The remark was a half-truth, since the controller had also made it clear that he understood the reasons for this failure (rising labor costs and rising materials costs, plus some unexpected taxes). The president, however, failed to report this. The controller immediately was attacked by the manufacturing group.

A vendetta was thereby created, and the president found himself to be the focal point in control of communications and influence. He reported that he was "not unhappy about this healthy competition." He was apparently less concerned about the lack of teamwork and coordination. But inevitably a boss weakens an organization when he creates conflict situations that splinter the group into noncommunicating factions.

The "jurisdiction fighter"

At the top level of far too many organizations—including corporations, governments, and universities—are the chronic "jurisdiction fighters." These are the people who see their membership in top management as being rooted in protection of the rights and interests of the group they manage. They see no necessity to approach the top-management role as a dual one—which it must be in large and complex organizations.

Take the case of the electronics company president who found that at all of his management committee meetings he was forced to referee attempts by his executives to grab more territory, power, or resources. After several months of such squabbling he announced to them: "Each of you has two hats he must wear. The first is the management of your own department and the execution of its affairs; the second is to serve as management committee members, at which time you drop all loyalty to your department and think solely in terms of the company as a whole." He then went on to cite specific examples where several of the managers had fought for their own departmental interests at the possible risk of ultimate loss to the company.

The selfish executive may often be more personal in his self-seeking than in the case where he is pushing his department. It is a certain mark of immaturity to be unable to give and only be able to take. Young men pushed too fast may therefore be expected to need some help in over-coming a "gimme" approach to the managerial job. The brash young executive who rides roughshod over the mangled bodies of his colleagues is a source of conflict that must be dealt with strongly, both from the top and by his peers.

Young M.B.A.'s from some of the leading business schools often re-quire some taming along these lines. "The young Turks fresh out of the business schools all push for vice presidential titles before they are ready," one president complained recently. "They don't see the hostility they generate among the old hands who have been slogging along, doing a solid job for years. Until they learn how to give as much as they get, they aren't worth very much to us."

As companies grow larger and more susceptible to bureaucratic red tape, they tend to breed too many petty administrators. These are the men stationed somewhere athwart the communication lines who emit vetoes, usually for violation of some rigid procedure. The fights usually arise when more active leaders at lower levels find their activity blocked by tight application of a small rule, often in a context far removed from its original intent.

This kind of administrative mentality works best at preventing things from happening. Often the things it prevents are bad things—inconsistent practices, for example, where inconsistency would be wasteful and damaging. Far too often, however, the kinds of things they prevent are the very actions that make for healthy growth and change, and such administrators comprise an important weakness in organization.

In one company the controller was such a person. He would deny payment of vouchers spent for purposes that actually made money for the firm. The personnel manager, for example, was recruiting a new sales manager and bargained with the man on the basis that the company would pay certain extra moving costs. The controller disapproved the voucher when it was filed. It led to a bitter fight, which the personnel manager finally won, but it left the new sales manager with a sour attitude.

When the fight is between the people who are making things happen and administrators who are only watching what goes on, it can have an enervating effect upon more positively active executives. Since the company usually lacks the latter and can find plenty of the former, such battles are bad for the firm.

The well-entrenched petty administrator, moreover, is a source of a great deal of politicking. As a politician and infighter, such a breed may develop impressive skills and acquire undue influence. When confronted boldly, most such persons will back down, but the little stingers in their tails will be working with some agility in the process. Given too much management backing, they may acquire enough influence to win major fights, thereby driving the competent action-getters into the hands of competitors who appreciate the necessity for action and the people who can produce it.

The culprit: organization

It is a common management practice to look first for the *person* at fault when a fight occurs. Frequently, though, it is simply the way the organization is set up that accounts for brawls.

Take the case of the chemical company in which the president assured both the research and engineering managers that they would have ample authority over the construction and operation of the pilot-plant stage of operation. In practice, each tried to reverse the other, and cries of anguish echoed throughout the firm. Nevertheless, each was right from his own viewpoint; the difficulty lay in an unclear definition of who was responsible and who had authority. Such built-in collisions occur in most firms and require some positive action to correct the flaws in organization that cause them.

A ready-made situation for this type of conflict is where a quality-control department, assured that it has control over the shipment of goods of high quality, is matched off against the production department, which is told it will be measured by its ability to turn out goods fast and cheaply. Trouble can also occur when the sales department schedules a plant and requires overtime but the plant manager is charged with holding his costs down within standards. Pointing fingers and angry accusations are sure to follow.

A variation of such fights occurs when the various department heads are so specialized they do not know what the department before or the department following them must do.

For years, one division in an instrument company that bought valves from another division, complained constantly about receiving them in dirty condition. Formal complaints about the supplying division flowed upward to top management, without effect.

The matter was solved when the two divisions were placed in a single managerial group for other purposes. The new manager of the two divisions began regular meetings and exchanges of personnel between the two. To their amazement, the instrument group learned that the people in the valve division had supposed that all valves were cleaned after receipt anyhow, and their attitude quite naturally had been: "What was the use of our paying special attention to cleaning them if they were going to be washed before they were used?" The new manager found it simple to define responsibilities for this task to both parties, and a fight of many years' standing was cleared up.

Other paired groups where trouble spots due to organizational conflict are sometimes wrongly defined as "people-centered" problems include: industrial engineering and industrial relations; sales and credit; maintenance and production; sales and marketing; personnel and public relations; purchasing and traffic. Such areas of point accountability are natural clusterings for fights. Every intracompany battle should be checked early to see whether it is caused by intractable people or simply by defective organization planning.

The rebel

A vanishing breed in most large firms, and especially at the higher levels, is the surly and rebellious man whose temperament naturally leads him to oppose others. Often a valuable professional or technical contributor, he is a man of deep convictions—or at least he would appear so in his own eyes. Usually his conviction is developed and strengthened only after he discovers what certain other people's views are, in which case he takes a solid position against them.

In one large firm such a man held down the post of research director for many years and fought hard against management indifference to research. He constantly overspent his budgets, defied direction, and generally swam upstream. As times changed and his budgets increased, he found the other side of the coin equally distasteful. He fought the measures to expand research, declaring that brainpower "cannot be pushed."

In another company such a hardhead held a plant management position and was often observed in the center of heated disputes. A careful analysis of his practices by a management development expert from corporate staff resulted in this analysis: "Mr. Smith may be expected to be opposed to ideas that were not thought of by himself or his immediate staff."

This did not add up to a total indictment of the man. He did not always resist change; only when it was suggested by outsiders. His own staff found him an eager and willing recipient of their ideas, and he was generous with credit. The prognosis was that corporate staffs must plant their ideas at lower levels and let this man believe that it came from within his own organization.

Disputes involving such a person are particularly liable to occur when he runs into another individual of his own make-up and habits. Then, again, he may automatically resist experts. In one automobile company the plant manager of one of the most successful plants resisted visits from staff men from the head office over a period of many years. This attitude was not based on any sound logical foundation; rather, it was a kind of stubborn pride typified by the drug commercial: "I'd rather do it myself." Actually this man maintained a network of informers who kept him apprised of the latest thinking of the staff, and he usually tried to beat the gun in installing their suggestions.

In one radio firm a very famous manager, who shall be identified here as Mr. Sammer, appeared to enjoy sending wires to the home office each time a new policy was circulated. "Received your policy statement on so-and-so," they would run. "Well written. We will not use it in this division." As time passed, these became known as "Sammergrams" to the corporate staffs. Since he ran a good plant, it was only the new and the uninitiated manager who entered into debates with Sammer.

Where the man of stubborn traits is successful in operating his part of the business, he can erect a barrier of folklore to protect himself against serious reprisal. He may be identified as "colorful," and other managers accommodate themselves to his positive ways. The trouble with such an arrangement is that a company cannot afford many such people, even though a couple add interest and style to the firm.

Staff departments also are not without managers who create destructive conflict. Surprising enough, he is often one of the most intelligent members of the management team. His intelligence, in fact, may be part of his problem. As an intellectual harbored in an organization that is oriented towards action, he scorns the rather simple-minded nature of many managerial decisions. As one Ph.D. in business rather arrogantly stated to a consultant: "The kind of conceptualizations required to manage are of a less lofty order than those in my major specialization. It irks me to have to answer the buzzer call of a man who is considerably less intelligent than myself."

What price the intellectual?

The intellectual in the corporation often finds himself an outsider, and his rebelliousness turns not against a single individual but against his condition. He spends an increasing amount of his time in sniping at the management and at the stupidity of present practices. He has a keenly developed sense of the absurd which he sees about him. Very seldom is he genuinely a leader or top operating man himself, but is an adviser to them. He reviews what they have done, perhaps starts a scene or two, and is cool and meticulous in his judgments. If a rebellious group starts, he is able to provide some intellectual basis for their schemes. In this sense he is often at the storm center, although he less often appears in the front line of combat than do his co-plotters.

The intellectual's contribution to the corporation sometimes grows out of his sharp critical powers, and much has been said about his valuable role in this respect. Less has been said about his function as a source of rebelliousness against management.

From this discussion of the evils of infighting and of the specific forms it can take, should we assume that every company dispute is harmful? Not entirely. Certain forms of conflict can result in change, improvement, and new vitality.

CONFLICT AS A VITAL CORPORATE INGREDIENT *

Constructive "inside" ferment toughens a firm for the struggle outside

In an economic system that counts on competition between business corporations to achieve a constantly rising standard of living, it would be strange indeed if there were not some inward turning of the competitive skills that make for a forceful company's outward success. Indeed, the manager who sharpens his talons on competing companies may have arrived at the top because of his combative nature, and it would be expecting too much of such a person to restrain his competitiveness inside the organization; after all, he was hired or promoted because of his pugnacity when confronted with other firms.

Nor would it necessarily be desirable to curb the fighting spirit of such a man vis-à-vis his own colleagues. For while many kinds of corporate infighting can be harmful, conflict can also breathe life into the most moribund of enterprises and act as a catalyst for progress.

---

* Adapted from an article by the author originally printed in *Dun's Review and Modern Industry* (March, 1964). Used by permission.

Take the case of one highly successful company in which there is perpetual conflict. With research expenditures up in the millions, there is constant pressure to get new products out of the scientists' hands and onto the market. Cost-reduction programs press plant managers into keeping the lines running; at the same time, customer demands for high quality impel the quality-control men to shut lines down when the products do not meet specifications. Sometimes the controller cannot find the cash to buy a new piece of equipment, while the manufacturing manager declares that the plant must shut down without it. People get intensely partisan, tempers flare. The result of these clashes: some personal friction, to be sure, but also a continuing rise in the level of productivity, higher quality, lower costs—and one of the best returns on capital in the industry.

Perhaps the most valuable contribution of internal battles is that they can sharpen a company's competitive stance and fortify its defenses. If, for example, the treasurer brings in a financing plan that is attacked by the management committee, he will be forced to reexamine it carefully, and any shortcomings will probably be discovered before the plan has been tried in the money markets. In collective bargaining, a heated discussion between the various plant managers and the labor relations manager may result in the original strategy for bargaining's being ripped to tatters; but although feelings may be ruffled, the strategy will have been tested when the negotiators meet with the union. And the new product that is ruthlessly screened by the critics on the new-products committee is unlikely to be as vulnerable a target for competitors.

The idea that harmony and sweet reasonableness should always prevail just does not stand up in practice. Too much unanimity in a new idea sometimes means that one person so dominates the situation that nobody else dares to stand up and shout "nonsense." As Chairman Charles B. Thornton of Litton Industries puts it: "All of us know of companies that are dominated by sales or manufacturing, by engineering or finance. Whenever management is dominated by a specialist group, on a long-term basis, it will be dead wrong."

"Swamped with advice"

But more than anyone else, it is usually the dominating top executive who kills the ferment and dissent that would separate the good ideas from the bad before they go to market. The top man who has reacted to competition by overpowering it on the way to the top does not ordinarily brook much competition or opposition once he is ensconced in power. As Burroughs Corporation's Vice President Milton Mengel puts it: "Top management is often swamped with an abundance of contradictory advice."

If freely accepted as evidence upon which the top man can base his decision, this contradictory advice can be a healthy kind of competition inside the firm that will strengthen its competitive posture. But if the chief executive has a hostile attitude toward his more enterprising subordinates, he may reject any ideas that are either not his own or not immediately attractive to him. Consequently, when the big crisis comes, as it seems to for every corporation, the corporate muscle may be too flabby to withstand the competitive onslaught.

Playing politics may sometimes be the only way of pushing through major reforms, and there are times when the best executives, like leaders in government, must engage in intrigue in order to do the right thing for the firm. Take the case of the vice president of personnel who developed a new method of handling a tough labor relations problem, which involved promotions of union members. He had calculated the advantages against the possible losses and saw immense gains to the firm in getting his plan installed. But he met with a massive wall of apathy upstairs and simply could not get his idea on to the executive committee agenda for discussion and approval.

Finally he decided to bypass the regular channels and talk privately with several top union officers. They saw the advantages to themselves in his plan (fewer strikes and slowdowns, more orderly contract administration, and less pressure on union officers from the membership) and immediately confronted management with a ferocious demand that such a plan be installed forthwith; serious trouble was threatened if action was not taken. The executive committee changed its next agenda at once and the plan sailed through without a hitch. By boldly stirring up trouble, the vice president provided his company with highly valuable union cooperation for years to come. As Cyrus Ching, veteran labor conciliator, once said: "You can get a lot done in this world if you aren't particular who gets the credit."

In another company the director of management development conducted a lengthy study of the company's future manpower needs and found that the age of the officers—a cluster of retirements was due in a few years—warned of a serious situation ahead. He attempted to use the regular channels for getting a sound program of promotion and hiring up before the board of directors. But the president, more interested in other things, never really listened, and certainly did not pass along the full story to the top group.

So the management-development man resorted to manipulation. He persuaded an old friend, who happened to be a company stockholder, to attend the next stockholders' meeting and to ask the chairman this question from the floor: "I have studied the age of the officers of the firm and note that more than three quarters of them are over 60. What specific plan are you following to provide for orderly succession? What is your management development plan to protect the stockholders after you have all retired?"

He got only a perfunctory answer, but shortly thereafter the management-development director was hauled on the carpet and to his delight was instructed to get a plan under way immediately. "I would have been fired if I had been caught," reported this otherwise noncombative staff man, "but I think my duty to the company is to get my job done, even in spite of my boss."

A comparison of two divisions in one large consumer products company illustrates the values of competition and conflict inside the organization in stretching men's abilities. The first is an old and staid division that for many years has been something of a problem to top management. It returns about 2 percent on sales and less than that on investment. It is staffed by good, solid, comfortable old performers. The demeanor of all is placid. They are led by an amiable man of great experience but little zeal for change. Turnover is extremely low, and procedures are immune to change.

In the other, newer division, however, an entirely different air prevails. Numerous young college recruits apply to get into this division because of its spirited and energetic air. The general manager is prodding and pushing, cajoling and persuading everyone to keep moving. Campaigns for sales, cost reduction, supervisory training, and new methods are in the air. Arguments and fights are commonplace. A walk through their wing of the building makes it obvious that this is an alive and vital organization; people move faster, work harder, bang their fists in anger more often—and laugh more often. Their growth and profits are carrying the company, with a sustained 10 percent return on sales.

Many a successful executive can recall a particular colleague in years past who was his fiercest competitor. Behind a surface air of geniality and good fellowship, the two would watch one another like hawks. When one scored a coup, the other worked overtime to even the count by performing feats that he would never have tried without the spur of competition.

The company shares richly in the rewards when such pairs of competitors work side by side. The conflict is in trying to outrace and exceed the other in excellence, and in small groups such competition has the general effect of raising the group's standards and spurring the would-be laggards to meet the norms of their fellow team members. Just as athletes scrimmage or box against sparring partners, the manager who has no opportunity to push himself against internal competition may be ill-prepared when he meets the buffeting from other firms in the field. Such internal conflict may also make the job more interesting and sharpen performance—if it is properly managed so as to avert destructive conflict.

Operating successfully in the marketplace, of course, is quite different from working inside a company, where the emphasis is on keeping harmony, good fellowship, and unity of purpose at all costs. And it is the realities of competition in the marketplace that force management to fire men, use power politics to achieve efficiency, make enough profit to pay dividends that attract capital, close down excess plant capacity—contribute, in fact, to what economist Joseph Schumpeter once called the "creative destruction" that pervades the free market.

The ideal concepts of professionalism in management, in human relations, and administrative practices, can be used to run a going concern when competitive pressures are scarce. However, a company may fall on harder times when it must function less like a luxury liner than like a Sherman tank, bristling with armor and rolling on grinding treads.

Internal conflict between managers, when focused upon excelling in their jobs, develops a capacity for hard work. Stress and pressure developed in attacking a tough technical or commercial problem develops habits of long hours and personal effectiveness. Harvard's J. Kenneth Galbraith has said that business managers seem to think leisure is immoral. There is little doubt that many of the good jobs—the ones everyone aspires to attain—are associated with long hours and devotion to the job.

Nothing, moreover, brings home to the executive the fine points of his job more than being challenged on his actions. Pressure of the kind that puts decisions to the test sharpens decision-making ability, and the quality of decisiveness itseslf is enhanced. The stress that comes from having to defend decisions against internal attack is most valuable in learning to make what management writer Perrin Stryker calls "the decisions that grievously test the character and understanding of the decider."

In extreme cases, nonmalicious fighting or politicking forces to the wall the executive whose inherent weakness of judgment or strength of purpose is producing a corresponding weakness in the firm. If such strife forces men out of the company from time to time, the chief executive can console himself with the thought that perhaps they should not have been there in the first place.

Strife inside a company is also valuable when it knocks the rough edges off capable but overly headstrong men. "Genius management" in a complex corporation almost inevitably leads to disaster. As psychologist Norman Maier puts it: "Aggressive, dynamic, decisive leadership will be proclaimed desirable in certain parts of the organization, but only in certain parts."

The headstrong individualist who wants to get things done will find opposition aroused against him when he tramples others in his assault on the top. The maturity that permits a man to give as well as take, to serve others as well as himself, is neither learned from books nor taught in classes. It comes from bumping heads with others who want similar things. Without such opposition, the manager may well remain arrogant, immature, and defenseless against serious knocks when they occur.

Any plan, even if it looks fine at first blush, needs some internal working over before it is ready. This requires managers who are ready to "shoot" when they see a fuzzy idea. If a project is basically sound, it may merely have some corners knocked off. If it has a basic flaw, it may crack into pieces. This is sad for the author, but the company avoids pouring resources into a rathole. Staff departments sometimes are guilty of developing grandiose schemes that look fine on paper but have basic flaws. "Before we try out a full-scale installation of a program," reports Elmer John, director of personnel services at General Mills, "we try it out on a few tough critics in the line departments."

In another large company, any selling project proposed by the purchasing people is always tested on a group within the same department, which takes the opposing role of supplier negotiators. In fact, this system has been endorsed on a national level. Secretary of Defense Robert S. Mc-Namara is reported to have established a "red team" and a "blue team" to fight out the merits of a proposal before going before a congressional committee with it, where the game might be played for keeps.

This deliberate establishment of "role-playing" sessions, used to sharpen the skills of salesmen in meeting customers, of financial men in meeting security analysts, or simply to preview an executive presentation to the board, is pretty tangible evidence that many firms see the value of opposition in the polishing of ideas. Learning to face opposition within the house prepares the man to learn from a disastrous encounter rather than be panicked or disillusioned by it.

Management is not wholly one grand fight, nor is it simply the art of compromise. It is the discriminatory art of seeing which approach is appropriate and not flinching from taking it. "Conflict in industry can never be eliminated," says Oswald Knauth, former treasurer of R. H. Macy & Co. "Nor is it desirable that it should be."

ᘒᘒᘒᘒᘒᘒᘒᘒᘒᘒᘒᘒᘒᘒᘒᘒᘒ

THE MANAGEMENT OF CORPORATE CONFLICT *

Astute managers ride herd on both good and harmful infighting

A close scrutiny of the pros and cons of corporate infighting shows that competition, conflict, and backbiting may have many damaging effects. It also shows that under the right circumstances, disagreement is healthy. The ideal situation, of course, is one where the top man manages the organization in a way that brings out the stimulative effects of fighting without also catching the wasteful, debilitating effects.

Experience in firms where this adroit balancing act is best performed shows that seven major control points must be maintained over infighting: (1) Communications networks and practices must be managed effectively.

---

* Adapted from an article by the author originally printed in *Dun's Review and Modern Industry* (April, 1964). Used by permission.

(2) The relationship between winner and loser must be carefully handled. (3) The manager must realize that as a solution to disagreement, compromise has many limitations and should not be looked upon as the ideal outcome. (4) He must seek to head off destructive conflict before it occurs. (5) The boss himself must act as the chief assuager of destructive conflict. (6) Executives should be kept "problem centered" rather than "personality oriented" in their jobs. (7) The manager must be aware that the organization itself can be a cause or cure for corporate infighting, and he should see that it is structured accordingly.

In business, as in the world at large, it is easier to fight with hostile strangers than with competitive friends. The physical separation of offices, plants, and divisions create a fertile breeding ground for disagreement and misunderstanding. In one large firm where all the executive offices had formerly been located in the main plant, a new home-office building was constructed to house the executives separately. The volume of bickering between executives and major department heads rose appreciably. Loss of personal contact is certain to be paid for in such tussles.

Social moats, which prevent frank speaking between different levels of the corporate hierarchy, are also apt to lead to corporate warfare. If a single rule to prevent destructive conflict were to be issued in the large organization, it would go something like this: if you have a misunderstanding with a man, go and talk to him about it.

Naturally, this rule bars the writing of blind memos by the executive as a way of giving vent to his feeling. In fact, the memo should be reserved for confirmation of a verbal agreement arrived at in face-to-face discussion. The only practical use of "cold" memos aimed at an adversary is to fan the flames of dissension. The businessman who wants to break a lease, or force an adversary into some kind of retributive, hostile, or emotional behavior, should sit down and state his grievances in writing, without discussing the topic face to face. To throw the opponent into a state of helpless rage, he should make this note official and businesslike: "I have noted with some regret that . . ."

Where a blind memo stirs up trouble, a personal visit will normally have the opposite effect. Keep the face-to-face communication going, and listen to him attentively. A conciliatory and reasonable discussion will reduce all but the most serious fights to businesslike differences of opinion. Even if nobody changes his mind, a tacit agreement that any differences are limited to ideas and not to personalities will probably be reached.

Fights do not end a war

One of the most frequent drawbacks to winning a battle is that only a temporary advantage is gained. Winning one fight does not end a war, and it stimulates thoughts of revenge. Indeed, vengeance is far sweeter for the man who comes back off the deck from a previous brawl than for the victor. The nature of revenge is that in the mind of the avenger it atones for previous defeats. It also challenges the victim of revenge to shape an even worse fate for his antagonist during the next round in order to get even.

The potent mechanism of revenge makes it pretty important to the company that its effects be avoided wherever possible. Every effort should be made, therefore, to help the protagonists keep their business differences and personal feelings separate.

The manager should also see that no move is made that would indicate one person has been a winner and the other the loser, for simply being labeled as a loser may goad some people into seeking revenge. In some instances, indeed, where feelings run high, it is more important to deal with the hostility than with the original issue that provoked it. Finally, if one of the combatants is guilty of "winner behavior," and crows too loudly in the "I told you so" vein, he should be discouraged immediately and emphatically.

Unfortunately, just as a fight that ends up with one man winning and another losing sometimes means that the company also is a loser, so too can compromise hurt the company. The mechanics of a compromise go like this: two people have taken diametrically opposed positions; they commit themselves publicly to that posture; they start throwing verbal punches at one another; somebody steps between them and suggests that each concede a few points; under pressure they do so. As a result each man is half-satisfied, which means that each is also half-dissatisfied. Such an outcome may be the best that can be achieved, but while it may be better than having a clear-cut winner and loser, it is scarcely ideal. Since both are sullen over the unsatisfactory outcome, hostilities may open once more at any time.

A possible solution is to get the two men talking, trying to find some common grounds for agreement. Take, for example, the case of two staff department heads who got involved in a jurisdictional battle. The matter reached the ears of the general manager, who sat down and talked it over with the two opponents. His first step was to ask each to define areas that he saw as being clearly in the other man's bailiwick; this established that there were some areas of agreement. From this point the general manager moved to less clear areas where "the other department *might* legitimately have an interest"; this narrowed the scope of the disagreement further. Finally he asked each department head to define some areas in which he felt the other man had no justification for meddling. In this particular case, by the time all these questions had been answered, the problem had virtually disappeared without any further bickering.

This method, of course, will not work as neatly if both antagonists have a strong case to be made for their own point of view. Take the case of the squabble in one firm between the industrial relations manager and the public relations manager as to who was responsible for the content of the house organ. The industrial relations manager declared that he should have veto power over any story that might have any implications for employee relations. The public relations manager, on the other hand, stated that he "couldn't run a periodical with such veto power held outside the department."

The executive in charge asked each man to identify the areas in which the other had clear-cut jurisdiction. The industrial relations manager identified such matter as press releases, production and printing of the house organ, and product news as the other man's domain; the public relations man clearly labeled collective bargaining, contract negotiations, wage and salary matters, employment, and training as the industrial relations manager's field. The two men finally narrowed the dispute to certain kinds of stories that mentioned plant operating personnel belonging to the union. Each man felt that such stories fell in his bailiwick.

Here the boss found them still in disagreement, and was forced to make a decision. "The public relations manager," he decided, "will forward such stories to the industrial relations department 24 hours before deadline, and if he does not hear any objection within that 24 hours, he may proceed to publish."

Once a dispute has been resolved by such a decision, it usually pays the arbiter to leave an avenue of appeal to the apparent loser of the dispute along the following lines: "We'll try it this way, and if it isn't working in a week let's bring it up again. If I don't hear from you, I will assume that this procedure is working out."

To prevent destructive fighting, a company may have to look back beyond the immediate issue, for the basic source of trouble often revolves around definitions of authority and responsibility in the organization, or in the organization itself. Here are two basic rules for conflict prevention: every person in managerial or staff positions should have an agreement with his boss on what his major areas of responsibility are for the coming year (they should be checked annually, usually at the time of the annual performance review); for each area of responsibility there should be a statement of how the results in that area will be measured at the end of the period at hand.

The answer: tight planning

In particular, defining measurement methods will solve many of the problems that grow out of joint accountability and duplication of responsibilities. It is possible that many persons have the same responsibility; the differences will be in the way they are to be measured for its discharge. The credit manager may be responsible for credit. The sales manager also has some credit responsibility. The sales manager is responsible for letting the credit manager know of his plans for soliciting a customer in time to have the proposed customer's credit checked before the goods are delivered—or perhaps even before the order is accepted. The credit manager is responsible for carrying out fast and accurate credit checks and getting the information back to the sales manager promptly.

With such a definition, the possibilities of an account going sour—and a fight over whose fault it is—are reduced appreciably.

Above all, however, the chief executive himself must act to prevent harmful fighting. Executives often unconsciously imitate their boss, either present or past. If he is a ready antagonist, quick to tear into anyone who crosses his path, the chances are high that his subordinates will do likewise.

Moreover, if he chooses to set different parts of the organization against each other, his control of communications and information places him in a remarkably effective position to do it. And since he allocates the rewards and punishments, he can reinforce cooperative behavior if he so desires. On the other hand, he can encourage combative behavior by ignoring or even rewarding it.

His supervisory skill and practices, moreover, will have a substantial effect on whether or not the conditions that breed conflict will arise. He can arrange duties so that nobody understands his own clearly, thus ensuring misunderstandings. On the other hand, he can spell out purposes, goals, and standards in such a way that fights can be averted. In selecting people he can build a team that is usually in agreement, or he can introduce mavericks. The latter course is more apt to lead to discord and conflict; at the same time, it may introduce a welcome spark of vitality and tension.

Just how much turmoil the top man wants may be dictated by the kind of business he is in and the performance level of the group. If his executives are so placid they are vegetating on the job, he might do well to accept some conflict in order to get action.

Perhaps the best device for keeping aimless infighting at a minimum is to focus the attention of every person on his work. The organization in which people do not have enough to do all day is more apt to turn to mischief than the one where employees are too busy working to pick quarrels.

It is axiomatic that the man who has too little to do will begin to find fault with the actions of others. The presence of several such persons in any company, moreover, is certain to encourage everyone else to begin judging the work of the others around them. This can tear the organization to tatters.

"I find this can be avoided by keeping every man about a week behind himself in jobs," explained one president. "When my executives leave town I expect them to have their secretaries programmed up tight for the time they will be gone; otherwise the girls will start bickering. I keep enough routine jobs packed into every man's work load so that he won't be lacking for things to do. On top of that I ask him to help out in emergencies in other areas and to have innovative projects on the back burner at all times. It's amazing how this keeps the fights to a minimum."

The ill-effects of bad organization are not limited to squabbles and infighting; this is merely one of the major results. The organization that has not clarified its goals may find people so buried in their work they have lost sight of its purpose. Fanatics—people who redouble their energy when they have lost sight of the goals—thrive in such an environment. When this type of executive feels he is right in a dispute, it is a safe bet that he has not considered the other man's position.

Organization planning to build smooth teamwork starts with defining the goals of the organization, breaking this goal into logical smaller parts, and defining specific responsibilities. But once the formal aspects of organization are agreed upon, it is vital that the informal aspects of organization be taken into account as well. Cliques, informal organizations, cabals, and the natural clustering of interest groups must be catalogued. Their modus operandi, their communication systems (the grapevine), and their informal leaders must be clearly identified by the supervisory staff.

Cliques cannot be wiped out, but this is not necessarily all to the bad. They set standards for the group's performance level and police the activities of their members. This can work in two directions: if a powerful clique is favorably disposed to top management's aims, it can product more action than the toughest authority would dare demand; if it is hostile, it can circumvent the tightest controls and procedures.

This chapter has spelled out the practical insight into handling conflict that experienced managers have learned the long, hard way. In reality, of course, the perils and advantages of corporate infighting are little different from the pros and cons of human conflict at large. Hospitals, universities, armies, navies, governments, and races all have their infighting, for better or for worse. It is only in the details that the management of corporate strife differs from the resolution of conflict in other and wider spheres.

QUESTIONS AND PROBLEMS

1. How does the clarification of objectives assist in conflict resolution?

2. What is the difference between management practices designed to bring about conflict elimination and conflict resolution?

3. You are plant industrial relations manager in a large plant. One of your department has been placed under a new boss. In the first six weeks after his arrival there are no grievances, where there had been several per week

prior to his appointment. What might you want to know about this sudden improvement? How would you go about finding out?

4. Why are disputes between managers more important than disputes between lower level employees?

5. How could a company policy designed for one purpose have an unintended side effect of causing disputes and conflict?

6. What are some of the healthy byproducts which can emerge from organizational conflict?

7. How would you describe the difference between healthy competition and destructive conflict?

8. Why should discussions and dialogue precede memorandum for resolving conflicts, making bargains, or changing somebody's opinion?

9. Are cliques unavoidable, and if so how would a manager handle them? Identify how some cliques you know about work, and what their effect has been.

10. How do you achieve unity in an organization?

11. Give an example of conflicts you have seen, how they grew, and what the effects were. How could the effects have been changed by action of one of the parties?

THE EXPLORATORY FISHING PROJECT: A CASE STUDY *

I. PROJECT GOALS

Based on the results of a short feasibility study, the Agency for International Development (AID) contracted the services of the Bureau of Commercial Fisheries (BCF), U.S. Department of Interior, to undertake exploratory lobster fishing operations in the Republic of Sartinia. The purpose of these operations was ". . . to determine the best methods of fishing for the several species of lobsters, their seasonal and depth distributions, as well as the general areas of best fishing in order to provide sufficient information concerning the resources for Sartinia's private industry to develop a strong industry in spiny lobster, and training potential spiny lobster fishermen." The original agreement was signed in June, 1962 and was to cover a 14-month period.

The agreement also contained the following provisions on relationships

---

* Prepared by James R. Brady in September, 1965 for the Bureau for Latin America, U.S. Agency for International Development. The years given in the case are not those in which the events actually occurred.

between the BCF field team and the "USAID" or AID Mission in Sartinia:

The detailed technical and administrative direction of the BCF technicians and of their operations is the responsibility of BCF.

BCF personnel visiting Sartinia under the terms of this agreement are responsible to the director of USAID or his designee with regard to all contacts with the participating country. In general, however, it is expected that BCF personnel will be in daily contact with local government personnel.

II. STAFFING AND FINANCE

The BCF team was to include a Fishery Methods and Equipment Specialist (Project Leader), a General Fishery Biologist, two Fishery Research Biologists, and a Vessel Master. (It is not known how many of these authorized positions were actually filled at any given time). One hundred sixty-two thousand dollars was allotted to the project, of which $39,000 was to be used for chartering a fishing vessel and crew. The government of Sartinia contributed $13,000.

III. INITIATION OF OPERATIONS

The project vessel accommodated ten persons and was operated by a captain, four Sartinian crewmen, and two fishery specialists. The three remaining berths were generally filled with observers from industry or fishery stations or other interested persons. Fifteen cruises were made between August, 1962 and October, 1963, with brief written reports on each cruise being submitted by the BCF Team to the USAID Mission.

In May, 1963, the USAID Mission asked for a meeting of representatives from USAID, BCF, the Sartinian government, and the Sartinian fishing industry to discuss progress. At this meeting, agreement was reached to extend the project for one year, but the USAID asked that the Sartinian fishing industry provide some tangible indication of support for the project. According to BCF representatives, agreement was not achieved on the exact form such support was to take.

In July, 1963, the agreement between AID and BCF was extended to September 1, 1964. Ninety thousand dollars was to be provided to cover operations for FY 1964 (from July 1, 1963 until June 30, 1964). Another $12,500 was budgeted for the period following June 30, 1964 if the Mission received adequate appropriations for FY 1965. A project implementation order (PIO) issued by USAID in August, 1963, to provide the actual FY 1964 funds for the project, indicated that BCF's activities would be conducted on behalf of the Sartinian Industrial Development Center, the Sartinian Department of Fisheries, and the "private sector." The first two organizations were under the Ministry of Agriculture, Commerce, and

Industries, but no specific organizations were identified for the private sector.

In the revised agreement, the general goal statement had been altered:

The purpose of this project is to train Sartinian officials and commercial fishermen in lobster fishing methods, continue exploratory fishing operations . . ., and provide government and industry information concerning the areas of best fishing to foster development of spiny lobster fishing industry.

IV. USAID REQUESTS CANCELLATION OF THE PROJECT

In October, 1963, the AID Mission suddenly requested AID/Washing-to (AID/W) to terminate the BCF project by December 31, 1963. When AID/W pressed for further explanation, the Mission replied as follows:

1) The USAID felt it was necessary during the second year to include simulated commercial lobstering, as well as scientific exploration, to teach local fishermen modern methods.

2) Since the first year's work had identified three distinct areas with commercial lobster potential, the USAID felt very strongly that the private sector should participate in and contribute to this phase. Two companies and two individuals agreed in principle to do this, but when we asked them to sign a contractual commitment, they backed off. At Mission's suggestion, a National Fishing Association was organized to represent the fishing industry. After this association discussed the project at a series of meetings, its principal officers and the head of the Department of Fisheries came to the Mission and regretfully stated that the association could not participate or contribute in any way to the project. At this meeting the head of the Department of Fisheries did not say that his organization was prepared to support the exploratory work, so the Mission accepted his silence as concurrence with the views of the association. Furthermore, financial and personnel problems in the Department of Fisheries give little reason to believe it could participate on any meaningful and continuing basis.

There will be other projects in which we will ask the private sector to participate in and suport. Quite obviously any weakening of the Mission's position in our first effort would tend to undermine future efforts.

3) The Mission planned to assist the two companies and two individuals showing a concrete interest in lobstering by making the BCF vessel and staff available to them for training. An intensive 60-day training program would enable these groups to begin commercial lobstering, which was the objective of this project. However, the BCF Project Leader refuses to proceed on this basis, and the crew and staff are idle. He contends that he must have additional personnel to complete the requested training work (no exploratory work) within 60 days or by December 31st as a maximum. This stand came as a complete surprise to us, as he has been working alone for four months without registering any complaints known to the Mission. Moreover, three months of the second year had passed without BCF providing the additional personnel required under the agreement. This failure to furnish the necessary manpower has thus

resulted in the boat being tied up at the dock for three weeks completely idle.
4) In addition, the BCF Project Leader is under the impression that the USAID
Mission has no jurisdiction whatsoever over his activities. Mission requests that
AID/W clarify this at once with BCF/Washington. The BCF should accept the
fact that their operations here are subject to policy determinations and guidance
by the mission director or his designee.
5) We have indicated to the BCF team that action now rests with AID/W.

V. BCF RESPONDS

In late November, 1963, BCF/Washington, sent one of its regional directors to Sartinia to review the project. His November 29th report included the following observations:

1) Because two of the approved BCF personnel have not been cleared by AID
to go to Sartinia, the project has not been as productive as it might have been.
2) Our BCF staff is held in high regard by Sartinians in government and the
fishing industry, for the accomplishments already realized. Highly valuable
information has been collected on potential lobster sources and the effectiveness
of traps in catching them. A by-product of one cruise was information on abundant scallop resources which led to the start of a new industry. Fourteen ves-
sels are now catching an average of 14,000 pounds of scallops and 8,000 pounds
of snappers per four-day cruise.
Representatives from the Industrial Development Center, Department of Fisheries, National Fisheries Association, and private fishery interests all expressed
the hope that the lobster exploratory project would be continued as originally
planned. The head of the Fisheries Association is having a boat built for lobstering and another operator plans to build one. Others were less definite but
thought more information should be available for industry use when conditions
were favorable.
3) In discussions with members of the USAID Mission, I referred to the agreement reserving to the BCF administrative and technical direction of the project
since there apparently had been some doubt about this feature. I reported the
apparent wide-spread Sartinian interest in the project and said that I had become convinced the project was sound. I pointed out that progress was being
made and that the relatively small expenditures made during the balance of
the fiscal year would yield tremendously greater returns than earlier expenditures because the latter had largely gone for outfitting, survey type work, etc.
After some discussion, I stated that the amount being spent by Sartinian private
industry for the new scallop industry was greater than the amount they had
tried to get the private firms committed to in the their draft contract. I also
explained that, in the U.S., the BCF goes far enough in exploratory fishing to
take out as much risk as possible by doing just what we are doing in Sartinia,
and going a step farther by assisting with product development and marketing
if necessary. I assured the AID staff that at no time did we try to get a written
agreement from industry associations or individuals. I also told them that some
Sartinians were aware of our methods of operating and were puzzled as to why
something different was being insisted upon in Sartinia.

4) Termination of the project for the reasons given by the AID Mission will bring sharp and, in my opinion, unanswerable criticism from the Sartinians of AID and the United States (but not BCF). The Mission is apparently willing to let the final decision be made by AID/Washington, so I recommend we make a forceful approach there through the assistant secretary, if necessary, for continuation of the project.

chapter 17

PARTICIPATIVE MANAGEMENT AS A GAME

DURING THE DECADE of the fifties, and well into the sixties, much of the thrust of behavioral research dealt with the question of management styles. Among the key issues to be resolved was that of the autocratic versus the democratic styles. Despite the vigor of the debate, no one found time to put forth a clear or commonly accepted definition. Thus, it's necessary to make one's own.

Autocratic style can be defined as management behavior in which the leader sets the goals, defines the ways in which they will be accomplished, tightly supervises to be certain that his methods are followed, and uses rewards and punishments directly for compliance.

Participative management includes several kinds of behaviors of bosses which are not autocratic. In degrees, this lessened control could be defined in these ways:

Level 1. *Directive:* The boss sets the goals and defines the methods, but doesn't really follow up, and those who wish to use their own methods may do so.

Level 2. *Democratic:* The boss sets goals and gives general expectations about methods to be used, but doesn't police and check tightly upon compliance with methods. He does, however, check upon results. Democracy is customarily associated with extensive discussion and individual choice by the governed.

Level 3. *Permissive:* The boss lets people set their own goals and choose their own methods of getting there, and generally uses results as a measure of success. His function is to help as requested, create the proper climate, and pay the bills.

Thus, the definition of autocratic and permissive is itself hardly a polarized, black or white, *X* or *Y* set of options, but a continuum of behaviors, including nonmanagerial.

FIGURE 17–1

Behavior	Participative levels				
	Autocratic	Directive	Democratic	Permissive	Non-manage-ment
Sets goals	Boss	Boss	Jointly	Subordinate	None
Defines methods	Boss	Subordinate	Subordinate	Subordinate	None
Uses tight controls to assure compliance	Boss	Jointly	Subordinate	Subordinate	None
Uses results to rate success	Boss	Boss	Jointly	Subordinate	None

Key: Who initiates behavior?

What advice should personnel departments produce?

Personnel programs have a tangible effect upon the behaviors of managers within this grid. If the appraisal system sets up discussions between managers and subordinates in which the agenda is subordinate performance, some combination from the grid becomes an ideal toward which managers will be coaching their subordinates. Salary administration and bonuses will be arranged so that rewards are issued or withheld for one pattern of behavior and not for another pattern. Training sessions will issue behavior-change instructions to managers to behave in a certain fashion according to a position on this grid. Managers who behave according to the approved style will be promoted and those who do not will be left behind.

Yet the choice of the proper managerial behavior is difficult for many reasons. The first has already been alluded to—the experts in behavioral science can't seem to agree upon a definition of participative management. A conference on the subject at Cornell University in the late sixties nearly collapsed under the confusion of attempting to define participative management. Secondly, the difficulties of weighing the pros and cons in order to use participative management is immense when it cannot be defined behaviorally. Thus, the definition suggested in Figure 17–1 is not intended to resolve the definition problem. Rather, it is intended to define the behavior of the manager and his subordinate for purposes of discussing its application in this chapter. The definition then?

Participative management is managerial behavior which is not autocratic in at least two respects:

(a) defining subordinate methods of work, and

FIGURE 17–2

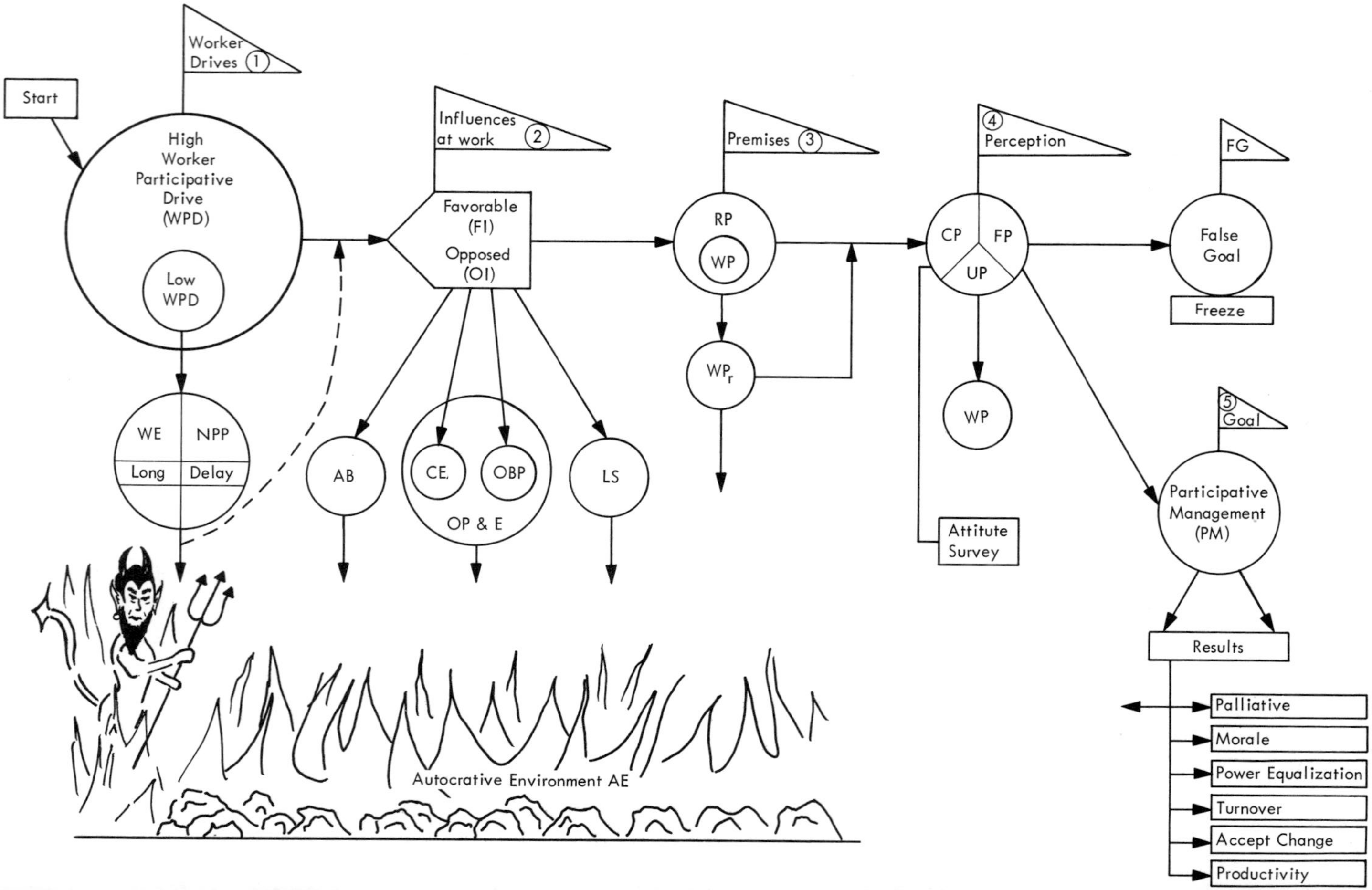
Start
Worker Drives (1)
High Worker Participative Drive (WPD)
Low WPD
WE
NPP
Long
Delay
Influences at work (2)
Favorable (FI)
Opposed (OI)
AB
CE
OBP
OP & E
LS
Premises (3)
RP
WP
WP_r
(4) Perception
CP
FP
UP
WP
Attitute Survey
FG
False Goal
Freeze
(5) Goal
Participative Management (PM)
Results
Palliative
Morale
Power Equalization
Turnover
Accept Change
Productivity
Autocrative Environment AE

(*b*) control of subordinate conformance—and may extend to more than these.

Autocratic behavior is the behavior of a boss in which he sets the goals, defines the methods, uses controls to assure compliance, and uses results to rate the subordinate's success.

The three degrees of participative management, shown in Figure 17–1, cover many, but not all, of the various definitions which have been used in behavioral research and include directive, democratic, and permissive.

The fourth column in which the boss doesn't do anything is not managerial behavior.

THE GAME OF PARTICIPATIVE MANAGEMENT

The path to the participative management game, showing its attendant pitfalls, snares, traps, and finally the triumphant achievement with corresponding payoffs, can be illustrated in Figure 17–2. Each of the milestones in the game will be discussed later in terms of the behavioral research which demonstrates why the outcomes of the game at each stage are valid. First, to the game. The objective is to arrive at PM (Participative Management). If you fall into AE (Autocratic Environment), you lose.

Step one

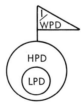

Move smartly onto the board to square number one, labeled Worker Participative Drive (WPD). If the workers have high participative drive (they want to be in the act), you win and can move on to the next square. If they have Low Participative Drive (LPD), you lose: move into either Wrong Environment (WE) or (NPP), NonParticipative Personality. If you get stuck in either of the latter, your progress is slowed considerably, you are in great danger of falling into AE, if not at a dead end. For one thing, if the environment is wrong for participative management, such as being aboard an airliner with two engines on fire, you must first put out the fires before you can expect the captain to call a passenger conference for advice on safe landing techniques. In fact, the other passengers will probably have rather strong feelings about your attempts to take charge, and may sit firmly upon you. If you land on NPP, you are faced with people who want to be dominated, are low on independence drives, and would rather have the boss give the orders and do the thinking for them. To change such people is complex and slow and your game is delayed considerably. For example, you might have to teach them the advantages of their participating and in some severe cases might have to resort to psychotherapy, which is time-consuming and costly.

It should be noted that both pitfalls here are centered in the worker himself, and that he is the reason for participative management not working, he battles strongly against it.

Step two

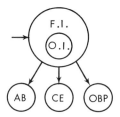

Having hurdled the possibility that the workers might not want to participate, you now land in step two, which is the most treacherous spot in the game. More participative management players are dropped here than anywhere, since it is the site of the dreaded two-headed Personality-Environment (PE) serpent, which has an amazing ability to eat up participative behavior. If, of course, all influences at work are Favorable (you land in FI territory), move immediately to step three. If influences are Opposed (OI), however, you may fall into one of three bogs (AB, OCE, or OBP), which, if not circumvented, could lead to your downfall into Autocratic Environment.

AB is the Autocratic Boss, who simply likes to be the big cheese, relates to the world by overpowering it, is determined not to lose control, or, for one of a host of other reasons, is autocratic and has learned to like it. You may have to replace him, which is not easy, especially since he has power and sometimes owns the company which he founded. If, however, he can be sold, you'll win, because he'll immediately *order* participative management.

CE is the pit of a Cultural Environment, which calls for autocratic management and opposes participative management. Such a trap includes total cultural factors such as tradition, history, customs, mores, and accepted practices which militate against participation. Military organizations, automobile assembly lines, and the like, are locales of such a cultural environment. They are very difficult to change since they have succeeded in the past using that cultural framework.

OBP *consists of an Opposing Boss Personality* and is another snare.

He has a deep-rooted desire to dominate people, especially those who depend upon him for a living, and has flunked his Adorno Scale. To change such a man requires therapy. Such a man is the favorite target of sensitivity training groups, although the track record in changing such people by this means is pretty weak. Despite the unfavorable publicity he receives in places like the Harvard Business Review and other scholarly journals, he seems to have immense powers of resistance and survival.

• *OCE plus OBP is a malevolent combination.* And perhaps the most difficult of all of the traps in the game. It is a combination of an autocratic boss personality with an opposed cultural environment and almost surely will lead the player who falls into this bramble to being dropped permanently into the pit of autocratic environment. Since many pits exist in our most successful organizations, and the two seem to have a natural attraction for each other, they combine often to make a formidable obstacle. The reason for its difficulty seems to lie in the self-feeding nature of the combination. To break out of it often requires changing both boss and culture. Sometimes in their attempt to break out, people themselves become autocratic and end up autocratically ordering the firing of the autocratic boss, and autocratically ordering that democratic or permissive methods be applied. Every South American dictator has this trap.

• *LS (Leadership Style) is perhaps the most easily escaped.* Since it involves a rational and conscious choice by a manager, it can often be affected by training. The potentially participative leader behaves autocratically simply because he doesn't know that any other style exists, or what the advantages of an alternative style might be. When he finds out the advantages and how to apply participative management, he changes.

Step three

Move to the Premises Square. The awful possibilities here are that Wrong Premises (WP) can drop you into autocratic behavior, whereas the Right Premises (RP) can carry you onward to your winning position. While quite serious, the WP trap is somewhat less dangerous than the previous step, and if caught in time can be remedied (WP_r). For one thing, wrong premises are rational, for the most part, and may be corrected by rational discussion and clear information. However, where wrong premises are fixed and not subjected to dialogue and rational discussion, this trap can be fatal. Sound communication is reported to be beneficial too. Given the right premises, move to the next step.

Step four

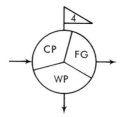

Go to the Perception Square. Here the player may land on one of three sectors of the square. CP is a winner since it means Clear Perceptions of reality and can go right on to the goal. However, UP or Unclear Perception does not. CP sees things as they really are, has a clear fix on what the condition of his organization is, knows what his people really want. Escape from this trap requires a new outlook. This is often reinforced through survey research and attitude surveys, which are a navigational system to clear perceptions. Such surveys can be obtained (at high prices) from academic and consulting organizations who will conduct attitude and morale surveys of your employees. As a result of these surveys you will have brought to bear the powerful tools of the questionnaire and the interview on obtaining clear perceptions. The answers to these questions are purified by running them through a computer, which makes them extremely scientific. Without such an attitude survey you may go happily along with the illusion that your employees have exactly as much participation as they would like, and not modify your behavior accordingly. If you are lucky enough to return to CP, go right on through into the Land of Participative Management.

A third possibility on the CP square is that you may suffer from the worst fate of all: you may land on the FP sector, which means you are routed permanently to the *False Participation* box, where you go into a freeze. The danger here is that you will delude yourself that you have arrived at True Participation and will be so happy with your circumstance that you won't even try to take evasive action or move to escape. False participation is the condition in which the employees *think* they are participating, whereas actually the boss, sly manipulator that he is, makes all of the decisions. To say he is able to pull this off is to act like a benevolent autocrat, or even worse he *manipulates* people through charm, persuasion, or even applied behavioral science.

If you escape the last pitfall, or have fallen but regained grace, you are now ready to enter to magic land of participative management.

WELCOME TO PARTICIPATION LAND

Having survived the rigors of the journey and the perils of managing wrongly, you are certainly entitled to a tour around this land of milk and honey. Where is the payoff for all the grief?

The *Palliative Pavillion* is a center in which everybody gets a lot of satisfaction from his work in lieu of pay and benefits. He gets a seat at the board room table, a chance to tell the boss he is an idiot, and opportunity to take part in the co-workers cooperative council. He sits on junior boards. He speaks his mind freely. In exchange for this he gets a very light pay check, which naturally means that the boss has more numbers at the bottom of the statement. There is a fog which surrounds the PP, and lots of members of the management of Participation Land would rather you didn't talk about it.

The *Morale Museum* is the next point of interest. People in Participation Land find this of great value, especially people with middle-class backgrounds and values. Thus, you are very apt to find such people as engineers, scientists, staff people, and professionals generally hanging out in the High Morale Museum in the Land of Participation.

Right next door is a similarly satisfied looking crew, with a connecting passage to the Morale Museum. This is the *Low Turnover Tower*. These people have been around a long time, in fact if you tried to get rid of them you'd have to pour hot water on them (or cut off their participation) because they are so hung up on participation that they just couldn't leave.

It's a short walk from here to *Accommodation Avenue,* where everybody is terrific on accepting change. They spend most of their time participating in things, and are most obliging when it comes to accepting any changes, as long as they themselves thought of them. This accomodation, of course, doesn't extend to accepting change if the idea is thought of at the top and crammed down their throat, but that is one of the beauties of Participation Land, nobody gets told much. Since nobody dictates change or even suggests too firmly what changes should take place, the friendly folks there are very nice about accepting change.

It's just a few steps into the bowels of the utility works at participation land, where we find the *Power Equalization* machines working constantly. This is the giant engine which makes certain that a steady flow of adjustment occurs so that the boss and the subordinate are always equal in power in the Land of Participation. If a boss should lose his head and start acting without involving his subordinates in the decisions which affect them, the PE machine goes immediately into action, and infuses the air around the boss with clouds of guilt, which he inhales regularly until it has affected him to return to normal participative behavior. In severe cases where the boss holds his breath and stays autocratic, it may take some time before the PE machinery works, but once in action it seldoms fails. A suggested beneficial side effect of the PE machinery working on employees is that it might extend itself into the world outside of the job. If such is the case, it makes the worker a better voter, citizen, and member of a democratic society. He will probably vote a liberal democrat ticket, of course. This is, of course, speculative, and isn't really advertized very much anymore as a feature of Participation Land.

We come now to a nameless and rather sad location, now undergoing major alterations. It seems that for many years a number of behavioral scientists were bent on proving that *Higher Productivity* comes without delay or uncertainty from participation. The climate in participation land, it was proposed, was so much more conducive to high productivity that the output there would beat the pants off productivity in autocratic behavior territory. The trouble with this appealing idea is that sometimes it works and sometimes it doesn't. In fact, the scientists who designed and built this center contradict each other terribly. One man studies some railroad workers and proves that close supervision leads to low productivity. Another man studies another group of railroad workers, using the same methods, and finds that close supervision leads to high productivity. We leave the scene as one group continues to pump murky fluid into a sump and another group works just as vigorously to pump it out.

Reports from down below in the land of autocratic behavior come filtering into this nirvana occasionally. Here the boss runs the show, makes all the decisions, and second guesses himself. He tells people what to do, how to do it, and raises hell if they didn't. Unfortunately, nobody has spent much time studying autocratic behavior, since apparently it is naughty and should be eliminated, and therefore what is the sense of studying something which is probably going to be eliminated anyhow? Travelers from 'down there,' however, report anecdotes about companies that make considerable sums of money, grow like mad, buy other companies, their stock prices shooting skyward making millionaires of investors, and generally make their stockholders and owners ecstatic, all the while sticking religiously to outmoded autocratic methods. There are also verbal reports, not verified by the powerful tools of the questionnaire and interview and purified by the computer, that the land of autocratic behavior produces an astonishingly high number of the leaders of industry and business at the very top levels.

THE RESEARCH EVIDENCE ON KEY QUESTIONS ABOUT PARTICIPATIVE MANAGEMENT

While the game is amusing, it has value only if it has some hard basis for each of its positions. Indeed this evidence would be necessary to construct such a game. What follows then is a summary of the research evidence of behavioral scientists for the statements and conclusions stated so categorically in the game. This is presented here as answers to a series of questions which are essential to shaping and giving sound advice to management.

1. Is participation desired by workers?

One of the first branching points for decisions on participative management is that of the level of desire for people to take part in decisions which affect them. Maier and Hoffman (1962) [1] assert that such a desire is widespread and should be assumed present. Vroom (1960) [2] presents research evidence that the desire to participate is a function of the personality of the worker. Those with high independence drives want to be consulted, and those with low independence drives really don't wish to be asked their views. Gurin, Veroff, and Feld (1960) [3] in a national study report that their research shows the desire to participate a middle-class value, to be found more frequently among college graduates and similar middle-class groups than among laborer and lower socioeconomic groups.

2. What opposing influences can block participative management?

Several kinds of opposing influences will work to bar participation of subordinates in decisions affecting them. The culture as such an influence was studied by Harbison and Myers (1960) [4] in their research into management styles in different parts of the world, most specially in the underdeveloped countries, but also in the Western industrial and postindustrial civilizations. Mason Haire (1966),[5] in studies of comparative practices in the United States and abroad, especially France, found that cultural differences affected the extent to which management adopted certain styles of managing, such as participative management. Carlisle (1967) [6] studied the differences in culture between French-speaking Canada, English-speaking Canada, and American firms operating in both the United States and Canada. He found that while the application of each differed, the expectations of people also differed.

---

[1] N. R. F. Maier and L. Hoffman, *Group Decisions* (New York: Wiley, 1962).

[2] V. Vroom, "Some Personality Determinants of the Effect of Participation," *Journal of Abnormal and Social Psychology,* Vol. 59, 1959.

[3] Gurin, Veroff, and Feld, *Americans View Their Mental Health,* Basic Books (New York, 1960).

[4] F. Harbison and C. Myers, *Management in the Industrial World* (New York: McGraw-Hill, 1960).

[5] Mason Haire, E. Ghiselli, and L. Porter, *Managerial Thinking: An International Study* (New York: John Urley, 1966).

[6] A. E. Carlisle, *Cultures in Collision* (Bureau of Industrial Relations) (Ann Arbor: University of Michigan, 1967).

Seashore and Bowers (1963) [7] and Marrow, Seashore, and Bowers (1967) [8] also contributed to the evidence that where the environment is not conducive to participative management, it is not likely to be in evidence.

Adorno (1950),[9] in his well-known book *The Authoritarian Personality,* attributes much of the behavior of autocrats to their autocratic personality. He has also proposed a widely used test to uncover this autocratic personality, which provides the tester with a position on an F scale (F purportedly meaning "Fascist"). In one application Vroom (1960) [10] applied this to determine the effect of personality upon leadership style and concludes that authoritarian personalities are in part an explanation of autocratic behavior by bosses.

Management styles might be considered as significant as an opposing influence to participative management. Fleischman (1955) [11] constructed a grid in which managers and leaders could be plotted with respect to the leadership style. Along one axis of the grid was the fact of "consideration" usually for employees' feelings and desires. Along the other axis was the factor of "structure" and discipline applied by the boss. This resulted in a position on the Fleischman LOQ grid. This grid has been widely discussed and applied by consultants in modified form. The ideal, some suggest, is an exact middle ground at the extreme ends of each of the axes of the Fleischman scale.

Blake's *Managerial Grid* (1963) [12] bears a striking resemblance to the Fleischman LOQ grid, although the test of fitness on Blake's grid, the instructional material for behavior change, and the practical examples and proscriptive materials found in Blake are not present in Fleischman.

3. What premises are necessary to affect participative management?

Simon (1957) [13] points out that for participative management to exist, certain premises are necessary on the part of management and of the worker as well. These premises include some intuitive or empirical judgments about the nature of man, his needs and wants, his character and nature, and the like. McGregor (1961) [14] has popularized best the exam-

[7] S. Seashore and Bowers (*Monograph 33,* Institute for Social Research) (Ann Arbor: University of Michigan, 1963).

[8] A. Marrow, S. Seashore, and D. Bowers, *Management by Participation* (New York: Harper and Row, 1967).

[9] T. Adorno *et al., The Authoritarian Personality* (New York: Harper and Bros., 1950).

[10] V. Vroom, *op. cit.*

[11] E. H. Fleischman, E. Harris, and H. E. Burt, *Leadership and Supervision in Industry,* Bureau of Educational Research, The Ohio State University, 1955.

[12] R. Blake and J. Mouton, *The Managerial Grid* (Austin, Texas, 1963).

[13] H. Simon, *Administrative Behavior* (New York: Macmillan, 1957).

[14] D. McGregor, *The Human Side of Enterprise* (New York: McGraw-Hill, 1960).

ples of premises which can be assumed about people. He refers to them in two polarized statements. One premise about people he refers to as Theory *X* and the other the Theory *Y*. Theory *X*, says McGregor, assumes the average person dislikes work and avoids it when he can, therefore works must be directed, coerced, intimidated, or controlled if we are to successfully manage them. Theory *Y*, on the contrary, starts with a different premise. It presumes that the average person finds work as natural and pleasant as rest or play, and thus can be relied upon to be productive and creative at work if he is not put off from such behavior by unfavorable circumstances, policies, or boss behavior.

Certainly such premises can have an effect upon the behavior of people. The black revolution of the sixties was in large part a product of a premise by the residents of the ghetto that jobs, individual freedom, and equality were rightfully theirs. Without such premises their efforts would have been lessened. The worker who starts with the premises that he is entitled to participate in the decision which affects him, will battle to obtain the things he presumes to be rightfully his. As Likert (1961) [15] has pointed out, for the generation which emerged from the schools during the sixties, a whole new set of premises came into the workplace. Such premises, spelled out as options, often relate to the role of the boss and subordinate, and affect policy, advice, procedure, and practice. Appley (1951) [16] has listed a range of premises which could prevail with respect to the relationship of order givers and order takers, boss and subordinate . . . He lists these as having an ascending level of civilization built within them, ranging from a lowest form "The other fellow is my enemy and should be destroyed," through successive stages:

Savagery—The other fellow is my enemy and should be destroyed.

Slavery—The other fellow is an object to be used for my purposes and discarded when used up.

Servitude—The other fellow will serve me for a consideration and ask no more.

Paternalism—I will help the other fellow improve his lot, without asking what put him in his present state.

Statesmanship—The other fellow has capacities and abilities which can be developed and it is my job to help him develop them.

This ascending scale of premises about man is seldom dealt with in the behavioral research respecting participative management, for it is clearly a matter of *values*. The mixture of ethical, cultural, social, and religious values with science tends to make such values more normative than scientific and objective. It also opens the conclusions to more challenge,

---

[15] R. Likert, *New Patterns of Management* (New York: McGraw-Hill, 1961).

[16] L. Appley, *Management The Simple Way* (New York: American Management Association, 1951).

for the acceptance of the premises becomes a necessary part of the validity of the scientific results.

It has been the heavy infusions of premises into the behavioral research about participative management that has led to its being suspect among behavioral scientists.

For those who understand the premises, and agree with them, there is no problem in accepting the findings of the research which is centered upon such premises. Yet, the premises have often led the conclusions of the researchers to categorical conclusions which can be easily controverted out of the common experience or day-to-day observations which are contrary to the evidence of the questionnaires and interviews.

If you start with the premise that human beings have a responsibility to help one another grow, learn, and live fully and express themselves as human beings, you don't need much scientific evidence that it works. If you inherently believe that people are objects to be used like tools, that they basically want little except food and sex, dislike work, and are probably a little dishonest, you really don't need any evidence to show you that participative management works or does not. Your solution is easily made.

This is the significance of premises in participative management systems.

4. What part does perception play in participative management?

In ordinary scientific discussion it is presumed that the findings of complex research should be readily evident in everyday observation. That is, if some meticulous research were to have shown that the moon is made of green cheese, the visit of astronauts there, bringing back samples of rock, would be considered proof of the opposite conclusions. In the behavioral research, however, an anomalous kind of logic has emerged.

1. The behavioral scientists have proposed a form of management based upon insights available to them which are not available to the operating managers on the scene in plant and office.

2. They suggest that the perceptions of managers with many years of experience are wrong, and that even though they are physically on the spot, they really don't know what is happening in their own organizations, with their own people, and among their own employees and customers.

Such conclusions are not without scientific precedent. The astronomer who proposed that the world was round, flew in the face of strongly held belief and of on-the-scene observations of sailors and farmers who spent their lifetime observing.

The perception question is whether or not managers know what reality in management consists of, or whether the behavioral scientists know what reality consists of.

REALITY IN MANAGEMENT

In one executive development course an eminent behavioral scientist, whose research in the practices of management is renowned, expounded his theory that present managerial practices are all wrong, and that behavioral science research had discovered entirely new principles for the conduct of managerial duties. Since his conclusions were quite contrary to the experience of the members of the executive audience, they politely suggested that perhaps the academician had missed something important. The researcher was adamant: "Whether or not you like it, the facts show that present-day management methods are wrong!" One of the more outspoken members of the class then delivered himself of a pungent opinion along these lines:

Professor, you and your academic colleagues are running around naked with a bag over your head yelling. "We'll save you, we'll save you!" You can't even save yourselves until you punch a couple of eyeholes in that bag and see what's really going on.

While such confrontations over reality in management are unfortunately all too infrequent, the literature of management is becoming increasingly devoted to the debate over managerial methods. Three 1967 books, all from the same publisher at about the same time, illustrate the dimensions of this dispute.

Marvin Bower's views

The first is by the head of one of the world's largest management consulting firms.[17] For over 30 years he has made his living advising top corporations on organization, management personnel, planning, and general management practices. He has the perspective of the outsider who has seen numerous firms, and has built a successful business himself, based upon his ability to go into sick companies and make them well. His detachment, his objectivity, and his knowledge of what makes managers succeed or fail make up his stock in trade.

Bower's view of reality is that managers who fail do so because they have not tried managing. They have been so busy making operating decisions they have had no time for improving managerial processes in their firm. He cites one president who said: "I have worked up from the bot-

---

[17] Marvin Bower, *The Will to Manage* (New York: McGraw-Hill, 1967), 276 pages.

tom of this business, and nowhere along the line has anybody told me anything about how to be president. In fact, no one has ever told me anything about being an executive, although I've had some instruction in how to do each job."

To Bower the successful executive emerges as a man whose decisions and actions are "fact-founded." He gets on with it, he doesn't fiddle around, yet without engaging in frantic haste. He works with zest, sets a good example, makes considered decisions, seizes and exploits opportunities, and is interested in building on strength, not shoring up weaknesses. He seeks out and faces up to problems, and does not shrink from difficult personnel decisions. He is fair but not ruthless and knows that unless poor performance can be overcome (as it often can) it is fairer to the company to remove the poor performer sooner rather than later. He focuses upon increasing the company share of market at a profit.

The source of these conclusions? A well-stocked memory and company files of thousands of clients; managers of well-run corporations. The examples he cites include General Motors, Du Pont, A.I.&I., General Electric, Unilever, IBM, and countless others. Page after page is filled with examples and quotations from well-remembered experiences and good files. He unites these into what he calls "fourteen basic and well-known managing processes from which a management system for any business can be fashioned." These points start with setting objectives, and wind up by activating people. As managing director of one of the largest management consulting firms, he is presumably summing up his organization's approach to turning sick firms into well ones and preventing decline of the most successful.

Douglas McGregor's perceptions

McGregor's book, on the other hand, begins with the statement that the manager's view of reality is an illusion.[18] Today's manager, he states, sees reality through a distorting device in his own cosmology and beliefs, however implicit, concerning the meaning of it all. McGregor and Likert alike challenge management view of reality in business. Conventional management practice (Bower's "basic and well-known principles") is what McGregor calls an "elaborate unrealistic game." "Why does the game of logic persist?" asks McGregor.

"Why do we pretend that reality is what we know it is not? There are undoubtedly many reasons, but one of the more important ones, I believe, is the anxiety that man experiences when he cannot perceive order and predictability in his world. The process of selective perception and

---

[18] Douglas McGregor, *The Professional Manager* (New York: McGraw-Hill, 1967), 202 pp.

memory in combination with his emotional needs enables the manager to *impose* this view on reality although it is something of a mirage."

Nowhere in the literature to date have I seen a more direct assertion that the leadership in our industrial society is out of touch with reality. Clearly, if McGregor, and Likert, and their followers, who are the core of the respectable academic behavioral sciences researching in management, are right, then Bower is wrong. If Bower is wrong, so then are the vast majority of today's managers who fancy that they have a fair idea about what the situation really is in business. *The question of who knows what is really going on in business has now been laid on the table.*

The manager sees the firm as an input-output machine. The inputs are labor, materials and supplies, and capital. The outputs are goods and services. In between inputs and outputs are activities such as production and selling and staff work which add value to the inputs. This value-added comprises the profit which is distributed to owners or plowed back into the business. The purpose of the owner and his hired managers is to enlarge the volume and the surplus. Everything in between is an independent variable, and might be achieved in a wide range of alternative actions. McGregor and Likert stress that the internal operations and methods of getting there are most important, especially the human relationships between the people engaged in the various activities.

To McGregor, an industrial organization is a "sociotechnical system, and consists of the organization of people around various technologies. Such a system is open, organic, and represents reality more fully and more adequately than the conventional picture of the formal organization." This new picture of reality has arrived through the behavioral sciences, which have studied firms through interviews and questionnaires, often supplemented, however sparsely, by observations and impressions.

Nowhere is the difference more apparent than when McGregor describes the manager's role. It's not that he denies the truth and usefulness of many management (conventional) ideas. It is merely, he states, that operating managers have overlooked many important new facts that the behavioral scientists have discovered, and therefore aren't using them. Likert explains this as a communications gap from bottom to top that conceals the truth from higher management. Many of these new facts require that managers fly in the face of their own experience. To do so might have a temporarily depressing effect upon profits and growth, but time would prove them best. Science is on the side of the academicians, state both McGregor and Likert. The idea that the world was flat appealed to the senses of the citizen of the 15th century. If Bower can cite hundreds of practitioners, so can McGregor and Likert cite hundreds of behavioral scientists, whose interviews and questionnaires led them to conclusions which are in many instances diametrically opposed to those of present-day successful managers.

Bower's view of reality has a special place in the literature because it isn't written by an operating executive whose experience is generalized from long service in one or two firms, perhaps some directorships and friendships with others. It is similar in method to that of the psychiatrist, who stocks his memory-drum with cases, and generalizes from his own case load. Would this exempt Bower from the "anxiety" which McGregor says causes most managers to live in a mirage? Has he caught, like an infectious disease, the "selective perceptions" and acquired the same "emotional needs" of his clients from having rubbed elbows with them over the past 30 years? Or could it be that in being on the scene, and actually engaging in the process, he knows what is really going on in ways that interviews and questionnaire can never uncover? This will be debated vigorously for many years to come.

Rensis Likert's perceptions

Of the behavioral scientists' works, Likert's is perhaps the more dogmatic of the two.[19] "All the activities of any enterprise are initiated and determined by the persons who make up that institution." Thus opens his work. Bower, on the other hand, declares that "user strategy" is the key, and that the customer and his needs are the initiators and determiners of activities. Yet Bower's ultimate conclusions about human relations are similar to Likert's. In his 14th point in his management system, Bower outlines that of activating people, and he presents an eight-part "activating package." The most important of these points, Bower believes, is "self government," which is but one of eight ways of getting people going. All are available and must be used in a discriminating fashion, depending upon who the manager is, who his followers are, what markets they are working in, and what the situation is at the time. Bower doesn't exclude Likert, but reduces his main thesis to one of eight available options when the activating packet is being constructed. Likert suggests that "most organizations today base their standard operating procedures and practices on classical organization theories. These theories rely upon key assumptions made by well-known practitioners of management and reflect the general principles they expound." While the wording is similar to Bower's, the conclusions are poles apart. Bower concludes that today's managers fail because they haven't tried managing. Likert concludes that they adhere tightly to an obsolete set of principles for managing.

Likert provides an interesting test of his system, which he labels System Four, which is "science based management" in contrast with "System One," which is conventional practice. He asks the reader to

---

[19] Rensis Likert, *The Human Organization* (New York: McGraw-Hill, 1967), 258 pages.

think of the most productive organization he has ever known and rate it on seven major variables as high or low. The present reviewer applied this to several of the largest and most profitable firms of his acquaintance and found the results mixed. This shouldn't surprise anyone. If Likert's survey has seven criteria and four degrees of compliance on each, it offers quite a cafeteria of possible outcomes. Four to the seventh power (4^7) at least. There are probably that many ways of managing well. It is clear that few, if any, of the *Fortune* 500 firms are following Likert's System Four.

Success stories and management systems

From the better documented stories of firms that were in trouble and turned around by a change in top management, one might speculate as to the universal application of System Four and "science-based" management. Would George Love have turned Chrysler around from a 40-million-dollar loss to a 186-million-dollar profit in a year using System Four? (Over 10,000 white-collar people were fired in one week to cut the break-even point by $100 million in 1961). Could Henry Crown have turned General Dynamics around after its 490-million-dollar loss on the 880 and 990 without surgery? Didn't Pierre du Pont, John J. Raskob, and Alfred P. Sloan save General Motors from too little control that was ruining the corporation in 1920? When Ernest Breech went to TWA and applied his "conventional wisdom," would he have turned multimillion-dollar losses into a 50-million-dollar profit in a year by System Four? Was General Ed Rawlings pursuing a mirage when he turned General Mills from a desultory performer into a high-return food business by lopping off the unprofitable feed division and closing down flour mills that weren't paying? If one applied the Management System Scale in these cases, I'm afraid that all of them were very close to System One. Yet, not all firms are sick, and managers of well-run companies generally aim for a style of management which is about "System Three," which provides for consultative management insofar as possible, Likert reports.

There is ample evidence also that the leading profit makers such as General Motors spend more money on improving the quality of their work force than do less profitable firms. The quick inference which might be made from Likert's book that "rigorously conducted" (a favorite phrase) research has perfected human asset accounting would be an error. Likert cautions the reader against such an assumption, but in later places leaves one with the impression that his organization has "proven" its value.

Some further misconceptions which could easily be drawn from Likert are found in the statement that "The highest productivity, best performance, and highest earnings appear at present to be achieved by System

Four organization." If the definition of a System Four organization is any organization which is profitable and productive, then System Four must include the General Motors and Ford assembly lines, as well as the service departments of the Telephone Company, the research department of Du Pont, the marketing department of P & G, and a host of other firms whose styles of management vary widely.

Since the issue in these books is *reality,* it leaves one somewhat less than satisfied that he has found any universal prescriptions for corporate ills.

Sources of data

Bower notes Likert's prior works in his appendix, commenting "This outstanding (but not outstandingly readable) book contains several useful chapters on measurement and also covers other aspects of management creativity." Neither Likert nor McGregor make any extensive use of practitioners' writings. They are more apt to cite other behavioral scientists, who in turn cite Likert and McGregor in their footnotes. The examples from firms which they cite are hardly typical of the leaders: a controversial pajama factory in North Carolina, a textile mill in India, a coal mine in England, a southwestern electronics plant, and a handful of notations about national corporations. Likert's work is derived from the substantial research conducted by the Institute for Social Research at the University of Michigan, a part of which has been in managerial behavior and organization behavior. McGregor's work, published posthumously, was edited by his wife and a colleague and is more speculative and eclectic in sources. Bower names corporations, executives, and cases on every page. He refers to 42 corporations in the first chapter alone.

Which group has a grip on reality?

The issue in these three books is stated: Are human values being subordinated and destroyed by present methods of management?

Make no mistake about it, the dispute will continue. The attack on management is now almost frontal.

Within the behavioral science establishment, however, there has arisen a group of dissident researchers, who, using their colleagues' methods, have arrived at different conclusions, closer to the reality views of the empirical observer. Within corporations, especially personnel departments, there are, here and there, men who seriously apply the behavioral theories in new forms of organization. Inside the schools of business, the behavioralists have made great strides, and young MBA's of the future will bring new ideas to corporations, some of which can only breed frustrations for them and irritation to their bosses.

What difference would it make?

Suppose you wanted to apply Likert and McGregor in your company, what would you do? System Four is larded with phrases which describe your proper feelings and values and is somewhat short on descriptions of your behavior. In brief form: you would have complete trust and confidence in your subordinates in all matters, would listen freely to subordinates, always get their ideas and try to use them, and pay them according to plans which they took part in shaping; everyone would feel responsible for the organization's goals, there would be much communication between individuals and groups—up, down, and sideways—and the upward communication would be accepted and would be honest. The superiors would know and understand the problems of subordinates very well, there would be extensive friendly interaction and high cooperation throughout the organization, decisions would be widespread and not centralized, and the top decision makers would know the problems of the lower levels. Knowledge everywhere in the organization would be used for self-control by subordinates, and not used punitively.

Bower proposes that a system which produces constancy to purpose would look something as follows: Objectives must be set, strategy planned, choice of specific goals as sub-objectives made, a company philosophy developed of how things will be done, and policies as guides to action must be established and promulgated. The organization structure must be shaped, staffed with high-caliber people, and procedures for operating defined. Facilities to carry out the business must be provided, capital accumulated, standards of performance defined, management programs and operational plans devised, the provision of control information to the affected people so that they can measure their performance, and the people must be activated. To oversimplify, Bower suggests that having a goal and a plan are the essentials for managers who wish to succeed. Likert and McGregor suggest that primary attention be paid to the human organization, and the goals, plans, and activities will of necessity follow. Bower suggests that people are vital, but are one of several means of achieving goals.

5. What practical effects will participation have?

From the viewpoint of the operating executive who might be seeking advice upon the effects of participative management on his organization, there are some hard bits of evidence, and some further research which is more speculative. What exactly will happen if you manage participatively? If all prior requirements are fully met?

It works to the extent that it raises morale and makes people more satisfied with their status and function, and turnover is lower.[20] You can probably count on less pressure for wages, salaries, and benefits where people are finding heavy doses of satisfaction from taking part in the decision which affects them.[21] People become more hooked on their work, and find that it becomes an end in itself. This is of some advantage when it comes to bargaining or discussing pay and fringes. However, since the condition grows out of people doing their *own* thing, it is entirely possible that certain objectives of the firm may not be accepted, and therefore the savings in labor costs are more than lost in their choosing their own objectives to the detriment of company goals.

Morale and productivity are not specifically related.[22] Nor is participative management a certain or even efficient method of improving productivity. Tight technical organization and tight discipline have an equally good record of productivity, and in certain emergency, temporary, or short-term situations, autocratic methods have a far better chance of improving things.

The idea that participative management causes high productivity is an easy mistake to fall into. High-producing units are often supervised less tightly than low-producing units. However, statistical proof doesn't explain the reasons for the relationship between production and looseness of supervision. Every supervisor knows that when things are going well you can afford to leave them alone. When they are going badly, you move in. You might issue orders, give instructions, train somebody, or merely ask questions. In any event, you will hardly ignore the situation. Thus, the worse the situation is doing, the more close your supervision.

This should not be inferred as meaning that loose supervision produced the high productivity, nor that tight supervision produced low productivity.

Patchen (1964) [23] and Rubenowitz (1961),[24] among others, conducted studies upon the effects of supervision on productivity and all found that high productivity could be generated along with tight supervision if certain other conditions also existed, such as enthusiasm for the goals, clear requirements, and a generally supportive approach. This contradicts earlier works by Bavelas (1947),[25] Katz, Maccoby, and Morse,[26] and

---

[20] F. Wickert, "Turnover and Employees' Feelings of Ego Involvement," *Personnel Psychology,* Vol. 4, 1951.

[21] Brayfield and Crockett, "Employee Attitudes and Employee Performance," *Psychological Bulletin,* Vol. 52, No. 4, 1955.

[22] Likert, R., *op cit.*

[23] M. Patchen, "Participation in Decision Making and Motivation," *Personnel Administration* (November-December, 1964).

[24] S. Rubenowitz, "Job Oriented and Person Oriented Leadership," *Personnel Psychology,* Vol. 15, No. 4, 1962.

[25] A. Bavelas, "Acceptance of Change Through Participation in Group Decisions," *Human Relations* (June, 1947).

[26] D. Katz, N. Maccoby, & N. Morse, *Productivity, Supervision and Morale in an Office Situation,* Institute for Social Research, University of Michigan, 1950.

others, which showed that tight supervision is associated with low productivity.

What can we learn from apparently contradictory evidence such as this? While it isn't as contradictory as it seems at first, we might well conclude that tightness or looseness of supervision isn't a major determinant of productivity.

The fact that people, most especially middle-class people, prefer to work in a place where their opinions are sought, leads to some further conclusions about participative management. If middle-class people do not have their opinions asked, they will leave their post either permanently or temporarily more often than where they are asked.

Overcoming resistance to change. Where acceptance of change is important, the evidence points toward participative management as a means of obtaining acceptance.[27] There is some difficulty here, however, if one presumes that participative management is a sure-fire method for selling ideas to works. For one thing, the very act of participation means that you listen to their suggestions and ideas, which could presumably modify your own. Thus, when they accept new ideas, they may be accepting their own ideas and not the bosses. The illusion that by simply *asking* people what they think should be done means that they will arrive at *your* conclusion and pursue it aggressively, simply isn't so. If you ask people their opinion, they may give it to you, and it may differ from your own. Once you have asked them, however, and implied that their opinion is sought and valued, you can't then suppress theirs and substitute your own for it. You will at that point be worse off than if you had never asked them in the first place.

The act of asking for opinions implies that the asker intends to *listen* and having heard will act upon the responses received. This also implies that one shouldn't even ask questions if he knows what the answer *must* be.

Summary: Participative management includes a wide range of behaviors on the part of managers in their relationships with subordinates. An optimal level seems to be that with middle-class people, the manager and subordinate should jointly confer on identifying goals for the subordinate, should jointly agree on results, but the subordinate should be free to choose and apply his own methods and control his own performance to the extent that he is trained to do so, and has demonstrated a will to perform.

QUESTIONS AND PROBLEMS

1. Have you ever known an autocratic person? Write a brief descriptive sketch of his behavior. Be specific. Use examples.

---

[27] L. Coch, and J. U. French, "Overcoming Resistance to Change," *Human Relations,* Vol. 1, No. 4, 1948.

2. How would it be possible to mistakenly label nonmanagement for permissive management? What is the key ingredient in permissive management to distinguish it from nonmanagement?

3. List several kinds of circumstances where you would prefer that the boss be autocratic. Why?

4. How would you rate the "participative drive" of the following people: rate from a low of 1 to a high of 5.

    Students_____
    Janitors_____
    Librarians_____
    Salesmen_____
    Factory Workers_____
    Engineers_____

5. In your hometown, or where you now live, how would you rate the cultural environment with respect to the acceptance of participative management?

6. What are the influences in college or training classes which make for a participative climate? or opposition to participation?

7. How could participation be used as a palliative?

8. What are the conditions which could cause participative management to produce low productivity? High productivity?

9. For the world at large, do you think that Theory X is truer than Theory Y? Why?

10. Off Appley's scale of interpersonal relations, which one do you see as being most predominant in the world today? Why?

11. If you were charged with changing an organization which was autocratically run to a participative one, what would your strategy be?

THE HARRISBURG PUBLISHING COMPANY CASE *

Facts about Harrisburg

Harrisburg (present population 18,000) was at one time a small town about 10 miles from one of the midwest's largest cities.

As the central city grew, Harrisburg became a suburb of that city. Yet it retained its own identity as a community whose activities were apart from those of the central city.

---

* All names, locations, and dates have been changed.

There is little industry within the corporation limits and the town consists mainly of residential and shopping areas. Further, Harrisburg is the home of a well known liberal arts college whose campus represents about 5% of the total land area in Harrisburg.

Because of the cultural environment and proximity to the central city, Harrisburg has become the home of many of the central city's professional population. (Doctors, lawyers, and engineers)

Adjoining the city limits of Harrisburg is a major U.S. Government research facility. As a result many government scientists are now living in Harrisburg.

The average income of family heads is $13,000.

Harrisburg residents are proud of their cultural achievements and are likewise proud of the *Harrisburg News* (published by Harrisburg Publishing). Residents like to think that the News helps to keep the town distinct from the city. It *concentrates on issues and events of local interest which get little if any* coverage in the central city papers.

History of the Harrisburg News

The Harrisburg Publishing Company has published a weekly community newspaper in Harrisburg for over 40 years. During that time it has grown from an organization which employed 3 people to one which now employs 34.

Gross receipts from the publication of the newspaper in 1961 totaled $195,000. Besides this the company does other job printing which ups the total gross revenue to considerably over $300,000.

The company has changed hands several times in the last 40 years. It was owned by E. Z. Worker from 1953 to 1958. In 1958 it was purchased by Peter Johnson who subsequently sold 10% of the corporation stock to Tom Miller.

In the five years since Johnson and Miller have owned the company, it has shown a loss in 1958 and 1960 and a gain in 1959, 1961, and 1962. All in all, however, the operation has lost more than it has earned in the last five years.

For over 30 years the *Harrisburg News* had a woman editor. Ann Henderson had spent her whole life in Harrisburg and knew about everything that was happening. Under her editorship the paper was considered one of the outstanding community newspapers in the state. Her assistant, Charlie Hudson, was also considered one of the top men in the area.

All things were running well until one morning in late 1961 when Ann was rushed to the hospital. When she died within the week the editor's job fell on Charlie's shoulders. He was an older man and had not been in good health for some time. It took about two weeks for him to realize that his health would not permit him to assume the duties of editor.

Less than three weeks after Ann's death Charlie came into Peter Johnson's office and announced that he was retiring immediately. He agreed, however, to assist in any way he could on a part-time basis.

Thus Johnson and Miller were left without anyone with editorial experience. Miller had invested in the company solely as an investment and at the time was not interested in the management of the operation. Johnson had spent most of his time and energy since acquisition in obtaining advertising and handling the job shop business. He had little contact with the editorial side of the operation and relied completely on his editor.

When I. M. Goodguy applied for the position as editor both Johnson and Miller were elated. Johnson knew Goodguy and he had over 18 years experience in editorial work and the best of recommendations from his former employers. He left his last position only because the paper went bankrupt. (Note that the editor has nothing to do with the financial operation of a newspaper.)

Goodguy was 50, married, had no children, and was a "devoted Christian." His father had been a minister and he had briefly considered becoming one himself.

Editorially things began to run smoothly again and Johnson was able to return to considering the problem of corporate profit.

After a comprehensive analysis of the company's current financial position and its forecasted rate of growth, it was decided that the only way to increase profit was to cut expenses. If the *Harrisburg News* was to remain a quality paper, the only way expenses could be cut would be to change over to new and improved printing methods.

The *News* had always used the letterpress method of printing, sometimes called the hot metal process. (See description of process in Exhibit A) Johnson decided that for a paper of the *News'* size (20,000 circulation) the offset or cold type process (also described in Exhibit A) could prove a substantial money saver. When all the factors were considered it was found that the savings would more than offset the initial $100,000 investment, and could get the company back on the profit-making road.

Johnson called everyone together and explained that he was ordering the offset equipment. He reassured his workers that no one would be laid off as a result of the changeover and that the reduction in costs would enable the *News* to lower advertising rates, sell more advertising, and subsequently expand business. He did note that some of the workers would have to be retrained to operate the new equipment. At the time all the workers seemed to like the idea and were willing to learn to operate new equipment where necessary.

It was decided to extend the changeover throughout a six month period. The first of the equipment was installed in late December of 1961.

Union enters the scene

The workers at the *Harrisburg News* had never been organized. In fact the Central City International Typographical Union local had never shown any interest in the Harrisburg operation.

At this time, however, the local union was becoming concerned about the lack of demand for linotype operators. When they heard that the *Harrisburg News* was changing over to offset they decided that it would be an excellent time to extend their authority over offset workers in the community newspaper field.

Central city linotype operators and other typographical workers were making considerably more than suburban workers doing the same types of jobs. The I.T.U. saw this as an important reason for organizing the *Harrisburg News* workers and accordingly sent all *News* workers the letter appearing in Exhibit 3.

One of the *News'* workers took the letter to heart, contacted the I.T.U. local president and began acting as organizer at the *News*. As it turned out this same worker was the assistant shop superintendent and, unknown to him, was next in line to become the shop superintendent.

On the morning of January 3, 1962, Johnson received the following telegram in his office.

To: Peter Johnson
Harrisburg News

From: George Anderson
Pres. Central City Local 24
I.T.U.

Be advised that as of 12 noon today. Your composing room employees are officially on a strike, authorized by Central City Typographical Union and the International Typographical Union representing a majority of the employees for the purpose of securing proper recognition of the Union as collective bargaining agent for said employees.

At 12 noon seven members of the composing room walked out and set up a picket line outside the *News*. The ITU then filed a petition asking the National Labor Relations Board to conduct an election to determine the representative for the employees. At the same time the ITU filed another brief asking the NLRB for a ruling which would include all offset workers as well as composing room workers under such representation. Thus in effect the Union wanted to represent everyone in the operation except professional, clerical, and supervisory personnel.

The *Harrisburg News* filed objections on the grounds that the NLRB should decline jurisdiction over the issue since the total revenue from the sale of a newspaper was under $200,000. (The NLRB has jurisdiction only over publications with gross revenues of $200,000 or more.)

Further, the *Harrisburg News'* labor counsel contended that the offset workers' jobs were sufficiently different from composing room workers' jobs and that they could not be mutually represented by the same union effectively.

The NLRB ruled that since the Harrisburg Publishing Company had a total gross revenue in excess of $200,000 even though it was not all attributable to actual publication of a newspaper it was still subject to NLRB regulations and that the NLRB could and would conduct an election to determine representation. Further the NLRB ruled that "all workers . . . on standard letterpress and "cold type" operations are pooled in a single unit for bargaining purposes."

This decision was based on a principle established in the *Ocala Star Banner* ruling in which the board stated:

"We now believe that a dual function employee devoting less than 51 percent of his time to unit work may have sufficient interest in the unit's conditions of employment to be included in the unit. Thus the board recognizes the existence of an economic strike, which began January 3, 1962 at the *Harrisburg News* by the employees it has included in the bargaining unit."

Actually what the Board was saying was that even though the *Harrisburg News* did not derive $200,000 in revenue from a newspaper it did derive more than $200,000 in revenue by using the same workers who print the paper, in its shop work and as a result these dual function workers were helping to earn revenue in excess of $200,000 for the *News* and could request an NLRB election. Since they performed more than one function and might be transferred from offset work to hot metal process work both types of workers must be represented by a union if such union is elected representative in an NLRB election.

At this same time the ITU got the Allied Printing Trades unions of the central city as well as several other unions to respect the picket line and all deliveries were stopped to the *News*.

When the composing room workers went out on strike the union was sure that the *News* would have to stop publication and would quickly come to terms, states Mr. Johnson. But he and the remaining workers continued through the night and by morning the paper went out on schedule.

The ITU did not know that all the offset equipment was already stored in the *News'* plant. Once the strike had started it was decided to complete conversion to offset immediately rather than over the proposed six month period. With the help of installation men from the offset equipment producer the *News* was able to complete the change-over in about two weeks.

From this point on with the help of some out-state labor the *News* was able to continue publication without hardship to any of the workers remaining.

The ITU then appealed to the advertisers and readers of the *News*. They were not prepared, however, for the complete disgust which the advertisers and residents showed toward the strikers. The Union then began to threaten suppliers. This was stopped when the *News'* labor counsel filed charges of secondary boycott with the NLRB. The Union cross-petitioned charging unfair labor practices. Both these and the secondary boycott charges were dismissed by the NLRB.

A lack of leadership

As Johnson looks back on the entire problem he feels that the strike was partly caused by Goodguy's lack of leadership. Goodguy knew about the organizing attempts for several weeks prior to the strike but failed to tell Johnson because he didn't want to get anyone into trouble. He thought he could handle the job himself and solve the problems. When the strike actually came he didn't know what to do.

Johnson noted that Goodguy became emotionally disturbed at the outset of the strike. Johnson came in one night as they were rushing to get the weekly edition out and found Goodguy, who was supposed to be in charge, sweeping up the back room. At this time Goodguy told Johnson he could no longer take the pressure and resigned.

By now Tom Miller had begun to take an active interest in the operation and he took over as editor until late 1962 when A. C. Hill was hired as editor and Miller became general manager.

The election

The strike lasted from January 3, 1962 until the election January 29, 1963. Because of the unusual nature of the case the NLRB ruled that the regular restriction of 12 months would be extended. (The regular restriction reads: Also eligible to vote for representation are those employees engaged in an economic strike which commenced less than 12 months before the election date and who have not subsequently changed their status as of the date of the strike.)

By the time the election was held there were 19 workers who were eligible to vote. (The NLRB permits replacements to vote in an economic strike.) Of the 19 eligible 17 votes were cast. Although a total of 10 workers had gone on strike only 8 votes were cast for union representation. The 9 remaining workers and replacements voted against union representation.

Mr. Johnson does not know why the other two workers who went on strike did not vote but assumes that they secured other employment and knew they would be challenged if they voted.

The aftermath

Since the strike the *Harrisburg News* has prospered and is doing a better business than ever before. Mr. Johnson notes that circulation is up, expenses are down, and it looks as if profits will be up for 1963.

The operation has been tightened and there is considerably better morale among the workers according to Johnson.

Of the ten strikers who left the *News* only two are known to currently have jobs in the printing industry.

Looking back on the entire situation, Mr. Johnson cannot help but wonder how all the trouble could have been avoided. He lost 10 good workers and a good bit of money in legal fees. Ten men lost jobs they had seemed content with until the Union came along.

The ITU lost thousands of dollars in strike benefits which it paid the men over the year's time. Even though the Union did get a ruling allowing it to petition for representation of both offset and letterpress workers in this operation the NLRB has already indicated that this decision will not apply to other offset operations as a general rule.

Mr. Johnson is sure of one thing. This is the first time the union tried to organize such an operation. They will try again. While he feels that they will leave him alone for some time he is confident that other small community newspapers are about to face the same type of problem. Every few days he receives letters from other small publishers all over the country telling him that they expect to encounter the same sort of problem soon and asking for advice.

Is there any way such papers can survive the necessary changeover without facing problems like those at the *Harrisburg News?* "Can harmony be achieved between the ITU and community newspapers without increasing wages to the point where community papers will be forced out of the publishing field?" asks Mr. Johnson.

EXHIBIT A

**Comparison of letterpress and offset
printing production processes**

News stories, advertising and other copy is processed out of the front office and then goes through the following steps:

Letterpress	*Offset*
The shop supervisor assigns the material to the linotype operator or hand compositor.	The shop supervisor assigns the material to the Justowriter operator or hand compositor.

EXHIBIT A (continued)

The linotype operator keyboards the copy and casts molten metal into slugs (column width lines of type) while the hand compositor assembles the remainder.

The slugs are proofed, read, and where needed, new lines of type are set and substituted for the incorrect lines.

Slugs and hand-composed type are assembled in newspaper page format and locked up for printing.

The locked-up type forms are made-ready on the bed of the letterpress machine for the press run.

The Justowriter operator types the copy into column width lines on ordinary paper. Meanwhile the hand compositor assembles the remainder as in letterpress.

Justowriter copy is read and, where needed, new lines are typed and pasted over incorrect lines. Hand composed proof is read and corrected.

Corrected Justowriter and hand-composed proofs are pasted up into the page format.

The pasted-up pages are photographed and the negatives used to transfer the image onto flat sensitized metal plates.

The offset plates are wrapped around the cylinders of the offset printing machine for the press run.

EXHIBIT B

(Below appears the context of a letter sent to News employees by the president of the central city I.T.U. local union.)

Dear Friend:

In coming weeks you will receive literature explaining the benefits of membership in the most honest and most democratic trade union in the world, the International Typographical Union, in continuous existence since 1852.

We request that you study carefully the advantages of membership as against the disadvantages of nonmembership. You will find a vast difference in economic, fringe, and fraternal benefits.

The ITU through the years has consistently secured, through contract, for its members Job Security, Freedom from Discrimination, Better Wages, Shorter Hours, Paid Vacations, Paid Holidays, Paid Sick Benefits, Paid Hospitalization and Surgical Benefits for Employees and their Dependents, and Good Working Conditions.

The ITU offers its members a sound, secure Pension Plan, Mortuary Benefits, Services of the Union Printers Home, free training at the ITU Training Center for new and related processes, and many other benefits too numerous to mention.

Central City Typographical Union No. 24 supplements the ITU benefits with a Local Union Pension Plan, Sick and Accident Benefits, Mortuary Benefits, and a Local Training Center where members are trained to master technological and substitute printing processes. All of these benefits, both ITU and Local, are available to members of the ITU in Central City.

We know that your conditions of employment are not what they should be. We know that your wages, hours, and fringe benefits are not what they should be.

You know that as an individual you can't do much to change these conditions. If you don't like them, you have only one course open to you—to quit and HOPE that you can find a job that gives you the benefits you deserve.

In numbers there is strength. The ITU has 113,000 members who stand ready to help you attain the goals you deserve. We would like to help you achieve the strength you need. The only way is to join the ranks of the thousands who have helped themselves by joining the oldest, most democratic trade union in the world—the ITU.

EXHIBIT B (continued)

While we are operating under amnesty authority during this organizing drive, you will be able to join the ITU at far less cost than at any other time. If you are interested, please contact me at the above address or phone me at 299-4573. You can rest assured that any action you take, or any contact between us, will be kept in strict confidence.

Fraternally and sincerely,
George Anderson
President

EXHIBIT C

Listing of *News* employees by job type

Administrative	2
Editorial	4
Advertising	5
Circulation	1
Offset Department	6
Composing room	7
Press room	2
Bindery	5
Proofreading	1
General office	1
Total	34

EXHIBIT D

Length of service at end of strike

Employees with the News for over 15 years	2
Employees with the News for 10 to 15 years	0
Employees with the News from 5 to 10 years	3
Employees with 1 to 5 years service	26
Those with under one year service	3
Total	34

EXHIBIT E
Organizational Chart for the Harrisburg Publishing Company

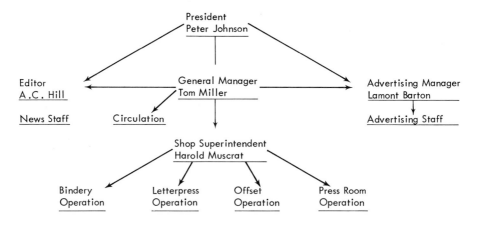

chapter 18

DISCIPLINE BY OBJECTIVES

THE OLD FASHIONED approach to discipline was that of the old testament dictum: "an eye for an eye and a tooth for a tooth." The purpose of such discipline was to exact punishment for sins, maintain conformity to old customs, and sustain the authority of the old over the young. Punishment was defined to fit the crime. Retributive justice drew upon a kind of natural law which provided that certain actions were forbidden to lower classes of persons, and when such offenses occurred and were proven, the guilty party would naturally be subjected to the punishment which had been designated for that crime. In the Far East theft was punishable by amputation of a hand; in the American West theft of a horse was punishable by hanging, and so on. Aboard the old British navy sailing ships the punishment was generally the lash, with a specified number of strokes for specific offenses, and hanging for another group, including murder, mutiny, and combat cowardice.

While it is entirely conceivable that such a system in its origin may have had some behavior-change objectives, over time such exacting kinds of punishments acquired a character quite apart from the behavior-change effect, and became an almost divinely inspired system of cause and effect, as if the crime itself produced the punishment.

The objective—behavior change

Modern discipline is forced to meet a number of new requirements beyond punishment.

1. Modern values tend away from excessively physical forms of punishment. The decline of capital punishment in many states and foreign nations is matched in declining levels of physical punishment for lesser levels of offense as well.

2. Greater protection of the rights of the accused than ever before are

415

being developed and applied. The belief that it is better to allow many guilty persons to escape than to punish one innocent person prevails in society at large, in our courts and police system, and in industrial and business discipline.

3. The decline of arbitrary individual judgments and the movement toward group judgments of guilt or innocence of acts requiring disciplinary procedures is rising, even in the school system, the last bastion of dictatorship. The trial by jury of one's peers, the right to counsel, the right to confront accusers, the right to cross examine witnesses, and the use of evidence in systematic fashion, are now widespread. Industrial discipline in many instances entails methods of redress, especially through the grievance procedure and the arbitration process.

4. The right to protest unilateral judgments is also rising in disciplinary cases. Even in those cases where no labor union exists, the skeletal outline of the arbitration system, the grievance procedures, and the right to appeal are increasingly being used in disciplinary cases.

DESIGNING THE DISCIPLINARY SYSTEM

Two major segments make up the modern behavioral approach to discipline: *a*) defining a list of actions, regulations, rules, behaviors, or offenses which shall trigger the corrective and remedial process and *b*) a set of procedures which shall be put into action when such offenses occur. This may also include some of the powers of persons and creation of groups to deal with and apply the procedures.

The clear listing of a catalog of rules and regulations

In all human organizations there will be kinds of behavior which cannot be permitted, for they keep the organization from going toward its objectives, bar individual members from being free to do their own work, or interfere with the personal rights of others. Traditionally, listing such offenses is done in the order of seriousness, and according to the severity of the ultimate punishments which might be used in the corrective process. These may be noted as falling into categories such as "Major," "Moderate," and "Minor," or some such classification.

Traditionally, listing of such offenses is posted in places where they can be seen and referred to by employees, without flaunting them in a threatening manner. They are reviewed at the time of employment as part of the induction process. They are available to every manager and discussed with all supervisors from time to time. Notes or memoranda upon their interpretation are circulated to all managers who have responsibility for their application.

Discipline by tradition

At this point we can see little to differentiate the rules and regulations of the modern factory or office from the work force of the Pharoahs in their structure of application. The rules were different and the punishments certainly more severe, but the basic design of the disciplinary system was similar. List the crimes—note the punishments attached to each—and promulgate and apply each.

This old-fashioned discipline had several basic assumptions which require updating in the new climate for discipline. These assumptions could be listed as follows:

1. Discipline is what superiors apply to subordinates and never the reverse.

2. The past is the arbiter of present and future actions.

3. Discipline is punishment for forbidden actions, and the severity of the punishment should, when practical, be exactly proportional to the severity of the offense.

4. The end effect of punishment is deterrence of others who have not sinned, who will be halted in their tendencies to do so by the example of those who have sinned, been caught, and punished accordingly. Punishment for "principles" should be more severe than punishment for the act itself.

5. Where the prevalence of wrong behavior increases in the entire group, it may be necessary to accelerate the severity of the punishment for the next person caught violating a rule in order to set an especially impressive example for the others.

6. When a single individual who will admit responsibility for the violation cannot be isolated, then the entire group should be punished, which will strike the guilty individual's conscience, as well as motivating the group to turn in the violator, or perhaps even punish him themselves.

7. Absolute consistency in punishment should be maintained *at all times* in all cases. If this is not done, the group will protest, feel that injustice is being done, and seek ways of circumventing the disciplinary system.

8. The severity of the punishment for a second offense should always be much more severe than for first offense, even though the offense is identical to the first in nature and severity.

9. The announcement of punishment and its administration should be given the maximum possible visibility and exposure, in order that the deterrent effect shall be maximized.

While there are, of course, many other specific details which could be noted, these are illustrative of the traditional philosophy, and the format and structure of the traditional disciplinary system. It has permeated the school system, the work place, and the life of the citizen.

Discipline by objectives

While the systems of discipline in law enforcement and in school systems would be worthy of some discussion, the applications of interest to the personnel manager relate to the work place, and personnel policies relating to discipline of people at work. Discipline in such an environment has some special features which are not characteristic of discipline elsewhere, such as the home or the church. This difference centers around the objectives and purposes of the business firm. The presumptions of discipline by objectives in the work environment could be listed as follows:

1. Discipline at work is for the most part voluntarily accepted, and if not voluntarily accepted is not legitimate. The recruit aboard a whaler out of New Bedford in the early 1800's was subjected to ferocious standards of discipline, which could be considered voluntary if the seaman signed the articles, and was fully aware of the strict requirement of being a sailor on a whaler. If he were shanghaied aboard, however, or beguiled by lies from a recruiter, or forced into accepting such a job because he was starving ashore and could only find a single alternative to starving, he could hardly be identified as a volunteer.

Such a voluntary bargain implies that the person entered it freely and willingly, with full knowledge of the demands which were to be made upon him, and the rewards and punishments for success and failure. Yet, if he understood and accepted the stringent requirements, the need for barbaric punishment is questionable. The discipline thus becomes a harsh reminder of the penalties for trying to escape a trap into which he unwittingly stepped.

Yet, the human memory is fallible, and the young accountant who was reminded again and again during the hiring interview that his position with the accounting firm entailed extensive travel and long hours at certain times of the year, cannot expect to remake the bargain after employment to which the employer committed funds and time. If after entering the business he sees more clearly after the fact that which he did not foresee with such clarity, he cannot selectively break the bargain without penalties of one kind or another.

2. Discipline is not a punishment system, but a shaper of behavior. Like the operant conditioning of B. F. Skinner, the disciplinary action should serve to provide favorable consequences for the right behavior, and unfavorable consequences for the wrong kind of behavior. This means that not only are verbal or physical punishments used in a response, but all of the elements in the system which can be conveniently arranged to produce the desired behavior will be employed, and not merely the judicial-like system of accused, prosecutor, judge, crime, and punishment.

On a military base it was noted that young soldiers were slipping over the fence after hours in violation of regulations. Some officers proposed stiff court-martials. Others proposed issuing live ammunition to sentries. The wise commanding officer, however, discovered that they were visiting local bars. He ordered that beer be sold in the PX throughout the entire evening. The rate of fence jumping dropped considerably.

While we really don't care about the details of the case, the principle is important. You find the causes of the behavior and arrange the situation so that it won't occur. Nobody was punished, for that is not the objective. The objective is to keep the soldiers in camp. The avoidance of "principles" to be upheld, but rather a concentration upon behavior and results is the difference.

3. The past provides useful experience in defining and changing behavior, but is not an infallible guide to right and wrong. The fact that something has been done consistently in the past is, of course, no assurance that it is the best behavior for the present. While it often is, the greatest uses of precedents are in positions where danger, high cost, or excessive losses could result from failure to use the right principle voluntarily the first time. The boss who suggests "do it my way the first time, then, after thinking about it, introduce improvements if you can," is sensing the importance of using experience, while encouraging innovation. He is providing a base point for departure.

4. Contribution to objectives is a reasonable guide as to when to depart from rules and regulations. When the subordinate is well aware of his own objectives and those of his unit, variation from rules and regulations becomes a part of his professional or occupational skill. The engineer who knows when to depart from rules and when not to is a better engineer than he who adheres slavishly to every rule simply because it is a rule. The breaking of a rule, however, when such violation has the effect of being counter-productive, and carries the man or his organization away from the desired objectives, should be the subject of some unfavorable attention on the part of his superior. Equally culpable is the individual who adheres strictly to regulations, when the effect of his behavior is such that the organization is served poorly, and its movement toward its objectives is impeded or halted.

The tiny voice of the bureaucrat inevitably cries out to establish the presence and presumably sacred nature of the rule and regulation. When he is in charge, he punishes or reprimands offenses against consistency, precedent, or rules for rules's sake. His memory for the details of such rules is formidable. His belief in their sanctity impressive. His contribution to objectives is marginal, perhaps ranging as high as nominal.

Yet, the man who breaks the rule or the regulation does so at his own risk. He may have done so without full knowledge of objectives, either his own or the organization. He might make a change for what seems to be a contribution to objevtives when, in fact, he is diminishing the total contribution. He may, indeed, on occasion hash the whole plan. It is this latter unseen possibility that should deter responsible people from casual variation for its own sake, just to be different. Not to worship laws and rules as having a special mystique of their own is excellent. Not to hate them blindly is equally sound.

5. Charts, lists, and compendiums of rules and regulations should be reviewed periodically against organization objectives to see if they are still productive.   In organizations where the system of management by objectives is being utilized, it makes good sense to review the rules periodically and revise the regulations of the organization to prevent absurdities in behavior being enforced upon employees. Where there are no stated objectives, then, of course, such review against them becomes impossible, and the mere listing of activity guides is perfectly logical. Organizations tend to conduct their affairs in a way that is *activity* centered, or *input* centered rather than *output* centered. For such organizations it thus seems important to keep all of the activity under control. If input centered, organizations emphasize discipline to prevent nonconforming use of inputs. The control of expense accounts is the most common application of an Input-Centered system of management. The manager who makes a trip to New York City where meals and lodging are higher than in Dodge City, Kansas, for example, will be bound by identical regulations for both locations. The possibilities that the objectives of gain attributable to the New York expenses may be far greater than for the Dodge City trip, and therefore should be treated as having different requirements is contrary to every traditional rule. To the office manager who would prevent such variances, the ultimate logic lies in a statement, "But we simply can't have everyone setting his own expense rates. Else we would be victimized by excessive expenditures." To which the response might well be, "We expect everyone to set and achieve his own objectives, otherwise we would not achieve breakthroughs and innovations to new heights of organizational achievement."

6. The application of individual discipline by objectives makes each individual responsible for his own output, and the individual differences are explainable in individual results.   It is reported that Alfred P. Sloan, for 28 years chief executive officer of General Motors Corporation, used the expression: "Did he get the job done?" in response to ordinary complaints that individuals had varied from customary practice or rules on his job. Abraham Lincoln, when told that General Ulysses S. Grant drank whiskey regularly in large amounts, is reported to have replied: "Tell me what kind he drinks. I should like to buy a case for my other generals. I can't spare this man; he fights!"

The point is clear. The exceptional performer in achieving exceptional results should be treated with far greater tolerance when it comes to violation of rules and regulations. This implies a converse rule. The cavalier treatment of ordinary rules of conduct is permissible only to people of exceptional competence and those whose achievements of results against goals is exceptional. Ordinary and below ordinary people should abhere to the rules until their exceptional excellence is proven. The exceptional should be given greater tolerance.

Are all forms of discipline obsolete?

The steps of short-cutting to reach a goal can be constructive for one person, where for another it can be destructive. Having made this distinction, we now face the procedural matters in dealing with destructive kinds of variation. About 2 million crimes take place in this country each year. Every day over 300 people are killed or feloniously assaulted. Over 3,000 reported thefts occur in an average day, in addition to over 500 car thefts. Clearly, this is destructive behavior, and law enforcement is a growing problem.

While the rates of crime in the work place are proportionately less than in the population at large, where crimes are mainly of unemployed and underemployed persons, there is needed a comparable kind of legal system inside the plant and office to the one outside. At the same time, this system of legal codes should draw sharp distinctions between the customary antisocial behavior, and the finely honed requirements of conformity to the will of the boss on the job.

The requirements of discipline

To make the disciplinary process into a teaching and behavior-change action, some conditions must be met.

1. Rules and regulations should be devised and made known, as has been outlined in the section above.

2. When an apparent violation has occurred, the action taken should occur as close to the time of the violation as is feasible. Holding off discussions of personal behavioral lapses until the "annual performance review" or some future time, lessens the behavior-change effect. The hot stove principle, which states that the cat that jumps on a hot stove will not jump on any stove again, illustrates this principle of immediate feedback.

3. The accused person should be presented with the facts, and the source of those facts. "Mr. Smith of the Eliot Store called this morning and stated that you have not taken inventory in his store for two months."

4. If a specific rule is broken, you should state that rule. In the above

case, for example: "As you know, our rules call for an on-site inventory every two weeks, with a signed report turned in certifying the inventory."

5. The reason for the rule should be given: for example, "Three things can occur if this rule isn't followed. First, the company could lose money because it puts goods in stores on consignment, and the store could go out of business and leave us a big bad debt. Second, the store manager likes to have their billings accurate, based upon inventory and not on estimates. Finally, we need the accurate inventory to schedule our production for the month ahead."

6. Ask the apparent offender if he agrees that the facts as you have stated them are correct. Then ask him what was his objective in following the behavior he did.

Asking an apparent offender for his "excuse" or his "alibi" or even for the reasons places him on the defensive and can quickly lead to a fight. Asking his objectives in behaving as he did opens the door to future improvement. By wording, we turn the context from backward-looking to forward-looking behavior.

7. State the corrective action in positive and forward-looking form: "Given your objective of covering more stores in the territory, how can you do that and at the same time meet my three objectives for getting inventory taken?"

Periodic review of shop or office rules

A continuing source of discontent, especially among young employees, is the existence and enforcement of rules which apparently have no reason. Rules which were made for a long forgotten purpose continue to be enforced, without noticing that the objective for which the rule was devised has long since become outmoded and forgotten.

Development of sound disciplinary policy requires that the personnel department initiate and maintain a review of rules of conduct for the plant or office. Such a review should deal with two specific questions for each rule.

FIGURE 18–1

The rule stated as it presently exists	The contribution to objectives which this rule makes
1.	1.

In the first column, as shown in Figure 18–1, the rule as it now exists should be stated. In the second column a brief statement of the contribution of the rule to objectives should be listed. Where the rule makes a contribution, or prevents something from happening which could diminish contribution, it stays. Some typical contributions to objectives of work rules could be the following:

Prevents line shut-down
Prevents spoilage and repair costs
Prevents customer complaints for quality
Safety of fellow workers
Safety of the employee
Improves yield of line
Prevents tool breakage
Prevents overexpenditure for small tools

There are, however, certain rules which have vast powers of survival for which only the following responses can be found, and should be eliminated unless further study shows them making a contribution to objectives:

We've always done it that way.
It's our policy.
That rule was made out of many, many years of experience.
The boss (now retired) installed that one.
Because I want it, dammit.
It's generally a good thing.
You wouldn't really know why, so let's not discuss it.
Don't make waves.
I don't have time to explain it to you, just do it.

Further study might well reveal a legitimate reason, in the form of a contribution to objectives. It might even be found that rules that are absolutely necessary in one location or department won't be necessary in another. Smoking is not allowed in the plant where volatile liquids are used, but may be allowed in the office.

Creative development of discretionary and selectively applied rules is evidence of good management, not bad management.

Just as was the case with the no-smoking rule, there may be discretionary application of rules affecting attendance, starting and stopping times, time cards, and other matters. There is no inherent and automatic virtue to consistency when the making of rules is concerned. *Consistency of application* among all of those employees covered by the same rule is, however, necessary to avoid charges of injustice and disputes between employees. You might, for example, suspend the attendance-keeping rules for engineers, by eliminating time cards, if it is done for all engineers. You can't selectively single out Jim and make a rule for him alone (unless he is a Steinmetz, a Shockley, or other genius).

Using progressive discipline

For certain kinds of offenses, such as murder, rape, felonious assault, major thefts, deliberate damage to company property, and the like, the first offense is the last, since it is a cause for immediate discharge.

Another category of offense which is worthy of disciplinary attention is less than a cause for immediate discharge, and here the use of progressive discipline applies. Progressive discipline means that the employee is subjected to several stages, each one moving closer to the separation stage, but each one in turn designed to effect a behavior charge prior to that move. The stage used in many firms, such as General Motors, Ford, Chrysler, and numerous other large firms, has grown for the most part out of successive tests of its success, as reviewed by arbitrators for equity and fairness to the employee. These steps generally include:

Step 1—First offense.   Instruct the employee in the proper method, explain the rule and its reasons, and explain what the next level of discipline will be for a reoccurrence. *Write the incident in his personnel record.*

Step 2—Second offense.   This could be a repeat of the first, or it could be a different offense of a similar magnitude. If a repeat of the first, summarize the instructions, tell the individual that his is a second offense, tell him that this is a reprimand and that the third step will be a temporary lay-off without pay. Explain the reason for the rule. *Write the incident in his personnel record.* If the offense is a second offense of a similar magnitude, but different in specifics, instruct him in the proper method, warn him of the next step which will follow a third offense. *Write the incident up in his personnel record.*

Step 3—Third offense.   The first line supervisor should at this stage consult with his superior and the personnel department since the issue might become arbitratable. Having verified that the stage is clear, he instructs the individual and gives him a lay-off of two to five days without pay, with the warning that a repeat of any similar level offense will result in discharge and his record being marked to prevent reemployment. Write the incident up on the person's personnel record.

Step 4—Discharge.   Following a confirmation from the supervisor's superior and the personnel department, the supervisor should tell the man he is discharged. *This should be written up in the man's personnel folder,* with recommendations for rehiring or not rehiring.

This brief description of the stages of discipline is based upon successful experience of employers in unionized and in government supervision who have discharged employees and been upheld. Throughout the entire process it should be borne in mind that each move may be subsequently subjected to close scrutiny of an arbitrator, a review board, or a top manager.

Some umbrella rules for discipline

In addition to knowing the general stages, the supervisor should now apply certain rules which hang over the entire disciplinary process itself like an umbrella. Failure in any of these rules could result in the action being reversed.

1. Be certain that the rule exists, is clear, and that the employees know the rule.

2. Use a structure of limitations rule for writing up disciplinary incidents. If a man, for example, breaks a rule and has this entered in his record, after six months of good performance without further incidents, remove the record from his file and clear his slate. Do not carry minor incidents over from year to year. Layoff reports could be kept for periods of two to three years.

3. Avoid behavior which creates further incidents. Using profanity (even where it is the ordinary language of the shop) in disciplinary proceedings, or physically touching the person invites explosions, anger, and physical responses.

4. Don't apply the procedure inconsistently to individuals such as adding a step between 2 and 3, or shortening the lay-off period for one person unless the facts are sufficiently different to permit toleration.

5. *Listen* carefully to what the other person says at all times, and note the substance of his remarks in the record.

6. *Be certain of your facts* before making your decision. In the rushed life of the business world wrong perceptions, garbled information, and errors in fact will come easily. Dig as deeply as is necessary to get all of the necessary facts before moving into action.

7. Don't jump the stages for less than discharge offenses under emotional pressures. This is the most likely cause of reversal by an arbitrator, who will reduce the penalty to the level at which the offense should have been handled. To discharge a man for spoiling work twice would probably result in the man being reinstated with full pay since ordinary practice would call for this stage first, before jumping immediately to the ultimate offense.

8. When the laid-off employee returns to work, don't continue the punishment. He has been instructed, warned, and seen the effects of his own behavior upon himself. Treat him like any employee, don't spend any special amount of time checking on him. Be business-like, neither clubby nor aloof.

9. Avoid entrapment. Setting snare to encourage employees to violate rules in order that the boss may administer the next stage of discipline is bad business. It breeds distrust in the equity and justice of the whole system.

Handling the nonrule offense

Certain kinds of behavior of employees require supervisory attention which does not fall clearly into the rule book, but need correction. Take the case of a salesman who habitually told racist jokes. This offended certain of the customers, and the president of one large company called to tell you of the salesman's behavior.

1. If no rule has been broken, don't invent one to cover the situation.
2. Treat nonrule violations as behavioral problems which need coaching and training rather than discipline.
3. Use feedback and discussion of objectives to effect a behavior change.

In the case of the salesman, the dialogue might go something as follows:

Joe, I received a call from Mr. X, president of the Apex Company this morning. He said that you have offended several of his people because you tell jokes about Jews, Negroes, and Italians while you are on their premises. He says, further, that they have many such employees, and that they are insulted by what you say.

I don't mean anything, it's a joke. Where is their sense of humor?

I wanted you to know that Mr. X had called, and exactly what he said.

It's only a joke.

What would you say your objective is in calling upon Apex?

To get orders, of course, but you know you have to have good relations with people, and a sense of humor and being cheerful is part of getting good relations.

Given your objective of getting orders through being cheerful, using jokes, how would you say your action is working in getting you to your objectives?

Notice what the boss didn't say or do:

He didn't preach about racism.

He didn't lecture Joe on his stupidity.

He didn't use satire or sarcasm.

He didn't agree or sympathize with Joe.

He didn't prescribe, "Now here is what you must do."

The emphasis here is upon behavior change, through concentrating on responsible behavior in the future. He presented the facts as he heard them, avoided generalizations and sweeping charges, and used a Socratic discussion to permit Joe to obtain insight through seeing his own problem. Once Joe sees the objective and the problem, he can start discussing some *optional plans* for solving the problem.

What do you think you should do next, Joe?

Well, I guess I better quit using jokes, even become a sourpuss if that's what they want.

All jokes?

Well, at least the ones about race and religion. I guess I could also apologize over there to some of the people I run into. Maybe I could get a new stock of jokes, too.

Sounds as if you have a good plan, Joe. Now is there anything you think I can do to help?

Sure, Apex is a big account and makes up a large hunk of my business. If you could call the president and tell him you talked to me, and I was startled and plan to apologize and lay off the bum jokes in the future, that might help. Tell him I appreciated the call, too.

The details of the case are, of course, more complex, but it illustrates the principles. What appears to be a discipline case becomes a teaching and coaching incident. There is no useful purpose to writing up this incident. The personnel-centered manager who builds his subordinates through coaching has hundreds of such incidents each year. They comprise the ordinary fabric of management and should not be treated as disciplinary incidents.

This blending of discipline and coaching, or remedial rather than punitive discipline, is centered around the achievement of objectives rather than the extermination of sin.

QUESTIONS AND PROBLEMS

1. How does the modern concept of discipline differ from traditional?
2. What has been the form of discipline used in the school systems in which you have been enrolled? Have you noted any changes in your school career?
3. What have been the social and cultural forces which brought about this change?
4. What is the structural similarity between discipline and good teaching or coaching?
5. Is law and order an end in itself?
6. How could a leader justify differences in treatment of different individuals? Isn't this discriminatory?
7. Divide the class into two groups to debate the following question: "Resolved that no smoking rules in classes should be enforced uniformly." Take pro and con with rebuttals permitted.
8. What is progressive discipline?
9. Give an example of entrapment.

10. Give an example of a nonrule offense which you were guilty of and for which you were punished.

11. Why shouldn't one generalize about behavior to an offender?

CASE—"BREAKING POINT FOR 'A' COMPANY" *

Song Chang Valley, Vietnam (AP)—"I am sorry, sir, but my men refused to go—we cannot move out," Lt. Eugene Shurtz, Jr. reported to his battalion commander over a crackling field telephone.

"A" Company of the 196th Light Infantry Brigade's battleworn 3d battalion had been ordered at dawn Sunday to move once more down the jungled rocky slope of Jui Lon Mountain into a deadly labyrinth of North Vietnamese bunkers and trench lines.

For five days they had obeyed orders to make this push. Each time they had been thrown back by the invisible enemy, who waited through the rain of bombs and artillery shells for the Americans to come close, then picked them off with deadly crossfire.

The battalion commander, Lt. Col. Robert C. Bacon, had been waiting patiently for A Company to move out. Bacon had taken over the battalion after Lt. Col. Eli P. Howard was killed in a helicopter crash with Associated Press photographer Oliver Noonan and six other men. Ever since the crash Tuesday, the battalion had been trying to get to the wreckage.

Sunday morning, Bacon was personally leading three of his companies in the assault. He paled as Shurtz matter-of-factly told him that the soldiers of A Company would not follow his orders.

"Repeat that, please," the colonel asked without raising his voice. "Have you told them what it means to disobey orders under fire?"

"I think they understand," the lieutenant replied, "but some of them simply had enough—they are broken. There are boys here who have only 90 days left in Vietnam. They want to go home in one piece. The situation is psychic here."

"Are you talking about enlisted men or are the NCO's also involved?" the colonel asked.

"That's the difficulty here," Shurtz said. "We've got a leadership problem. Most of our squad and platoon leaders have been killed or wounded."

---

* Reprinted by permission of AP from a release by Horst Faas and Peter Arnett.

A Company at one point in the fight was down to 60 men—half its assigned combat strength.

Quietly the colonel told Shurtz: "Go talk to them again and tell them that to the best of our knowledge the bunkers are now empty—the enemy has withdrawn. The mission of A Company today is to recover their dead. They have no reason to be afraid. Please take a hand count of how many really do not want to go."

The lieutenant came back a few minutes later: "They won't go, Colonel, and I did not ask for the hand count because I am afraid that they all will stick together even though some might prefer to go."

The colonel told him: "Leave these men on the hill and take your CP —command post—element and move to the objective."

The lieutenant said he was preparing to move and asked: "What do we do with the ammunition supplies? Shall we destroy them?"

"Leave them with them," the colonel ordered.

Then Bacon told his executive officer, Maj. Richard Waite, and one of his seasoned Vietnam veterans, Sgt. Okey Blakenship of Panther, W. Va., to fly from the battalion base, "LZ Center," across the valley to talk with the reluctant troops of A Company.

"Give them a peptalk and a kick in the butt," he said. They found the men bearded and exhausted in the tall, blackened elephant grass, their uniforms ripped and caked with dirt.

"One of them was crying," said Blakenship.

Then the soldiers told why they would not move.

"It poured out"

"It poured out of them," the sergeant said.

They said they were sick of the endless battling in torrid heat, the constant danger of sudden firefights by day, and the mortaring and enemy probing by night. They said they had not enough sleep and that they were being pushed too hard. They hadn't had mail. They hadn't had hot food. They hadn't had the little things that make war bearable.

Helicopters brought in the basic needs of ammunition, food, and water at a tremendous risk because of the heavy enemy ground fire. But this was not enough for these men. They believed that they were in danger of annihilation and would go no farther.

Fear in eyes

Maj. Waite and Sgt. Blakenship heard them out, looking at the soldiers, most of them a generation apart, draftees 19 and 20 with fear in their eyes.

Blakenship, a quick-tempered man, began arguing.

"One of them yelled to me that his company had suffered too much and that it should not have to go on," Blakenship said. "I answered him that another company was down to 15 men still on the move—and I lied to him—and he asked me, 'Why did they do it?' "

With fists raised

"Maybe they have got something a little more than what you have got," the sergeant replied.

"Don't call us cowards, we are not cowards," the soldier howled, running toward Blakenship with his fists raised.

Blakenship turned his back and walked down the bomb-scarred ridge line to where the company commander waited.

The sergeant looked back and saw that the men of A Company were stirring. They picked up their rifles, fell into a loose formation and followed him down the cratered slope.

A Company went back to war.

APPENDIX I: COMMANDER OF 'ANTIWAR' GI's LOSES JOB IN S. VIET SHAKEUP

Saigon (Wednesday), (AP)—The company commander who had a small antiwar revolt on his hands in the battlefield Sunday has been relieved of his job and is being transferred to a new post, his battalion commander said Wednesday.

Lt. Eugene Shurtz, Jr., 26, of Davenport, Iowa, commander of Alpha Company, will be given a new assignment with the 196th Brigade of the American Division.

The battalion commander, Lt. Col. Robert C. Bacon of Falls Church, Va., said in a telephone interview from Landing Zone Center south of Da Nang that he went out into the field Monday morning to relieve Shurtz.

The battle-worn and understrength Alpha Company at first refused Sunday to move again down the jungled, rock slopes of Nui Lon Mountain into a deadly labyrinth of North Vietnamese bunkers and trench lines after making the same push and being driven back five days in a row.

But after calm persuasion by Bacon, his executive officer, Maj. Richard Waite of Reynoldsville, Pa., and Sgt. Okey Blakenship of Panther, W. Va., the company finally moved out.

Bacon said Wednesday he made the decision to relieve Shurtz Sunday night.

"I went out to relieve him personally," said Bacon. "I wasn't satisfied with the progress the company was making in the two or three days I had them."

"I made the decision for a lot of reasons. I didn't think he—Shurtz—had the experience to handle the job. It became more apparent as time progressed that we needed new blood in the job."

"The company wasn't responsive, it was dragging its feet. It was slow getting its gear together. I didn't think the company moved when I wanted it to. I would tell them to move out at 6 a.m. They would move out at 6:30. The company was not responsive."

Bacon said he talked to Shurtz about the company personally and "explained the situation."

"He—Shurtz—fully understood," said Bacon. "He told me he wanted to visit the men in his company who had been wounded."

At the same time Bacon relieved Shurtz he brought with him a new company commander, Capt. Bernard F. Wolpers, a native of Germany, now a U.S. citizen.

Discussion questions

1. How well was the problem handled?
2. What might have been done to avert it?

chapter 19

COMMUNICATION BY OBJECTIVES: THE EXCHANGE OF MEANING

COMMUNICATION is being in touch with other people. You might quickly conclude that this means talking, or perhaps writing. It's far more than this.

Communication includes all of your behavior which results in an exchange of meaning. It includes everything you do which transmits intentions or ideas to another, or by which he transmits ideas and intentions to you.

> It could be making a speech at the PTA.
> It could be reading your daily newspaper or a book.
> It might be listening to your wife or to a speech over TV.
> It could be making a presentation to the board.
> It might be a gesture, a snort, a sneer, a scowl, or a nod of approval.

Communication is closely tied to stirring up what you have received in your memory drum and spinning it out later.

Running the entire gamut of behavior and actions, communication is hard to manage. You'll do it better if you have a *system*.

The employee and the human condition

More than 2 billion people cover this planet. They live, work, raise families, exploit minerals, sail the seas, and probe the hemisphere and beyond. Being part of the human race, we must relate to the environment. If we are to be leaders, we must make things happen in one tiny segment of the world. This means that we can keep from falling off the roster of the human race.

432

Wars erupt periodically among these humans. Organizations split into squabbling groups, companies fail, families break up, and racial strife develops at various times and places. The big issues of our times are the issues of human relationships. Scientific progress doesn't seem to assure growth and happiness for men. What is the cause of these undesirable conditions? People aren't in touch with one another. Misunderstanding, failure to persuade, quick conflict, lack of unity in groups and nations and open warfare are the consequences of the failure to communicate.

Closer to where we live, people operate at less than their full potential as humans. They live in half awareness; they live lives of monotony, fear, or anxiety because they aren't in complete vibrant control of themselves and their environment. Their senses are limited, and the extensions which other people make of themselves into new and self-fulfilling activity aren't realized.

Economic man

Adam Smith, the philosopher-economist who is generally credited with being the father of capitalism (at least of the theory of modern capitalism), made an interesting assumption. He stated that the cause of the wealth of nations was "the invisible hand" which operated without the need of central control by government. It was the marketplace where each man, carrying his own "private interests and passions," communicates with others of similar aims. The result is a self-regulatory kind of competition which leads to a higher standard of living for all.

Although he wrote this in 1766, and his theories are not accepted except in vastly modified form, Smith pointed up the importance of a mechanism for communication if we are to prosper economically.

While the Western world lives now in a kind of administered capitalism, the importance of communication in the marketplace is greater than it was in the day of Adam Smith. A message to another continent, which took months in Smith's day, now flashes in seconds. For Smith to have traveled from his home post in Glasgow, where he taught moral philosophy, to London would have been a major undertaking of weeks' duration. Today, by jet, the professor at Glasgow may be in New York in hours. A fast train ride to Prestwick and a comfortable jet flight to Kennedy Airport can be made in six hours on the clock. Cutting across time zones at a speed near that of sound, he moves so swiftly that his body's metabolic clock reels at the unsettling collapse of time and distance.

The problems of communication have not been alleviated by this constriction of time in media and transmittal, however. On the contrary, our apparent improvements have left us closer to the brink of destruction, and the problems of economics—how people make a living—haven't changed very much in the world at large, aside from the West, since Smith. Starvation, plagues, wars, and other disasters seem to have accelerated their pace in much of the world.

For the man who works for his living the problems of communication seem greater than they ever were. Large organizations take on the apparent characteristics of dinosaurs, often too large to draw sustenance from their environment. Conflicting groups fail to reach understanding in matters of labor-management relations. Inside firms there are products which are invented but not brought to market in time to meet competition. Errors, failures, and people working at less than full potential are all too common. In the world of creative chemistry, of mass transport, of electronics and space technology, communication is not an incidental process. It is a natural resource which we haven't studied, explored, and developed adequately. Canadian scholar Marshall McLuhan declares that "our human senses, of which all media are extensions, are also fixed charges on our personal energies. These media shape the awareness and experience of each one of us."

We face our inadequate skills in communication daily. As radio, TV, the telephone, and printed media expand our senses, they emphasize our shortcomings as communicators.

THE MODEL FOR DIRECT ACTION COMMUNICATION

In shaping this chapter, and the subsequent one which builds upon it, we follow a model. A model is simply a working framework around which the specific ideas are draped. The model used is one that's been developed by the informational theorists. These are the scientists who have studied communication at the deepest scientific levels.[1] When they communicate with one another about communication, they use mathematics. Since we're more concerned with day to day communication in the marketplace, we'll skip the formulae, but the model remains.

Figure 19–1 depicts what the model looks like as it will affect you.

The model is really an analogue of communication in its basic process. In telephone and electronic communication, or in the diciplinary process as applied by a supervisor, the process is much the same. When a scientist makes a presentation to a sponsor, when a salesman makes his pitch, or when ten men enter a conference room to solve a problem or make a policy, the model is at work. Here's how it works.

• A *sender* is the fellow who initiates the message. He's the fellow who has something to say, or an idea or intention he wishes to place in the mind of a *receiver*, or several receivers. What he hopes to achieve is under-

---

[1] For the technically oriented reader: Claude Shannon, and W. Weaver, *The Mathematical Theory of Communication* (Urbana, Illinois: University of Illinois Press, 1949).

FIGURE 19–1

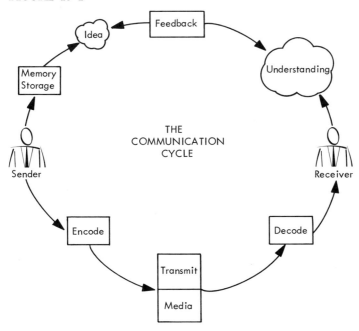

standing of his idea and, consequently, perhaps a change in the receiver's behavior. We say he wants to persuade him.

• *The message* is an idea which exists in the mind of the sender. It's pretty obvious that before a person can communicate he'd better have an idea. If that idea isn't clear, it should be clarified inside the sender's head before he starts to *transmit* it to others. If he doesn't understand it himself, he won't stand much chance of creating understanding in the mind of the receiver.

Information is stored in the memory of the sender, and he must be able to pull this information forth in coherent form. Often people "forget," which means they don't have a set of memories to manipulate. Note this about so-called intelligence—without a memory drum stored with information you have nothing to manipulate. Sharpening your ability to memorize, especially faces, names, and people, is essential in dealing with problems in human relations.

Plain talk. When we convert our ideas into words in our own minds we use a code. The code may be written words, or numbers, or verbal (spoken) words. We usually think in words and numbers, with occasional symbols which are neither. This skill in transforming our ideas into words and numbers isn't an academic exercise. We choose the code which fits the receiving person. When talking to a child we may use small words; when talking to a technical expert in our field, we probably use some special jargon unique to that field.

The trick in coding a message is to put it into that code which the listener (or reader) must use in decoding it. Suppose we don't? The message will go right past his decoding equipment and won't reach his mind at all. The result—no communication, no exchange of meaning, no understanding, and no change in the other fellow's behavior.

A simple lesson? To be sure. But it is often violated.[2]

Being an effective receiver

Not all of the responsibility for communication lies with the sender. The receiver, too, has an obligation to develop his decoding equipment and use it effectively. There may be skills of listening which he can develop. He may enlarge his own vocabulary. His emotional barriers to listening can be recognized and allowances made for them. The mechanical techniques of receiving, collecting, classifying, sorting, and comparing information received can be sharpened through desire and practice.

Filters may be applied, often unconsciously, to messages which come to us. These filters are often emotional and psychological and can be controlled to increase our effectiveness in human relationships.

The importance of feedback

Communication efficiency decreases drastically when the receiver and the sender fail to check back with each other to see how well understanding has been achieved. This takes us into dialogue, interviews, conferences, and questioning. The failure to achieve dialogue is at the root of so many human relationship problems that the list could be endless. Marital, military, industrial, educational, and mental health problems would be substantially reduced if more dialogue at a gut level could take place.

Feedback completes the communication cycle. It is the basis of information theory and rounds out the model with which we'll be dealing in some detail.

How do we summarize this matter of feedback? As a general guide in business, two major means are required to make communication work: a *dialogue* and a *memo*.

Dialogue means simply "talking to the guy." There are three major types of situations in which the written communication—the cold memo— won't work and will probably do more harm than good:

1. You can't solve a conflict with a memo.
2. You can't strike a bargain with a memo.

---

[2] Rudolf Flesch, *How to Write, Speak and Think More Effectively* (New York: Harper & Row, 1960) is perhaps the best total compendium on clarity of communication.

3. You can't change another's behavior with a memo, if that behavior is at all deeply rooted.

Of course, if the information being transmitted is routine, a memo might do; "The office will be closed on Christmas day," doesn't need a discussion. The above three classes of communication require the dialogue, because it involves feedback. *A memo* confirms in writing what has been agreed during the dialogue. The faintest ink is stronger than the best memory. If a bargain has been made, it should be put on paper and sent to the other party. If a conflict is solved, the new conditions should be described in writing and sent to the other party. If changes have been agreed upon, summarize the agreement in writing. It can be a good point of reference later.

Understanding other people

Modern behavioral science has produced many new insights into human behavior. In fact, research studies which explain and define human behavior are going on all the time. University centers like the Survey Research Center and the Mental Health Research Center at the University of Michigan spend millions annually studying various facets of human behavior.[3] They try to find out what causes consumers to buy (or to hoard), what makes voters act the way they do at the polls, and what makes engineers act like engineers.

The specific details of this research are pretty technical stuff. You'd find yourself wrapped up in statistical calculations, tests of significance, two-tailed tests, and the like. For our purposes, suffice it to say that you needn't be a scientist, psychologist, or sociologist to tap this rich body of knowledge and apply it to making yourself more effective in your actions in day to day living.

In this chapter you'll find a model which will help you explain human behavior. This is pretty useful knowledge when the time comes to act—to move things along where other people must be moved along with you. You see, if you understand human behavior, you can do a better job of predicting what other people's behavior will be. If you can predict what it will be, this gives you a means of controlling the events ahead, for you'll be able to allow for the future. You might even be able to control that behavior by making allowances for it and perhaps by changing it.

Our model for understanding human behavior is what we'll call the *Block T* model. This isn't one the scientists have invented, but it is an applied model which has been developed for use in this book and in the courses which use this book. Clearly, the underlying theories are much

---

[3] R. Likert, *New Patterns of Management* (New York: McGraw-Hill, 1961) is a summary from much of this research.

FIGURE 19–2

An action model for understanding human behavior

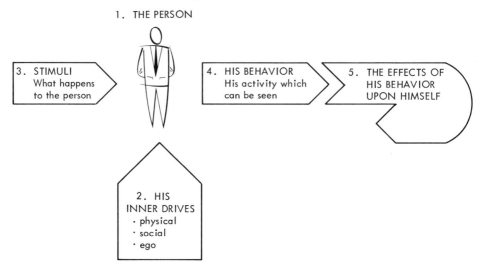

1. THE PERSON

3. STIMULI
What happens
to the person

4. HIS BEHAVIOR
His activity which
can be seen

5. THE EFFECTS OF
HIS BEHAVIOR
UPON HIMSELF

2. HIS
INNER DRIVES
· physical
· social
· ego

more complex, but the basic ingredients in the Block T are all scientifically sound. Figure 9–2 shows the components of the Block T.

As you can see the T isn't perfectly symmetrical; its something like an unbalanced line but close enough to resemble a T. Let's look at the components which make up the T.

(1) At the crossroads of the cross-bar and the vertical line is "The person." *This is man.* (2) *Inside himself* there are certain needs or drives which impel him to behave in a certain way. (3) From outside there are cues and prods—we call them stimuli—which move him in one direction or another. Sometimes (2) and (3) occur simultaneously. A man is hurrying across the street to meet his girl and is honked at by a car horn. (4) What follows these stimuli is what he does as a result of the stimulus being applied—we call it *behavior*. Behavior is very tangible; you can see it, measure it, count it, take a picture of it, or record it in some way. It is "*activity which can be seen or measured.*" (5) Once the man has behaved in a certain way, some result caused by the behavior occurs. He whistles at a girl, and her husband punches him in the eye. He touches a hot stove and immediately finds his hand is burned.

These five ingredients, all surrounding and affecting the *person*, comprise the subject of this chapter and the T model for understanding human relations and human behavior.

IS MAN A MACHINE?

Man is an animal and has all of the characteristics of an animal, but he isn't limited to those conditions. He has the skeletal, circulatory, muscular, integumentary, reproductive, nervous, glandular, and digestive systems of other mammals. This isn't intended to be a medical text, but man's physical make-up is closely related to the explanations of his behavior. It's apparent that changes in his physical plant affect everything else about him. A high fever, a serious physical injury, or four double martinis will transform him into a different person for the duration of the change.

It's not a bad idea to look here first when you see significant changes in yourself or your close friends. When you feel lazy, or when there is a change in your outlook, a check-up with your physician is probably a sensible first step. If you find that all's well here, the next step is to turn to the needs you have at a psychological level. These needs appear to fall into a hierarchy; that is, when one of them is satisfied, the next highest come into play and become urgent.

Physical needs take precedence over others. People who are very hungry or very thirsty probably will pay little heed to their social standing or their pride. They will make any necessary move to satisfy that physical need. Once that need is satisfied, however, the whole man is not necessarily satisfied. Another kind of need rises into a more prominent position. This can be illustrated in Figures 19–3 and 19–4.

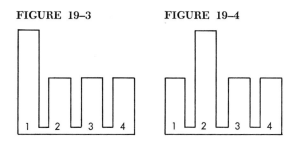

FIGURE 19–3   FIGURE 19–4

In Figure 19–3 the subject has an unfilled physical need, and this physical need takes a dominant position in affecting his behavior. In Figure 19–4 we see what happens when that physical need has been satisfied. Another need which has previously been subordinated rises into the dominant position. He now wishes to satisfy this need; and the effects of this unsatisfied need are just as great in shaping his behavior as those of the previously unsatisfied physical need.[4]

Once man has satisfied most of his pressing physical needs, he will still remain desirous of finding social, ego, or "self-actualizing" (self-expressive) satisfactions.

We should note that an unsatisfied need is an internal cause of a man's outward behavior and that without needs he would become a vegetable. A satisfied need is no motivator, and man always has new needs. Most of

[4] Abraham Maslow, *Motivation and Personality* (New York: Harper and Row, 1954).

our physical needs are met in our affluent society. This doesn't mean that people are without needs, however. Social, ego, and self-expressive needs are constantly pressing them for more goals to be achieved.

Ego needs are those which make a person feel important to himself. A man feels that his sense of worth and his liking for himself call for certain kinds of behavior on the part of others. As a practical matter, this drive in people means that we avoid those actions which rob others of self-esteem. Rob a man of his self-respect, and in defense he must react in kind. For a boss to deride an employee in public, to downgrade his efforts, to belittle him, reduces the possibility of getting that person's best efforts. He will turn his attention to getting even with his boss and hating him, rather than trying to help him achieve his goals.

Social needs grow out of what psychologists call the instinct for gregariousness. This means simply that man is a social animal, likes to be with other people, needs their companionship and friendship. The worst form of punishment for a normal human is to be isolated from human contact. If this isolation is forced on a person and extended, he is said to be "alienated," and his effectiveness drops. The simple human value of being friendly and extending kindly words has the same effect as stroking a pet. We all like what psychologist Eric Berne calls "stroking behavior" in others, and, when we extend it to others, to get it in return.[5] Saying "good morning" to everyone is a kind of necessary social cement which makes the condition of being born an individual more bearable. Letting people know you recognize them as members of the group, making them feel "in," is an important key to effective human relations. Simple stuff? Surely. Yet it's sufficiently important to all of us that without it we die a little.

Self-actualization. Every person has a kind of activity at which he feels adequate, or at which he can do better than most people. It may be running a lathe, tying a trout fly, or chipping shots onto the green with an eight iron. This need to express ourselves through something we do is a basic need in normal people. Bosses who deny people this opportunity to express themselves kill initiative, incentive, productivity, and creativity in employees.

The important point about this hierarchy of needs is that such needs are common to normal people, and they afford us clues to predicting the behavior of others and to getting others to do things we'd like them to do. Why shouldn't they? You are helping them at a fundamental level. We shouldn't underestimate the power to affect people through meeting their needs. Often they will sacrifice many valuable hours, preferences, or even tangible possessions for the person who helps them retain their human capacities through meeting these needs.

---

[5] Eric Berne, *Games People Play* (New York: Grove Press, 1966).

Demagogues, manipulators, con men, and great lovers have often mastered this knowledge and used it to exploit people. The needs are neutral, and their use is under the control of the user. They natrually should be used for ethical purposes. Yet, knowing about them means one can avoid being manipulated, and, at the same time, can use them for good purposes.

Suppose you decide that your knowledge of human relations permits you to "con" people into going against their own long-term interests. Almost inevitably you will acquire such an unenviable reputation that you will be mistrusted.

Thus, this knowledge of human behavior and motives should be coupled with a general value system of using it to help others rather than to exploit them to their own disadvantage, or the entire system will merely serve to damage your own reputation. The fictional character of Sergeant Bilko on TV was recognized by all as exploitative; at the same time, we could marvel at his ability to size up the raw humanity of his appeal and his skill in using an extensive knowledge of human behavior to trick others. As watchers, we could see through his machinations and laugh at the innocence of others. This ability to see our motives as we apply our human-relations skill to affecting the behavior of others is far more widespread than is supposed.

QUESTIONS AND PROBLEMS

1. If "communication is behavior that results in an exchange of meaning," give an example of nonverbal communication you have used successfully. Give one that failed.

2. What are some of the undesirable business effects of communication failure?

3. Use the communication cycle shown in the chapter through describing a case study from your experience.

4. What are some of the barriers to effective listening?

5. What is the hierarchy of needs? Can you give an example of how this hierarchy has applied in your own experience?

6. How would Maslow explain the son or daughter of a well-to-do home becoming a hippie, or other alienated person?

7. What would Maslow predict as being the prime motivator for a peasant in an Indian village?

8. How do the motivational forces acting on a person at the moment affect his communication skill?

9. Can you describe a time or an experience when you felt that you were actualizing yourself? When was it? What happened?

10. How does the clarification of your ideas bear upon your communication skills?

11. What are the major communication problems you see in society? In the educational system? At work?

THE CASE OF THE
OVERWEIGHT FOREMAN

Frenchy Smith had always been considered a capable man from the days when he had been a young apprentice. He had been a hustler, willing to learn anything new or to take a new job. When the boss asked him to do anything he usually took off at a trot. Even as a journeyman he had been known as a very hard worker. Long hours and hard work apparently never deterred him. Because of this willingness to put forth extra effort, a pleasing way with people, and a generally smart air, he had been made foreman. Two years later the superintendent was considering removing him. Frenchy had become a genial loafer. He was now 45 pounds heavier and often complained that his feet bothered him. As a result, he spent more and more time in his office, often just sitting or doing some minor paperwork. He spent less and less time on the floor.

1.   What would be the first suggestion you would make to the super?
2.   Do you think Frenchy's motives had changed?
3.   What specific program would you outline for Frenchy?

THE NOVEL READING
SECRETARY

After graduation from college, Mark A entered the army and was assigned as a second lieutenant to the Finance School at Fort Benjamin Harrison. He was in charge of a group of employees who prepared statistical reports. The work tended to be concentrated in certain days of the month when the books were closed. At other times the work was often slack, and the girls didn't have enough to do. Mark thought that this would be a good time to try some new ideas, and he developed several projects which he hoped to complete, using the available slack time between rush periods. He found, however, that he couldn't get any work out of one group of girls. One of them sat openly reading *The Agony and the Ecstasy* all one day. At the end of the day Mark called her into his desk area and explained to her why he wanted to level out the work and get some innovations made. The girl shrugged. "The colonel walks by and doesn't say anything; why should you make trouble? We work hard all day and sometimes overtime when the rush period is on. I think we'll just keep things the way they are, and I think the colonel will back the girls."

1. What should you say immediately?
2. What is the cause of the situation?
3. What are some of the alternative solutions?
4. Which one would you choose and why?

THE CASE OF THE SALESMAN WHO FAILED

Harry Brothers was a salesman for Consolidated Drug Company, a wholesale firm in upper New York State. One day he was called into his supervisor's office and told that he was being terminated. "The sales in your territory against the potential are less than half of what we expected. The average size of your order is too small, and the number of contacts you have made is less than 60 percent of the possible number of market outlets we wish to have covered in that territory." Harry was later telling his sad tale to a manager of an employment agency. "The trouble is, I never knew they wanted those things. My territory was too big for me to cover, and I was always rushing to catch up. As a result, all I could do was try to sell the store owner another case when he ordered one, or a whole case if he asked for a partial." Harry was placed with a petroleum products firm as a salesman and was very successful.

1. How would you explain Harry's failure?
2. How could the company have averted this incident?
3. What could Harry have done?

THE CHICKEN COLONEL CASE

The commanding officer of an air base in Africa during World War II made a habit of appearing at the post movie with an attractive blonde on his arm. He always came late, and when he walked in, the GI's had to stand at attention while he and the blonde walked down the aisle. After they were seated, the GI's could be seated and the movie started. Since there were no other women available, the GI's often whistled and howled during the "walk-down." The colonel commanding tried to scowl down the crowd but couldn't identify anyone in particular. The day following such an incident, a memo was sent out by the commanding officer to all wing commanders and service unit commanders. It was terse:

"All members of this command will change their attitudes immediately. Unless they do so, movies will be stopped."

B. G. Chicken
Colonel Commanding

1. How effective do you suppose the order was?
2. Were there any hidden effects you can imagine?
3. How might the situation have been handled differently?

THE CASE OF THE DISCONTENTED HEIR

Jack Palon had started his company in a garage and had built it into a multimillion-dollar business. He had failed twice but had snapped back and finally had made it big. Sales in the most recent year were $17 million, with a respectable rate of profit. During the summers between semesters in college his two sons had worked in the business. He hadn't pampered them but had demanded that they put out at an above-average rate. He often called them in and chewed them out when they slacked off. After college Bill, his older son, announced that the was going to study law and probably wouldn't enter the business. Two years later Danny, the younger son, announced that he was going to attend graduate school, study for a Ph.D., and become a history professor. Jack was disconsolate. "I built this business for my sons and now they desert me. What's wrong with them?"

1. Why do you suppose Bill and Danny didn't elect to join the firm?
2. What could Jack have done to avert this?
3. What lessons might an ordinary supervisor learn from Jack's experience?

THE CASE OF THE UNGRATEFUL HELPER

Jamie Smith came from a depressed region of the state into the big city and looked up a cousin. Hack Smith owned a nursery and employed men in cemetery maintenance, in the greenhouse, driving the truck, and in other handyman chores. He created a job for Jamie and paid him a pretty fair wage. Jamie paid off some of his bills, rented a nice apartment, and sent for the wife and kids. He was a good worker, and Hack was pleased with the work he did. One day, however, Jamie came and told him he was quitting to take a job driving for a large department store. "I just don't like the funeral work, and my wife keeps telling me working in the cemetery makes people think I'm a grave-digger." Hack was indignant. "Now that I'm short of help he quits. When I took him in he was almost down and out; now he leaves me flat!"

1. Is Jamie an ingrate?
2. How valid is his reason for leaving?
3. What could Hack have done to avert this?

chapter 20

PRACTICAL
FACE-TO-FACE
COMMUNICATION

ACADEMIC RESEARCHERS who have investigated the use of time in business have found that people in technical, managerial, professional, or sales positions spend almost 75 percent of their time meeting and talking with other people. These are activities which involve the individual and which can be improved upon and developed with practice and coaching. Much of personal effectiveness in the symbol manipulating world in which we live is in word skills. The kinds of conversations in which we engage can easily be classified into the three categories we discussed in the previous chapter. You may converse with people to tell 'em, or sell 'em, or consult 'em.

CONVERSATIONS THAT INSTRUCT

The principal use of the one-way conversation is in that kind of in-structional conference in which an informed speaker is transmitting knowledge to an uninformed listener.[1] This presupposes several conditions:

1. The teacher is transmitting a kind of factual knowledge which doesn't require any attitude change, nor upset any prior learning on the part of the listener. For example, if a physicist is going to explain atomic energy to a group of laymen, he would hardly want to conduct a demo-cratic discussion. He knows the principles, and the listeners don't. We should avoid faking democratic discussions when transmission of new

---

[1] Robert J. House, *Management Development, Design and Implementation* (Ann Arbor: Bureau of Industrial Relations, University of Michigan, 1967).

knowledge to an unlearned person is the objective. *Just go ahead and tell him.*

2. The person receiving the information is intelligent enough to be able to understand the information. This may also imply that he knows the jargon which will be used. Nothing is more irritating than listening to somebody explain something in a vocabulary which is totally foreign. "The cut-edge overlap of the side seam should be within a plus or minus tolerance of two-tenths." Such a statement would have great value to the experienced person who has worked in a particular shop for years and might even be helpful new knowledge; but to the completely new person it would only be confusing.

A variation of this is a habit which many people persist in pursuing. They use inside jokes, local terms, or first names of people whom the listener couldn't possibly know, just as if he were fully aware of every term, every name, and every past event with which the speaker is familiar. Take the conversation which I heard recently between the young GI and a motherly lady in an airport.

"I'm lucky to be here. The CQ was supposed to have my TD orders cut, but they'd been sent to Regimental CP with the morning report." The lady looked neutral. "That's nice," was all she could reply.

The principle of show-and-tell is helpful when you are presenting new information for the first time. The old World War II method of Job Instruction Training is still the best method of presenting job information to new people. This was an orderly process of teaching people who had never worked in industry how to perform factory jobs for turning out defense products.[2] Over 13 million workers were trained by this system. It has three specific steps:

1. Prepare

a) Break down the job to be taught into definite steps.
b) List all of the key points which will be important. Remember, a key point is any feature on the job which can make or break the job.
c) Get all of the tools, equipment, and location ready before instructing the worker.
d) Prepare the worker to get him ready to learn. Tell him the purpose of the job, its importance, and the reasons for doing it your way. Stress benefits to him, such as promotions or bonuses, if they exist. Find out how much he already knows about this kind of work.

2. Present

a) Patiently show and tell the worker the job one step at a time.

---

[2] Walter Deitz, "Spotting Training Needs" *Manpower Review,* Vol. 12, 1965, pp. 11–13.

b) Demonstrate each step as you describe it, and permit him to ask questions constantly or ask to repeat your instructions. Stress the key points and make him repeat them.

3. Performance try-out

a) Immediately following the instructions, have the worker do the job and explain each step as he does it.
b) Correct every error as it occurs and have him go back over it until you know that he is doing it the right way.
c) Have him teach the job to you as he is demonstrating.
d) Put the man on his own.

4. Follow-up

a) From time to time audit his actual performance to see if he is using the proper method.
b) Arrange a way for him to get his questions asked and answered.

It is a key ingredient of this method that the responsibility for communicating lies with the teacher, and *if the learner hasn't learned, the teacher hasn't taught.*

At this stage, you should take some time out from your reading and try applying the instruction method suggested to teach some simple operation familiar to you to some person near you who will cooperate—some member of your family, an employee, your secretary, or a colleague. Go back over the four-step plan and apply it to any of these simple jobs. It may not be as simple as it looks. Try these.

Opening a fresh pack of cigarettes and lighting one.

Tying a windsor knot in a necktie.

Tying your shoelace.

Braiding a little girl's hair.

Changing the cartridge in a ball point pen.

If it seems costly in time to do it right the first time, match it against the time consumed by doing it over, by patching up errors, or by filling out accident reports when the job is not done properly.

When you are in instructional situations with individuals, practice this JIT four-step plan. The payback is immense.

CONVERSATIONS THAT SELL OTHERS

There are numerous formulae for selling. "AIDS" is shorthand for "Attention-Interest-Desire-Sale," for one example. More valuable, however, is the rule proposed by Dr. Arthur X. Deegan, whose courses in personal persuasion have been of invaluable assistance to others. Deegan emphasizes that selling conversations involve a person-to-person relationship.[3]

This approach is based on four basic needs which have been found by psychologists to be common to all of us.

Recognition.   We all desire to be told that we are important, even if it is only temporarily. The customer feels that he should be treated as an important person and wants the kind of recognition that indicates he is respected and his business is valued. This doesn't require groveling nor subservience, but respectful and sincere interest and attention.

Belonging.   Everyone desires to feel that he "fits in," and when he is meeting a salesman for the first time, he wants to know that the relationship is normal and that his performance as a customer is OK. Growls, indifference, or mere tolerance of him destroy this relationship.

Adequacy.   Many people live in fear of being wrong or being found inadequate. The high-hat sales person who makes the customer feel out of place gives the customer feelings of inadequacy. To eliminate embarrassment and make the latter feel comfortable, his ignorance and helplessness should be dispelled quickly.

Security.   We all desire to be able to predict with reasonable certainty what will happen to us and what our relationships will be. In selling people, we put them at ease so that they feel confident and relaxed in their relationship with the seller.

Deegan has developed 12 rules to cover the situation which revolves around the maxim "people sell people." it applies to more than product selling.

People sell people

The key to successful selling and to repeat sales is the establishment of a personal relationship between you and the customer. The objective is *persuasion,* whether to actually buy a product, or an idea being "sold" to a colleague. In recent years, it's said, selling has become a lost art.

The trick is to make each customer feel important, and to give him the red carpet treatment. The technique for putting a welcome mat in front of your customer is very simple—just act the way you do when a friend calls at your home.

These twelve steps are for more effective person-to-person selling:

Step one.   *Don't keep the customer waiting,* just as you wouldn't keep a guest waiting at your front door after the bell has rung.

Step two.   *In greeting the customer, avoid the trite expressions, or questions which invite a negative answer,* such as "May I help you?"

---

[3] Arthur X. Deegan, "People Sell People" (Ann Arbor Michigan: Chamber of Commerce, 1967).

Step three.   *Avoid small talk that invites negative or uncomfortable feelings.* If you are looking for fill-in conversation, don't talk about the heavy snow, the bitter cold, the downpour of rain, the football defeat, etc. Such topics only make the person feel depressed, self-protective, bitter, or even hostile.

Step four.   *Remember to listsen.* What friend of yours doesn't desire the opportunity to do some (or most) of the talking! This will give you an immediate line on the *human* need she is trying to satisfy.

Step five.   *Point out the advantage of the item or position for the buyer, rather than all the features claimed for the product by the manufacturer.* While it is important to have product knowledge, it is more important to be able to translate this into an understanding of how, where, and why it fits human needs and desires. Advertising men speak of "key ideas." Take any magazine at random and open to some ad that catches your eye. You'll find one special advantage that is featured in the headline, the copy, or the picture. The appeal is not based on the excellence of the product as much as on how it satisfies some human need, offers some benefit to the buyer as a person.

Step six.   *Try to do that something extra.* In a competitive atmosphere it is often the little extra service that makes the difference.

Step seven.   *Try to learn and remember names and faces.* Most of us are insulted when people don't remember our name or our face. These are among our most personal assets. Learning the name and face will help you to deal with a person and not an anonymous browser.

Step eight.   *Issue a quality return invitation.* If you want the customer back again, say so. Not "Come back again," but, "I've enjoyed serving you, Jim. I hope you'll come back soon so I may personally help you."

Step nine.   *Take an interest in people in between business discussions.* When we don't see friends for awhile, we send them a note. Take a cue from insurance and other sales persons who send cards on special days (birthdays, anniversaries) to renew friendships. All it takes is a few five-cent postcards around all the time. Try sending out just ten a week for a month and watch the results.

Step ten.   *Make an effort to win new customers.* Ask others to come buy from you. Ask those you buy from to patronize you in return. You'll be pleasantly surprised at how flattered they will be. Staff work needs selling as well as products.

Step eleven.   *Follow the Golden Rule*—treat the customer the way you like to be treated by sales persons. Probably in your shopping you see many examples of the way not to treat people. Make a mental note not to do the same to your customers.

Step twelve.   *Establish a personal goal or objective* to improve your person-to-person selling. If you really want to move ahead, you need to set a goal, write it down, and constantly refer to it. How about: "I am going to try conscientiously, every day, to follow the Twelve Steps to More Effective Person-to-Person Selling."

These 12 principles work just as well in other situations, too. The customer may be an actual customer in a store or purchasing department, or he may be a boss, a peer, or a subordinate.

FACE-TO-FACE CONVERSATIONS THAT MOTIVATE PEOPLE

The third category of face-to-face conversation is that which involves treating another person consultatively.[4] The main idea here is to help the other person help himself. You hope to discover with the other person *insights* which will cause him to change his own behavior. Here's a three-step plan for conversations that motivate people through consultation.

1. Become involved with the other person.
2. Use nondirective listening methods.
3. Summarize the conversation and action agreed upon.

Let's look at each step in a little more detail.

1. Become involved with the other person.

The first step in consultative conversations that motivate people is to make the person feel important by showing sincere and friendly interest in him and his problems.

Make the other person the central figure. Treat his opinions as more important than your own. Find out his objectives and the obstacles to his reaching them. Learn how he feels about the situation.

Recognize your own prejudices. If you have prejudices, know what they are and recognize what effect they could have and are having upon effective listening in face-to-face conversations. You can't get rid of all of your likes and dislikes, but keep them under control.

Listen in order to understand. You have one purpose in this situation: to understand the other fellow's position. You might not agree with it, but at least you'll understand it from his viewpoint at the end of the conversation. Find out what are his priorities.

2. Use nondirective listening methods.

The second step is learning the technique of active listening, which isn't natural for most of us. In normal conversation we usually listen only long enough to wait for a break so we can jump in with our own views.

---

[4] Carl Rogers, *Client Centered Therapy* (Boston: Houghton-Mifflin Co., 1951).

This is a barrier to good listening. Nondirective listening is active, attentive listening to what the other person is saying.

Try to keep him talking by keeping your own trap shut. Nod attentively that you understand, and perhaps make noises of understanding such as, "I see," or "Uh-huh." If he pauses, prompt him to tell you more.

Encourage expressions of feelings. Don't fight back when he expresses emotional concerns. Simply accept them and don't argue or rebut or you'll bottle up the most useful kinds of information he can divulge.

Repeat or phrase in different words what he says. Try to state his position as you have heard it in exactly his own words. "I see. You felt let down because you didn't get the city territory."

Don't use cross-examination methods of questioning. Avoid leading or loaded questions such as, "Wouldn't you be better off . . . ?" or "Have you considered doing . . . ?" Don't ask questions which can be answered yes or no, but only those which will start the conversational flow of words from him.

Listen for insights. When the conversation is flowing smoothly and he is spilling forth his ideas, goals, emotions, and problems, somewhere in the midst of the stream will come some words of insight. "Now I see my problem as being . . ." At this stage you might move toward the third phase of consultative conversations. You are now ready for the action payoff. Be patient in waiting for insight to come and permit him ample time to keep talking. Once insight has come, don't let it get away.

3. Summarize the agreements.

In your rephrasing of his comments keep coming back to insights. Emphasize that it was *he* who stated the conclusion, and that he has developed his own solution. "To summarize, what you have told me is that you feel that perhaps your failure to get the city territory was due to mediocre performance in your present job?" He may then go back to previous tirades, but keep rephrasing his insights until he accepts his own conclusions. Then state the problem to him for him to solve: "What do you think you could do to improve your present performance and perhaps be ready when the territory opens up again in the future?"

The whole idea is to help the person see his own problem and develop his own solution. This identification of problems and their solutions won't emerge in crystal clear form. They are apt to be mixed in with lots of irrelevant, emotional statements. You must listen to it all; and, by becoming involved and by mastering nondirective listening, you'll be able to get genuine commitment.

Simply pointing out the problem in the first place will do nothing but antagonize him and increase the emotional fervor. When a man is emotionally charged up, nondirective conversations are the only way out for you.

Professor Earl Brooks of Cornell University has catalogued a list of phrases which he calls "boomerang phrases" in such situations. Here are a few ill-chosen words which will wreck any conversation. We might call them, "Famous Last Words":

"If I were you, I would . . ." or *"When I was . . ."* This is the use of the "BIG I." Actually, you are making the decision for him, whereas what you want to do is to have him make his own decision, whereby he is likely to take action for improvement.

"What you say just isn't so . . ." This one has proven to be a complete and long-remembered barrier to successful communication.

"This is what you are going to do . . ." This is another effective communication stopper. If you must use it, be sure you mean it and can back it up.

"If you would do. . . ," or even worse, *"If you would do what Jim does . . ."* Compare him with standards, not with other persons.

"Fine, but. . . ," or *"Yes, but . . ."* This is the technique of a fast pat on the back followed by a knife in the same place.

"I told you so . . ." You know the under-the-breath response to this one, too.

SMALL GROUP COMMUNICATION

More than a decade ago an important group of conferences was held at Harvard in the Social Relations Department. Unlike some momentous conferences of heads of state, these were meetings of variously composed small troups of Harvard students. Every word and action was observed by trained social scientists, who were studying what actually came out of this research.[5] They were originally published in a book written for other social scientists but were more recently woven into industrial and business training courses for conference leaders and conference members. They include some practical aspects of being a conference member and a conference leader, and of communicating with small groups.

Understanding the nature of groups

The research on small groups is extensive and would take more time and space than are available here even to outline in major principles. Suffice it to say that the group has characteristics and behavior which can be studied, predicted, and managed. The group, like the individual, develops purposes and norms of behavior for its members, and can use these norms to move the individual members forward energetically, or can subvert them into position movements of considerable influence and power.

---

[5] Robert F. Bales, *Interaction Process Analysis* (Boston: Addison-Wesley, 1951).

Cliques, or informal organizations, often grow up inside formal organizations and can affect the behavior of individual members as much as the policies, pay systems, and regulations of the formal organization.

In addition to this, the behavior of members of the group is reasonably predictable. There are roles that appear in many—or even most—groups, which, if recognized, can make small—group communications more effective. One such role is that of "convenor," the person who calls the meeting and opens it, suggesting the purpose and agenda. Often he serves as chairman throughout the meeting, but he isn't the only ingredient in its performance. Another role is that of the "idea man," who puts forth a veritable barrage of new and acceptable ideas that advance the meeting. Another role, played by a member, may be that of "best liked man," whose ability to ease the tension or to solve a puzzling block in the conference makes him liked by the other members of the group. Finally, there is a "blocker," whose opposition to what the rest of the group apparently wants slows down the progress and sometimes blocks the success of a small-group meeting.[6]

Small groups are usually considered to be "primary groups," in which the number of people in the session is small enough that all of the people can see and talk with one another. Usually this comes to no more than a dozen. One research study indicates that the most effective group size is five members. When it gets beyond that, the simple mechanics of getting everyone to take part are hampered. When it drops to four, the chance of a two-two split is present; and, when there are three, the term "consensus" can have no meaning, and the group simply doesn't jell as a group.

Conferences as typical small-group sessions

The most familiar of the business and voluntary association small-group meetings is the conference or committee. Based upon the research and the experience of many such groups, we can now identify what makes for effective membership and leadership in a conference.

Three reasons for conferences: the three major purposes of conferences are to solve problems; to define policy; or to train the participants.

Three requirements of a good conference: a good conference starts with a reason for being called. It should include *people* who can make a contribution. It should be conducted systematically to move it toward a *result.*

The most common conference is one which is designed to solve a problem or several problems. The idea is to achieve several kinds of objectives. You want to achieve not only a solution of high quality in terms of logic

---

[6] *Ibid.*

but also to find one which will work because it is acceptable to the group members. A conference, when well conducted, can be especially valuable in terms of this latter aspect—gaining *acceptance* of the solution. It is a form of participative leadership and permits all those available with informed opinion to discuss their own interests and to incorporate these contrary views into a solution through which group unity can be achieved.[7]

It provides for a pooling of experiences not readily obtainable through individual interviews.

It draws on the power of suggestibility. The idea of Member *A* elicits a new idea suggested to Member *B* when he hears *A*.

It blunts the criticism of the absent member who "wasn't consulted."

Importance of the leader in a conference.   The leader plays a special active role, but he doesn't dominate or manipulate the session. His main job is to serve in the capacity of a PBX switchboard operator in a live session, where he gives everyone who has an opinion an opportunity to present it. He stimulates the dull members of the group who might not say anything. He also shuts off adroitly the monopolist who would dominate the whole meeting.

The tools of the conference leader.   Like any skilled craftsman the leader has certain tools which he uses. They include the following:

An agenda.   A list of things which should happen at the meeting and the order in which they should occur. The agenda is prepared in advance and is distributed so that the conferees will have a chance to prepare themselves before they arrive. If there is any detailed reading to be discussed, copies of it are sent out far enough in advance that meeting time needn't be consumed in reading it. If there are any questions which are to be resolved, they are stated in the agenda.

Visual aids.   If something to be discussed can be visualized by making a chart, preparing a handout, or using a blackboard, these items are on hand when the meeting starts. During the meeting the leader uses such devices as the blackboard or chart pad to note in written form what the discussion has concluded; and common areas of agreement can be displayed for all to see.

Questions, not lectures.   It's important to remember that a conference is not a "tell 'em" kind of session. The problem-solving conference is designed to get acceptance as well as to solve the problem, and sermons won't do the job. This doesn't imply that the conference leader is mute. He uses the basic tool of *questions*. He uses questions to steal the topic from the monopolist (turns to another man and asks, "What do you think, Harry?"). He uses questions to clarify points, to stir up differences of

---

[7] R. Bellows, T. Gilson, and G. Odiorne, *Executive Skills* (Englewood Cliffs: Prentice Hall, 1965).

opinion. He uses bland questions to stimulate further expression. He uses questions to summarize. He uses questions to get commitment to action.

Behavioral skills. As the leader continually leads conferences, he works hard at sharpening certain kinds of skills:

Thinking quickly and responding quickly.

Sufficient vocabulary and effective expression.

Thinking systematically (This means starting at the beginning, proceeding to the middle, and going to the end.).

Controlling temper and emotions.

Learning to wait out the slow movers.

Resisting the temptation to "bop" people.

Maintaining a ready store of quips and cheery soothers.

No one, apparently, is born wtih these behavioral skills, and learning them takes time and practice. They aren't learned in isolation but in the give and take of conferences. The learning comes from trying them and gettting feedback of successes and failures.

Procedures.   Certain rules of the road which should be used if a conference is to be effective:

Advance notification of conferees and distribution of agenda.

A telephone reminder to the office of the late arriver, then *convening of the meeting without him* (He'll show up on time at the next meeting, and you won't penalize those who were prompt.).

A visual display of the meeting's objectives on the board or chart pad throughout the meeting.

Introduction of conferees to each other. They might introduce themselves, and among complete strangers name cards are a sensible idea.

A review of the entire agenda; of the expected course of the conference; and of the ground rules, if any.

A statement of the hoped-for closing time for the session (Planning meetings an hour before lunch or quitting time will expedite matters.).

A statement at the beginning of the meeting of any limitations on the group's decision-making or problem-solving powers.

A periodic summary at logical points in the conference of agreement reached, perhaps even of disagreements.

Assignment of someone to take notes for the record.

Later distribution of the record, with any agreements reached, to the conferees.

Your own evaluation of your own performance, or an evaluation by the conferees.

Here's a widely used form for rating:

1. It is only natural that one has a desire to know just what progress he is making. To satisfy this desire in conference leadership, a check list has

been prepared whereby an efficient evaluation of a leader's performance can be made.

2. Who evaluates the leader: Because the leader is too busy with the details of leadership, it is impossible for him to observe in detail his own performance. It becomes necessary, therefore, that the service of a conference critic be utilized. But conference critics must be made, just as conference leaders are made. It is commonly accepted, however, that the good leader and good critic can be one and the same individual, performing in one instance as a leader, and, in another, as a critic. The check list then has a two-fold purpose: (*a*) to evaluate the leader's performance and (*b*) to train the conference critic.

3. In the development of the evaluation sheet, the introduction, the leader, the conference, the charts, and the room conditions are determined as components of the conference. Each component is then broken down into its major factors.[8]

EVALUATION SHEET

Conference Leader_____ Date_____
Topic_____ Evaluated by_____
Place a check ( ) in the blank space opposite each point in which you feel the leader appeared to be definitely lax or in which he revealed a weakness. (While more than one weakness may be indicated in a statement, the presence of any one in the leader's work is reason enough for checking that statement.)

A. The introduction

1. Inadequate introduction to topic; group did not understand . . . 1. _____
2. Lecture type of introduction too long, stilted, biased . . . . 2. _____
3. Conference not made aware of a real problem to be solved . . . . 3. _____

B. The leader

4. Leader nervous, erratic, or ill-at-ease . . . . 4. _____
5. Referred too much to notes or manual . . . . 5. _____
6. Apparently ignorant of topic; unprepared, no planning . . . . 6. _____
7. Lectured or expressed own opinions too much . . . . 7. _____
8. Lacked zest, enthusiasm, and humor . . . . 8. _____
9. Slow to grasp and develop pertinent points offered . . . . 9. _____
10. Vocabulary inadequate for group . . . . 10. _____
11. Boresome over-use of pet phrases . . . . 11. _____
12. Too talkative (wordy, not condensed) . . . . 12. _____
13. Poor tone or modulation of voice . . . . 13. _____
14. Kept group too long after closing time . . . . 14. _____

---

[8] *Ibid.*

15. Abrupt or tactless in handling individuals .... 15. _____
16. Did not announce next meeting and topic .... 16. _____

C. The conference

17. Discussion not well distributed, monopolized by a few .... 17. _____
18. Failed to arouse and/or sustain lively interest in topic .... 18. _____
19. Failed to establish and clarify purpose of successive charts .... 19. _____
20. Side-tracking and lack of attention not energetically checked ... 20. _____
21. Permitted too much wrangling over words .... 21. _____
22. Dangerous topics or offensive argument permitted to run ...... 22. _____
23. Too many lags in the discussion .... 23. _____
24. Not much thought indicated by group in responses, a
    tendency to agree with others .... 24. _____
25. Shortage of pertinent and interesting case material .... 25. _____
26. Failed to clarify and analyze points or cases developed .... 26. _____
27. Numerous questions left unanswered .... 27. _____
28. Deviated too far from standard outline .... 28. _____
29. Poorly framed questions not designed for timely answers ..... 29. _____
30. Poor distribution of time among various phases of topic .... 30. _____
31. Not enough ground covered in available time .... 31. _____
32. Failed to draw conclusions and drive them home in closing .... 32. _____
33. Failed to place charted points before group for approval ...... 33. _____
34. Did not secure understanding of important terms .... 34. _____

D. The charts

35. Charts and spacing poorly planned and organized .... 35. _____
36. Lettering not legible enough .... 36. _____
37. Entries too long .... 37. _____
38. Work too slow .... 38. _____
39. Entries not sufficiently clear or precise .... 39. _____
40. Abrupt or awkward transitions from one chart to another ...... 40. _____
41. Not headed in advance .... 41. _____

E. The room conditions

42. Laxity in controlling seating arrangement and interruptions .... 42. _____
43. Started late without good reason .... 43. _____
44. Topic title not displayed .... 44. _____
45. Inadequate chart (as mentioned under "D" above) facilities ... 45. _____
46. Poor lighting .... 46. _____

The efficiency of various small-group forms

While we've been concerned up to now with the conference, mainly because it's the most common form, there's more to small-group communication. The form of communication will follow the way in which the group is organized by the leader. Professor Alex Bavelas of M.I.T. performed some pioneering experiments on the effect of various structures of small groups upon their communication efficiency and the morale of the group.[9] The details aren't important here; the experiments were done under laboratory conditions using naval cadets as subjects; and the problem being solved was that of finding a common color in a group of six marbles. The important point relates to the ways in which small groups can be arranged to permit flow of communication by the leader. Each form has a different kind of effect.

The leader as the center. The first organization form is one which we find in groups where the leader contacts each person individually, and each has little cross-communication with the others. This form would look something like Figure 20–1.

FIGURE 20–1

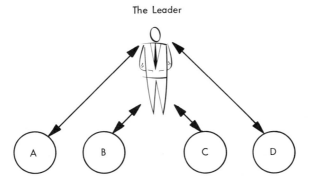

The Leader

This means that *A,B,C,* and *D* can all communicate with the leader, and he can communicate with them. It also means that they are dependent upon him for their information about what is going on elsewhere in the organization, what the objectives of the group might be, and practically any other kind of news about what's happening. This, of course, puts considerable authority in the hands of the leader, since his communicative system is itself a kind of power.

What are the effects of this kind of group upon group performance and efficiency?

The centralized group will be the most efficient of any form getting the job done as long as the group is doing routine repetitive work, such as on a production line.

If the job is constantly changing, and cross-information is important to adapting to the changes, the centralized group is the least efficient.

---

[9] For a full report, see Alex Bavelas, "Communication and Organization," in *Management and the Computer* (Schultz and Whister, Free Press, 1961).

The group members will tend to dislike the part they play in the group and will want to get out of it. The leader, however, always enjoys his role in the group and thinks it is just great. If this relationship continues, the group may slow down; or, even more likely, the members will quit when they can do so.

When you have a production routine job to do, line your followers up this way but try to overcome the natural distaste they feel for their role.

The shared information group. The second organization form is one in which each member of the group has equally good access to all other members of the group and to the leader. The leader doesn't have any special leverage over the members because of his position in the communication system. Such a group might look like Figure 20–2.

FIGURE 20–2

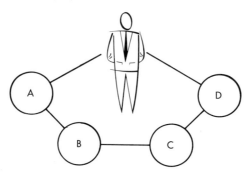

The diagram might be complicated by giving everyone access to everyone else, but the effect is what we're interested in, not the details. Here's how the experiments showed this group would behave:

In production work it would be very inefficient but the members would enjoy the part they played.

When the job to be done was a constantly changing one, it would still be pretty slow and inefficient but would be more efficient than the first type, which often broke down when confronted with changes.

Even when the program was changing, the members of the group would be happy about their roles.

The divided lines of authority group. The third form of group is actually a mixture of the two listed previously. It would look something like Figure 20–3.

Such a simple form actually resembles that organization where there is one man at the top with two lines of subordinates who work apart from each other. An example of this is the general manager who has production people in the plant and sales people in the field, and they seldom, if ever, get together. He is the focal point of communication. What effect does this have upon performance?

FIGURE 20–3

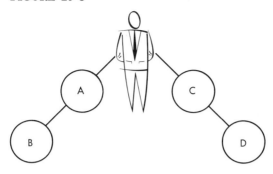

The leader enjoys his role in the group, and the people who report to him enjoy their roles fairly well but somewhat less. The guys at the bottom enjoy theirs not at all and would like to quit. Often they aren't even certain who the real leader is.

In terms of efficiency it falls midway between the first two. It isn't as efficient on production problems as the first group, nor as efficient on changing problems as the second. The morale of the people ranges over a wider scale than either of the others.

QUESTIONS AND PROBLEMS

1. Make a list of some insider terms used by you and some of your friends.

2. Prepare an instruction outline for teaching another member of the class one of the following tasks:
    How to tie a shoelace.
    How to open a milk carton.
    How to sharpen a pencil.

3. Go through a sales speech using the IDS formula to sell one of the following to another member of your class:
    Joining a fraternity or club.
    Attending a show with you.
    Going into business with you.
    Eating at your favorite restaurant.
    Reading a magazine you like.

4. Take the twelve steps described in "People sell People" and visit twelve stores and check sales persons performance in each. Which industry, group, or type of store has the best selling technique?

5. Choose some person whom you know only slightly and apply the three step formula for obtaining insights into his behavior. What insights came forth that you might not have obtained if you hadn't handled it systematically?

6. What are some of the conferences or small group meetings you attend? What are some of the shortcomings of these sessions?

7. Organize a class or small group to discuss "How this course could be improved." Follow the procedures outlined in the text in conducting the conference. Have the members rate the conference leader using the checklist.
8. What is the most important role of the leader in small group activities?
9. Should the officers of a voluntary group such as a lodge or fraternity adhere to Figure 20–1, 20–2, or 20–3? Why?
10. How could you use face to face communication skills to improve organization effectiveness?
11. How could good face to face communications improve labor relations?

THE OFF-COLOR
RED TIN CANS

Mike Grazzo was an old, experienced plant manager and had always run his plants with an iron hand. His people knew him well and had been led to expect that he would be tough on loafers, but he was generally fair and always honest. One month the corporate training director convinced Mike that he should attend a course in conference leadership at a trade association meeting. Mike went to the conference. The day he came back he discovered that a whole carload of tin cans which should have been lithographed fireman's red had been lithographed the wrong color and were crimson. The customer had rejected the whole lot. Mike assembled his crew with a few phone calls. As the lithograph foreman, chief inspector, assembly supervisor, and shipping superintendent sat down in his office, he opened the meeting with a few words. In quiet tones he explained the problems involved in the mistake, the cost, and the seriousness of the matter. He then made a temple of his fingers and gestured to the cans on his desk as he had found them. "Okay, Gentlemen, I'm ready for your comments and suggestions." He waited silently for a full minute. Not a soul opened his mouth. Mike shrugged, then barked, "Okay! Okay! Get the hell out of here, you nincompoops!"

1. What went wrong with Mike's first conference?
2. Why was the group silent?
3. How should Mike have handled the conference differently?

THE TROUBLESOME
COLONY CASE

George III of England was having trouble in the colonies. He imposed one tax levy on the colonists, and the citizens of the Americas howled in protest. He let up and relaxed on the tax. Needing money, he ordered another tariff imposed, and this time the colonists were even more violent. In order to appease them he withdrew the tariff. To save costs he ordered the colonists to house soldiers in their own homes without pay. They protested this invasion of their privacy, and he relented on the order. Then he ordered a stamp be bought and pasted on all shipments of tea. The colonists this time dressed up like Indians and threw the tea into the harbor. Each event brought successively more violent reaction, and each time the Crown withdrew. Finally the people organized a rebellion and fought the British army for independence.

1. What was George III's major mistake?
2. How could he have averted antagonisms which built up as they did?
3. What lessons for modern managers are there in George's behavior?

BARRETT HIMBER'S DILEMMA

Barrett Himber was manager of quality control for a large electronics plant. After many months of study he developed a statistical quality control system for the plant. This system required that foremen and workers post hourly measurements on charts near the machines. It also required them to average the readings each half day. The charts were to be picked up just before quitting time at the end of each shift. Despite written instructions posted with each chart, they were often filled out incorrecly, and many were never filled out at all. When asked about this lapse, the foremen declared that they were too busy getting out the work and solving problems to supervise the charts. Himber was furious. "Stupid foremen! I think they should all be disciplined to make them follow the policies and rules of the shop."

1. What is Himber's real problem?
2. How could the incident have been averted?
3. In the light of what has happened, what choices has he?

THE MIDWEST
INSTRUMENT CASE

Jim Perez attended a conference where he met a brilliant young engineer. This engineer expressed an interest in joining a new firm, since he was unhappy with his present lab's location. His wife wanted to get back to the town where Jim's lab was located. He was an experienced valve designer, and Perez recalled that on several occasions he had considered the idea that his development group might someday get into valve design. He invited the young man to visit his firm and possibly to interview for a position as supervisor (and only member) of a new valve design group. When Jim told this story to the president upon his return, the president objected mildly. "We shouldn't drift into a new line of business because we accidentally run into a fellow who would like to make his wife happy by moving to our town. If we want to go into valve design, we should think it through and make it a goal, rather than backing into it."

1. What should Jim say to the president?
2. Do you agree with the president? Why?

INDEX

INDEX

*This book has been set in 10 and 9 point Cale-
donia, leaded 2 points. Part numbers are in 24
point Helvetica Medium. Part titles and chapter
numbers are in 18 point Helvetica. Chapter
titles are in 16 point Helvetica Medium. The
size of the type page is 27 by 45½ picas.*